This Is Not a President

This Is Not a President

Sense, Nonsense, and the American Political Imaginary

Diane Rubenstein

NEW YORK UNIVERSITY PRESS

New York and London

NEW YORK UNIVERSITY PRESS
New York and London
www.nyupress.org

Library of Congress Cataloging-in-Publication Data
Rubenstein, Diane, 1953–
This is not a president : sense, nonsense, and the American
political imaginary / Diane Rubenstein.
p.   cm.
Includes bibliographical references and index.
ISBN-13: 978-0-8147-7602-5 (cloth : alk. paper)
ISBN-10: 0-8147-7602-7 (cloth : alk. paper)
ISBN-13: 978-0-8147-7603-2 (pbk. : alk. paper)
ISBN-10: 0-8147-7603-5 (pbk. : alk. paper)
1. Presidents—United States. 2. Political culture—
United States. 3. Popular culture—United States.   I. Title.
JK516.R83 2007
973.920922—dc22   2007029770

New York University Press books are printed on acid-free paper,
and their binding materials are chosen for strength and durability.

Manufactured in the United States of America
c 10 9 8 7 6 5 4 3 2 1
p 10 9 8 7 6 5 4 3 2 1

In memory of my parents,
Natalie and Gilbert Rubenstein.

To Philip and Rachel.

Contents

Acknowledgments

This Is Not a President addresses those endeavors that Freud designated as *interminable*: government, psychoanalysis, and (obliquely) pedagogy. It is thanks to the support and generosity of many individuals and institutions that this book was finally brought to completion.

This book began (as I recount in the introduction) as a thought and teaching experiment. It was my former Yale student Tom Levin who made me a gift of two slim, black *semiotexte* volumes and our mutual comrade Tom Keenan who discussed Baudrillard and Reagan with me in the mid- to late 1980s. Students in my "Reification, Semiotics, and Everyday Life" course at the University of Wisconsin-Madison, as well as participants in Murray Edelman's 1987 NEH summer seminar, gave me early feedback. Some of these undergraduate students, Jim Knipfel and Tom Vanderbilt, have inspired me with their own book-length contributions to cultural theory and memory. Other colleagues, such as Chip Stearns and Bill Chaloupka, organized the first North American Baudrillard conference, in Missoula, Montana, in 1989, where I presented an earlier version of chapter 2 of this volume. I am grateful to the others present at this event: Jean Baudrillard, Arthur and Marilouise Kroker, and Tom Dumm, who (along with Bill Connolly) provided editorial assistance in revising that paper. Siba Grovogui, who also was a participant in Murray Edelman's seminar, has remained a beacon of intellectual and professional integrity.

It was at Purdue University that the occasional essays on Baudrillard, Reagan, and Bush began the evolution into a book. A grant from the Purdue Alumni Research Fund enabled me to visit both Disneyland and two southern Californian presidential libraries. A fellowship from the Center for the Humanistic Studies provided a semester's leave from teaching. Colleagues such as Berenice Carroll (in Women's Studies) and Janice Lauer and the late Jim Berlin (in Rhetoric) invited me to present early versions of chapters in their departmental colloquia series. Robert

X. Browning placed the considerable resources of the C-SPAN archives at my disposal. While at Purdue I began an institutional involvement with the graduate program in American Studies, where I benefited from Susan Curtis's always deft and gracious leadership. I had two superb initiators into the field's core with my co-teachers, Siobhan Somerville and Patrick O'Donnell. I remain grateful for their intellectual friendship and pedagogic example. Michael Weinstein was all that one could wish for in a senior colleague; his Nietzschean daring inspired so many aspects of this project. An outstanding cohort of dissertation students produced an invigorating intellectual environment: Andaluna Borcila, François Debrix, Margaret Hirschberg, Alon Kantor, and Dave Read enriched my work by theirs. Lisa Shaffer, Julie Webber, Ramon Soto-Crespo and Deems Morrione remain vital interlocutors. One could not find a better close reader or editor or a more loyal friend than Geri Friedman.

The chapters written during this time were presented to audiences at various annual meetings of the American Political Science Association, the Western Political Science Association, and the Midwest Political Science Association. I wish to thank Rod Hart and Jim Glass for their astute comments, as well as John Nelson for his invitation to participate in the Shambaugh Symposium at the University of Iowa, where "Oliver North and the Lying Nose" was first presented. Barbara Biesecker was the best respondent I have ever had on a paper, and I also benefited from my time with William Corlett and James DerDerian. I was fortunate to have Jacques Derrida read an earlier version of this chapter.

My move to Cornell was contemporaneous with the 2000 election. I am grateful to the creative efforts of Jonathan Culler, Phil Lewis, and Biddy Martin in constituting a home for me here. I am thankful to my friend and colleague in government Susan Buck-Morss for suggesting that visual studies could be a part of that home. The political theory group provided a congenial context for sharing work. Luke Terlaack Poot and Ajay Chadhury were able research assistants. Cary Howie's friendship makes being here fun.

My knowledge of psychoanalysis, as well as my appreciation of ambivalence, has been greatly enhanced by Rod Deaton and Paolo Huober. Philip and Mary Hyman have provided superb ex-pat readings of American politics, served up with a suggested subtitle change along with their home-cooked Parisian meals. My sister, Susan Rubenstein, and brother-in-law, Carl Sabath, have supported me in too many ways to enumerate here. But I can at least publicly thank them for serving as my Washington "reliable sources" and for providing a superbly edited transatlantic clipping service during the impeachment process. It was an act of pure collegial generosity on the part of Dwight McBride that brought my book to the attention of my editor, Eric Zinner at NYU Press. I thank Eric, as well as Emily Park, for their careful attention to my manuscript and for the excellent anonymous readers Eric found. Jerilyn Famighetti was a superb copyeditor, and Despina Papazoglou Gimbel attended to my book with great care.

I would like to acknowledge the affirmative lives and supportive presence in my work of those who have not lived to see its completion: my dear friends Phyllis Jordan and Maria Tai Wolff, my cousin Barbara Richards, and my early mentor Elaine Marks. I was very fortunate to have Barbara Hinckley as a colleague both at the University of Wisconsin and at Purdue University. She encouraged my work on the presidency and first gave me the idea to work on first ladies. Chapter 6 is dedicated to her memory. Michael Rogin was a continual interlocutor, setting the standard for fearless, truly innovative, critical cultural and political work on the most urgent questions in American ideology. I was in Berkeley the night the first Gulf War started, and I remember his passionate activism. There has not been a week during the present administration that I have not wondered, "What would Mike think and, more important, *do*?" Another of Mike's durable legacies to me is those friends I first met because of him: Anne Norton, Jeff Tulis, and Linda Zerilli. I have dedicated Chapter 8 to his memory.

Both of my parents died during Clinton's second term. The first chapter on Hillary was the last one I ever discussed with my father, Gilbert Rubenstein, a scholar of Shakespeare and American literature. We talked on the phone about *Macbeth* and the gender instabilities of some of its more famous lines. My father was not a literary theorist but the kind of English professor who could recite vast amounts of text from memory with only slight provocation. He loved vernacular American culture, especially its popular genres of film, Broadway shows, the American songbook, and television, as much as high European literature. My mother, Natalie Rubenstein, a chemist by training and a research science librarian by later profession, was a passionate observer of politics. Her analyses, idiosyncratic and beyond binary partisanship, were often brilliant and never mundane. Her ethical core derived from Hillel, with an Antigone, "take no prisoners" twist. She would have told Monica she looked fat in that blue dress. But, as a Hunter College graduate of a certain era (the same one as Bella Abzug), she would have done it with a hat and gloves on and only if asked. I have always imagined she would be comfortable with the extreme theory of Baudrillard or Lacan. This book is dedicated to their memory.

My husband, Philip Protter, and daughter, Rachel, have lived far too long in the shadow of the presidential object. I am grateful beyond words for their love and cheerful endurance in the face of innumerable State of the Union addresses and presidential debates and funerals and for the way they have shared the remote control without colluding in my symptom. This book would not exist if it were not for them.

1

Introduction
My Own Private Presidents

The object casts its shadow on the subject.
—Christopher Bollas

This book is about the vernacular use of the American presidency. For the American presidency enters into the every day life of its citizens in myriad ways, both marked and, often, oblique. Presidents figure in the currency we use as we go about our tasks (in contrast to pre-euro France, whose currency featured both St. Exupéry's *Little Prince* and Berlioz, and Germany, which put the mathematician K. F. Gauss on the ten-Deutschmark note). Every President's Day we see the representations of Washington and Lincoln hawking furniture and discounted Chevy Blazers. "George Washington" himself advertises the new one-dollar coin, seemingly nonplussed about his replacement, dancing in a disco or driving through a highway tollbooth ("I look good on paper"). "Abraham Lincoln" (played by Martin Short) does a quick star turn for the Biography Channel ("But I always wanted to be a dancer"). People increasingly consume biographies and nonfiction books about the presidents in both popular and scholarly versions and read about the difficulties with "plagiarism" that plague public presidential historians (e.g., Joseph Ellis, Doris Kearns Goodwin). It is indeed difficult to open the *New York Times Sunday Book Review* or cable-surf (the History Channel, A&E, the Biography Channel, Turner Classic Movies) without experiencing a "presidential moment" even if one is not watching *24, Commander-in-Chief,* the Emmy-winning *West Wing,* or *Battlestar Galactica.* Commercials for a sleep-inducing pharmaceutical (Rozerem) feature dream sequences starring Lincoln (alongside an astronaut, a talking beaver who accuses Honest Abe of cheating at cards, and a human).

In a younger niche market, there are punk groups ("Dead Kennedys") and pop recording artists ("The Presidents of the United States"), and most of my undergraduate students can sing all the words to the "mediocre presidents' song" from *The Simpsons*. ("We are the mediocre presidents / You won't find our faces on dollars and cents"). Presidents appear in animation cartoons, making cameo appearances on *The Simpsons* and on *Beavis and Butthead*. Their real counterparts, both candidates or elected leaders, make the round of the talk shows or do bit parts in Hollywood releases, as Bill Clinton did in Bob Zemeckis's film *Contact*. More recently, they appear on reality shows such as *Extreme Makeover: Home Edition*, as Laura Bush did after Hurricane Katrina, or both Bushes on *American Idol*. Families on vacation at Disneyland, in California, can share some "great moments with Mr. Lincoln." On a recent vacation, one family traveled from Disneyland to visit President Gerald Ford's body, lying in state at Rancho Mirage. Alternatively, families can drive either to Yorba Linda, where they can select from an array of Nixon-Elvis souvenirs (mugs or watches, the most popular item) at the Nixon Birthplace and Library museum shop, or to Simi Valley, where they can interact in a simulated situation room or push a button and end the Cold War via holographic images of Mikhail Gorbachev and Ronald Reagan in a Geneva cabin replete with a fake burning log. Or they can visit one of President Reagan's brown suits from his Hollywood days. In Orlando, an animatronic Bill Clinton joins the roll call in the Hall of Presidents, situated right next door to the Haunted House at Disney World.[1]

While the presidency has always served as a subject for the great Hollywood directors and actors (Henry Fonda as *Young Mr. Lincoln*, Spencer Tracy as aspiring candidate in *State of the Union*, Gregory Lacava's *Gabriel over the White House*), its presidential monuments, such as Mount Rushmore (*North by Northwest*), the Jefferson Memorial (*Born Yesterday* and Hitchcock's *Strangers on a Train*), and the Lincoln Memorial (*Mr. Smith Goes to Washington*, Tim Burton's *Planet of the Apes*), perform a crucial diegetic function for a plot's narrative tension. These monuments often appear heroically as metonyms for normative citizenship or, in postmodern fashion, as in *The Simpsons*' "Mr. Lisa Goes to Washington" episode, where Lincoln's "father function" is ironically underlined by a throng of citizens asking Mr. Lincoln such questions as "How do I get my kids to brush more often?" and "Do you think I should grow a mustache?"[2] The Lincoln Memorial serves as a tragic backdrop in Oliver Stone's *Nixon,* or it frames the "infantile citizenship" of Forrest Gump's address at the March on Washington, a film that splices in actual presidential footage (in *Zelig* fashion) within a traditional fictional narrative.[3]

Lincoln has functioned as well in avant-garde performance pieces, colorized in blackface in *Holiday Inn,* impersonated by African American actors and women (a recent performance piece begins with a woman draped alongside a black Lincoln Continental, only to have a "car crash" into history and survive in the form of a "female Lincoln"!). There are "Lincoln impersonation conventions" where an array of Lincolns and other people in period dress chant "Ready and Abe-L."[4] Lincoln also enters, in a very displaced way, in Ben Stiller's *Zoolander,* in which a male-model conspiracy theory of presidential assassinations is proposed, with John Wilkes Booth characterized as a "male model." (Oswald wasn't a male model, but a viewer is shown some footage and asked to check out "those two guys on the grassy knoll" who are filmed in postures reminiscent of *GQ* and *Esquire* layouts.) The assassination is fodder for a Sondheim musical, *Assassins,* and going to that musical is part of Sarah Vowell's best-selling *Assassination Vacation.* Most recently, Lincoln appears as a depressive in the biography by (and marketing of) Joshua Wolf Shenk's *Lincoln's Melancholy: How Depression Fueled His Greatness* and in the History Channel's two-hour documentary derived in part from the book (and is also presented as potentially "queer" for his intense homosocial friendship with Joshua Speed). A review by the *New York Times* theater critic Patricia Cohen asks: "Can the generally disappointing crop of national leaders today be attributed to the Prozac generation's addiction to cheeriness . . . ? The emotionally suffering artist stokes our imagination, the emotionally suffering politician evokes panic; who wants to think about Eeyore nose to nose with bin Laden?"[5] Doris Kearns Goodwin's popular *Team of Rivals* fuels speculation about improbable fusion tickets in the 2008 presidential race, such as a McCain-Clinton pairing. Lincoln becomes a talking-point comparison after George W. Bush's "new" Iraqi surge policy (like Lincoln, he had to change some generals). This meets up with its hilarious *Daily Show* counterpart, a found recording of Lincoln mangling "A house divided" ("You can't stand in a divided house") to illustrate yet another similarity between W-Bush and Lincoln.

The Kennedy assassination itself could supply material for several books about the vernacular use of the presidency. From the more literary "novelizations" such as James Ellroy's *American Tabloid* or Don De-Lillo's *Libra*, to Oliver Stone's film *JFK*, the assassination itself, as well as its dispersive metonyms and part-objects—Dealey Plaza (site for the ending of DeLillo's first piece, *Americana*) to Jackie's pink Chanel suit and pillbox hat (forever emblematized in *The House of Yes*, where a reenactment of the motorcade scene and shooting serves as a prelude to acts of brother-sister incest and repetitive family trauma), pervade popular culture. In David Cronenberg's *Crash*, a protagonist, Vaughn, suggests that the Kennedy assassination is just another iconic car crash, along with those of James Dean (DeLillo sees Oswald as a poor man's James Dean), Jayne Mansfield, and Albert Camus. These mergers of national history and family or personal trauma are increasingly played out during the Clinton presidency films (even in comic ones like *Dick* that ostensibly treat other presidents), such as *Absolute Power, Murder at 1600*, and *The Contender*. Moreover, we might locate a Lewinsky affair legacy in the increasingly forensic view of the White House, in particular, in the siting of the Oval Office as crime scene, and in the beginnings of the procedural or reality TV shows that have displaced earlier detective genres. For the Lewinsky affair did demonstrate, as shows like *CSI* do so ably, that "truth" resides outside consciousness/cognition in the forensic object—the blue dress or the bloody glove, to cite just two Clinton-era relics. There is even some speculation that the popularization of the Lewinsky affair made the revelation of the Catholic Church abuse scandals easier because of the Clinton scandal's matter-of-fact presentations about oral sex.

The Clinton presidency marked an intensification of these cultural trends in more conventional ways, as well. Michael Rogin's insightful reading of *Independence Day* discusses not only how the film entered the 1996 campaign (where both Clinton and Dole felt obliged to "endorse" it) but its most popular trailer, which shows the blowing up of the White House.[6] Tim Burton's *Mars Attacks!* covers much the same territory; alien invaders destroy most of monumental Washington, with a president played by Jack Nicholson and Glenn Close as first lady (dressed in Nancy Reagan red). The president became an action hero to identify with when Harrison Ford took on the role (in *Air Force One*, Clinton's personal favorite). Clinton claimed that the best perk of being president was not Air Force One or Camp David but the inhouse movie theater. Bill Pullman (in *ID4*) forgot his constitutional role and flew an airplane himself to defeat the aliens. W-Bush's "Mission Accomplished" photo op on the deck of the USS *Abraham Lincoln* mimics Pullman's presidential performance.[7] Great comic actors such as Jack Lemmon and James Garner played unwitting ex-presidential heroes in *My Fellow Americans.* Kevin Kline played a convincing (GHW) Bush-style president in *Dave* and exposed corruption in the executive branch while his friend Charles Grodin, as Murray the accountant, balanced the budget. John Travolta convincingly portrayed Clinton, fictionalized as Jack Stanton, in *Primary Colors,* and Jeff Bridges was in many ways an even more compelling Clinton in *The Contender.* Gene Hackman was the president in *Absolute Power,* promoted from his cabinet position in *No Way Out.* Clint Eastwood didn't get to be the president but was at least in the Secret Service in *In the Line of Fire.* Morgan Freeman comforted the nation in the comet-disaster film *Deep Impact.* Of all the demographically viable popular Hollywood actors, perhaps only Mel Gibson did not get a presidential role (although it could be argued that he did pave the way historically in *The Patriot* or that he was preparing to appeal to a "higher authority" in the W-Bush years with his *Passion of the Christ*).

At other times, the merger of Hollywood and Washington could be dizzying. Marilyn Monroe's singing of "Happy Birthday, Mr. President" is endlessly circulated in biographies of Marilyn, of JFK, of Jackie, and of the Rat Pack (the Peter Lawford connection). It is decontextualized and recontextualized in an eerie impersonation by Drew Barrymore on the cover of John F. Kennedy Jr.'s *George* magazine. And, to return to my opening example, an ad for a car-leasing deal on President's Day 2001 claimed that the offer was democratically available, even to those who weren't "big shots" like the president: "You don't have to be a Washington or Lincoln to get the presidential treatment and there is no residency requirement" (intimations of Hillary Clinton's Senate campaign—where the ad also appeared—in 2000). Even the Florida recount after the 2000 presidential election became grist for the mill, as in the Doritos Chip inspector ad where chips, substituting for ballots, are held up to a light while the inspector says, "I've lost count." Bob Dole's public-service (erectile dysfunction) ad for Viagra is indexed in his Viagra-inflected Pepsi ad shown during the 2001 Superbowl, in which he extols his "little blue companion" and seems to be having a lot more fun on the beach than he did in the original public-service announcement/ad, in which he was shown alone in his office with an American flag. Bob Dole made his first Viagra disclosure on *Larry King Live,* and, again in 2001, a NASCAR with the Viagra logo is shown racing around a track and then stopping, the driver opens the door, takes off his protective helmet, and asks, "Who were you expecting—Bob Dole?" One can argue that W-Bush did a lot of product placement in his appearances for the 2002 Winter Olympics. The ubiquity of these examples is not just a recent effect of a celebrity culture or some epiphenomena of infotainment.

Scholars such as Murray Edelman, Barbara Hinckley, Jeff Tulis, and Anne Norton have noted the specifically rhetorical or symbolic aspects of the American presidency.[8] Norton quotes Alexis de Tocqueville to the effect that the presidency is a *semiotic* function and links its signifying forms to practices of everyday life, from shopping and eating to popular court and lawyer television series. My presentation of the American presidents in this introduction focuses *less* on representative or semiotic (signifying) functions (which are addressed at length in chapters 2, 3, 5, and 7) than on their position as a site for an existential or experiential form of knowledge. In other words, one of the implicit claims I develop is that the *dialogue* between president and citizen is an *operational* as well as a *representational* form of knowledge.

When a major novelist like DeLillo in *Libra* speaks to us as Oswald, or a debutant author like Lydia Millet, in her more frivolous *George Bush, Dark Prince of Love,* stages an erotic transference, or a Pulitzer Prize–winning biographer such as Edmund Morris in *Dutch* casts himself in a Reagan presidential primal scene, these are self-conscious and publicized aspects of the daily use we make of our presidents, living and former. This "use" is often not conscious. Its logic is not necessarily linear and may be diffusely associative (what Deleuze might call rhizomatic),[9] but it can perhaps be best designated by what Donald Winnicott calls a transitional object and Christopher Bollas a transformational object.[10]

For Winnicott, transitional phenomena, both objects and spaces, "refer to a dimension of living that belongs neither to internal nor external reality; rather it is the place that both connects and separates inner and outer."[11] Transitional objects and spaces are places of cultural experience, invention, and creative play, developmentally necessary for symbolization. In other words, in addition to a person's intersubjective relations and intrapsychic world, "which can be rich or poor and can be at peace or in a state of war," there is an intermediate (or third) area of expertise to which both inner and outer worlds contribute: "It is an area which is not challenged, because no claim is made on its behalf except that it shall exist as a resting-place for the individual engaged in the perpetual human task of keeping inner and outer reality separate yet interrelated."[12] The transitional object marks an important step in psychoanalytic theory between object-relating and use of an object; "from an observer's point of view it is an aspect of the infant [subject's] experience of his environment."[13] What the pediatrician-psychoanalyst Winnicott designates for a child-subject as an intermediate area is one between objective perception (i.e., that which is based on the reality principle or reality testing) and primary creativity.[14] It relates "subjective" reality to communal, "objectively perceived" shared reality and forms.

In Winnicott's later writings, *The Place Where We Live,* he attempts to extend his insights from the child world to adult life, as a third way between behavioral therapy's insistence on conditioned learning and traditional psychoanalysis's exclusive focus on an inner life to the exclusion of environmental conditions (poverty, hunger): "If we look at our lives we shall probably find that we spend most of our time neither in behavior nor in contemplation, but somewhere else. I ask where? And I try to suggest an answer."[15] The everyday spaces in which we live our lives are suggestive of those adumbrated by Anne Norton and Lauren Berlant, spaces in which daily citizen acts perform and reiterate ongoing processes of national identity construction (Norton) or form what Berlant designates as the national symbolic: "the National Symbolic is there for use, for exploration to construct a subjective dependency on what looks like the *a priori* structures of power." Or, more generally, in a Walt Whitman-like formulation: "a National Symbolic, the common language of a common space."[16]

Winnicott is attentive to the ways psychoanalytic theory does not adequately address the places and, more important, the kind of activity that goes into living one's life as a citizen. Winnicott asks:

> What for instance are we doing when we are listening to a Beethoven symphony or making a pilgrimage to a picture gallery or reading *Troilus and Cressida* in bed or playing tennis? . . . What is a group of teenagers doing participating in a pop session? It is not only what are we doing. The question also needs to be posed: Where are we (if anywhere at all)? Where are we when we are doing what in fact we do a great deal of our time, namely enjoying ourselves?[17]

Winnicott and certain object-relations analysts would argue that our transitional spaces are circumscribed by the national cultures we find ourselves in, and in engaging in these daily spaces we constitute ourselves as subjects/citizens. I am calling the "vernacular" what Winnicott and his followers would designate by the terms "culture" and play." "Playing and cultural experiences are things that we value in a special way; they link the past, the present, and the future; they take up time and space. They demand and get our concentrated deliberate attention, deliberate but without too much of the deliberateness of trying."[18] If I am insisting somewhat on using Winnicott's conceptualizations, it is because his idea of the transitional phenomena is enunciated in a fashion similar to the presentation of those "rights" in the American Bill of Rights. Transitional phenomena allow for the pursuit of happiness: "In the normal person, a highly satisfactory experience such as may be obtained at a concert or at the theater or in a friendship may deserve a term such as ego orgasm, which draws attention to the climax and the importance of the climax."[19] While I do not recall finding the exact expression "ego orgasm" in the documents of our Founding Fathers, Winnicott's follower Christopher Bollas uses a more legally resonant language: "*Jouissance* is the subject's inalienable right to ecstasy, a virtually legal imperative to pursue desire."[20] And what I find most constructive in Winnicott's formulation is a certain unresolved question about transitional phenomena: whether it was solely a result of a subject's volition or simply a felicitous accident, a found object creatively utilized: "*Of the transitional phenomena it can be said that it is a matter of agreement . . . that we will never ask the question: Did you conceive of this or was it presented to you from the start?*" (italics in the original).[21]

How the President Came into My Life: Screen Memories of a Citizen Theorist

> *Anthony De Curtis*: The Kennedy assassination seems perfectly in line with the concerns of your fiction. Do you feel you could have invented it if it had not happened?
> *DeLillo*: Maybe it invented me.[22]

The American presidency functions as a transitional object for me in yet other ways. As I have argued, the American citizen meets or discovers the president while going about her everyday life, or, as we say in the American idiom, going about one's business. My business or "day job" is that of a theorist trained in nineteenth- and twentieth-century continental thought and, more specifically, in contemporary French cultural and literary theory. My graduate training began with structural Marxism (Louis Althusser), Marxist semiotics (early Roland Barthes and Jean Baudrillard), and, in later moments, Michel Foucault, Jacques Derrida, and Pierre Bourdieu. I later found "practical applications" of these theorists in my study of French fascist intellectuals and elite educational institutions. I spent the years 1979 to 1982 in France doing research, and I went back at every possible interval when I was not teaching French theorists or European institutions.

To make a long story short, I encountered the American president not in my early graduate training or teaching but in a far more banal and exemplary American way—on television. Returning from a summer's research trip to France, I arrived in America in time for the 1984 Republican convention. While watching the play of screens through which Reagan introduced himself via videotape (a photo of this moment was on the original book jacket of Michael Rogin's *Ronald Reagan, the Movie and Other Episodes in Political Demonology*), I was finally able to appreciate the two little *semiotexte* books by Jean Baudrillard (*Simulations* and *In the Shadow of the Silent Majorities*) sent to me by an enthusiastic Yale student of mine, now a professor of German at Princeton. Tom Brokaw's frustration as a TV anchor ("I don't know what's real and what's electronically real") perfectly illustrated Baudrillard's notion of the "hyperreal," which I had previously found of little use in my research or teaching lives. As I began to read more Baudrillard, certain aspects of Reaganism that seemed to mesh perfectly with the idea of a hyperreal simulacrum became more salient.

Baudrillard enabled me more closely to engage with what was going on in America during Reagan's presidency, to pay attention to a situation that I had previously just hoped would go away. It would not be an exaggeration to say that Baudrillard made me a more informed American citizen and initiated a series of activities (paper giving, independent studies, conferences) that led to a professional involvement with American Studies. But Baudrillard (and later Lacan) functioned as a transitional object for me in another way, as well. While teaching a course on ideology at a large Midwestern university, I discovered that many conceptually difficult and verbally abstruse ideas of contemporary French theory could be explicated to a heterogeneous undergraduate student body (without the requisite history-of-philosophy formation of my Yale students) by using the 1988 campaign as a sort of *lingua franca*. As the Reagan presidency gave way to that of George Herbert Walker Bush, I increasingly saw the American presidency as enacted or performed French theory. And, if Baudrillard improved my citizenship and teaching life, it was the first Bush who made me a Lacanian.

In other words, the postmodern presidency of George H. W. Bush drove me to Lacanian psychoanalysis, and Lacanian psychoanalysis in turn enabled me to watch Bush for four years. Bush was the medium through which some of Lacan's most seemingly opaque pronouncements (e.g., "the unconscious is on the outside," "I identify myself in language only by losing myself in it as object") finally made sense. Indeed, I began to wonder what people who did not read Lacan could possibly make of Bush. Indeed, Bush's parapraxes, what Lacan calls "linguistricks" ("*linguisterie*") or the "wacky lyricism" that Mark Crispin Miller has described as "a weird patois: the pidgin English of an old preppy on acid,"[23] necessitated a theoretical shift in my treatment of presidential rhetoric away from the semiotic and toward a more psychoanalytic approach. As will be explained at greater length in my reading of Bush's failed 1992 campaign (chapter 6) and of Clinton's botched first hundred days in office (chapter 8), parapraxes exemplify the unformalizable or unsymbolizable side of language that is most obvious in unconscious utterances, dreams, omissions, jokes, interruptions, and verbal or behavioral slips (bungled or symptomatic actions).

Bush, read in conjunction now with Lacan, initiated a shift in my critical standpoint that highlighted my divergence from linguistically inflected understandings of other scholars such as Edelman and Rogin. Edelman's description of leadership as a "banal dramaturgy"[24] whose major function was its sign value could accommodate a Bush as easily as a Reagan. Rogin was less willing than Edelman to see the presidency as an empty sign and placed greater emphasis on the referential or contextual in the service of a grand meta-narrative of American demonology. Rogin's brilliant knack for discovering and incorporating the often absurdist aspects of historical coincidence enriched his historicist perspective. Rogin did appeal (as we will see in chapters 2, 3, and 8) to Freudian and Kleinian psychoanalytic concepts and ably described the repetitive process of historical trauma and disavowal.

Lacanian psychoanalysis shifted my reading away from the rhetorical or symbolic politics tradition that focused on *purposive signs* or *intentional* framings of the speech situation and toward symptomatic effects or what is unconscious. The priority of the unconscious is subtended by a claim about the nature of knowledge: "Knowledge is what is already there, but always in the Other." Knowledge, in other words, is not a substance but "a structural dynamic . . . (which) comes about out of the mutual apprenticeship between two partially unconscious speakers which *both say more than they know*" (emphasis mine).[25]

Baudrillard Goes to Washington

> It is no longer theories which adapt themselves to events, but the reverse. Events now adapt themselves to the most hostile environments, like species adaptation. —Jean Baudrillard, *The Perfect Crime*[26]

The first Bush presidency not only displaced my critical posture from semiotics to psychoanalysis. I also became increasingly aware that the presidency was telling a meta-theoretical story about Baudrillardian sign theory where presidents would mark different moments of the simulacrum. "The Mirror of Reproduction: Baudrillard and Reagan's America" was my first attempt to situate the presidency away from discussions of representation and toward a more radical recasting of the semiotic object. Ronald Reagan has remained for many the iconic postmodern president, raising the scripted or televisual Kennedy communicational legacies to the new art form of the photo op. In his Simi Valley Presidential Library, there is a room dedicated to the "second Reagan revolution," resplendent with displays of television sets tuned to CNN and VCR machines, reminiscent of a Nam June Paik installation. So it is perhaps not inappropriate to organize my narrative around Baudrillard's concept of the simulacrum as the "iconic postmodern concept."[27] I am not doing this to reduce Baudrillard's theoretical contribution to a narrow "simulation" fashion moment (which would play as the bad "irresponsible" episode in a parallel-universe theory genre series "I Love the Eighties"). Rather, the simulacrum is key to Baudrillard's critique of the real as a semiotic category. It is this category of the "real" and its putative erasure or endangerment that has increasingly become an object of concern in our political culture today—whether in derogatory references to the "reality-based community" found among

W-Bush's advisers[28] or generative of inventive neologisms such as Stephen Colbert's "truthiness." It also became an issue when John McCain made a cameo appearance on 24, provoking charges of genre-blurring induced propaganda.

This critique of the real can be related to his earlier works of ideology critique such as *For a Critique of the Political Economy of the Sign,* where Baudrillard performs a deconstruction of sign value analogous to that of Marx on exchange value and money in *Capital.* A secondary content in both sign and commodity first appears "natural" (or "external"). This is the signified or the referent for the sign, or use value or needs for the commodity form. This "secondary" or derived form then is shown to be actually *internal to* and *produced by* the hegemonic form that serves as its effective support. The exchange value (Marx) or sign value of the president (Anne Norton) "is not external, but is a product of the sign and its prior reduction of this complex experiential symbolic relationship."[29] Thus, "reality" or "reference" is like the money form for Marx—a phantom, a spectral effect, or a trace. In other words, what we call the real—this semiotic real of the president designated by Tocqueville and Norton—is only a "semiotic reality effect." Baudrillard uses the same example of the table as Marx. "The 'real' table does not exist. If it can be registered in its identity (if it exists), this is because it has already been designated, abstracted, and rationalized by the separation that establishes it in this equivalence to itself."[30] It is this "equivalence to itself" that marked Reagan's career as president, according to his biographer Lou Cannon. It was *the role of a lifetime*: himself!

One narrative trajectory in *This Is Not a President* tracks this semiotic critique of the real through presidencies read against turns within Baudrillard's theory of the simulacrum (as well as the defensive—or symbolic—resistance to this process of semioticization). Understanding of this concept is often obscured by Baudrillard's dual and at times inconsistent genealogies of it. As both genealogies frame my analysis of presidents, I will briefly outline pertinent aspects of each, retaining the original French publication date next to the translated English title.

Baudrillard's first genealogy, "The Order of Simulacra" (*Symbolic Exchange and Death,* 1976), begins in the Renaissance. Signs exchange against each other, rather than against the real. This is due to the structural revolution in value that he had previously outlined in *Critique of the Political Economy of the Sign.* Semiotic processes (like those of economic-capital formation) accelerate and absorb the referent. This leads to hyperreal forms that are conceived from the point of view of their re-productivity or model. Ronald Reagan begins here at this moment of the hyperreal simulacrum. The second genealogy, detailed in "The Procession of Simulacra" (*Simulation and Simulacra*, 1981), is more Nietzschean. It has more import for later presidents such as Clinton and W-Bush, who conform to the theories of Baudrillard's recent formulations of virtual and integral reality (respectively, *The Perfect Crime*, 1996; *Paroxysm*, 1997; *Impossible Exchange*, 1999; *The Lucidity Pact*, 2004.) Here the story is about the sign's *dissimulation*. We can begin with Reagan as a sign that dissimulates *something* and turn to signs (such as the first President Bush) that dissimulate *nothing*. The starting point for the second genealogy is with the Christian iconoclasts and addresses the divine referential or code-DNA (or its French homonym, *adonai*-ADN).

The sign that dissimulates nothing rather than something is the switchpoint that separates my presentation of Reagan in chapter 2 as a hyperreal (hologram) from my reading of Bush in "This Is Not a President: Baudrillard, Bush, and Enchanted Simulation" (chapter 4) as a *trompe l'oeil*. For the *trompe l'oeil* referenced in the title of this chapter (and the larger book title) responds to the oppositional logic Baudrillard names "seduction." The hologram and *trompe l'oeil* both master the world of appearances, but they do so differently; *trompe l'oeil* withdraws a dimension, while a hyperreal hologram disturbs visuality by projection. Seduction disrupts the ideological process, which has been brilliantly resumed by Mike Gane as "the semiological reduction of the symbolic." It is in *Seduction* (1979) that Baudrillard sees the sign itself as offering, in Charles Levin's words, "the best available medium for the irruption of the symbolic."[31] Another way to mark this turn is to see it as a reversal of the Levi-Straussian opposition between sign and symbolic order; now the sign becomes necessary to the symbolic's realization. Baudrillard denotes this anthropological turn within the sign itself by the seemingly oxymoronic term, "the *enchanted* simulacrum." The enchantment or charm comes from turning the "evil forces" (*le malin génie*) of appearance against truth itself. This is part of my reading of Bush's otherwise politically tone-deaf response to the fall of the Berlin Wall.

The next stage of Baudrillard's sign theory sets a "disenchanted" simulacrum against the enchanted one and comes to the fore during the Clinton presidency. As outlined in *The Perfect Crime* (1996), reality has become excessively realized in a virtual order that is so technically perfect and absolute in its semio-realization of "reality" that it eclipses it. To distinguish this from Reagan hyperreality, I refer to this as "ultra" reality (as well as virtual reality or digital reality). It might be useful to consider another synonym for such technical perfection, first utilized in *Seduction*: "high fidelity" as the trope of the real's relation to itself in time and dimension. High fidelity is, of course, also a homonym for the exciting cause of Clinton's impeachment.[32] Baudrillard's language is resonant here: "Something else fascinates (but no longer seduces) you: technological perfection, 'high fidelity,' which is just as *obsessive and puritanical as the other conjugal fidelity*" (emphasis mine).[33]

This virtual order described as the next level of the simulacrum is one of high definition and real time. Baudrillard sees it not as a flight from or overcoming of realism but rather a veritable *orgy* of realism: "rage . . . to summon everything before the jurisdiction of signs."[34] This could be a better way to read the mania of the Starr report and all the investigations that plagued the Clintons, from the travel office inquiry to Whitewater to questions about the death of Vince Foster to the haircut logs, all of which are analyzed in the second half of chapter 7. Pornography becomes the condensation figure for this obsessive ultra realism, otherwise denoted as a "voyeurism of exactitude,"[35] where both the symbolic scene and relationality vanish.

Hypervisibility replaces previous modalities of spectatorial reciprocity. Saturation by absolute reality in the form of twenty-four-hour news channels on cable and satellite television and of the Internet exacerbate reality to the point of paroxysm, where it involutes of its own accord and leaves no trace. If Reagan was for Joan Copjec "the Shroud of Turin" (and *Spy* magazine, contemporaneous with his presidency, ran a visual gag—a cartoon of "guest towels of Turin where there was some traces left"),[36] the virtual revisits this figure in a more abyssal form: "In the shroud of the virtual the corpse of the real is forever unfindable."[37] What Baudrillard's title *The Perfect Crime* alludes to is the murder of reality by virtual reality. "Honey, I Shrunk the President: Psychoanalysis, Postmodernism, and the Clinton Presidency" (chapter 7) examines the way the real has now become an extreme phenomenon once it has been expelled from its own principle in the form of theories of wound culture and other practices of abjection I designate as "tabloid liberalism." I read the pathologization of Clinton's body and presidency, as well as the state-of-emergency tenor of the impeachment process as signs of a virtual order in which referential substance has become increasingly rare and even events have adapted themselves to theory. The first part of the Clinton chapter in particular examines what happens in an era of ultra reality, when the political spectacle gives way to the reality show and the president shifts from serving as mirror to serving as a screen. In ultra reality, we no longer fight shadows but transparency.

Baudrillard's more recent writings (immediately pre- as well as post-9/11) have tracked the metaphysical disappearance of reality in ways that anticipate and disturbingly resonate with life in W-Bush's America. For it is not that the real itself no longer exists but rather that its *principle* has faltered (or, perhaps, reality has overwhelmed its principle). In *The Intelligence of Evil or the Lucidity Pact,* Baudrillard designates this as *réalité intégrale* (complete or integral reality), a specific form of virtual reality predicated upon the deregulation of the reality principle. The virtual has become reality's ultimate predator: "The differential of time having disappeared, it is the integral function that wins out."[38] Baudrillard relentlessly tracks "immaterial" technologies of immanence, immersion, and immediacy as operational fetishes that absorb exteriority, reabsorb interiority, and no longer allow for adequate representation. The mirror gives way to the "cold epilepsy and overcharged inertia"[39] of screens. And irony is no longer ours to exercise, as it now resides in the object.

Baudrillard states clearly that hyperreality is the simulacrum's last stage (Reagan will be its last president). And virtual reality (to which we have become accustomed since Clinton) is decidedly not a simulacrum. Computer-generated equivalents and images are not signs. Moreover, even the sign is not what it used to be, "since there is no longer any 'real' for it to be the sign of. . . . This is the era of the digital, where the technologies of the virtual accomplish this miracle of abolishing both the thing and the sign."[40] *Impossible Exchange* provides further philosophical elaboration of Baudrillard's insights concerning the virtual in *Perfect Crime*. These are discussed in chapter 7, on the Clinton presidency, but can be briefly summarized as the idea of *telepresence* (how the collapsing of time and distance short-circuits "real" life and how the media, and especially television, now inhabit real life from the inside, on the model of a virus and cell): *high definition* (real time is hi-def time; porn is hi-def sex, the human genome is hi-def body). The world described in *Impossible Exchange* is that of speculative capital: "As for the sign, it is passing into the pure speculation and simulation of the virtual world, the world of the total screen, where the same uncertainty hovers over the real and virtual reality. *Once they go their separate ways, the real no longer has any force as sign and signs no longer have any force of meaning*" (emphasis mine).[41] This also changes the very nature of the object. "In all areas it evades us. It now appears only as a fleeting trace on computer screens. At the ends of their experimenting, the most advanced sciences can only register its disappearance."[42] Reality itself has become simulative in ways that have unmoored semiotics and the possibility of a critical approach to presidents and to events.

In simulation, the real object is taken for a sign. "But in a subsequent stage the sign becomes an object again, but not now a real object; an object much further removed from the real than the sign itself—an object off-camera, outside representation, a fetish. No longer an object to the power of the sign but an object to the power of the object—a pure, unrepresentable, unexchangeable object, yet a non-descript one."[43] Baudrillard references Agamben and says one can use the language of fetishism or perversion (as I do in my reading of W-Bush in chapter 9), but he marks this process otherwise. This transmutation of a sign into an object (a redoubled simulation) redoubles the abstraction (as it does in Marx's analysis of commodities), rendering the fetish even more invulnerable and immunizing the subject from his object of desire. The metaphysics of fetishistic investment is at work in the presidency of George W. Bush (although the Democrats do help), which places him in a different relation to the truth and the real than Reagan, who also seemed at times untouchable by history or fact. Fetishistic investment is an extreme form of singularity and literality. (Singularity, in Klossowski's definition, is "a sign without content.")

Events (such as 9/11) increasingly displace the object, as they alone are real, as opposed to the nonevents of the news/information/media: "If we see history as a film, . . . then the 'truth' of information consists in the post-synchronization, the dubbing and subtitling of the film of history."[44] The event resists or is recalcitrant to the nonevent of news/information. These mutations of the sign and the object into the more compelling figures of the fetish and the event suggest that there are more than surface dissimilarities between the conflation of fact and fiction or the exposure of presidential lies (Iran-Contra for Reagan, WMDs for Bush). This only underscores the temptation to read and reread these narratives in terms of their denouement or retrospective illusion.

Enjoy Your Presidential Symptoms

> Terrorists never stop thinking of ways to hurt the American people and
> neither do we.   —G. W. Bush, August 11, 2004[45]

Our second theoretical trajectory concerns presidential subjectivity and
the types of unconscious national identifications that undergird a president's appeal. For the president is less a symbol or a sign than what
Lacan denotes as a master signifier, a locus for projections and desires
that constitute our identity. In his recent book *Cruel and Unusual,*
Mark Crispin Miller calls the current President Bush "our projector-in-
chief."[46] The term "master signifier" arises from a homonymic play between being and mastery. "*M'être à moi-même*" is the urge to master/be
master [*maître*] myself by being myself [*m'être*] to myself.[47] Lacanian
psychoanalysis is concerned with the intersubjective dialectic of identity
construction, that is, the president as stand-in or avatar, our fetish in
practice as well as in theory.

I move from an early presentation of the first President Bush in the
1988 electoral campaign (chapter 4) that uses his parapraxis as a signifying form (i.e., a *trompe l'oeil*) as illustrative of male hysteria to the
interpellative appeal of his presidential performance as male masochist
in 1992, the subject of "Bush, the Man Who Sununu Too Much: Male
Trouble and Presidential Subjectivity" (chapter 5). My attempt to enjoy
Bush's symptom (in Zizek's terminology) led me ultimately to read him
as an *enactment* of what were (at the time) cutting-edge queer cultural
studies and feminist film studies theories. Bush becomes in this chapter,
as Hillary does later on (in chapter 6, " 'Chicks with Dicks': Transgendering the Presidency"), a performance artist of contemporary 1990s
theory concerning (possible) gender subversions—in the appropriation
of formerly female-gendered pathologies (male masochism for Bush) or
masquerade and drag (for Hillary).

There is also a meta-narrative about Lacanian theory in my presentation of presidents as related to the three registers—symbolic, real, and
imaginary. Reagan exemplifies a symbolic identification. He was an "in-
imitable" figure. Symbolic presidents are great condensation symbols,
serving as points of identification: "from the point from which I am being observed to appear likeable to myself." The first President Bush and
Bill Clinton are presidents illustrative of imaginary identification: "the

way I see myself in order to appear likeable."[48] We identify with "imaginary" presidents (in Zizek's formulation) to the point at which he is like us. (This is why Kerry, Gore, and Lionel Jospin never had a chance in an age of imaginary and not symbolic leadership.) The second chapter on Hillary Clinton (chapter 9, "Hillary Regained") tracks the first lady's successful transformation into senator and asks if her story is one of gender and its tie to the imaginary register. Or is her "electability" a question of sexuality linked to the real? (This is a question we also could ask about Barack Obama's appeal.) A gender-oriented reading of Hillary would still be refracted from the masquerade and would situate her more coherent performance along the lines of "extreme" imaginary makeover. A reading premised on the real would see her less as an ego ideal than as an object of desire or *jouissance*. W-Bush's war presidency (as discussed in chapter 8, "Father, Can't You See I'm Bombing? A Bush Family Romance") is situated on the terrain of the real. Successful presidential contenders for 2008 will be on the register of the real—displaying either perversion (McCain) or the Other *jouissance* (Hillary, Obama).

Another way of viewing the difference between Bush *père et* Bush *fils* is tied to the changing status of the Oedipus complex in Lacan's work, which views it less as a Levi-Straussian myth than as a "dream" to be interpreted. Different presidents represent different father figures. The contrast is greatest between Ronald Reagan and W-Bush. Ronald Reagan is the canonical Oedipal father. The Oedipal father establishes law, which comes before transgression. The father in the Oedipus complex is subject to the same law that he has transmitted to his child (e.g., the prohibition on incest). W-Bush, in contrast, is the model's inverted figure—the Oedipal father as *père sévère* or pervert, as I argue in chapter 8. In Russell Grigg's formulation, "the pervert is not limited by any submission to the law of an order transcendent to him."[49] (He is "the decider.") Perversion specifies a relation to the law, and we see this in W-Bush's unprecedented use of signing statements to evacuate the contents of a law; in the crafting of the Military Commissions Act, which enables the president to, in effect, make law through his interpretation of Article 3 of the Geneva Convention; in his preemptive firing of U.S. Attorneys and his replacing them with others who are subject to no confirmation process or court approval; and in his attempts either to circumvent or to perform an end run around the FISA court.

This different Oedipal figure is presented in Lacan's *Séminaire XVII* as a "father retroactively created as the father who enjoys" in *Totem and Taboo*. (It is interesting to note that this 1968 seminar of Lacan, first published in 1991, has achieved prominence in the years of the W-Bush presidency in the works of Joan Copjec, Slavoj Zizek, Alenka Zupancic, and others of the Ljubljana school.) If the aim of paternal prohibition in Oedipus was to contain, regulate, or otherwise pacify the ferocity and omnipotence of the m/Other, this revised father takes on all this maternal power, cruelty, and omnipotence. My Bush family romance retrospectively reads the first George Bush as a primal father who enjoys (in chapter 8) and tracks the rhetorical displacements of the Bar m/Other from strong maternal superego holding AIDS babies during the 1992 State of the Union to a cold and cruel counterpart, revealed to devastating effect by the First Mother's remarks concerning the effects of Hurricane Katrina and on the Iraqi dead. On *Good Morning America*, Barbara Bush issued a preemptive strike against showing full war coverage on television: "Why should we hear about body bags and deaths and how many, what day it is gonna happen? . . . It's not relevant. So why should I waste my beautiful mind on that?" Her remarks on the displaced Katrina victims in the Houston Astrodome received similar media attention: "So many of the people in the arena here, you know, were underprivileged anyway so this is working very well for them."[50] This was not the strong, reassuring maternal figure of chapters 4 and 5 but a figure of sovereign enjoyment: haughty, cold, indifferent, and cruel.

Séminaire XVII dramatically realigned the prior relation between the master signifier and enjoyment in Lacan's previous writings. *Jouissance* is a difficult notion to give an account of. It is, by Lacan's own statements, not definable, as it is precisely that which escapes symbolization.[51] In seminars such as *The Ethics of Psychoanalysis*, the signifier was in an antinomical tension with enjoyment. Later, in *The Four Fundamental Concepts*, both concepts were put together along the lines of a structural analogy of heterogeneous elements. It is with *Séminaire XVII* that enjoyment and the signifier are posited together as "an essential element of every discursivity."[52] And this co-imbrication reveals that enjoyment is a political factor. Lacan makes explicit the linkage between *jouissance* and politics in this seminar at the moment when he interrogates the place of psychoanalysis in politics.[53] *Jouissance* takes place in the body through *invasions* and *inscriptions*. One of my favorite analyses is that of Parveen Adams, who says that there is no direct relation to *jouissance* and that we attain access to it through its leftovers. She issues a caveat: "I will add that *jouissance* isn't very nice, and . . . your mother should have warned you against it."[54] While the body is the "enjoying substance" (as Lacan discusses in *Séminaire XX: Encore*), one can know enjoyment only through the detour of a signifier. Paul Verhaeghe describes how this comes about in a language resonant of Bush as "wartime" president. *Jouissance* takes place in the body through *invasions*. But they are inscribed on the body through the *intervention* of the Other. "Walking along the road to *jouissance*, one will inevitably follow the signs that have been previously erected along the road. This instinctual knowledge is then grafted onto this mapping."[55] This occurs through repetitions—as attempts to attain *jouissance*—yet with inevitable detours.

I conclude my situating of the chapters anachronistically—by recasting my first Lacanian reading, "Oliver North and the Lying Nose" (chapter 3), last. This chapter takes as its target a covert operation, Iran-Contra, that functioned as a surplus object to my earlier account of Reaganism. That this is what Zizek might call an "excremental remainder" or *objet a* might be confirmed by the fact that it was (once again) a "missing portion" during the necrospective extravaganza of the Reagan funeral media blitz. Iran once again figures prominently in the news. Mark Crispin Miller cites the rehabilitation of perpetrators of Iran-Contra; John Poindexter, Otto Reich, Elliot Abrams, and John Negroponte all work or worked in the Bush government. Fawn Hall's testimony in support of Oliver North sounds very familiar in a post-9/11 world: "Sometimes you have to go above the written law."[56] This necessary duplicity is invoked by the use of a religious figure: "What Ollie North did was basically the moral equivalent of what spies and Rahab did in Jericho. Rahab lied to protect lives."[57] Robert Gates (an Iran-Contra protagonist) is now Donald Rumsfeld's replacement as secretary of defense; Daniel Ortega is even president of Nicaragua again.

Daily news is punctuated with public disclosures of governmental "breaches" (a movie recently opened with that name): of secret rendition, warantless wiretapping, the "outing" of an intelligence officer, Valerie Plame. Both the Iran-Contra affair and the W-Bush presidency share issues of dubious legality, obsessive secrecy, and hypocritical "leaking." They both expose the relative impotence of hermeneutic unmasking gestures. In this chapter, I present two nonhermeneutic models with which to interpret Iran-Contra: either as Derridean "open letters" or according to a model of such a radically designified text that it must first be fantastically reconstituted. (Abraham and Torok). I suggest that we do the same for the current administration. Reagan vowed that he did not exchange arms for hostages; he parsed a health bulletin to the American people: "I did not have cancer. I had something in me that had cancer in it and it was removed." W-Bush tells us about the Iraq war: "We are not winning. We are not losing." We can read this media-critiqued "bubble of denial" as a crypt (as outlined in chapter 3): as a designified utterance, along the lines of an *anti*-semantics. One of the lessons of Iran-Contra concerns not just the political robustness of an Oliver North or a Robert Gates—as recent cabinet choices have shown, there are second and third political acts, and you can go home (to Washington) again and again. Iran-Contra (like Operation Iraqi Freedom) is a story about how language in a national-security state is not about signification; neither metaphors nor literal meanings are used in an ordinary language sense. The meaning of signs now radiates in a radically undetermined way. This goes beyond Orwellian "doublespeak," which is why that felicitous concept cannot apprehend it. (Partly this is no doubt also due to the processes described by Baudrillard as outlined earlier.) "Language is set at an angle with itself and shatters all linear correspondence." Would this aphorism of Derrida's provide a more productive framing than "hypocrisy" or "lies," albeit a framing that drives Keith Olbermann nuts and provides grist for Stephen Colbert or Jon Stewart's objective irony?

> It (*Ça*) begins with a tickle and it finishes in a blaze of *gasoline*. That's *jouissance*. (*Séminaire XVII*: 83)

Language set against itself and language inextricably linked with *jouissance* are my apparent alternatives to a more conventional study of presidential politics as symbol, media effect, or institution. But these are also ways of becoming more intimate with language's "real," its non-sense. Lacan's most directly political *Séminaire XVII* demonstrated how closely bound were the signifier and enjoyment, but also how they exist in a paradoxical tension: "the signifier is both the cause of the impossibility of reaching *jouissance* and simultaneously, the path to its attainment."[58] In these new times of war and death (to trope on Freud), psychoanalysis presents a different way of "enjoying something that is not transcendent, but which lies within the subject, *though not hidden in its depths.*" I concur with Eric Laurent in finding Lacan's teachings a warning against forms of prevalent fascist desire: "There are many ways of enjoying something besides the Other's signifiers in me."[59]

Organizational Note

This Is Not a President takes its title from the figure of the *trompe l'oeil*, celebrated in numerous artistic works, such as Holbein's *Ambassadors*, which is subject to a lengthy discussion in Lacan's *Séminaire XI: The Four Fundamental Concepts of Psychoanalysis*.

In this painting, two viewpoints are proffered. The frontal (or geometric) view reveals a manifest political content of two diplomats. When this frontal view is surrendered, a previously blind spot (in this case, a death skull image) emerges. This book can also be read perspectivally. The chapters follow a sequence of theoretical texts (Baudrillard, Lacan, Zizek, Butler . . .) and moments in a presidential administration. They can be read "geometrically" to see how well ideas of Baudrillard or Lacan serve as explanatory matrices for the political examples. But the chapters can also be read "anamorphotically" or awry (as a type of presidency journal) to see how what momentarily appeared as an explanatory cultural theory (semiotic readings of Reaganism, feminist Lacanian writings on male hysteria and male masochism, Butlerian gender performativity, Zizekian approaches to seemingly everything cultural) inflected the Baudrillarian theoretical progress narrative that provides one line of the book (tracking the presidency from the point of view of the object) or the shift from the Lacanian registers of the symbolic to the imaginary to the real that punctuate the narrative from the point of view of presidential subjectivity. To facilitate a historicist or aesthetic inquiry into the interplay between frame and narrative, I have signaled the date of composition of each essay. I have tried to restrict revisions of the essays to points of clarification that draw upon the same texts that were originally used but have signaled newer literatures as well as more contemporaneous examples in the footnotes. Each chapter is an attempt to read the president in "real time." Moreover, as my reading of Clinton's presidency is also a story about the shift from symbolic to imaginary identifications with the president and about how our investments are less along the lines of what Lacan would designate as desire and more about the "falling into the frame of reference of the Other" constitutive of the drive, the chapters on both Clintons enact some of the problems of "presidential transference and countertransference" that they partly seek to describe.

The chapters are also somewhat diverse with respect to authorial voice. Lacan's *Séminaire XVII* outlines four discursive possibilities, each of which enacts both a knowledge claim and a subjective positioning in relation to that enunciation. The introduction and more expository moments are examples of university discourse that attempts to link several fields of knowledge but that resists precipitating a key signifier or concept out of these disparate fields that might totalize or order them. Several chapters (these should be recognized by their titles!) adopt what Lacan calls the discourse of the hysteric, which contests the dominant frame of reference in which concepts are traditionally ordered. Chapter 3, on Iran-Contra, is an example of analytic discourse, which adopts the standpoint of the *objet a,* or unsymbolizable excess, as are parts of chapter 9, on Hillary Clinton's Senate campaign, which describes her transition from a body that matters to a *jouissive* body that mutters.

2

The Mirror of Reproduction
Baudrillard and Reagan's America (1989)

A universe where the image ceases to be second in relation to a model, where imposture pretends to be the truth or finally, where there is no more original but an eternal sparkle where in the glitter of detour and return the absence of origin is dispersed.

—Maurice Blanchot

It's a re-ron.
    —Gil Scott Heron

It should not be surprising that Ronald Reagan intrigues semiologists and rhetoricians. He serves as a convenient *topos* of many structuralist and poststructuralist themes. The "Great Communicator" consistently argues for voice over text, for phonocentrism over logocentrism. His early career of sports "visualizations" put into question the difference between discourse and referent, original and copy. His first presidential spokesman, with the felicitously homonymic surname Speakes, would argue for a new Lacanian reading of a pseudo-crossing of the bar between signifier and signified. And, most recently, the latest White House revelations echo that question dear to both astrologists and semiologists: "What's your sign?"[1]

The most insightful theoretical analyses of Reagan have been those of Michael Rogin and Anne Norton, which have treated the president as a sign. These readings have been largely meta-analyses of other texts, such as Hubler, Cannon, and Leamer,[2] and their explicit central problematic is the conflation of the cinematic signifier with the cinematic signified: "An uncanny slippage between life and film marked Ronald Reagan's entry into the movies";[3] "The easy slippage between life and his early films meant, in William James' terminology, that in Hollywood

Reagan was only once born";[4] "Reagan, . . . found out who he was through the roles he played on film."[5] Indeed, in a peculiarly appropriate twist, Reagan is given back as a stage name his real name. " 'Ronald Reagan, Ronald Reagan' repeated the headman, and the others around the table said it after him. 'I like it' the boss decided, and gave Ronald Reagan back his own name."[6] While other stars receive stage names, Ronald Reagan gets his "real" name back, paralleling the confusion between original and copy that we will see in Charles Matton's works as characteristic of simulation. For Ronald Reagan, the real comes back as a double of a self that never was. Indeed, this is consonant with the logic of the Platonic simulacrum as defined by Fredric Jameson: "the identical copy for which no original has ever existed."[7]

As my presentation of Reagan as a hyperreal object is a radical displacement of the semiotic argument, a discussion of Baudrillard's notion of simulation and the hyperreal is in order. Baudrillard's notion of the simulacrum marks a significant departure from the representational basis of signification. The model of simulation has three characteristics: the substitution of (or precedence) of the model for the referent; the neutralization of the signified by the code; and the priority of reproduction over production. It overturns the relation between the signifier and the signified and is a next step in the radical questioning of the priority of reference at the heart of Saussurian linguistics.[8] The adoption of Saussure's paradigm entails a revision of the question of reference, a revision of the relation between word and thing as conventional and not phenomenal. Baudrillard's notion of simulation is yet another turn of the linguistic screw, which designates reference prior to designating the referent. Reference is now self-referential. Baudrillard's notion of the hyperreal resumes these philosophic concerns.

In *Symbolic Exchange and Death*, Baudrillard defines the hyperreal as the meticulous reduplication of the real, preferably through another reproductive medium—photocopying, photography, film, Memorex. Moreover, the hyperreal is not only that which can be reproduced but that which is always already reproduced. The real is "[T]hat for which it is possible to give an equivalent representation."[9] The hyperreal opposes itself to the concept of representation and its twin notion of the simulacrum. It opposes itself to the idea of a false representation and, by extension, to the distinction between original and copy. Baudrillard begins his undoing of the concept of representation with Borges's fable of the mapmakers who construct such a detailed "map" of the empire that it is coextensive with it. This absolute coincidence of referent with reality marks the end of our "representationalist imaginary," an imaginary replete with second-order "simulacra" such as "the map, the double, the mirror, the concept."[10] In an era of hyperreality, the territory no longer precedes the map but is generated by it. Simulation and hyperreality are genetic and nuclear categories, not specular or discursive ones. One reads the entire logic of American society, already there reproduced and imminently reproducible, in any gas station, any Burger King, any Midwestern American street, as if it were inscribed in a societal genetic code.[11] There is no longer the reflexive or critical difference between the real and its concept, between reality and appearance; rather, there is operational miniaturization. The real is produced via the miniaturization of its model. Enlargement/reduction replaces the specularity of reflection.

These features are present in the work of Charles Matton's miniature reconstructions. Matton first miniaturizes old studios in meticulous fetishistic detail. There are newspapers the size of matchbooks, miniature paintings, painted wallpaper with graffiti, tiny furniture—all the accoutrements of a tiny doll's house. Matton then paints canvases based on blown up photographs of these reconstructions. Baudrillard, in his introduction to the catalogue of a Matton exhibit at the Palais de Tokyo, sees this miniaturization as an attempt to make realism credible.[12] Perfect miniaturization creates the illusion of actual rooms when photographed. By manipulating the camera angle, Matton can quickly complete a big canvas that gives the illusion of a realist painting. The photographic step is crucial in the move from realism to hyperrealism. Matton's work relies on the camera angle to seemingly displace subjectivity and to confer visual authority. Moreover, these reconstructions displace the notion of the original. It is difficult to know exactly what is an original in Matton's work. Is it the sketch, the model, the Polaroid? Are these originals or reconstructions of an original?

It should also be noted that the hyperreal is opposed to the surreal, as well as the real. The surreal was an attempt to break down the distinction between the "dream" and the real, between sleep and nonsleep, the unconscious and the conscious. The surreal asserts that the banality of everyday life could be surreal, but only in privileged moments of art and imagination. This privileging of art and the imaginary serves as an alibi for the reality principle. In circumscribing when the banal can become transcendent (surreal), the surreal reinscribes the distinction between art and "life" in negation. Hyperreality refuses the surrealist's implicit separation of the real and the imaginary. What is unreal? The real's hallucinatory relation to itself? Wills asks the rhetorical question concerning Reagan's thespian prowess: "Could he act? Of course he could. . . . He always acted like Ronald Reagan. It is a heartwarming role."[13] How much Reagan resembles himself recalls Deleuze on the Eternal Return of the simulacrum—that is, "the same which returns as the like," which attacks the world of representation. For in the Eternal Return (and in its Reagan *Back to the Future* re-ron), "everything happens as if a latent content blocked a manifest one."[14]

Rogin and Norton's readings of Reagan oppose themselves to Baudrillard's conceptions in their persistent attachment to the reality principle and to the "alibi" of reference. The line between fiction and reality, between original and copy, is underscored by the preoccupation with quotation and attribution of quotes. For Rogin, Reagan knows what reality is because he normally credits the lines he is using. (Similarly, in quoting from a movie, Rogin infers a "real" as well as a cinematic homage.) Reagan would have a cinematic reality principle if not a historical one. Norton counterargues that, although Reagan makes the attribution, he ascribes the lines to the actors and not to the fictional characters. For example, Reagan attributes the line "Make my day" to Clint Eastwood, the actor who plays Detective Harry Callahan. On the one hand, this slippage between fiction and reality is pervasive in the Reagan era. Shirley MacLaine plays herself on the televised version of her autobiography, as does Ron Reagan Jr. in the American Express advertisements. The comedian David Steinberg's joke that "I'm not a president, but I play one on TV" reads as an apt empirical description of the Reagan presidency. Yet, at the same time, this concern with accuracy (in media, in academe), plagiarism (Joe Biden), and falsification and verification ("Trust, but verify") all seem to be futile attempts to rejoin the signifier to the signified, to track down a referent and make it responsible—in short, as so many heroic attempts to deny the breakdown of the signifying chain.

Both semiotic accounts are recuperations of two different theoretical projects and serve different theoretic agendas. For Norton, the concept of representation as exemplified by Barthes underwrites liberal regimes and the realist aesthetic they presuppose. "What is particularly useful about Barthes' theory is his contention that the signifier and the signified are finally inseparable and that their interdependence . . . is entailed in the concept of representation and hence in the act of signification."[15] Representation is a key concept for understanding liberal regimes and liberal institutions. Norton's focus is on representative strategies made available to presidents through interplay of signifier and signified. This focus (like that of Garry Wills) is semantic—that is, concerned with reconstituting networks of meaning. Reagan is especially "representative" as an exemplar of Whitman's "divine average" and in his rhetorical use of office. Rogin's treatment is a recuperation of neo-Marxist critical theories. His reading presents a history of a countersubversive tradition in which signifiers and signifieds of American demonology retain the binary structure so necessary to the social construction of Others. There is a diachronic procession of groups that are then constructed as the Other. The signifying form remains the same; its contents (or, in this context, discontents) change color. If both treatments aim on the semiotic level to recuperate, there is also a psychoanalytic subtext that precludes this and works against the more positive formulations.

Let us consider for the moment both treatments of Ronald Reagan as a representative figure, a sign, indeed, a trope. For Garry Wills, he is the "great American synecdoche,"[16] as he is also implicitly in Norton's formulation as "head of state." "Head of state" and "commander-in-chief" are both expressions that designate the president as either the momentary representative of the nation as a whole or the permanent commander-in-chief of some part of the whole. Rogin alludes to "Ronald Reagan's self-presentation as a *figure*" (trope) and sees this slippage between movies and "life" as "synecdochic" for a political culture increasingly impervious to distinctions between fiction and history. Reagan's tropological status is thus tied to his person and to his office.

Synecdoche is a rhetorical figure that designates part-whole relationships. It is a figure of integration suggestive of a qualitative relation. The example "He was all heart" does not designate a part of the body (literally) as much as it designates a quality (empathy, compassion). Hayden White notes that "it is possible to construct the two parts in the manner of an integration within a whole that is qualitatively different from the sum of the parts and of which the parts are but microcosmic replications."[17] Reagan, as synecdoche, is a microcosmic replication of American popular culture.

The trope of synecdoche intrudes on both Rogin's and, to a lesser extent, Norton's reading of the presidency. It is important for Rogin's reading of Nixon in the discussion of the king's two bodies. The head of state is the figure employed to designate the body politic, and the Oval Office is the "heart" of the executive branch. This heart is indeed a heart of darkness, with a richly anal erotic subtext. One of the great merits of Rogin's figuratively informed reading is that the Watergate break-in and bugging, as well as the Nixon tapes, can no longer be seen as accident but must be viewed as essential to (at the heart of) the Nixon presidency. "Like Wilson, Nixon gave up his home for the White House heart. The heart was the heart of the king's royal body. The taping system aimed to gain Nixon secure possession of the king's royal body." The tapes were "love letters to the White House heart."[18] As with Norman Mailer's DJ, the bug is an inverted form of the heart, a part that names the (ass)-(w)hole. Thus, it is a synecdoche that is also (and quite literally) an interior duplication, a figure called a *"mise-en-abime"* placed into the abyss. Stephen Melville defines the *"mise-en-abime"* as an interior duplication, originally of heraldic origin and "referring to the settling of a smaller version of a given shield at the center of that shield. . . . [M]ise-en-abime implies an infinite perspective on and reduplication of the initial motif."[19]

For Rogin, the trope of synecdoche underlines the shift toward a royal executive. "Far from gaining independence from its occupant the office gave transcendent importance to the person. It placed him above the law. It transformed rational independent citizens into the limbs of a body politic, governed by their head."[20] The president as head of state, as synecdoche, underwrites metonyms of power as it conflates the royal with the actual body. This conflation is rhetorically produced and maintained. Presidential efficacy is tied to corporeal integrity—the ability of a president to maintain and control his body parts. Nixon describes the loss of his two right-hand men: " 'I cut off one arm and then I cut off the other arm.' These were the limbs of the king's royal body."[21] Genette notes the precarious status of the trope of synecdoche: "We see that at the limit all metonymy is convertible to synecdoche by appealing to the higher ensemble, and all synecdoche into metonymy through recourse to the relation between the constituent parts."[22] This rhetorical figure is *strategically* constituted and can be strategically undermined. With Reagan, we witness an interesting development. Here the (rhetorical) struggle is not between the heart and the limbs, between synecdoche and metonymy, but between two synecdoches: the heart and the head. In admitting an arms-for-hostage trade (another tropological exchange), Reagan states: "I told the American people that I did not trade arms for hostages. My heart and my best intentions still tell me that it is true, but the facts and the evidence tell me it is not."[23] I will argue in the second part of this essay that this two-headed, doubly synecdochal (dare we say schizo?) presidency is emblematic of the postmodern presidency. We should note in passing, however, the rhetorical perversity of the reliance on Reagan's autobiography (*Where's the Rest of Me?*), for all figurative assessments of him as synecdoche distinguish themselves from metonymy by linking the part with the *rest*. In the second part of this essay, we will see that Reagan is a stand-in for the rest of American culture. *Where's the Rest of Me?* underlines this synecdochal status and is an interior reduplication (an *en-abime* as opposed to a conflation) on both the narrative and the formal levels.

If commentators have concurred on the characterization of Reagan as a synecdoche, they have also noted his status as a signifier. For Ronald Reagan was elected as a signifier—that is, elected for his "representation of leadership and not for his possession of qualities of leadership." He is thus not just a signifier but also an autonomous one. He represents the nonobligation of the signifier to the signified. And it is precisely in tracking this autonomous signifier that we see that charges of either hypocrisy (i.e., he doesn't do what he supposedly represents) or vacuity are epistemically inappropriate. "What is at work here," as Norton aptly argues, "is neither delusion nor ignorance but something far more interesting."[24]

One could read the history of twentieth-century American presidents as a gradual loosening of the signifier from the signified. Indeed, from the interdependency of the signifier/signified in the Elizabethan doctrine of the king's two bodies to the radical semiurgy of the sign (the hysterical exchange evinced in Reykjavik),[25] we can evoke parallels. Nor is it surprising that for both Norton and Rogin, FDR plays a pivotal role. Roosevelt does represent a limited case of grounded nonarbitrary signification. His physical paralysis literalizes the economic paralysis of an America crippled by the Great Depression. With Roosevelt, there is congruence between signifier and signified. The counterintuitive reading that to elect a crippled president in a time of economic depression was unthinkable becomes understandable when read as a remedy (*pharmakon*) to the arbitrary political economy of the sign exemplified by the stock market crash. "The collapse of faith in signs necessitated a return to non-arbitrary signification, it demanded a congruence between signifier and signified. Roosevelt offered this."[26]

FDR marks one extreme of signification, what Baudrillard calls a natural simulacrum and Foucault, a signature. (Indeed, Baudrillard's outline of the succession of simulacra reads at times like a parody of Foucault's orders of representation in *The Order of Things*: "counterfeits" parallel "signatures"; "series" parallels "table.") Signs have an absolute clarity within the natural simulacrum. Each sign refers to a determinant status. Or, as Ronald Barthes would have it, here the sign is full. Gerald Ford represents the empty signifier. Who can forget such Fordisms as "Things are more like they are now than they have ever been"?[27] We witness a passage from the surrealism of Ford to the hyperreality of Reagan, passing through Jimmy Carter as the master of the nonsynchronous gesture. Democrats are tied to motivated signs and metonyms such as interest groups and constituencies. Republicans are synecdochic, tied to the *reste,* the remains. This is the potlatch theory of Republican presidents.

For Baudrillard, this representational view of language and politics intrudes into the order of political assassinations. Only those who represent can be assassinated—Kennedy, Martin Luther King. Ford and Reagan have a right to a puppet or simulated murder. Reagan is shot by an assassin acting out of a movie script (*Taxi Driver*) for the love of a movie heroine (Jodie Foster) on the night of the Academy Awards. These simulated assassinations reempower. "In the olden days the king . . . had to die—that was his strength. Today he does his miserable utmost to pretend to do so."[28] Reagan's unsuccessful assassination preserved his "blessing of power" as it previewed the split-screen 1984 Republican convention. The scenario of split screens was similar to the convention of 1984 and in many ways anticipated Nancy and Ronnie's nonsynchronous exchange of greeting.

"The television audience watching a screen saw a Hollywood audience watch another screen. One audience saw the other applaud a taped image of a healthy Reagan while the real president lay in a hospital bed." Rogin recounts the whirling *en-abimes* of the attempted Reagan assassination. "The shooting climaxed the film's ingestion of reality. In so doing, it climaxed in an uncanny way Reagan's personal project: the creation of a *disembodied* self that, rising above inner conflicts, would reflect back to the president and all the rest of us not only how he looked and sounded but more important—how he felt and who he was."[29]

This view of the president as an autonomous signifier is different, however, from saying that the president has charisma. For charisma is

Original jacket cover for Michael Rogin's *Ronald Reagan the Movie and Other Episodes in Political Demonology.*

grounded in the body. The pure sign is, on the contrary, disembodied. As Arthur Kroker describes it, the pure sign is relational, tautological, signaling a move away from a grounding in the body to a nonsexually based power. Michael Rogin's book jacket of Reagan's truncated head and shoulders on the convention screen underscores his status as a truncated, disembodied figure. Indeed, Reagan's asexuality becomes noteworthy when juxtaposed to that other Hollywood version of the presidency, Camelot. The Kennedy years, for Garry Wills, represented an unhealthy union of Hollywood and Washington, where "political shame is tickled and played for the story's sake," from the shot of the assassinated Kennedys in *The Parallax View* to the revision of Chappaquiddick in *Blow Out*. Wills sets up an image of Reagan as the sanitized Disney version of the union between Hollywood and Washington in which Nancy and Ronnie both get to continue playing their roles as "chastity symbols."[30] The Kennedy-Reagan opposition also applies when we consider terms such as "charisma." Kennedy was charismatic. Kennedy's problem was that he "got the girl"; Reagan was always a peculiarly asexual leading man in romantic comedies. Rogin recounts: "Resenting accusations that he 'never got the girl' in his movies, Reagan listed the heroines he got." The question was how "his list included girls he got by losing his legs, by nearly dying of epilepsy and anthrax and by undergoing other forms of humiliation."[31] For Rogin, these movies revealed Reagan's psychological attractiveness: He got the girls by being dependent. Moreover, there is an uncanny slippage between these roles and his "real" domestic life. After surviving anthrax in *Stallion Road*, he comes down with viral pneumonia in "real life." In this reading, his roles become "precreations" of his life as his dependence and domesticity (especially his leglessness) become *en-abimes* of his need for corporate support (from both MCA and GE).

Nor should "truncated" be confused with "legless." Although crippled, Roosevelt was never disembodied. Seen as a pre-polio playboy ("footloose") or as a brave crippled president, there was none of the slippage between personal bodies and the body politic so desired by Reagan. The importance of Roosevelt for both Norton and Rogin is the importance of a bounded sign, either in its Nietzschean guise ("revaluation of values") or in its Marxist form (tied to an ultimate transcendental signified, the people). FDR becomes a springboard for a psychoanalytic reading that itself serves as an alibi for a bounded sign.

The problem of leglessness relates both to the question of disembodiment (the president as pure sign) and to articulation in general. Articulation is the focus of both authors. Indeed, articulation is something that both limbs and mouths do. We witness a division of theoretical labor; Norton concentrates on oral aggression, while Rogin unpacks the surgical and corporeal metaphors involved in leglessness. Both are psychoanalytic accounts. Norton's focus is on Reagan the corporate sponsor and talking head, while Rogin's is on the Oedipal cutting off of the family. Moreover, Reagan's surgical metaphors evince slippage in both directions, so that Reagan can embody punishment and still claim that his programs have hurt no one. He can, in other words, have his cake and eat it, too.

Having his cake and, especially, eating it is the *topos* for Norton. Reagan is presented as an American with Promethean orality, on a par with Davy Crockett and the other great oral compulsives of the westward expansion. Norton focuses on Reagan's primal screams and his costly china. "He could consume more on the plates than Crockett could by filling them."[32] Although she focuses on the metaphorical significance of ingestion, the form is more akin to Georges Bataille's description of the potlatch and of "senseless expenditure" (*dépenser,* that is, nonutilitarian). Norton prefers a model of identification, however, and Reagan thus "represents" America in eating. Eating stands in for speaking. Reagan is a talking head for GE, for MCA, for the Hollywood unions. We witness a historical shift from a territorial, land-based first moment of American history (i.e., the westward expansion). This is displaced to a period of treaties and verbal agreements that parallel and complement oral aggression. Reagan is situated at a later moment of consumer capitalism.

Norton's attempt to relate corporate America to consumer society is an attempt to rebind the sign while acknowledging polysemy. Polysemy and pluralism make strange bedfellows in this (ultimately) liberal reading of the sign (albeit with a strange admixture of Nietzsche). Her reading is itself predicated on pluralistic exchange relations, a characteristic of a rational political economy. But what if Reagan's orality (which would comprise that of David Stockman and the most recent Pentagon scandals) was characteristic of a radical discontinuity within the exchange relationship? What if we take seriously the analysis of postmodernism (such as Jameson's) that the crisis of representation results from an overgeneralization of exchange value to the point where the memory of use value is erased? The disobligation of the sign, the detachment of the signifier, would then parallel the uncoupling of the economic sign. Reagan's enormous budget, the Carl Saganesque "billions and billions" of expenditures, the gargantuan sums involved in the Pentagon scandals (as well as Imelda Marcos's fantastic shoe and black bra collection—a veritable museum) attest to a break with this rational utilitarian view of the sign and a shift more in keeping with Bataille's notions in *La Part Maudite.*[33]

Bataille's notion would distinguish between real and symbolic (i.e., unproductive) expenditure such as that for luxury, cults, games, spectacles, art; all of these examples represent activities that "have no end beyond themselves." Moreover, the "loss must be as great as possible in order for that activity to take on its true meaning." Each type of expenditure represents two principles (homogeneity and heterogeneity) that are of different orders. Homogeneous elements are those "neutral and abstract aspects of defined and identified objects." Heterogeneous reality, which defined fascist regimes for Bataille, is one of shock or force. These two orders are mutually exclusive. Homogeneity underwrites useful, productive society. Commensurability is key here: "the common denominator, the foundation of social homogeneity . . . is money, namely, the calculable equivalent of the different products of collective activity."[34]

Norton's polysemic reading is predicated on a "homogeneous" notion of society and the pluralistic exchange economy. Within this productivist schema, political realignments are affected by changes in signification; changes in the party's representative change the meaning of the party. Political change also entails altering the mythic context and primary referents of political discourse. There is thus a fundamental commensurability. In place of arbitrary signification, we have "polysemy with a human face." Three alternatives present themselves: binding the sign, remotivating the signifier, or celebrating polysemy as liberalism's final sign.[35]

But what if we were to look at the form of articulation rather than its content: limbs, mutilation, castration, cutting? The signifier is cut off from the signified. This cutting also reveals what is at stake in a psychoanalytic reading. For Rogin, the problem of leglessness is clearly tied to the problem of articulation, forming an *en-abime*. Reagan's inability to draw arms and legs suggests the attendant irony that Reagan's legacy ("legs" in French) will be an arms agreement. On a first reading, Rogin's attentiveness to "leglessness" *literally* answers the question: How do you not follow in your father's footsteps if he is a failed shoe salesman? The answer: "By cutting off your legs!"

This "solution" to the Oedipal dilemma of killing the father who has trouble standing on his own two feet finds its ultimate cinematic expression in *King's Row*, but Rogin gives many examples from other films, such as *Knute Rockne* ("'I'd give my right arm for a halfback who could run, pass, and kick,' says Rockne, and he trips over the Gipper's feet"; in *This Is the Army*, Reagan plays the son of a legless George Murphy, in whose political footsteps he will follow). In *The Girl from Jones Beach*, Reagan plays an analogous role of magazine illustrator who "cuts up the bodies of twelve girls to make one perfect figure."

("But he broke his tailbone on the set of that movie," Rogin recounts.) Reagan breaks his leg after notification of his divorce from Jane Wyman. His happy second marriage, to Nancy (whose father is an important surgeon), is heralded in a picture of them in the GE home, with Nancy dutifully at his feet. As the concluding footnote, his autobiography ends with this: "The most important thing a man can know is that, as he approaches his own door, someone on the other side is listening for his footsteps."[36]

These surgical-amputation metaphors recur throughout the Reagan presidency, including his last term as a "lame duck." Rogin sees such terms as "tax ax," as well as Tip O'Neill's characterization of the budget as "cutting off your legs at the knees instead of the hips," as instances of a "slippage between personal bodies and the body politic."[37] There is another possible reading of these surgical metaphors. This reading is implicitly acknowledged in the next paragraph, which alludes to Reagan's "celluloid" world. For the images of amputees and severed limbs (or potentially lethal ones—for example, Nixon's phlebitis) also conjure up corresponding notions of prosthetics, important for our reading of Reagan as a simulacrum. Indeed, Rogin is concerned with prosthetics in his chapters on the presidency, for example, his discussion of Lincoln's beard. Moreover, this attendant focus on prosthetics is not out of place in a discussion of the doctrine of the king's two bodies, as this dates to the same period as the faked fronts of the Elizabethan theater, the counterfeit that for Hobbes marked both actors and sovereigns. Rogin's focus on the natural is in keeping with the emphasis on prosthetics: "It was thus with the Renaissance that the false was born with the natural."[38] Rogin's book is situated in the tension between the desire to go back to natural, motivated signs and Marx's notion of the fetish. The Leviathan serves as a preview of the radical hysterical semiurgy of the Reagan presidency, while theories of fetishism are invoked not just to empower forgotten subjects of history but also to point to the theories of symbolic exchange involved in an age dominated by the proliferation of codes and the fetishism of the signifier. "The severed head still signifies power," Rogin writes, and he is to the point, for the "head of state" is not just a synecdoche but also a fetish.[39] And it is with this recognition of the symbolic and fetishism that Rogin moves beyond the overt problematic of his book.

On the one hand (to continue with prosthetics and appendages), Rogin posits a continuity of demonology, an apparent belief in representa-

tion over simulation and demystification over dissuasion. His focus on
limbs and the edifice of remembering Reagan in the hope of empowering minorities (i.e., re-membering them) would be a diachronic history
of political repression. But is Reagan just another cold warrior? The
epistemic unevenness of Rogin's work (which is not to be confused with
its psychoanalytic coherence) would answer this rhetorical question
negatively, for, against the explicit text that works on the logic of demystification of repression as the dark other side of liberal representation, we have figural subtext whose rich metaphoricity suggests something beyond representation. At times, Rogin seems figuratively aware
of the *en-abimes* that affirm his argument, as, for example, in his hilarious treatment of "anty-communism" in the sci-fi movie *Them*.[40] The
psychoanalytic account both opens up and forecloses a more radical
reading of Reagan. If semiotic treatments were seen to be predicated
upon a classical political economy of the sign, psychoanalytic ones are
similarly circumscribed (or should we say circumcised).

Baudrillard writes: "As for psychoanalysis, although it acknowledges
the ghostly presence of the symbolic, it averts its power by circumscribing it in the individual unconscious, reducing it, under the law of the
Father, to the threat of castration and the subversiveness of the signifier.
Always the law." So, too, with Marx: "If Marx has tried *cutting* a path
through this law of value, it has in the end remained a revolution according to the law."[41] Alas, dismemberment is no facile solution: "The
severed head still signifies power" (Rogin); "Always the Law" (Baudrillard). In other words, psychoanalytic accounts are themselves tied to an
era of production and second-order simulacra, while Reagan represents
what Baudrillard designates as third-order simulacra. Secondary simulacra are tied to an era of serial technological reproduction. *Techné* is
their origin. Third-order simulacra appear when dead labor triumphs
over living serial production and we have generation by models. This
reverses origins and finalities. All is diffracted from the model. (DNA is
an emblem of this.) Third-order simulacra are neither true nor false but
operational, as in cybernetics and model-generated feedback. Industrial
simulacra are *operative.* Digitality is the metaphysics of this third order,
and the genetic code is its logic. Baudrillard's criticism of psychoanalysis
is implicit in his notion of the third-order simulacrum: "You cannot
beat randomness with finality, you can not beat programmed dispersion
with *prises de conscience* or dialectical transcendance, you cannot defend against the code with political economy."[42]

Norton and Rogin do provide fascinating, theoretically self-conscious accounts, but they fail to see what is epistemically significant about Reagan. Norton's reliance on Barthesian myth is insufficient. Reagan's success is only in part meta-linguistic, because of what Barthes called the "mobilization of connotations of affect."[43] A focus on secondary signification is not enough, nor is the positing of commensurability necessary for semiotic exchange appropriate to her hyperreal object. Rogin's use of a secondary simulacrum theory—(Freudian or Kleinian) psychoanalysis—to describe a third-order simulation is inadequate in a more profound way, as it heroically refuses the heroic depthlessness of the "Reagan thing." Richard Schickel's rhetorical question ("Did a man lacking the depth for a great role in the theatre somehow acquire a knack for filling the most responsible role in the world?")[44] is to the point here. To the extent that both Norton and Rogin strive to complete the hermeneutic gesture, they reveal themselves embedded in a problematic of representation inadequate to their object, an object whose hyperreality is lost or only briefly captured as simulation by its simulacrum on film. Rogin's history of repression is sufficiently superficial.

Yet the recognition of the absence of "depth" ("the idea that the object was fascinating because of the density of its secrets and that these were to be uncovered by interpretation")[45] is not without its attendant dangers for the possibility of socially responsible critique. How are we to proceed if the idea that the "inert" is a clue for something larger has now disappeared? And, if postmodernism and hyperreality are historical rather than stylistic notions—that is, cultural dominants in late consumer capitalism—how are we to normatively evaluate it? "The luxury of the old fashioned ideological critique, the indignant moral denunciation . . . becomes unavailable."[46] Cultural criticism based on earlier depth models becomes extremely problematic in a postmodern culture in which it is difficult to position ourselves. It should be noted in passing that this lack of depth parallels a death of feeling (necessary for moral tone), affect, and anxiety (seen as a hermeneutical emotion by Jameson). And is critical theory even possible if not scripted by an anxious, morbid subject?

What replaces the vantage point of critique, mystification, or judgment, which might have been effective in understanding what Barthes calls the level of communication (message) or signification (second-level symbolism) but remains recalcitrant in the face of the image (the obtuse meaning of Barthesian "significance")? Moreover, as we are increasingly confronted with this image as the final form of commodity reification in hyperreal America, interpretation of "the political" poses a double challenge, aesthetic and historical. In the place of the earlier critical categories we have pastiche, pseudocrossings of the bar (puns, homonyms), the *mise-en-abime*, and all the categories of the carnival—the useless, futile, trivial, fake. These are constructed as oppositional and disruptive in that they stand outside or challenge analytic reason. Barthes distinguishes between the symbolic and the "obtuse" meaning. The symbolic meaning is "intentional (it is what the author wanted to say) and it is taken from a common lexicon of symbols." Its temporality is specific: "It is a message which seeks me out."[47] Its logic is prescriptive and closed. This "obvious meaning" is the one prevalent in interpretation practiced by most linguistically oriented analyses of the presidency. The obtuse meaning addresses the unassimilable, that which of necessity invokes a general, open economy.

These Bataillian categories of nonproductive expenditure (i.e., expenditure without exchange)—"drinking, screwing, birth, eating and defecation"—are resumed in Murray Edelman's counterargument to theorists of political communication.[48] Drawing on Bakhtin's work on Rabelaisian laughter, Edelman sees the possibility for a short-lived collective resistance situated in carnivalesque forms of expression (i.e., popular culture) and works of art. This laughter is only fleeting—a brief meta-laugh, easily erased, as in Foucault's concluding moments of *The Order of Things*. For what is experienced in a postmodern era dominated by codes is a "non negating derision of the expression,"[49] a hollow, "false" laughter of pastiche as it raises precisely those sorts of questions that Baudrillard poses in reference to the absence of an original: "Parody capitalizes on the uniqueness of these styles and seizes on their idiosyncracies and eccentricities to produce an imitation which mocks the original." Pastiche "lacks parody's ulterior motive, without the satirical impulse, without laughter, without that still latent feeling that there exists something normal to which what is being imitated is rather comic. Pastiche is blank parody."[50] It is an irony without pathos. This absence of an original invokes Barthes's "obtuse meaning" as it also has no original reference: "It does not copy anything—How do you describe something that does not represent anything?"[51]

What replaces "critique" is, then, humorless, blank at the very least, nonironic. The impossibility of irony is underscored by the figure of *mise-en-abime* previously invoked. For the disruption provoked by *mise-*

en-abime momentarily blocks self-reflection (and might well result in the implosion that Baudrillard eagerly anticipates). For *mise-en-abime* is a profoundly disruptive figure:

> [A] disruption that can be thought of as a blocking of adequate self re-flection (the intervention within the field of reflection of something both necessary to it and radically heterogeneous with respect to it: the insis-tence of the general economy within the appearance of its general re-striction) or that which obliges the field of self reflection no rest, no mo-ment of self adequacy. (And this moment can be described as the always belated effort of a restricted economy to expand itself far enough to master and subsume the general system from which it is inscribed.)[52]

Humorless, Nonironic, but Also Inadvertently Hilarious: A Homoeopathic Presidency?

> At Disneyland, one can meet a real president, real as the racetrack on the television was "real," realer than the ordinary world. . . . Technol-ogy has brought us living history . . . its limbs disposed and moved arti-ficially but realistically (under the right light) delivering an ancient and beautiful message. Who would have thought, until recently, that such a president could be found outside Anaheim?[53]

It is, curiously enough, in a book with little claim to meta-theory that Baudrillard is most at home. For attempts to see the problem with Ron-ald Reagan as conflation of cinematic signifier and signified forget that the problem with Reagan is not Hollywood but that other American utopia, Disneyland. Garry Wills invokes the figure of a celluloid Moe-bius strip to describe Reagan. *Back to the Future* replaces *Where's the Rest of Me?*, especially in its *Saturday Night Live* Re-Ron version star-ring Ron Reagan Jr. and the *topos* of leglessness is replaced by that all-time American prosthesis, the car (i.e., "your father's Oldsmobile"). Prefiguration for Reagan is to be found not in other presidents or cine-astes but rather in Henry Ford's Greenfield Village, in southern Califor-nia reconstructions such as Knott's Berry Farm and Reagan's GE home, and in his first marriage to Jane Wyman, at Forest Lawn Cemetery. Wills understands implicitly that the problem with Reagan is not semi-otic but idiotic. And if Rogin has focused on the romance and politics of nature (always present as a first value), Wills situates Ronald Reagan within the revenge of technology with an almost Heideggerian insistence (as in his revision of Lynd's Middletown). In this reading, Heidegger's free path has become a freeway, and we riskfully collide in the aisles of our Safeways.

Readings of Reagan as a sign simply do not go far enough in acknowledging the challenge of his presidency. This theoretic challenge (to history, to representation) is addressed by European theorists of hyperrealism and simulation such as Jean Baudrillard and Umberto Eco, who see America as the home of the absolute fake and of artificial restoration. Eco and Baudrillard share a perverse "Europeanist envy" for the America of Disneyland, Marine World, Magic Mountain, the Hearst Castle, Knott's Berry Farm, and the Museum of Holography. Holograms replace Velasquez's *Las Meniñas* as frontispiece, as simulation displaces the episteme of representation. "For here the sign aims to be the thing, to abolish the distinction of the reference, the mechanism of replacement." Here Eco is writing about the reconstruction of the Oval Office—"for historical information to be absorbed, it has to assume the aspect of a reincarnation."[54] Eco presents a historicized view of American hyperreality, while Baudrillard hystericizes it. The hyperreal for Baudrillard is a sphere of absorption of the social and the political. Yet both are presentations of Reaganland. This "secret" America (Eco) or a "sidereal" one (Baudrillard) is that of the American dream realized as hologram (in three dimensions). Hyperreality in America is idiomatic. It is in microwaves (hyperspeed) and trash compactors (hyperspace). It is in the Ultra Brite smile, the blaze-of-headlights dentition of the Hollywood actor that, like the smile of the Cheshire cat, becomes the sign of an absence, the absence of any other than hyperreal American identity. "A défaut d'identité, les Americans ont une dentition merveilleuse."[55] Or, we Americans may not be incisive, but we have great incisors!

Indeed, our lack of incision is a result of our perfect embodiment of hyperreality, so perfect as to preclude a conceptual language. If Americans lack a meta-language of our meta-vulgarity, Europeans remain light-years away from comprehending the inanity and stupidity of American hyperreality, frustrated in their attempts to apprehend it on the secondary level of "unhappy consciousness" or reflexive thought. European readers of American hyperreality alternate between the shock of a first-level brute empiricism and a third level of absolute simulation. It is thus even more surprising that Wills reproduces this stance of the

European abroad. Or, he is an innocent abroad, a babe in Reagan's Toy-land, who convincingly presents us with his own amazement at this miniature, absolutely fake landscape of Reagan's and our minds. The entire problematic of the hyperreal is here: the identification of the completely real with the completely false that haunts Reagan's presidency and the rest of our American culture.

Wills traces the ambiguity about the real in Reagan's personal and professional life. His discussion proceeds in a fashion analogous to that of hyperrealist analysts of American society in that it is centered on the "real," on fakes and pretense. Again, it should be noted that although Wills does focus on Hollywood, it is not to discuss the conflation of the cinematic signifier and signified (as in Rogin's and Norton's readings) but rather that Hollywood here reemerges as a subvariant of American absolute fakery and pretense. Reagan's goal was not to construct a "Hollywood on the Potomac" but that technological dream object of Henry Ford, a "Greenfield Village on the Potomac." Greenfield Village, an ur-Disneyland, was the model of a "degenerate utopia" described by Louis Marin. What is at stake in Greenfield Village/Disneyland/Reagan-land is not a reproduction or approximation of some prefilmic reality but something that bypasses the logic of representation entirely, substituting miniatures, scale replicas, and signs of the real for the real itself.

The shift to simulacra underlines the other association of "pretense," a pretender to the throne. As we have outlined in the introduction, the Platonic dialectic is above all one of rivalry (*amphisbetesis*)—a dialectic of distinguishing the true from the false claimant. In Plato's *Sophist*, the simulacrum is not simply a false copy but that which calls into question the very notion of the copy and the model. Plato distinguishes between image idols (likenesses), iconic copies, and phantasmic simulacra (semblances). Copies, as "second hand possessors, authorized by resemblance,"[56] are in some respects well-grounded claimants. On the other hand, simulacra imply the false claimant, built around a dissimilitude; its dissimilitude is interiorized. Any analysis of Reagan's career as a simulacrum begins in Plato's cave.

Reagan's early career as a journalist and sportscaster was one of "visualizations" or "recreations" of baseball games (which he would later use as primary material for the evening news). His wedding to Jane Wyman at the Wee Kirk o' th' Heather in Forest Lawn Cemetery was on a level of pretense "of Reagan's telegraphed ballgames squared." Wills describes the scene for us: "A marriage made in the Hollywood Hotel issued from the very heart of Hollywood feigning." The wedding mimicked the simulated gaiety of the radio show ("The Hollywood Hotel"): "The paid actors described the mythical hotel's opulent interior and named the milling stars, including some who were not there."[57] Pretense marked not only Reagan's Hollywood career but also his homeopathic survival of Hollywood. Reagan dealt with his divorce by simply pretending not to be divorced and giving little speeches about successful marriages. He pretended he never pretended.

Feigning marked Ronald Reagan's war movie experience, as well. "War movies are hell," Wills ironically remarks about Reagan's wartime record.[58] (Wills's ironic engagement with his subject replaces a more traditional mode of engagement. Wills is not being snide or gratuitously sarcastic; rather, his sarcasm is a symptom of the inability of the observer to dominate the simulacrum.) Reagan's war record was hyperreal—he was "off to war in Hollywood." An early Culver City assignment was to produce fake bloopers. Was this production of "fake mistakes" an anticipation of "disinformation"? His war experience was one of meticulous miniature reconstructions (of Tokyo for simulated bombing runs in which, like Baudrillard's revision of Borges's map, the simulated bombing run preceded the "real"). Reagan was also involved in another form of absolute fakery, the propaganda film, for the Office of War Information. Indeed, facts do not matter for propaganda; the "feeling of truth" can substitute for the truth (or real) itself. Reagan's war service was a "strange mixture of real and make-believe war." This ambivalence toward the real underscored in his war career "explains" his bizarre anecdotal rendering of history, a sort of postmodern libidinal historicism that cannot be judged on the basis of truth or accuracy. Reagan *was* there at the liberation of the death camps because he saw the films. Lou Cannon and the Reagan spin doctors who tried to explain or decry this Reagan "gaffe" to Shamir simply do not realize that his episteme is one not of representation (in which the notion of "false representation" makes sense) but of simulation, in which the sign of the real, the absolute fake, is superior to the real itself.

Nancy was also not a foreigner to faking it. From the studio-created "artificial family" replete with "fake" friends to illustrate a fanzine (fan magazine) spread on her new apartment[59] to her lip-synching answers to reporters' questions directed at her husband, Nancy is a perfect co-star in feigning. Nancy and Ronnie spend their wedding night at the hyperreal Mission Inn and live in a technological GE home, a descendant of GE's House of Magic, which was designed in 1930 for the Golden Jubilee of Light to honor Henry Ford's hero, Edison. It is perversely fitting that Reagan, as postmodern emblem of the post-Cartesian post-Enlightenment, should have been a corporate talking head for GE (as part of the Enlightenment project of "bringing good things to life"). GE advertising is to the point in a postmodern era of esthetic recommodifications. "Outsiders say that the GE monogram is stamped on the rear ends of its people." We underline the importance of the GE logo for this critique of logocentrism. For GE is an emblem of Disneyland, the "original Boy Scout company."[60]

Reagan's hyperreal presidency must be situated in relation to Disneyland. For if America is the one invoked by Baudrillard and Eco, the America of K-Mart, Safeway, Hearst Castle, and Knott's Berry Farm, then Disneyland is its "Sistine Chapel." Moreover, the different ways of reading Disneyland invite analogous readings of Reagan—in relation to the frontier myth, as illusion, as dissuasion/simulation.

Louis Marin's *Utopiques: Jeux d' Espaces* presents the most detailed treatment of Disneyland and is the standard reference point for Baudrillard, Eco, and Foucault (on heterotopias). Marin situates Disneyland in relation to a frontier myth. It is a frontier town that "receives entering visitors and distributes them through various sectors of the Magic City."[61] (If Disneyland is a system of distribution for Marin, it is a system of ventilation for Baudrillard.) Disneyland is defined as a "degenerate utopia," that is, an "ideology realized in the form of myth." This semiological reading parallels that of Barthesian mythology as it parallels thematically Norton's situation of Reagan in the westward expansion. As her reading is theoretically predicated on Barthesian mythology, Marin is apposite on both formal and thematic levels.

In Eco's reading, Disneyland is a locus of illusion, both producing illusion and stimulating the desire for it. His is a dialectical treatment of humanization and dehumanization, of nature and technology. Disneyland teaches us that technology can be more realistic than nature or that the pleasure of mimeticism-faked nature—fake sea serpents—is more satisfying than its natural counterpart. Indeed, robots in Disneyland are there to instruct us that reality is a let-down, just as the pleasures of Forest Lawn cemetery similarly instruct us that death is a small price to pay for admittance. We can be "humanized" by the spectacle of technology, but there is a rub—we must leave our cars to do so! (Both Eco and Baudrillard give haunting images of the parking lot—as elephant graveyard or concentration camp.) The pleasure of the imitation is incremental—more real, better than the original. And a dialectical tension exists between the scale of the reproduction and the credibility of the object. The credible must be miniaturized in order to seduce (i.e., the fake New Orleans). Full-scale reproductions are allowed only for already incredible objects.[62]

This increment of "more" and "better" is idiomatic in our excremental culture. Eco notes that the two main advertising slogans of America are "real" (Coke is the "real" thing) and "more." "More" is a sign of a surplus in need of disposal. Disneyland is thus an allegory of consumer society (for Eco), and its passive visitors are allegories of the robotic state of American culture—the release without abandon of our leisure activities, the "dependent independence" of the Reagan persona or of Suzy Chapstick.[63]

Yet, implicit in Eco's allegorical reading of Reagan is the possibility for something that is outside Disneyland. One cannot establish a dialectic between two identities. Baudrillard realizes that the problem is not a binary opposition between fiction and the real (and the blurring of this line); rather, the fiction of the real is what is problematic. Far from being a locus of illusion, Disneyland preserves a reality principle, dissuading us that the rest of America is real. Indeed, Marin's view of degenerate utopia (and Eco's endorsement of it) obscures the fact that Disneyland is a third-order simulacrum. The mythological reading (as degenerate utopia) conceals the fact that Disneyland *is* the real America. We have realized a utopia that Europeans can only dream of. And this has nothing to do with fiction. Disneyland is no allegory; it is "America's objective profile in miniature and in comic strip form." Disneyland is a deterrence machine, neither true nor false. Disneyland is "an imaginary effect concealing that reality no more exists outside than inside the bounds of the artificial perimeter."[64] It is an imaginary used to regenerate a reality principle. It is no exception. Neither is Reagan.

The Reagan years have been full of extraordinary hyperreality: Max Headroom, Spuds Mackenzie, Vanna White, Joe Isuzu, the Dancing Raisins (Motown as Eternal Return), and the Stealth Bomber Honda ads. The two most important aspects of hyperreality/simulation in contemporary American popular culture have been the substitution of signs of the real for the real itself and the blurring of fact and fiction. John Ehrlichman plays himself in an ad for Dreyer's Ice Cream, which claims "unbelievable spokesmen for unbelievable products." (Melvin Dummar of the Howard Hughes will is another such claimant.) John Ehrlichman also feigns truthfulness as he "plays" a credible witness on a recent episode of *Divorce Court* (another hybrid show in which real people and bad actors and bad lawyers playing bad actors collide).[65] The only convincing candidate in the 1988 electoral campaign was the product of a cartoonist and director. Tanner was an absolute fake whose slogan was "Tanner for President . . . for Real." Tanner went to the actual primary states and to the convention in Atlanta and collided with "real" candidates.[66] All of these video exchanges do recall Deleuze on the simulacrum: that "folded into the simulacrum is the process of going mad."

If we have grown accustomed to this slippage in both directions between the real and the fictitious, we have also become adept in substituting signs of the real for the real, either in commodities or in narrative forms. False cellular car phones (Fauxphones) and cheap status objects in the Sharper Image catalogue (such as their car alarm) give us every sign of the thing (a decal warning label, lights that go back and forth on the dashboard—just no alarm!) except the actual thing the product was intended to do. Real car alarms go off; one can actually speak on real car phones. Yet, this noncommunication that the hyperreal product offers us is not just satisfying but may be downright superior in an age of noncommunication and (media) irresponsibility. Ralph Lauren creates pedigreed clothing with emblems that look like monograms until you realize that this tangle of lines doesn't actually form any letters. But is the insistence of the letter something we actually want from clothes that promise us "the whole atmosphere of the good life"?[67]

This promise of commodities to produce the true without the real is what enables Larry Speakes to make up presidential quotes and yet claim he is not lying: "I knew those quotes were the way he felt."[68] Similarly, the author of a book on the Getty Oil takeover explains in a biographical note that, "while many of his characters did not use the exact words we see in quotation marks . . . the journalist endows historical events with the feeling of truth—A feeling the reader intuitively appreciates."[69] Move over, Baudrillard! For these feelings may not be "true," but they are "real" and need not be obligated to any originary reference in an era of simulation. "Lauren apparently takes it for granted that by divorcing symbols from their contexts, he can unburden them of specific meanings and yet somehow leave their general sense intact."[70]

Sometimes an originary reference (or history) intrudes. This makes little difference. In Britain, a consumer electronics goods company chose a Japanese name and a rising-sun symbol.[71] The slogan "Japanese Technology Made Perfect" reinscribed the sign of Japan. All the signifiers were Japanese. None of the signified was. The product was made from components manufactured in South Korea, Yugoslavia, Malaysia, Taiwan, and Britain and assembled in various countries. "The Matsui goods are made anywhere but in Japan." However, the Matsui name also referred to General Iwane Matsui, who was responsible for the 1937 "Rape of Nanking" and who was hanged after the war. This aroused protests from some British veterans' groups, and a court ordered the company to drop its slogan and pay a modest fine but (and this is most significant) allowed it to keep its name, Matsui. "We won on the name," said the director of corporate affairs, and he is correct in seeing this as a victory.

What is it in this . . . that poses for me the question of the signifier?[72]

These instances invoke what Roland Barthes referred to as the obtuse meaning, instances in which we have a signifier but no signified. The isolation of the signifier is what Jameson speaks of when he calls the postmodern "schizophrenic." Let us conclude with a consideration of the challenge of Reagan's seeming depthlessness, of his superficiality, for interpretation, for perhaps commentators who have focused on the slippage between a cinematic signifier and signified are symptomatically accurate. In other words, there is something "filmic" about Reagan. The filmic should not be taken too literally. What is filmic about Reagan is not that he has appeared in film but rather refers to the Barthesian sense of filmic, as that supplementary signifier that stands for that which cannot be represented. "The filmic is that in the film which cannot be described, the representation which cannot be represented. The filmic begins where language and meta-language end. . . . The filmic, then, lies precisely here, in that region where articulated language is no more than approximative."[73] (Anyone who has ever tried to read a transcript of a Reagan press conference already knows this.) The filmic importance of Reagan is included in Rogin's book—but it is in his chapter on D. W. Griffith.

Indeed, Barthes's notion of the obtuse meaning addresses Reagan's hyperreality. As we "grin with the Gipper," we recall that the obtuse meaning is one of pun and buffoonery. It addresses the issue of pitiful and double disguise. What Barthes sees in Ivan the Terrible is an actor disguised twice, as anecdote and in dramaturgy, neither canceling the other. What we have here is not a doubling of cinematic signifier and signified but a fetish quality read as excess. This "nonnegating derision of the expression"—that is, "saying the opposite without giving up the contrary"—is *the* characteristic feature of the Reagan presidency.[74] Nor should it be surprising that Reagan's obtuse meaning has been misunderstood by most of his analysts, who have attempted to relate the Reagan sign to its "obvious" or symbolic meaning. For the obtuse meaning is discontinuous to discursivity (the Reagan story) and dissociated, denatured, and distanced in regard to the referent. The Tower Commission report's depiction of Ronald Reagan's "management style" exemplifies the independence of the signifier in relation to political or historical narrative. This signifier is not just empty but in a "permanent state of depletion."[75] Reagan's obtuse meaning is literally impertinent. This impertinence can be read not in some gaffe or anecdote but visually. We can read Reagan's impertinence, as does Mark Miller, in his hair: "[He] sports the same haircut he wore when Hitler took over the Sudetenland." We read Reagan as we do a still of Eisenstein: "the lopsided grin, the wavy thatch, the eyebrows impishly tilted."[76] What Reagan confronts readers with is something unoriginated and obsessive and disturbing. But perhaps what has been most disturbed by the Reagan thing, by Reagan as obtuse meaning, are his critics. For reading Reagan as Barthesian third meaning, as dissociated (and dissociative) signifier, is to give ourselves up to an impossible reading. "In short what the obtuse meaning disturbs, sterilizes is meta-language."[77] Reagan, the great communicator, leaves his critics speechless.

3

Oliver North and the
Lying Nose (1992)

The state system must be protected from Congressional investigations that rob the president of his covert tool which must be veiled from scrutiny to protect from embarrassing consequences. The Iran-Contra revelations, Secord lamented, publicly exposed the inadequacies of the President's "tool," have ensured that the whole world is laughing at us.   —Frederick M. Dolan

Ollie resisted all efforts by committees to housebreak him.
                                                            —Ben Bradlee

the malevolent movements of Uranus and Saturn [astrological reference for the Iran-Contra scandal]   —Kitty Kelley

Public disclosure of a covert operation simultaneously reveals and reveils a president's tool. Revealing and reveiling—separated by the difference of a letter: *a,* the "a" of *différance* and Lacan's little object "i," indivisible letter of the self and subject of a predication to follow.[1] The covert operation can be read as a letter (purloined or otherwise) contained in traditional notions of diplomacy (the courier's mail pouch) or the new postage of a media cyberspace (electronic mail, CNN). But how should we read such overdue mail/male?[2] Do we read Iran-Contra as Lacan reads the purloined letter, as the process of the course of a letter in its movement of rephallicization? Or do we read Iran-Contra as prefigured in Freud's Wolf Man narrative: as an attempt to preserve masculine self-esteem or aggression against the feminine threat or the passive (homoerotic) wish? America Standing Tall, holding its own against communist insurgency? The Wolf Man narrative here is the allegory of a secret, of "a drama of disclosure which veils yet another secret."[3] Two ur-texts that have been subjected to extensive and protracted readings correspond to the two pleasure zones of Iran-Contra—the phallic and the anal.

Iran-Contra begs for a literally symptomatic reading—somewhere between the president's tool and Oliver North's stool. My reading, like Nancy's astrologer, will, by a homonymic displacement, follow the saturnalia of Uranus/your anus. Iran-Contra is part of a larger Reagan policy, as Don Regan and others have written, of controlled leaks. Iran-Contra cross cuts and interrupts a presidential politics of bodily disorder. Read against a backdrop of Reagan's medical interventions—his nose, bowel, and penis—it is eerily reminiscent of the Wolf Man. Reagan's body, like Larry, speak(e)s. The story of Reagan's nose surgery and coverup recall the fetishistic obstruction of the Wolf Man's private nose language. I insist on the fetish quality of Iran-Contra: the construction of a fetish—a CIA outside the CIA, a "simulacrum of the national security culture."[4] Casey and North's "off-the-shelf" covert operation is a part object that both compensates for as it denies the fear of castration. It also incessantly reminds us of the apparent reality of castration after the Boland Amendment cuts off the purse strings. But if one examines the exact language of Casey's and North's wish, there is another erotics of the covert operation: an "off-the-shelf, self-sustaining, *stand-alone entity*" is also a turd/feces. Ollie's and Casey's "neat idea" is neat in two senses. It is both clever and anal. This "stand-alone, self-sustained entity" is what Freud designated by *Zwangsneurose,* obsessional neurosis, "a self-sufficient and independent disorder."[5] I would privilege the German term "*zwangsneurose*"; "*zwang*" refers to compulsive acts (*zwangshandlungen*) and emotions (*zwangsaffekte*), as well as the more common reference to compulsive thoughts (*zwangsvorstellungen*). But most important for our analysis is that this term as used by Freud points to a *symptom* rather than to a *structure*. Laplanche and Pontalis have noted: "The evolution of psychoanalysis has led to an increasing emphasis being placed on the obsessional structure to the detriment of the symptom."[6] The reading of Iran-Contra that follows reverses this traditional preoccupation with structure, placing considerable weight on the symptoms produced in the disclosure of the covert operation.

The reading that follows is framed by two texts, Poe's "Purloined Letter" and Freud's "Wolf Man," as well as by the subsequent interpreters of these works (Lacan, Derrida, Felman, Johnson, and Abraham and Torok). My two ur-texts are detective stories at one (Poe) or two

(Freud) removes. Moreover, we will see that these two narratives oppose differing strategies for reading the covert operation: a hermeneutic reading versus a hermetic one. The hermeneutic reading follows the logic of Lacan's "Seminar on 'The Purloined Letter'" and attempts to locate a meaning of the affair, even if it is only the positing of a lack of meaning as a transcendental signified. The hermetic reading situates the affair within a national-security culture figured as a cryptic text that is so radically designified to begin with that it must be (fantastically) reconstituted in order for interpretation to proceed. The question of hermetic versus hermeneutic readings underline the problem central to this chapter: (How) can the covert operation within a national-security culture be read? They remind us that questions of interpretation always presuppose a theory of readability at work in a text. I situate this question of the readability of the covert operation at the angle between the "clues" afforded within the detective-story genre (or the "symptom-clues" of the Freudian case study) and the explicitly psychoanalytic-literary reading of textual clues.

My argument for a psychoanalytic reading of the covert operation is not a traditional hermeneutic interpretation. Decipherings, de-scriptings, take place on the level of the *signifier*.[7] The secret is never fully disclosed—it was there in full view or, like the signed presidential finding always already there, locked in Poindexter's safe and burned upon discovery. In other words, this is not a disclosure of a hidden referential content or ultimate signified of Iran-Contra. The power of the signifier is apposite to the covert operation—it resides in the signifier's "transparent materiality, invisible in its very visibility."[8] "The Purloined Letter," like Iran-Contra, displays strategies of open concealment as well as duplicitous discourse. We will also note that, for Lacan, signifiers, as opposed to meanings, always point to the unconscious. Psychoanalytic readings, which follow the rhetorical displacements of the signifier (and, after all, arms for hostages is a rhetorical as well as a geopolitical deal), mime the notions of diversions and trace that are crucial to Iran-Contra.

I would also like to caution against any overly facile psychological reductionism. I am not saying that either Ollie North or Reagan is the Wolf Man or that they are Dupin or the Minister turning letters inside out. Moreover, I am not saying that we are Freud or Dupin. Rather, I would like to address the uncanny coincidence with these literary ur-texts that a symptomatic reading of Iran-Contra discloses. Coincidence here refers to "the coming together in a single moment of two entities belonging to two absolutely different ontological realms . . . which consequently can have no strict causal explanation, but which, touching, appear to be motivated by some significant necessity, some deep affinity of meaning . . . normally used to designate the accidental appearance of some resemblance between two heterogeneous events."[9] This resemblance with an appearance of motivated necessity is called "significant coincidence" by Jung and refers to an associational contiguity. This uncanny associational link between the language in which the affair is disclosed by commentators and that used by participants recalls many of the same *topoi* mobilized in these "literary" texts. What I am suggesting, then, is that this "coincidence" points not to any direct one-to-one correspondences but to different *models* of reading. If the language of disclosure of Iran-Contra recalls "The Purloined Letter" or "Wolf Man," then the readings of these texts in turn should double as model readings of the event, that is, of covert operations, in the national-security culture. My concern is primarily about the readability of the covert operation.

Psychoanalytic readings such as those of Lacan and Derrida are not the only possibilities for a rhetorical reading of Iran-Contra. Iran-Contra can be and, indeed, has been read otherwise. In Rogin's version, it is part of a history of racial demonology and the emergence of a specular foreign policy. Spectacle and secrecy are figured *chiasmically* within a model of historical trauma and amnesia: "Covert actions derive from imperatives of spectacle, not secrecy, but owe their invisibility to political amnesia."[10] Fred Dolan situates Iran-Contra as a moment in the history of metaphysics: "Such doctrines as 'rollback,' 'containment,' 'counterinsurgency' must be read as sketches for a metaphysics of contemporary world history as a permanent crisis requiring constant supervision and if necessary, intervention."[11] Both Rogin's and Dolan's accounts draw on Freud's theory of fetishism. Dolan's ostensible preoccupation is an analogy between the crisis manager's masculine subjectivity and that of the empirical political scientist. His claim, that the male crisis manager's badge of toughness is the mastery of a reified language, is apposite in some respects to that of Rogin. For Dolan, a crisis manager is an adolescent boy whose tough talk screens him from fears of inadequacies, thus enabling him to project power. Rogin's discussion of Iran-Contra is similarly framed by an incident of "tough talking," in this case "Make my day!" as challenge and mastertrope of Reagan's and Bush's racist policies. This tough talk is spoken as Eastwood dares a black man to murder a white woman in the context of a film whose subject is rape and revenge (*Sudden Impact*). "The lives he proves his toughness by endangering are female and black, not his own."[12] My reading overlaps with both Rogin and Dolan. The male crisis manager is a fetishist (Dolan). The covert operation is a form of therapeutic politics within a larger political culture of motivated disavowal (Rogin).

James Der Derian offers a third reading in his "Arms, Hostages and the Importance of Shredding in Earnest."[13] Der Derian's reading underlines the modernist frames of both Rogin and Dolan (Freud, Marx, Heidegger) as its exceeds them, situating Iran-Contra against the hyperreality of terrorism and counterterrorism. Terrorism is a deconstructive activity, and North is the simulacrum of the national-security culture. Iran-Contra takes p(l)ace in a chrono/geopolitical cyberspace—a covert operation in (Mona Lisa) overdrive. Terrorism has a proleptic quality as anticipation of a legitimation crisis to come. Der Derian reminds us that deciphering the contemporary culture of the national-security state requires attending to excessive writing/overwriting, briefing and overbriefing, the creation of the false Ollie chronologies, backdated bills, doctored IBM typing balls, magnetic messages (PROF notes), shredding machines, signatures on traveler's checks (emblems of both traceability/ countersignature and security: "Don't leave home without them"). The fabulous textuality is addressed by Representative Pascell in the Senate hearings when he says that Ollie deserves to be in the Guinness Book of Records: "Colonel, you have probably produced and disposed of more government paper than anybody I ever heard of."[14]

And yet, despite the hyperobtrusiveness of writing, the "epiphenomenology of terrorism" of the covert operation is to be read in shredding. Der Derian establishes an epistemological equivalence between knowledge and shredding, as we learn from "the smoke rising from the 'burn bags' of the executive branch."[15] What Der Derian implicitly addresses is another (cyberpunk) language ("at high orbit and in low resolution . . . and in lower orbit but at higher resolution") is the underlying question of my reading. Reading the covert operation of a national-security culture, in other words, requires that we confront the (in)ability of the trace to speak.

The Urinary Politics of the National-Security State: Reading Public Orifices/Offices

> Now, of course, the concern you expressed about leaks is a real one. . . .
> But let's be clear. The fact that a few members of Congress leak doesn't
> mean that all members of Congress leak, just as the fact that some
> members of the Administration leak cannot be fairly said to mean that
> all members of the Administration leak.   —Senator Mitchell[16]

Iran Contra signals a shift from the promiscuous Derridean dissemination (before AIDS hysteria) to the urinal politics of Der Derian national-
security cyberspace where archival secretions leak out, only to reappear
as pub(l)ic narratives. Dissemination in a safe-sex age with the condom
deterrence of SDI (nothing gets through this defensive shield) regulates
the flow and potentially risky exchange of valorized symbols and information. The archive of the national-security state accretes, secretes, and
excretes not only flows but *piles,* too: "But once obtained . . . (this) archive of the 'high' (political) culture of the national security state, that
is, the official currency of discursive practices which circulate, accumu-
late, *piles* up around the great power."[17] Not to worry. These excretory
"piles" will be cleared by the "shovel brigade."
    I am taking Der Derian literally when he suggests that "we must seek
out [the state's] most sensitive secretions." For Der Derian's epistemological equation of knowledge with shredding takes place in a post-
AIDS discourse of risk and safe sets: semantic sets as well as ethical,
epistemic, and practical sets for responding to crises within the national-security culture (i.e., disseminating terrorism). The (im)possibility
of safe (discursive) sets to "write/read about terrorism without a teleol-
ogy" affects the semio-critical reader: "reducing the possibility of any
metacritical and ethico politico response to it."[18] My literalization of
the post-AIDS metaphors of flows and secretions is an attempt to "excessively reinscribe this story of arms, hostages, and terrorism"[19] via a
reactivation of Bakhtinian categories of the carnivalesque (i.e., Rabelaisian laughter), of Bataille's categories of nonproductive expenditure
(i.e., expenditure without exchange), or of what Baudrillard refers to as
the "ob-scene." This new semio-critical strategy of overwriting deploys
the ludic and the scatological, which can be read either (critically) as
forms of resistance or as (postmodern) excess that momentarily disrupts
the domination of the code. A focus on the scatological in Iran-Contra

(as in Rabelais) provokes uneasy laughter. Bakhtin reminds us that "laughter liberates not only from external censorship but first to fall from the great interior censor."[20] My flagrant literalization of Der Derian and the Iran-Contra (con)texts of Speakes, Regan, Bradlee, and North posits excessive inscription as a carnivalesque writing of the body. Literalization becomes a form of em-bodiment, a rhetorical strategy to read a radically designified and designifying text.

The covert operation and its disclosure are indissociable from an administration that conducted foreign policy by leaks and was obsessed by leaks.[21] Regan writes: "Even though I had to admit, surveying the techniques invoked and the results obtained, that this policy of deliberate leaks was an interesting example of management by objective."[22] These "deliberate leaks" stand in contrast to the "indiscrete silences" of Regan's years on Wall Street, the "indiscrete silences" of insider trading. Regan offers a catalogue of leaks—from the unintended leak to the "officially sanctioned leak calculated to produce a specific effect."[23] This second category was not new to Ronald Reagan—the Kennedys used it —but, in Regan's words, "it was raised to an art form under Baker, Meese and Deaver." Both foreign and domestic informational material were leaked. Regan describes a situation in which there was a "remarkably free flow" of unsourced information out of the White House into the public domain as triads (Gergen, Darman, and Baker; Craig Fisher, Jack Svahn, Meese) acted in concert with media stars such as Bill Plante of CBS and Paul Blustin of *The Wall Street Journal*. "Paradoxically, these secret arrangements . . . created what was probably the most open government in history."[24]

Regan and Speakes present at times conflicting assessments of the ability of the trace (i.e., the leak) to speak (be traceable). For Regan, it is a question of knowing one's partners (and their histories) in this fluid exchange. For Speakes, there is a hermeneutic of generalized suspicion without unequivocal verification. Speakes believes that Gergen leaked the story of McFarland's Lebanon trip (after all, he's in a high-risk group), but "they never found out who was responsible for the leak or for any other leak."[25] Leaks also remain untraceable as Speakes consults his phone log.

The NSC team—Allen, Clark, McFarland, Poindexter—was obsessed by the possibility of leaks, making a fetish of secrecy and keeping the press "in the dark." Poindexter drafts a NSC directive on how to control leaks and punish them, including the use of polygraph tests and the creation of an FBI strike force. Casey's obsession with leaks underscores the link with a new late-eighties McCarthyite hysteria over clean bodily fluids, what Arthur and Marilouise Kroker in "Panic Sex in America" describe as urinal politics. In this body, McCarthyism loyalty oaths are displaced/replaced by mandatory drug testing in the workplace: this recyclage on "the terrain of bodily fluids . . . insists on the (unattainable) ideal of absolute purity of the body's circulatory exchange as the new gold standard of an immunological politics."[26]

Yet urinal politics is only one part of the flow. There are other orifices (nasal, anal) that leak and have their (body) part to play in a symptomatology of Iran-Contra. When reporters ask for permission to see President Reagan's scar after his colon surgery, Speakes says no, deflecting attention to another orifice: "He wants to show you the point of entry of yesterday's [proctoscopic] examination." Proctorscopophilia replaces the trace (scar) as it also displaces the tube in the president's nose: "The first photograph of the President after surgery was artfully arranged to conceal the nasogastric tube that had been inserted in Reagan's nose." Nancy's kiss "strategically covers the tube." (We will return to a discussion of the Political Father's Nos/Nose in our next section.)

A cursory list of "public" figures of secretion would include Cap "the knife"'s *Seaspray* covert operation of 1981 (clandestine air support for the CIA), which also prepares Cap to be the "mouthpiece" for the military brass in the Reagan administration.[27] It would also take note of the letter-writing campaign during Iran-Contra to the onamastically felicitous "Spitz" Channel.[28]

But it is North who has a privileged relation to the Iran-Contra body fluid/orifice narrative. First praised for his "tight, hands-on" control of the Achille Lauro command post (two pleasure sites of Iran-Contra), North becomes Reagan's alter ego and national hero. Described by Ben Bradlee as a "cold warrior soulmate" and "Ronald Reagan in miniature,"[29] he is psychohistoricized as an alternative son: "the desire for the aging Gipper to latch on to a surrogate son . . . who could play out his dreams." Ron Reagan Jr., "cavorting about in his underpants [briefs] on *Saturday Night Live*" (a *Risky Business* in a dangerous world) is, in Bradlee's words, "not quite the *Halls of Montezuma* stuff the President had in mind." North, as loose cannon within the self-sustaining entity of the NSC covert operation, returns in the Oedipal narrative as a form of Montezuma's revenge.

Through his Senate testimony, taking the stand (or, more accurately, stooling on just about everyone else but Reagan), North is able to shed his loose-cannon image. But he is never far from scatological figuration. No longer a "loose cannon" but a "national hero," Oliver North is praised by pundits as not "housebroken" by the committee.

The Name of the Nose

I never thought I'd see the day when the credibility of a White House news secretary would be put in jeopardy because of a pimple on the president's nose.   —John Madigan, WBBM commentator

A bit later, the famous symptom of the nose (= he knows) begins. . . . The scratched out pimple leaves a hole. Yes, he does know the whole business about the *hole.*
           — "A Lying Nose and the Tooth of Truth," in Nicholas Abraham
                   and Maria Torok, *The Wolf Man's Magic Word*[30]

Since Watergate, the hermeneutic question that underwrites the narrative disclosure of the covert operation is "What did the president know?" What the president knows becomes the ultimate transcendental signified, limit, or horizon for understanding the covert operation. To rhetorically displace this originary question to a focus on a signifier that functions as a bad pun—that is, the president's *nose*—may well seem extreme or frivolous. And yet, the president's nose (and other bodily symptoms) are hyperobtrusive in the textuality of the Iran-Contra Affair. The equation of knowledge with nose is crucial in a symptomatic reading of signifiers disclosed in the exposure of this covert operation. The different implications of these two epistemological equations—knowledge = shredding; knowledge = nose—will be discussed in a concluding section. For the moment, we will read Reagan's nose and the disavowal/cover-up of this particular cancer as a transparent literalization of the problem of his presidency and of his policies. It is a transparent literalization—as plain as the nose on the president's face.

This body focus is not an extension of the doctrine of the King's two bodies.[31] It is not an argument to develop the identification of the personal with the body politic along the lines of a hysterical somaticization.[32] Iran-Contra is metaphoricized as a cancer on the Reagan presidency. But most important for my reading is the uncanny parallels between the sites of Reagan's nonmetaphoric cancer and the Wolf Man's symptomatology. Both Reagan and the Wolf Man's sites of bodily dysfunction include the bowels and the nose. Can these sites be read as allegories of persuasion and disinformation? Do the bowels and the nose somehow mimic the problems of the larger context of Iran-Contra?

What is most surprising about narrative accounts by insiders such as Speakes and Regan is that the pathological policies of Iran-Contra are discursively framed by Reagan's hospital stays and surgical interventions. Decisions concerning arms for hostages, the signing of presidential findings, the staging of the possibility of nonrecall (deniability) takes place in the hospital ward. We may well ask if the primal scene of Iran-Contra is not a scene of surgical intervention and writing.

Regan's narrative account of Iran-Contra begins in the (cancer) ward. "Nancy Reagan stammers slightly when she is upset and her voice was unsteady when she called me from Bethesda Naval Hospital on Friday afternoon, July 12, 1985, to tell me her husband, the president of the United States, would require surgery for the removal of a large polyp in his intestinal tract." Regan's disclosure of the radical semiosis (i.e., astrology) at the heart of the Reagan presidency is interrupted by details of the colonoscopic examination: "the preliminaries for major surgery included measures such as fasting and cleansing of the bowel."[33] Reagan is operated upon, wakes up from anesthesia, becomes president again with a stroke of his dark blue plastic souvenir pen at 7:22 p.m., and, after a joke about Bob Dole, asks if there is any word on the hostages.[34] Over the next few days, between more jokes and Hollywood stories, the president is finally allowed, on July 18, to see Bud McFarland, who has urgent reasons to see the president. This meeting, Regan goes on to say, was "of course the first in a sequence of events that very nearly led to the fall of one of the most popular presidents of the United States."[35] Yet this meeting with McFarland passes out of presidential memory.

Speakes's account of the Reagan presidency also begins with a body focus—that is, an assassination attempt: "The gunshots thrust me from a relatively obscure job as deputy press secretary into the spotlight as the spokesman for the President, the White House and the nation."[36] The president is shot, and now Larry Speakes—a therapeutic conversion that is linguistically satisfying. Speakes's identification with the presidential body is direct. Speakes's chapter is simply called "A Cancer on the Presidency" and begins with simple declarative sentences: "It's cancer, it's big, it's black, it's ugly."[37] The hospital is just a setting for Reagan; the real presidential obstruction lies not in his colon but outside his body in the form of Nancy. It is a stage, a backdrop in which key meetings take place and are forgotten. But Speakes's narrative (and here I am favoring the un-derridean move of valorizing Speakes over writing/Regan's *On the Record*) implicitly recognizes the import of a truly symptomatic reading of the Reagan presidency.[38]

Speakes links the deniability of Reagan's surgical interventions with political deniability, the cover-up (of Reagan's cancer) with the covert operation. The analogy between the body politic and political policies is apparent to Speakes in Reagan's double disavowal. When Lou Cannon asks Ronald Reagan if he had cancer, the president says: "I didn't have cancer. I had something inside me that had cancer in it and it was removed."[39] This "unrealistic" and "incorrect" medical history is compared with Reagan's denegation that he did not exchange arms for hostages: "He believed that just as he believed he hadn't had cancer, but he was wrong each time."[40] Reagan believed that he was dealing with third parties and thus not directly negotiating with hostage takers. "Iran" here is in the position of "something inside me that had cancer in it." Reagan's disavowal of his cancer allows for Speakes's charitable reading of either presidential nonknowledge or misrecognition: "I know that the President and perhaps McFarland and Poindexter really believed that, but almost everyone else involved—Americans, Iranians, and Israelis—recognized the shipments for what they were: bribes that were intended to lead to the release of the hostages."

The president's colon cancer allows Speakes to admit that the president does not know. But the president's nose is another story. Just ten days after his colon surgery, Reagan developed a pimple on the right side of his nose. He thought that this was caused by irritation from the nasal surgical tape. We recall that the president tried to cover up his nasal tube—discursively deflecting attention to other zones. He compared his surgery to a wart on the end of a finger[41] and offered to show the hard-nosed press corps the point of entry of his proctoscopic exam. Why does Reagan prefer the anal orifice or the phallic-digital index? Does Reagan have, in the Wolf Man's words, a "lying nose"?

Yet another nasal cover-up ensues as the scab on the president's nose seems serious enough to be removed. A biopsy is performed under a false name—Tracy Malone, identified as a sixty-two-year-old white fe-

Photo by Judy Sloan/Gamma Liason.

male. Tracy Malone is the name of an actual nurse at Bethesda; forty years were added to her real age to make "her" sample fit with those in the president's age group. So far, so good.

"It was on Thursday, August 1, that all hell broke loose," Speakes writes. The scene is an address of evangelical broadcasters, and members of the regular White House press corps notice the scar on the president's nose: "What's the scab on the President's face?" Speakes disinforms under orders from Nancy, "The scab is an irritation from the tape that held the nasogastric tube in place." Speakes calls it by a string of euphemisms: "an irritation," "a gathering or piling up of the skin." Nancy engages in denegation: "Who has never picked a pimple?" She argues for the elision of certain words: "cancer," "biopsy." "Why can't we just say . . . He had a pimple on his nose which he picked at and scratched?"[42] Speakes refuses to sign the press statement of fifty words that omits the two crucial ones ("cancer" and "biopsies"), sending "a clear signal, though a subtle one, that I was not staking my credibility on these words." Attribution is generic: "The White House, Office of the Press Secretary," and without the endorsement of Speakes's proper name. However, these elementary semiotics were lost on the press corps ("No one noticed my signal").[43] Maybe it was not their fault. Having dealt with the linguistic complications of the pseudo-crossing of the bar between signifier and signified whenever Larry Speakes, they could overlook the rhetorical subtlety of his clear signal. In an epilogue, Reagan discloses the "basal cell carcinoma" on his nose on Monday, August 5. (Two more nose operations follow, in October 1985 and in July 1987—the month of North's testimony). Yet Sam Donaldson and Helen Thomas accuse Speakes of having a "lying nose." "They raised questions about my credibility."

This "lying nose" can be read as an emblem of the covert operation and disinformation that takes place in the national security culture figured as a "crypt." As we will see in our concluding section, the "lying nose" is not a conventional metaphor. The cryptonymic reading of the "lying nose" displays the radical semantic shift that psychoanalysis effects in language. Although my reading of Iran-Contra appears to proceed by a progression of literalized metaphors ("leaks," "cancer," "lying nose"), these are neither metaphors nor literal meanings in an ordinary language sense. Ordinary language will not help us enter the crypt, although it does enable us to zealously overwrite upon it.[44] The crypt, Abraham and Torok (as well as Derrida) tell us, necessitates a different t(r)opography. This new tropography proceeds by "anasemic conversion"; it *designifies* along the lines of an *antisemantics*.

The reading of the covert operation as crypt is thus a departure from the Derridean reading as an open letter/postcard. Derridean dissemination designated the process by which thought jumped along looser knots of syntax that resisted being unraveled into final sets of meaning. *Dichemination* (the term deployed in his reading of the postcard) underlines "writing's relentless will to divide and detach itself from sender and receiver."[45] Dichemination does offer a plausible model of reading Iran-Contra, but both terms—dissemination and *dichemination*—advocate *polysemia* over *anasemia*.

Anasemia was the mastertrope of Abraham and Torok's work. Anasemia is derived from "ana": "upward," "according to," "back," "revised," "backward," "again." "Semia" is defined as "that which pertains to the sign as a unit of meaning."[46] Anasemia is a process of problematizing the meaning of signs in a radically undetermined way.

Moreover, the various possibilities contained within the first part of the term "ana" point to the new topography that cryptonomy designates.

Abraham and Torok's anasemia is perhaps best known to the English reader through their analysis of the Wolf Man, *The Wolf Man's Magic Word*. Instead of the presentation of a catalogue of "deciphered hieroglyphic," that is, a dictionary of the Wolf Man's words, they present a "verbarium": an incredible and stupefying language that "sets language at an angle with itself and shatters all linear correspondence."[47] There is a tremendous temptation to construct a dictionary of Iran-Contra—a dictionary of euphemisms ("residuals," "management style," "strategic opening," "neutralize") or a catalogue of rhetorical tropes (*litotes,* the trope of negative relation and denial; "deprecation," pleas to obtain something; "imprecation," "conmination," and "apostrophe").[48] Oliver North's testimony deployed all of these rhetorical devices. (In that respect, North was a model reader of the CIA manual.) Yet I will stress the need for a *verbarium,* a term whose play in English translation repeats the French in another language. "Verbarium," or *verbier* in French, recalls the disseminating germs of "herbier." "Verbarium" in English contains "barium," the element used to trace the symptomatology of Reagan's body politic. Barium sulfate is an indicator in an x-ray photograph of the digestive tract.

Abraham and Torok's verbarium is constructed among three languages: the Wolf Man was a Russian emigré who undertook an analysis with Freud in German. Abraham and Torok's "discovery" is the importance of English in de-crypting. The Wolf Man had an English governess, and his dream is a rebus that is articulated in the play between these languages. Homonymic displacements, phonic similarity ("tooth" = "truth") enable Abraham and Torok to reconstitute the radically designified text and connect the Wolf Man's sexual knowledge (of coitus *a tergo*) to his nasal obsession (he knows = nose). This approach, relying on the poetic as well as the polyphonic capacities of language, is not to be restricted solely to polyglots. In other words, a verbarium can be constructed out of the differences *within* the same language. It is this latter possibility that intrigues Derrida in his foreword to *The Wolf Man's Magic Word*: "already within a single language, every word multiplies its faces or its allosemic sides and multiplies the allosemic[49] multiplication by further crossing formal grafts and combining phonic affinities."[50]

Let us again take up Reagan's "lying nose." There is a "coincidence" between Reagan's symptoms and the nose language of the Wolf Man. The Wolf Man had an obsessive preoccupation with his nose and teeth, continually seeing dermatologists for treatments of blackheads, swellings, wounds from picking pimples, and imaginary or exaggerated scars. On Easter, in 1925, between appointments with Freud, the Wolf Man develops a pimple on his nose. He consults a doctor, who diagnoses it as an infectious sebaceous gland and recommends a particular course of treatment. The Wolf Man consults another doctor, who squeezes his pimple, causing blood to rush out and provoking a feeling of great relief in the patient. (Some interpreters go so far as to say he experiences orgasm.) Nevertheless, a scar remains, and nasal symptoms remain an obsessional idea (*idée fixe*).[51]

The somatic parallels between Reagan and one of Freud's most famous patients include his other surgical site. In the course of his psychoanalysis with Freud, Freud promises the Wolf Man a complete recovery of his intestinal activities (i.e., chronic constipation). The psychoanalysis is so successful that the Wolf Man's bowel enters into the conversation! Stanley Fish reads this as an allegory of persuasion that is as transparently literal as my reading of Reagan's nose. Psycho(anal)ysis is an "emptying out" of preexisting convictions and doubts.[52] A bowel or intestine enters into conversation, and something is eliminated (doubt? belief?). Does Reagan's intestinal surgery eliminate doubts about the wisdom of exchanging arms for hostages? Does it raise the possibility of another strategic *opening*—one to Iran, paving the way for North's neat idea? Does the intestinal surgery somehow figuratively mime and enable the necessary elimination of doubt? Does it mime or prefigure an act of persuasion that in turn authorizes the covert operation—going private, finding channels, and creating the self-sustaining entity?

But what does the president's nose signify? Derrida writes about the Wolf Man's nose language: "the Wolf Man's desire had to become mute." The "nose language" is provisionally analyzed as a symptom in which no word can yet be read. Nose language/what the president knows in a covert operation in a national-security culture is "a sort of writing without language, a billboard or open book covered with unpronounceable signs—not yet a rebus."[53] "Bowel conversation" persuades the president to take part in the covert op. Nose language dissuades in the form of the cover-up.

Indeed, the unpronounceable signs point, like Reagan's lying nose, to the covert operation. A rhetorical reading should be attentive not only to silences but to parapraxes—mispronunciations. But McFarland[54] stumbles over the word "prescience" (saying "pre-science") shortly before he is forced to resign due to unforeseen events.[55] Casey's image is also that of a bumbling, inarticulate man: "The classic example was that he could not pronounce Nicaragua. He would say Nicawawa. He didn't apologize for it. When Casey would discuss Nicaragua, he would just say 'Nicawawa' and everyone present would know what he meant."[56] The nose language is covered with unpronounceable signs, "Nicawawa," yet Larry Speakes decrypts this writing without language. What was the president's nose as signifier? Speakes proclaims: "The President's nose was Grenada all over again." The press exchange with Donaldson and Thomas recalls the credibility crisis over Grenada as it anticipates Nicawawa. "There was no lie, but they were right. There was a glaring omission."[57] Glaring, like Freud's *glanz* (shine) on the nose.

The exchange among Speakes, Donaldson, and Thomas serves as a model for other post-Iran-Contra scandal disclosures. But there is one other body site that Larry Speakes of in the briefing room. In August 1986, the details of the president's bladder exam are disclosed. Under local anesthesia, "an instrument is inserted in the penis and goes up the urinary tract and it has a viewing apparatus where the doctor is able to examine the interior of the urinary tract." The word "penis" is mentioned in the briefing room, as the president is doubly de-briefed. Larry Speakes is jubilant about his narrative miming: "Public discussion of the president's penis? Yes—it happened—in the Reagan White House, on my watch."[58]

Filling in the Blank Check of the Covert Operation: Iran-Contra and "The Purloined Letter"

> Le manque a sa place.
>
> —Jacques Derrida, writing on Lacan's "Seminar on 'The Purloined Letter'."[59]

The disclosure of the covert operation simultaneously reveals and reveils the president's tool. The president's penis is de-briefed (by Speakes) as compensation for the nose language. Let us take up the threads of the Iran-Contra narrative again, with Oliver North and Grenada, within the frame of "The Purloined Letter."[60] For it is in reference to the crisis management of Grenada (i.e., the president's nose all over again) that North performs a key gesture of "The Purloined Letter,, a gesture that is repeated by two of Poe's most attentive readers: Derrida and Lacan. In Grenada, North *fills in the blank* of American foreign policy.

"More than anything else . . . North's role in the Grenada success established him as a man of rising influence within the national security council."[61] Grenada is North's opening into the epicenter of the NSC crisis management group. After the coup against Maurice Bishop, Bush convenes a special-situations group that plans to divert a twenty-one-ship flotilla headed by the aircraft carrier *Independence,* bound for Lebanon, to the Caribbean. Sentiment grows for an all-out invasion. Vessey argues that the rescue of Americans would be difficult without securing the whole island, and this needs a rationale. Fears about student safety and questions about airport construction prove insufficient legal grounds. North supplies a "neat idea" for a rationale. His solution is to use the Organization of Eastern Caribbean States (OECS) to press for American assistance. This "transparent justification" enables North to "fill in the blank." "North . . . pressed an idea that filled in the last legal blank."[62] North fills in a blank and, along with his fellow crisis managers Fontaine and Meages, places a bet on whether the president will sign the NSC directive for an invasion. Their bets are then sealed in an envelope. Reagan signs off on the invasion.

North, like Dupin inscribing a phrase from Crébillon in his facsimile of the letter, fills in a blank. If the covert operation, like "The Purloined Letter," is an allegory of the signifier, what role does this blank-filling play? A fuller reading of the Iran-Contra affair as purloined letter would discuss this role at length. It would fill in the gap, by discussing gender and symbolic determination. If "the shadow of Ollie North hung over the entire Iran Contra deal,"[63] is this a "great female body" to be read à la Lacan? It would read North's filling in a blank in relation to the plausible deniability of the diversion. No smoking gun is ever found because *a space is left blank.* "The evidence shows that at least one of Ollie North's memos about the diversion had a space for the President's signature and that space was left blank."[64] This draft of a memo that was sent to Poindexter to review was never passed on to Reagan. But does this mean that it never reached its destination?[65] Does the lack have (a) (its) place in the covert operation? Do covert operations circumvent the system of checks and balances, replacing them with blank checks? Was Reagan's euphemistic management style a "blank check"?

But there is a second structural parallel between Iran-Contra and Poe's story. For, as Johnson has so brilliantly analyzed in her account of Lacan's and Derrida's Poe-tic readings, the letter produces an automimetic effect. The key term of Iran-Contra: residuals, a euphemism for the word (diversion) that Oliver North does not like to say,[66] re-produces the figuration of Derrida and Lacan. "Residual" is tied to "residue," alerting us to the question of whether or not the trace can speak. "Residual," like "diversion," has two connotations, two registers of meaning. "Residual" refers to the corporate ("of, pertaining to or characteristic of a 'residue,' 'a remainder,' a qualify left over at the end of a process") and entertainment. A residual is the money paid to a performer whenever his performance is repeated. As entertainment, "residual" connotes the "always-already" diversionary: what is more diverting than a (repeat) performance? (Residue/residuum also has important associations for a cryptic analysis—a residue is what remains of a testator's estate after all debts and claims are satisfied. Residuum generates reside/residence, a dwelling. A crypt is a dwelling place for the remains.)

If "residual" sets off a chain letter of associational connotations, including the one it hides ("diversion"), "diversion" literalizes the Derridean enterprise of *dichemination*. Diversion denotes an act or instance of turning aside, as well as something that distracts the mind, relaxes, or entertains. It also connotes a military maneuver of deflection that turns an opponent away or astray (aside, distract or amuse). Yet this entertaining tactic need not distract us but rather points to how diversion relates to *dichemination. Dichemination,* as we have stated earlier, describes the way letters stray from their paths, (in Conley's words) "writing's relentless will to divide and detach itself from sender and receiver." *Dichemination* is part of a meshing of figures, and it stands in relation to dissemination as its trace. The breakout of the closed space of polysemy is accomplished by another neologism: *tranche/fer,* or axe-blow. *Tranche-fer* homonymically displaces and recalls transfer (as *dichemination*/dissemination). The relation between these "words" is pun, buffoonery, "parasitical dependence."[67] *Tranche-fer* (axe-blow) is a cutting trope deployed to slice through the intersubjective dialectic characteristic of *transference.*

North's activities partake of *dichemination* and the *tranche-fer* of funds to the Contras. The euphemism "residual" points to the "diversion" it covers up and etymologically includes. This amusing diversion is a *dichemination*: Oliver North fills in the blanks, writes "diversion memos" that are destroyed except for one found in his safe.[68] But, in this displacement of the letter, in the transfer, the *tranche-fer* comes down on him, too. He is continuously and simultaneously rephallicized and dephallicized, described as a "Marlboro Man without the Marlboro" and re-membered as a "rebel with a cause."[69] A reading of Iran-Contra in reference to "The Purloined Letter" would account for the movement of the letter in rephallicizing the male crisis manager to enable him to fill in the blank after a president's "management style" requires him to shoot blank checks.

Dances with *Wolf Man*

What we have here is a picture of someone who alternates between passive and aggressive behavior, now assuming the dominant position of the male aggressor, now submitting in feminine fashion to forms that overwhelm him."

—Stanley Fish, "Withholding the Missing Portion:
Psychoanalysis and Rhetoric"[70]

If the commander-in-chief tells this lieutenant colonel to go stand in the corner and sit on his head, I will do so.　　　—Oliver North[71]

Freud's analysis of the Wolf Man deploys a rhetorical strategy similar to that of Poe's "Purloined Letter"—a strategy of open concealment at work in Iran-Contra, as well. Freud offers to reveal the Wolf Man's secret as he also offers to share his doubts and intellectual uncertainty with us. Ollie offers full disclosure: "the good, the bad and the ugly," in a discursive power play as flagrant as Freud's. Both Freud and North demonstrate the way denial (*litotes*, plausible deniability) can function equally as a boast and a jubilant affirmation. Freud's narrative, like the textuality of Iran-Contra, is one of things withheld (by doctor and by patient) and lies told to advance the story and to cover it up.[72] Oliver North is part of a group at the NSC that "withholds the missing portion," in Fish's terminology, but with an interesting twist. North withholds even as he "stools." He takes the stand (he does not lie). The equivocal nature of North—as "compass point" (and the "magnetic North" that Daniel Schorr and James Der Derian speak of)—turns oxymoronic when we consider his full name. Oliver North, a non-place— olive trees do not grow in the north. No wonder that Oliver North is difficult to place. Let us frame him, then, by his testimony and by the Wolf Man's case.

Oliver North is a radically equivocal compass point. He wants, in Bradlee's words, to "have it both ways on the fall guy issue."[73] He wants to get credit for being able to "stand up and take the heat," yet his testimony smears everyone but the president. Now, Oliver North is not the first person who ever wanted to swing both ways, but what is peculiar to his case is that he draws a line on taking the fall when it is a criminal issue. He will take a "political" but not a "criminal" fall. How do we explain this fear of law? Does it relate to North's wish?

I conjecture that the law Oliver North is afraid of transgressing is his covert or veiled homoerotic wish. Contained within the often-cited boast of aggressive bravado "If the commander-in-chief tells this lieutenant colonel to go stand in the corner and sit on his head, I will do so" is a wish to sit on the president's face/head.[74] The indeterminate use of the pronoun "his" could refer equally well to the president as to North. Who is sitting on whose head? And why must this be done in a corner? (Veiled) North distinguishes between a "political" and a "criminal" fall —in one ("political") he is a "hero," in the other a "patsy." Clearly he does not want to be seen as acted upon. North overtly desires to be a "fall guy" on top, in control. The oxymoronic character of this wish ("a fall guy on top") produces a grammatical lapsus (indeterminate pronoun reference) as symptom. Bradlee reminds us that this was not North's first day in court; he flew back to Vietnam to testify for his friend Randy Herrod, accused of My Lai–type brutalities. North's testimony earned an acquittal for the friend who saved his life, and the description of his courtroom appearance is a prefiguration of the hearings:

> every bit the poster Marine with his high and tight haircut and his summer khaki uniform studded with combat decorations. He was articulate and had a relaxed yet earnest tone to his voice. But where Buckley, Carpenter and Bender decorously kept their legs crossed, North's legs were *splayed out, spread eagled.* It was the only flaw in an otherwise impressive performance, which did not go unnoticed at Marine headquarters.[75]

Oliver North, the (spread) eagled scout can be read as the large feminine (passive) body spread over this affair.[76] This oscillation between the passive and the hyper-male can be read against the hysterical male presidencies of Reagan and Bush.[77]

North's testimony reveals another affinity with the Wolf Man narrative, but this is a characteristic he shares with Reagan and Bush. For the Wolf Man narrative/dream is, in Rapaport's words, "an obscene and traumatic spectacle in a pathological staging of the refusal of an image to be either fully opaque or fully transparent, the refusal to fade and the inability to block yet another *mise en scene*."[78] It is this pathological staging that makes obsession possible. A reading of Iran-Contra through the frame of the Wolf Man, through the window (of vulnerability) that stages the Wolf Man's dream, would situate the covert operation in the seductive power politics of the *trompe l'oeil*. Reagan and Bush present a politics of the afterimage. Presidential subjectivity in an era of the *trompe l'oeil* is not the de-authorized "dead" father but rather a disappearing or fading one—as we will see in the next chapter, a ghost.

Conclusion

"The Wolfman," says [John] Waters, referring to Freud's famous case study: "I wanted him to be my friend."   —Paul Mandelbaum[79]

From then on, that particular pleasure, jealously preserved in his *inner safe*, could only be subject to total disavowal.   —Derrida, "Fors"[80]

Derrida makes the argument for cryptonymic readings in his introduction to Abraham and Torok, entitled "Fors." "Fors" is a word that is uneasily translatable: "for," an archaic meaning (outside, except for, save), and "for," always modified, the *for intérieure*, the inner heart(h) or the figure of a subjective interiority. "Fors," plural, invokes a play between an "inner safe" and "save" (except for) what is contained and what is left out. I will briefly suggest that his new t(r)opography is a model for an international relations that has displaced Cartesian coordinates, which no longer apply.

Cryptonomy is peculiarly suited for the covert operation as it concerns the secret/secrecy. The secret is given a new topolographical and metapsychological status. Indeed, *cryptonymy* (a neologism combining *crypto* and *metonymy*) is a strange psychoanalytic practice that replaces traditional metaphors of the unconscious (secrecy = latency = hidden) with a "false unconsciousness" (HUMINT), positioned as a first object or backdrop. Derrida writes: "an artificial unconscious lodged like a prosthesis, a graft in the heart of an organ, within the divided self, a very specific and peculiar place, highly circumscribed to which access can nevertheless only be gained by following the route of a different topography."[81]

The crypt as presented by Derrida is an emblem of an NSC culture with partitions and simulated situation rooms (built to look like what people in the movies feel a situation room should look like). The crypt, like the NSC culture, is an artifact, in whose partitions are enclosed enclaves such as the "executive junta." It is a figure of compartmentalization: "a place comprehended within another but rigorously separate from it . . . so as to purloin it from the rest." This construction of partitions, the cryptic enclose, produces, in turn, clefts in space. "In the architectonics of the open square within space, itself delineated by a general closure, a forum. Within this forum, a place." Inside this forum, an inner safe is constructed, "a secret interior within the public square." This inner forum, separated from the outer forum, where speeches and symbolic goods are exchanged, is a safe: "an outcast outside inside the inside."[82]

I suggest that, rather than read Iran-Contra as the simulation it presents itself to be—"a CIA outside the CIA"—we ask about its inner safe. A "stand-alone entity" still conforms to the topographic space of Descartes: inside/outside. Iran-Contra is about figuring the national-security culture as an "outcast outside inside the inside." And this outcast safe has everything to do with secrecy: "staking a secret place in order to keep itself safe somewhere inside a self."[83] I find it ironic that North's infractions are themselves symptomatic signifiers: the acceptance of money to build a security fence. I am alerted to the cryptic language of discussion: all the "spare parts" and "oil-drilling equipment" held in the small cargo area of one plane. Why insist on one single cargo plane? I think of Ollie encrypted in the inner safes of his car (in the many curb-side interviews) and of the physical layout of the briefing books at the Senate hearing, designed to create a "bunker effect."[84] North's testimony itself displays an encrypting effect. His rhetorical appeals build up a rationale and construct a record, a caulked and sealed room.

I read Iran-Contra ultimately as the construction of a cryptic safe that maintains, in a state of ritual miming and repetition, the conflict it is incapable of resolving. The secret fragments the topography of the crypt. (The crypt is no "solution"—it is a strategic compromise.) The difficulty in staking a secret place in order to keep itself safe somewhere within a self addresses the rationale of the covert operation and its operatives: "that we are at risk in a dangerous world."

Oliver North has learned much since then. No longer concerned with security fences and the construction of a cryptic enclave somewhere between his "dynamic unconscious and the self of introjection," North now wears his safe on the outside.[85] As a spokesman for bulletproof vests, North sheds his Marine officer's uniform and repeats the gesture of Poe and Freud (turning signifiers inside out). Resplendent in his bulletproof vest, Oliver North is (finally) safe.

4

This Is Not a President

Baudrillard, Bush, and Enchanted Simulation (1991)

Today *the trompe l'oeil* is no longer confined to painting.
—Jean Baudrillard, *Seduction*[1]

I mean, like hasn't everybody thought about becoming president for years?
—George Bush[2]

The end-of-the-millennium American presidency reads as a perverse rewrite of Baudrillard's sign theory: a gradual disobligation of the sign as we pass from the disenchanted and banal strategies of Ronald Reagan to the seductive, enchanted simulation of Bush and his most "fatal strategy," Dan Quayle, a man who "does not live in this century."[3] What has been lost in the nonvisible transition from Reagan to Bush is precisely this move from hyperreality to seduction. The apparent continuity of Reagan-Bush and their cabinet cross-dressing (the same men in different suits) mask an epistemic discontinuity. For Bush is our first hysterical male president. The first *trompe l'oeil* president of Baudrillard's fourth order of simulation: fractal (a thousand points of light) and orbital (yes, we will go to Mars). With Bush we move from the hyperreal in-difference of Reagan to an objective irony, from a president as hologram to the *trompe l'oeil*: Reagan, the ecstasy of the real in hyperreality; Bush, the ecstasy of the fake in seduction.

Umberto Eco evokes what is at stake in this realm of the Absolute Fake in his depiction of Disneyland's reconstructed Oval Office: "Elsewhere, on the contrary, the frantic desire for the almost real arises only as a neurotic reaction to the vacuum of memories, the Absolute Fake is the offspring of the unhappy awareness of a present without depth."[4]

We might as well insert the "id"—a president without depth. The scandal that the *trompe l'oeil* poses for political and esthetic representation since the Renaissance is situated in its "unreal reversion" (S, 60). The aim of the reconstructed Oval Office in both Disneyland and Washington is to supply a sign that will fool (*trompe*) the eye and abolish the distinction of reference. (Or, as in Bush's own words: "This isn't any signal. It's a direct statement. If it's a signal, fine.")[5] In the history of the late-twentieth-century presidency, Bush marks a peculiar instance of the relation of reference to signification. While American presidents since Gerald Ford have been empty signifiers, rarely has there been such a Lacanian relation to language as the one that Bush daily enacts. Bushspeak may be the closest approximation *outremer* of the Lacanian unconscious: *ça parle*: "It says what it knows while the subject does not know it."[6] With Bush, we have a presidential subject that cannot be understood as a signified (i.e., as objectively knowable). This is preparation for the final turn of the screw: Quayle as Baudrillard's fatal strategy, where "the metamorphosis, tactics and strategies of the object exceed the subject's understanding."[7] (Carter posed problems of a different psychoanalytical order. For he demonstrated the fissure between idea and affect. Carter always seemed to smile at the wrong time.)

The end-of-the-millennium presidency is a twin appeal to the "image repertoire" and the symbolic order. As image repertoire, it can be read as a litany of bad presidential performances: "LBJ abusing his dogs and exposing his belly; Nixon hunched and glistening like a concerned toad, Gerald Ford tripping over. . . ." Reagan, as a hyperreal president, could always satisfy our iconic interests: "Reagan was nice as Iago was honest because his image repertoire required it of him."[8] Moreover, Reagan was always tangible as symbol if not as image. In the difference between image repertoire and the symbolic order we can first glimpse the subtle passage from hyperreality to seduction. What sets Bush apart from Reagan is his intractable opacity. For Bush is a simulacrum without perspective. He appears as a pure artifact (our "environmental" president, our "education" president) against a vertical backdrop. Bush replaces Reagan's tangibility with the "tactile vertigo of the afterimage." Richard Goldstein concurs: "now we're in the grip of something that no longer requires a spokesman."[9] This tactile vertigo recounts "the subject's insane desire to obliterate his own image and thereby vanish" (S. 62). Life becomes a "Jeff Koons tableau." Koons the artist and Bush the seducer know how to let the signs hang. Bush/Koons, suspended in ether.

Bush not only follows the hyperrealism of neo-geo/Reagan but recalls the surrealism of Gerald Ford. Both share the same knack for the tautology: "Things are more like they are now than they ever have been" (Ford) [10]; "It's no exaggeration to say the undecideds could go one way or another" (Bush).[11] They juxtapose physical against linguistic slapstick: Ford trips; Bush slips linguistically. If Gerald Ford recalls the Jerry Lewis of the Lewis-Martin movies in which a subjective irony might still be possible, Bush is most reminiscent of the movies Lewis produced after his split with Martin.[12] An internally dissociated subject emerges in the linguistic parapraxis as Bush stages his own disappearance. Pronouns flee, then verbs, in the vanishing act of his State of the Union address: "Ambitious aims? Of course! Easy to do? Far from it."[13] We are left with nothing but the irony of the object, which underscores the tie between Lacan's *linguisterie* ("linguistricks") and Bushspeak: "what might be called a man, the male speaking being strictly disappears as an effect of discourse by being inscribed within it solely as castration."[14]

Ghosts that haunt the emptiness of the stage —Baudrillard (*S*, 60)

I'm going to be so much better a president for having been at the CIA that you are not going to believe it. —George H. W. Bush[15]

What seduces us with Bush, as in the *trompe l'oeil,* is its missing dimension. And if Ronald Reagan was a hologram, Bush is, in Baudrillard's words, "a superficial abyss." Opposed to Reagan's televisual sarcasm ("How do I spell relief? V-E-T-O"), Bush is a visual non sequitur. Bush affords the same perspectual pleasure as that of the *trompe l'oeil* (as well as its secret undermining of language), even as he takes us back to our earliest lessons of political representation. Since Machiavelli, power has always-already been a simulation model, only an effect of perspective. Baudrillard recounts that at the heart of the ducal palaces of Urbino and Gubbio were tiny *trompe l'oeil* sanctuaries, inverted microcosms whose space was actualized by simulation. These sanctuaries (*studiolos*) were blind spots in the palace and were placed at the heart of the prince's politico-architectural space. Through a subversive metonymy, they invite an allegorical reading: that the prince's power is only mastery of a simulated space. This is the prince's secret.[16]

And, we might wonder, who is better than Bush, a former CIA spook, to preside over the seductive presidency and guard this secret? Seduction is, after all, the realm of the *secret*. Production, for Baudrillard, is "to materialize by force what belongs to another order, that of the secret and of seduction. Seduction is, at all times and in all places, opposed to production. Seduction removes from the order of the visible, while production constructs everything in full view, be it an object, a number or concept" (*S*, 34). Those people who doubt Bush's popularity at the polls, who castigate his caution (or prudence), are like those critics of Ronald Reagan who saw him either as a hypocrite or as vacuous and thereby missed his remarkable sign function and theoretic challenge. The depthlessness and nonobligation of the sign is constitutive of the postmodern presidency. And if Reagan was conceptually tragic, yet hilarious, Bush proffers a no less metaphysical hilarity: the acute metaphysical appeal of the *trompe l'oeil*.

It may appear bizarre to characterize Bush as seductive. After all, this is the man whom *Newsweek* decreed had a wimp factor too strong for him to ever become president. But we should not make the mistake of confounding the autonomous or disembodied signifier with charisma or its lack. Charisma, like vulgar notions of seduction, has everything to do with the body; seduction, in contrast, connotes a whole "strategy of appearances" interpreted in terms of "play, challenges, duels" (*S*, 7). Indeed, the Bush presidency when read against Baudrillard's *Seduction* seems less an instance of the wimp factor than a transvestite oversimulation of femininity. The Bush impersonator on *Saturday Night Live*, Dana Carvey, is also the punishing church lady. This oscillation between the two Bush personas uncannily evokes both of Carvey's characterizations, especially that of the phallic mother and her appeal for the male masochist. This recentering around the strong mother entails a concomitant displacement of male subjectivity. Political pundits such as Peter Hart and the Texas senator Carl Parker have an idiomatic appreciation of Bush as feminine simulator. Hart calls Bush the "Don Knotts of American politics." Parker compares Bush's macho performance to that of Reagan: "Reagan can portray a real macho guy. Bush can't. He comes off looking like Liberace."[17] Both analogies are telling figures. Don Knotts was best known as Andy Griffith's inept deputy, Barney Fife, whose failed attempts to impose a law recall the hysterics of Al "I'm in charge" Haig. Knotts is the perfect second fiddle (as is Bush). His tremendous effort at and his failure to control become a caricature of male potency. Knotts, like Bush, exemplifies the masochistic self-victimization of one who is so visibly trying to please. Indeed, Knotts seems an ersatz, made-for-television (pre-telethon) Jerry Lewis. While Liberace is a rhetorically charged *topos,* he too can be read, like Knotts or Bush, as an oversimulation of the feminine.

The transvestite is an apposite figure for Bush. Like the transvestite, Bush parodies signs by oversignification. Bush, like Baudrillard, knows that "it is the transubstantiation of sex into signs that is the secret of all seduction" (*S*, 13). Moreover, what we witness with Bush, as with male hysteria in general, is not the recoding of men as men but rather a process of uncoding.[18] Like Jerry Lewis's, Bush's frenetic effort to "control the [political] spectacle finally yields to a male subject position which demolishes any prospect of a coherent masculine subjectivity."[19] Reagan's obtuse meaning was literally impertinent; Bush's persona is incoherent: Bush-wimp and the macho Bush; Bush with Barbara, Bush with Baker; the kinder, gentile Bush of the new WASP cultural hegemony against the macho cowboy Texan who puts Tabasco sauce on his tuna, "yet always seems to look as if he has just escaped from a dude ranch."[20]

What fascinates us in Bush is precisely this unresolved and contradictory self-formation—the self-canceling spiraling of signs that is also the fascination with the neuter: one libido? Or Barthesian nectarine that dampens oppositions? In *Sade Fourier Loyola,* Barthes discusses Fourier's classification scheme, in which there is always a reserved portion (1/8). This reserved portion is liminal or *neuter*: "The neuter is what comes between the mark and the non-mark, this sort of buffer, damper, whose role is to muffle, to soften, to fluidify the semantic tick-tock, that metronome-like noise the paradigmatic alternative obsessively produces: yes/no, yes/no. . . ." This portion is shocking as it is contradictory and disturbing. It is necessarily ambiguous, and it undermines meaning. The neuter is a "qualitative, structural relation" that subverts the very idea of norm and normality. "To enjoy the neuter is perforce to be disgusted by the average."[21] And, despite his many protestations, Bush is no average guy.

Yet, Bush is a transvestite-feminine dissimulator in a parodic sense: "The seduction is itself coupled with a parody in which an implacable hostility to the feminine shows through and which might be interpreted as a male appropriation of the panoply of female allurements" (*S*, 14). This repudiation of the feminine is most evident in a contest situation, such as the Bush–Geraldine Ferraro debate in which Bush "kicked a little ass" (a good ole Texas phrase) or in his televisual dual with Dan

Rather ("that guy makes Leslie Stahl look like a pussy").[22] His repudiation of the feminine is twinned with an overcompensation of masculine behavior that can look only to Jerry Lewis's Nutty Professor for an equally apt hysterical enactment. The Bush wimp is like the Lewis-Kelp character cured of what ails (Ailes) him via a substitute ego of simulated virility. Bush as wimp is transformed to macho-Bush only by an excess of masochistic self-victimization. Dana Carvey's brilliant parody of Bush's campaign self-management is to the point: "Voice low. Voice getting lower. Doctors tell me it can go lower still."[23] The exhibition of Bush-suffering throughout the entire 1988 campaign is enacted via the body: His voice is lowered, his mannerisms contained. Moreover, the oscillation between a passive and a hypermale (often misread as the opposition between Peggy Noonan and Roger Ailes) underlines the lack of a stable balance within a single male subjectivity, thus adding Bush to the ranks of other late-eighties male hysterics: Pete Rose, General Noriega, and Bob Saget.

Like the transvestite, there is nothing latent about Bush. It is only latent discourse that tries to hide the secret of appearances. Seduction is a manifest discourse offering us the lure (*leurre*) of the secret of appearances. What Bush offers is nothing less than the faker than the false —Oprah Winfrey's head on Ann-Margret's body on the cover of *TV Guide*. Bush becomes, in this reading, a blank, empty sign that bespeaks the anticeremonial of anti(political) representation. I repeat: Bush is a manifest character. Maureen Dowd and Thomas Friedman describe him: "When you sit across from the president, it is like holding an X-ray plate up to the light. You can see if he feels defensive or annoyed or amused. He is often distracted, toying with something on his desk."[24] Dowd's depiction of a distracted Bush makes him no less seductive in Baudrillard's sense: for the absence of a focused look, like the absence of a face, highlights the abstraction of the void that lies at the base of all seduction: "The mind is irresistibly attracted to a place devoid of meaning" (*S*, 75). As our *trompe l'oeil* president, Bush "bewitches" us with his missing dimension. And if Reagan simulated his constituency, Bush quite literally mirrors it. Like the seducer, Bush says, "I'll be your mirror." But this is not in some American interest-group liberalism sense of "I'll represent you or reflect you." Rather, Bush offers to be our deception. "I'll be your deception," the mirror ensnares us with its come-on of "Let's Pretend."[25] Bush is as transparent and false as the plastic bag holding the crack "purchased" in Lafayette Park—a wholly fake enactment with malfunctioning video equipment and a pusher who couldn't find the White House.[26] Rarely do we have a president with such camp potential. Yet the question still lingers: Which male hysteric, Pee-Wee Herman or Jerry Lewis? Male hysteria with or without anxiety?

> I do not like broccoli. And I haven't liked it since I was a little kid and my mother made me eat it. And I'm president of the United States and I'm not going to eat any more broccoli.   —George H. W. Bush[27]

> I'm legally and emotionally entitled to be what I want to be. That's what I want to be and that's what I am.   —George H. W. Bush[28]

It is this void, this missing dimension, that ties Bush the *trompe l'oeil* president to Bush the hysterical male president. For it is the inner absence that terrifies the hysteric. Bush is described by Steven V. Roberts as a man in his middle sixties who "still didn't know who he was or where he wanted to go."[29] This panic is sometimes evinced in a self-reflective comment: "I'm looking introvertedly and I don't like what I see." This uncertainty and terror over his fragile concept of identity are underscored by his manic 1988 campaign insistence that "I'm one of you." This rhetorical tick (like the hysteresis of Koch's "How'm I doing?") was repeated eight times in his New Hampshire speech and in numerous states: Massachusetts, "Born there. I'm one of them, too"; Texas, "I'm one of them, too" (or, in dialect, "Ah am one of y'all"); Connecticut, "I think it might be kind of nice to have a Connecticut kid in the White House."[30] So much insistence on Being (the *Dasein* in all its naked stupidity). Barthes notes that the hysteric asks, "Am I?" Bush's profound lack of a sense of self is momentarily assuaged by the appeal to voter registration: "I'm legally and emotionally entitled to be what I want to be." Bush displaces the question of identity to one of a posited self signified by documentation ("my Texas hunting license, my Texas driver's license and my voter's registration card")[31] for this gives him the freedom to play roles and to refuse any one fixed identity. The *trompe l'oeil* underscores the lack in male subjectivity.

Indeed there is a certain pathos in Bush's frenetic attempts to establish an identity (if not a residence—the *unheimlich*/homelessness of a suite in a Houston hotel serves as his primary address). Bush reminds us that hysteria is "the effect and testimony of a failed interpellation." Moreover, Bush's self-questioning recalls Lacan's reformulation "Why am I what you're telling me that I am?" Zizek situates the hysterical question in the failure of the subject to assume symbolic identification. "The hysterical question opens the gap of what is in the subject more than the subject of the *object in subject* which resists interpellation."[32] The Bush-lack is tied to the Lacanian (m)-other as Bush answers charges that he is a carpetbagger: "When I ran for office in Texas they said this guy's from New England. I said, wait a minute, I couldn't help that, *I wanted to be near my mother at the time.*"[33]

Baudrillard compares the hysteric and the seducer in their development of signs. The fear of being seduced leads hysterics to set up "booby-trapped" signs. Indeed, the entire 1988 campaign can be read as one long booby-trapped sign, as if Bush entirely lacked the capacity for secondary revision. With Bush, there is a dizzying array of parapraxes, elisions, and repetitions. Bush is aware of the problem: "I have a tendency to avoid on and on and on, elegant pleas. I don't talk much, but I believe, maybe not articulate much, but I feel."[34] Bush is self-conscious, defensive, and nonironic about his *linguisterie*. He fondly replays his Pearl Harbor Day lapsus when he gets flustered in the debate with Dukakis: "It's Christmas. Wouldn't it be nice to be perfect? Wouldn't it be nice to be the iceman so you never make mistakes?"[35] The Bush parapraxes can include foreign words: "muchissimo grazie" and thinking of "comme çi comme ça" as a popular Hispanic phrase.[36] But it is in electoral campaigns and contest situations that his unique rhetorical talent merges most fully.

The primal scene of the 1988 campaign is the May 1988 rally in Twin Falls, Idaho, when Bush admits to having sex with Reagan: "For seven and a half years, I have worked alongside him and I am proud to be his partner. We have had triumphs, we have made mistakes, we have had sex." Correcting this lapsus ("we have had setbacks"), Bush commits an even greater blunder, comparing himself to a "javelin thrower who won the coin toss and elected to receive."[37] Nor is this the first time the electoral parapraxes have concerned masculinity. In 1984, Bush offered to "lay his record on manhood against Mondale's anytime."[38] Or, commenting on the Anderson challenge in 1980, "If we win in Michigan, it would be like a jockey or a marathon man with lead weights in both pockets."[39] (The 1984 convention provoked considerable anxiety as Bush suffered from convention envy, forcing the phallic comparison "It doesn't have the drama of San Francisco. But our halo blowers are as good as theirs. Our flag wavers are taller, stronger and better.")[40]

As stated earlier, the Bush parapraxes range from elision (forgetting about Reagan's governorship while praising Deukmejian at a 1988 rally as the best governor of the state on record) to the just plain silly: "Tell me, general, how dead is the Dead Sea?" asked of the Jordanian Army Chief of Staff.[41] The explicit goal of Bush's administration is to "make sure that everybody who has a job wants a job"[42] (a much more ambitious aim than mere full employment). It is against this question of desire that Bushspeak should be read: not as overexuberance leading to "misspeaking," but as an excess of decoration (a linguistic surplus value) over meaning, which may be one reason he is so difficult to translate. Bush baffles his translators with his use of colloquialisms derived from popular culture (especially baseball) and Texas slang. Bush tells the Japanese to "stay tuned," the Soviets to "lighten up." He uses baseball references in a discussion of Panamanian strategy: "American will stay at the plate." Yet, it is Bush's rhetorical appeal to Yogi Berra, master of the tautology ("You can observe a lot just by watching"; "déjà vu all over again") and oxymoron ("No one goes to that restaurant anymore, it's too crowded") that most frustrates the French translator.[43] Yogi Berra's rhetorical duplication recalls that of Magritte's calligram[44] and once again underlines the figure of *trompe l'oeil* in Bush's presidency. Bush also enacts (with considerable hilarity) the difference between the logic of the unconscious and that of the ego. As mentioned earlier, Bush's slips exemplify Lacanian *linguisterie* (translated as "linguistricks"): "that side of language that language has left unformalized."[45] These are most obvious in verbal slips, jokes, interruptions, and dreams.

There is a manic insistence and disjointed character to Bush's discourse. (Mary McGrory notes that the non sequitur is the one grammatical form Bush has mastered.) Even more than President Reagan's anecdote about his drive down Highway One, Bush exemplifies the Lacanian *dérive* (or drift): "being dragged by currents and not knowing where it is going."[46] An emblematic Bush drift is the following quite literal *dérive* as Bush floats around the Pacific Ocean after his fighter plane is shot down near Japan:

> I was shot down and I was floating around in a little yellow raft setting a record for paddling. I thought of my family, my mom and dad and the strength I got from them. I thought of my faith, the separation of church and state.[47]

Or we can consider Bush on his goals for the summit with Gorbachev:

> We had last night, last night we had a couple of our grandchildren with us in Kansas City—six-year-old twins, one of them went as a package of Juicy Fruit, arms sticking out of the pack, the other was Dracula. A big rally there. And Dracula's wig fell off in the middle of my speech and I got to thinking, watching those kids, and I said if I could look back and I had been president for four years: what would you like to do? Those young kids there. And I'd love to be able to say that working with our allies, working with the Soviets, I'd found a way to ban chemical and biological weapons from the face of the earth.[48]

Bushspeaks as such typifies the split between *savoir* and *connaissance*: it is a *savoir* without *connaissance* inscribed within Lacan's discourse of the messenger slave: "the subject who carries under his hair the codicil that condemns him to death [who] knows neither the meaning nor the text nor in what language it is written, nor even that it had been tatooed on his shaved scalp as he slept."[49]

In other words, Bush's "linguisterie" shares with Barthesian "betise" the eruption of an unconscious truth in an unacceptable manner: incoherent, fragmentary, nongrammatical. At times Bush exemplifies something resembling a classic nineteenth-century hysteric such as Anna O. It seems as if English is not Bush's native language. While many of Bush's slips appear merely stupid or of trivial significance, it is at precisely such moments, when meaning is fractured, that we glimpse a "missing letter"[50]—a break in the cohesion of the ego. When asked if the economic decline is over, Bush states emphatically, "The slide show is over." Also, the possibility of no further Contra aid "pulls the plug out from under the President of the United States."[51] Both slips reinscribe the afterimage cyborg quality of his presidency. For Bush's digressions, non sequiturs, lapses, and repetitions recall those of an analysand, rather than the narrative closure of an authorial subject (i.e., the president of the United States).

One of Bush's most interesting and parodied linguistic tropes is his use of the word "thing"—"Did you go through that withdrawal thing?" (to a recovering drug addict)—or its numerous guises: the "feminist thing," the "hostage thing," the "vision thing," the "gender thing," the "ethnic thing,"[52] and so on. Bush's thing-thing is like Lacan's "*petit objet a*," a surplus object, a leftover of the Real that eludes symbolization.

And, like Lacan's "*objet a,*" it "partially represents the function which produces it."[53] This "thing-thing" allows a hysterical Bush to identify with the Other's lack, as well as his own. There is always something that escapes the presidential subject, and this lacking object releases his desire.

For Baudrillard, the seducer and the hysteric differ in their manipulation of signs. If seduction mocks the truth of signs, the hysteric plays with signs without sharing them (*S,* 120). Bush does both: seduction as challenge, hysteria as blackmail—an effective double-game strategy. Bush, like an hysteric, turns his body into a mirror. He is what he does and does not eat (pork rinds, broccoli).[54] But this is a mirror that has been turned against the wall by effacing the potential seductiveness of his body (after all, he is relatively good-looking and fit) by desexualizing it. This desexualization can be read against the classic scenario in which strong female subjects (Marilyn Quayle, Barbara Bush) are obligated to assume male lack. (To the extent that Bush is also a male masochist, as we will see in the next chapter, this is his fantasy, as well). The gaze of the sexual (m)other of the Bush presidency is quite different from Nancy's fawning. Barbara Bush answers the call to look upon and accept male lack. The denegation of her Wellesley commencement address acknowledges and embraces male castration (even and especially as it rewrites the First Lady as a man). Marilyn Quayle insisted during the campaign that she was not getting paid to be Dan's adviser even if she was doing what an adviser would normally get paid for. We witness a reorientation: a recentering of the Strong Mother and a combination of female magnanimity and male masochism.[55] Barbara Bush is so popular because she is so reassuring. But her reassurance is not that she allows herself to visibly grow old but rather that she encourages us to be passive without guilt.

If Barbara follows the Lacanian route of the acceptance of male lack, Bush in his desexualization offers us an ultimatum: "You will not seduce me. I dare you to try." Yet, as Baudrillard notes, seduction shows through in negation. The dare is one of its fundamental forms. A challenge is met with a response. This is the real sense of "read my lips," and not, as Peggy Noonan would have it, an attempt to establish unequivocal meaning.[56] Bush closes down the game by dramatizing his refusal to be seduced (i.e., cash in on his popularity), at the same time dramatizing a need for seduction.

Bush, seductive and oblique, is the perfect end-of-the-millennium president. If Ronald Reagan showed the signifier in a "permanent state of depletion" (the Barthesian third or obtuse meaning), then Bush proffers another sign strategy: the obliquity of the seducer who knows how to let the signs hang. Who needs a White House astrologer when you have a seducer who knows when signs are favorable and has the requisite male masochism to enjoy suspense? We recall Baudrillard's words with a poignancy for the events of last fall (1989). Bush is the luckiest man in the world, some say. I disagree. Bush appears lucky only because of the uncanny deployment of a seduction strategy:

> Signs are favorable only when left suspended and will move of themselves to their appointed destiny. The seducer doesn't use signs up all at once but waits for the moment when they will all respond, one after the other, creating a unique conjuncture and collapse. (*S*, 109)

5

Bush, the Man Who Sununu Too Much

Male Trouble and Presidential Subjectivity (1993)

I will explore the election of the fetish in the service of seduction,
particularly the way it stages a play of differences, or cuts a fine
line between affirmation and denial. Does this play of fetishism
have something to do with contemporary hysterical inscriptions
that serve to recode masculinity?
—Berkeley Kaite

What we must do is to isolate the *sinthome* from the context by
virtue of which it exerts its power of fascination in order to expose
the *sinthome*'s utter stupidity.
—Slavoj Zizek

Contemporary presidential leadership poses a problem for
critical analysis. Daily, one witnesses such a radical and destabilizing
deauthorization of the presidential subject that it goes well beyond the
capability of semiotics to read it as a sign *tout court*. The semiotic cou-
pling of signifier and signified (as well as the conflation between them in
the case of Reagan) cannot adequately capture the stupefying character
of Bush/Quayle, necessitating a shift in focus to terms encountered in
previous chapters, such as Barthes's third meaning (the obtuse or supplementary signifier that stands for that which cannot be represented)
or Baudrillard's insignificant or meaningless "seductive signifier," which
renders the "superficial abyss" or the "shiny surface of non-sense."[1]
The Lacanian phallic signifier, a signifier without a signified, offers yet
another interpretative possibility.[2] These three terms, like Bush's discourse and persona, confound meaning.

This reading of Bush and the postmodern presidency is indebted to Zizek's *Looking Awry* in several ways. Zizek's adumbration of the phallic signifier augments my previous analysis of Bush as a disenchanted simulation (i.e., as a Baudrillardian *trompe l'oeil*). Moreover, it appears that the presidency is a sublime object in Zizek's sense. Although Zizek does draw a connection between elections and the irruption of the Real in *The Sublime Object of Ideology*, I privilege his reading in *Looking Awry* as it applies to leadership—that is, "the gaze capable of seeing nothingness, i.e., of seeing an object 'begot by nothing.'" This attendant problematic relates to the hysterization of a king (*LA*, 9): "a process whereby the king loses the second sublime body that makes him a king, is confronted with the void of his subjectivity outside the symbolic mandate-title 'king' and is thus forced into a series of theatrical hysterical outbursts from self pity to sarcastic and clownish madness." This characterization is foregrounded by Zizek in *Richard II* and in the exchange between the Queen and the King's servant (who is felicitously named *Bushy*).

Perhaps the critical problem is the very attempt to account for leadership with reference to any purely representative model, however linguistically derived, rather than to see presidential subjectivity as *enacted* or *performed theory*. In the case of Bush, this is indeed a missed opportunity. For, I will argue, Bush has become a leading performance artist (or drag queen, if we choose to gender his hysterical enactments as feminine) of contemporary theory. Moreover, framing Bush in this way can raise many exciting theoretical questions, such as the possibility of "empowered transvestism" (is Bush a real man in disguise?), issues of fetishism (both male and female) and their relation to the space of theatricality, impersonation, and the masquerade of the modern presidency, as well as a more general problematic that concerns itself with subjectivity and lack (whether, indeed, lack must be a gendered term). And it is a most varied performance. Bush is equally at home in Baudrillardean seduction and as a Lacanian *sinthome* (i.e., a "signifier" permeated with idiotic enjoyment). The reading that follows privileges the Lacanian performance. Miming Jane Gallop's transferential relation to her object, Lacan, I now read Lacan as Bush.[3] The similarity is striking: those choppy little paragraphs, many of which are composed of only one sentence, the fragmentary nature of many of those sentences, which also tend toward discontinuity and isolation.

But apart from this transference, the preference for a Lacan-Bush may be due to the uncanny resemblance between Bush's performance and Lacanian-derived gender theorists' preoccupation with the construction of masculinities as "male trouble," "queer theory," or the study of "deviant masculinities"—masculinities whose "defining desires and identifications are perverse with respect to phallic structures."[4] Bush becomes, in such a reading, a *deconstructive practice* within gender theory's already deconstructive exploration of the "hegemonic ideology of compulsory heterosexuality" or the "phallic redundancy"[5] implicit in terms such as male subjectivity. Bush acts out (without working through) the theoretical insights and aporias of theorists such as Kaja Silverman, Constance Penley, Parveen Adams, Gaylyn Studlar, and Lynne Kirby, who transpose the Freudian monuments of hysteria and masochism with a male subjectivity in crisis. Both are apt depictions of Bush in 1992. Hysteria positions its (male) subject in the gap between "phallic plenitude and alienated dependency."[6] Male masochism addresses the "inseparability of pleasure and pain coincident with an exteriorizing identification and a dissolution of identity."[7]

The "Bush-performance" (it is more difficult to situate Bush as image than as attempted control of the image; in this way he prefigures Clinton's disturbance of the visual economies of the look and gaze) also enacts queer theory's motivation articulated by Jonathan Goldberg, that is, the "necessity for a post humanist ideology . . . for kinds of 'new people' who demand a place in the political—women of color, people with AIDS, etc.—people whose 'novelty' lies precisely in the ways in which their (our) own identities fracture the human/biological/heterosexual imperatives."[8] In such a way, Bush as deconstructive performance within theory belies the content of his own exclusionary (homophobic) policy formulations. To read Bush in such a way is destabilizing and potentially subversive to the normative assumptions that govern traditional masculinity and also those of authoritative leadership that they underscore. I maintain that Bush's incoherence as presidential persona is best read against theorists such as Zizek and Silverman, who focus on disavowal—the disavowal of sexual differences, as well as the defiance of castration. For Bush's "abject and enervated masculinity"[9] enacts the oscillation between lack and surplus meaning addressed by Lacanian feminist theorists.

Bush's foregrounding of male trouble in his last (1992) State of the Union address ("This will not stand"), as well as in his many rear-positionality electoral parapraxes, should not surprise us. The question

"Does Bush have an unconscious?" would be better reformulated as we have seen in the preceding chapter with Lacan: "Bush identifies himself in language only by losing himself in it as an object—*Ça parle*—it says what it knows while the subject doesn't know it."[10] Bush as presidential subject is not objectively knowable—he can be understood not as a signifier but rather as a *sinthome,* that is, "a signifier permeated with idiotic enjoyment."[11]

Yet I will argue that this very *méconnaissance* is indispensable for presidential subjectivity. For, as Slavoj Zizek notes, "knowledge in the real" depends upon a subject's nonknowledge either of something unintegrated into the symbolic network or something left unsaid. "As soon as the subject knows too much, he pays for this excess surplus knowledge in his flesh."[12] *Méconnaissance,* or not knowing too much, facilitates Bush's ability to either foreground or literalize precisely what is at issue. His lapses come to serve as meta-commentaries or hilarious *en-abimes.* This is especially pronounced in campaigning or contest situations (debates with Ferraro, battles with Congress), which can be read transferentially—as an analytical session in which the word is addressed to the other. Moreover, we will see that Bush's masochism—on display throughout 1992—doubly disavows the imperatives of "normal" masculinity as patterned in the positive Oedipus complex in ways that further radicalize the gender-destabilizing question of the hysteric ("Am I a man or a woman?").[13] Bush's idealization of Bar/Dorothy Walker Bush disavows maternal lack as it also allies mom with the law; his deidealizing disavowal of Pres(cott) Bush's paternal prerogative expels the father from the symbolic order (just as Prescott Bush was expelled from the Senate for his family-planning policy initiatives!). Paternal power, as addressed in the male masochistic performances of candidate (and president) Bush, is radically reconfigured and contested—a possibility that exists only to be repudiated.

While these enactments of theory/theoretical aporia might suggest other sites of pleasure and (subject) positions that circumscribe the authority (and appeal) of normative masculinity, I concur with Kaja Silverman in circumscribing the limits and direction (progressive or regressive) of a "subversive" presidential performance. One plays the Oedipal hand one is dealt, and, in this case, even "transgressive" possibilities are refracted from a given nuclear-family structure. And, although the moral masochist may put the authority of the paternal metaphor in doubt, the requisite punishing superego is produced through introjection of the paternal function to some extent. The question of whether these "perverse" enactments of masculinity destabilize, disorient, refract, or, rather, *hyperbolize* the drama of a subject's submission to the normalizing agencies of law/language remains an open question. The impetus behind this reading of Bush's performance shares with Kaja Silverman's attempt to conceive of "different psychic relations" to laws of language and kinship structure than those dictated by the hegemonic narrative deterrence machine she adumbrates as "the dominant fiction." My interest is somewhat specified and displaced: to the extent that the male masochism or hysteria on display is that of elected presidents (or candidates), what do these postures tell us about unconscious national identifications? (How) do these perverse enactments beckon toward other forms of *jouissance* than phallic *jouissance*? And what are the political possibilities and dangers of appeals to the surplus *jouissance* of the other? My approach to Bush in this chapter (and in his second campaign) shifts from an ideological reading attentive to his signifying form—as representation, synecdoche, *trompe l'oeil*—to the interpellative appeal of his performance (i.e., our identification with and enjoyment of his symptom). For what separates a delusional paranoiac who thinks he is president from any fool who happens actually to occupy the office, as Zizek notes, is less a distinction between those capable or not of direct identification than it is a question of social recognition. In other words, our concern here displaces the Freudian rhetorical question concerning femininity, asking in its place Freud's implicit question in his book on Woodrow Wilson: "What do the American people really want?"[14]

By shifting the frame of reference that surrounds Bush's electoral and presidential parapraxes from semiotics to "transference effects," Bush appears less as a theoretical fetish than a practical one—forming part of what Zizek calls the ideological fantasy. In other words, Bush is "not an illusion masking the real state of things" but is an "unconscious fantasy structuring our social reality itself."[15] Moreover, it is only as ideological fantasy that Bush can achieve his synecdochal function in American political culture. The tension in the Bush performance relies on the paradoxical structuring of the symptom/sign that begs for an interpretation and the enactment of a fantasy whose very naming renders speechless. Bush's presidential performance is itself predicated upon a fissure between apprehension/cognition and ideological belief—for both himself and his electorate.

Let us follow Bush on the campaign trail as he enacts Lacanian theory and gestures toward presidential abjection.

Going Behind

I'm not going to be the javelin catcher for liberals in Congress anymore.
—George H. W. Bush

As my reading in the preceding chapter indicated, Bush's male trouble should not be read as a relatively recent occurrence, a result of the historical trauma of a slow economic recovery and his concomitant inability (in the words of behaviorist American political science) "to pull his polls out." Bush released the results of his rectal exam in 1980 to show he was fit for the presidency. Although, in 1984, Bush offered to "lay his record on manhood against Mondale's anytime,"[16] it was Barbara Bush who "asserted his manhood" after the infamous *Newsweek* "wimp" article. Bush was figured in apposite fashion to Dora's Herr K as a "man without means" (the *unvermögender* Other): "To put it delicately, (as) something less than his own man." Impotent or spectral: "a good old boy under glass."[17] For Margaret Thatcher during the period of the Gulf War, the lack of phallic sufficiency was designated by the phrase "going wobbly": "But this is no time to go wobbly." Bush's "firm resolve" in the Gulf was fragile and needed "propping" by recurrent "joking" references to "going wobbly" by his backup men, Brent Scowcroft and John Sununu. Indeed, if Reagan was all too comfortable in the presidential posture of wielding the "tax ax," Bush preferred that his sword be handed off to others: he "wouldn't mind having a few other people pick up the sword and go to battle for him."[18] Even his son and unnamed campaign manager George W. bemoaned a lack of killer instinct in his father and, in perhaps the unkindest cut of all, said that George Bush (Senior) was a better dad than campaigner. George W.'s ability to objectify his father, to separate out his differing abilities in each of the king's two bodies, for me only underscores the importance of the Bush presidency as a study in object relations. As George W. put it succinctly: "I've got such a vested interest in my dad."[19]

Bush was expected to win in 1992 not because of the strength of his Gulf War performance but by *default,* according to his advisers. In contradistinction to Clinton's "high negatives," Bush's "negative electoral perceptions" were "soft" and hence more open to resignification. Bush's virtuosity in office stressed tactical nimbleness and flexibility in office, not mandated strength. Sununu aptly resumed the partial *jouissance* of the Bush administration: "If it looks like the president and the government are *juggling thirty small balls* that's because they are" (italics mine).[20] The phallic insufficiency of his administration was underlined by Bush himself in the words of his first inaugural (which, typically, as we shall see, got it backwards): "We have more will than wallet." This misperceived underendowment necessitates—albeit only provisionally—a different configuration: "Our funds are low. We will make the hard choices, looking at what we have and perhaps allocating it differently."[21]

This inaugural appeal of the Other without means (the *unvermögender* Other) can be read as a hysterical solution to the democratic paradox of American pluralism. By discrediting (or deflating expectations of) himself, Bush is able to make disavowal work: keeping a master signifier alive and yet flattering our own "uniqueness," our own sublime X or *agalma*. As Joan Copjec neatly resumes the contradictory pressures and demands of democratic citizenship: "the subject of democracy is constantly hystericized, divided between the signifiers that seek to name it and the enigma that refuses to be named."[22] In a hysterical posture ("Am I a man or a woman?"), Bush's disavowal here works in the service of imaginary identification. But does the shift from a hysterical imaginary to masochism reveal both the stakes and the historical contingency of any (successful) symbolization? Can we read Bush's trajectory as underscoring the importance of the fantasmatic in sustaining this space of symbolization? What happens when this fantasmatic is then "brought out"?[23] This is especially perverse in Bush's case, as the precise scenario brought out is condensed in myriad lapses involving "going behind."

As I have already argued, it was at the May 1988 rally in Twin Falls, Idaho, that Bush committed the most telling lapsus (one that eerily prefigures the sodomitical identification and masochistic ecstasy of the 1992 campaign) when he admitted that he had had sex with Reagan. "For seven and a half years, I have worked alongside him and I am proud to be his partner. We have had triumphs, we have made mistakes, we have had sex." Correcting this lapsus ("we have had setbacks"), Bush commits an even greater blunder, comparing himself to a "javelin thrower who won the coin toss and elected to receive."[24] In 1992, Bush was reluctant to leave this theme behind, refusing to be the "javelin catcher" for tired liberals in Congress and in his hilarious showdown over Gates's nomination: "They ought not to accept a rumor. They ought not to panic and run like a covey of quail because somebody made an allegation against a man whose word I trust. What I worry about is pusillanimity, faintheartedness—you hear a rumor and then you run for cover. *You get under a bush like a quail and hope you don't get flushed out for a while*" (emphasis mine).[25] Quayle is no exception to these presidential couplings. Reminiscing about inauguration day: "They asked me to go in front of the Reagans. I'm not used to going in front of President Reagan so we went out behind the Bushes."[26] The Bush-Quayle allied parapraxes build upon one another, recalling Barthes's adage in *S/Z*: "castration is contagious."[27]

How are we to read this? As a meta-commentary linking second positionality with feminization? Or, rather, as a Barthesian rejection of masculinity, as in the *Pleasure of the Text,* where, rather than speaking frontally from the place of the phallus, Barthes speaks of "that uninhibited person who shows his behind to the political father."[28] Is Bush deauthorizing or dispossessing the political father from the paternal legacy—mooning the political father—in other words: "Read My Hips"? Or is he a follower of Baudrillard's strategy, articulated in *Seduction*: "One must always wager on simulation and take the signs from behind."[29] It is all of this and more. The figures of the "javelin catcher" and the "javelin thrower who elects to receive" can be read as the emblematic parapraxis of the Bush presidency/candidacy/administration, namely "going behind." Kaja Silverman discusses the psychoanalytic stakes of "going behind": "The receptive position is an over determined site of pleasure." For in "going behind" (as a subset of narcissistic object choice), desire and identification converge upon one object: the "imaginary" or fantasmatic father. The "javelin thrower who elects to receive" gets at this equivocal aspect: "Going behind" is a "mechanism through which a subject who is marked by passivity and lack can lay temporary claim to an active sexual aim." But it is also an unacknowledged threat to "normative masculinity," as it expresses a desire to have the father, as well as be him.[30] The denegation implicit in the "javelin catcher" ("I'm not going to *be* . . .") underlines its continued psychic importance for Bush. Moreover, the first figure (the javelin thrower who elects to receive) retains the willful aspect of the hysterical discursive subject refusing a symbolic mandate (he has not yet been elected; he is still candidate Bush), whereas the javelin *catcher* ably condenses the disavowal of the presidential subject he has become. The peculiar (counter-intuitive) syntactic reversal—Bush is more passive as president than as vice president—underscores the paradox of the hysteric's desire (a desire that desire remains unfulfilled) as it also presages a shift from hysteria to masochism. This positional passivity is extreme and self-immolating in its consequences, recalling Vic Gold's assessment: Bush was so averse to confrontation that "you had to pour gasoline . . . and light a match to him in order to get him to counterattack."[31]

For Avital Ronell, the contiguity of sex and setback is significant. "The substitution of sex for setback, which in this context refers to Bush's secondary position within a structure of the couple, reveals as well the libidinal investment in the setback, in the reversal, postponement, delay which must be *surmounted*. It further shows that setback is beyond the pleasure principle and in the service of repetition and the death drive."[32] The "setback" becomes in this reading the predominant *trope* of the Bush Administration—the linguistic equivalent (and symptomatic substitute) for the turning point in his life, when the USS *Finback* (invoked in his 1992 nomination acceptance speech) saved his life. *Fin back* read in French and English would be "end back." (And we will see how prominently the backend and their reversals figure in Bush's discourse.) For Ronell, Bush has always been a secondary (or doubled) figure. (Even *Time* magazine hailed him as "*Men* of the Year" in 1991.) "At any rate, Bush had always been second and secondary. This was his nature, to be a second nature." Bush's rhetorical unconscious addresses the belatedness of American hegemonic power: "Everything that Bush does is a matter of presencing for a dead center that keeps on replicating itself. Catching up to first place, first couple, first Superpower. Bush is still running behind, fluttering and *second*.") In Ronell's reading, Bush's unconscious phantasmatic redoubles an American one that insists on "riding signifiers on the rebound."[33] As embodiment of the death drive, the Bush subject is frozen, arrested in time, anachronistic, unable to introject history and inhabited by a "ventriloquizing syntax."[34]

Bush's "arrest" within a cycle of repetition compulsion is visually conveyed in juxtaposition to his wife, Barbara, constructing a tableau of marital misalliance: "It was as if George Bush had been arrested, which is why his iconic relation to his wife looks as though he had struck a deal with a soul murderer, giving the couple the disjunctive look of a moment in *The Picture of Dorian Gray*." Lydia Millet's transferential reading in *George Bush, Dark Prince of Love,* maps Bar as a "virtual grandparent": "His own domestic order was not dissimilar to mine; he was also partnered with an individual who was, for all intents and purposes, a member of an older generation." Bush's "eternal youth" or boyishness is part of a narrative of "return and second chance" that, for Ronell, "tends to revert either to the happy few or the severely neurotic" and, for Millet, "marks only the scions of the leisured classes and the clinically insane."[35] Marked as eternal son to ineffectual fathers (Prescott Bush, Reagan), to his own mother (whom he called every day from the White House), and to his own wife and his eldest son, Bush reiterates a profoundly dehistorizing desire, in Ronell's iteration: "a predicament of (metaphysical and historical) non-closure."[36]

The proximity of sex and setback, then, underscores the "backside of projected progress, the place of impasse."[37] His rhetorical insistence on "Finback"—for Ronell another version of *Finnegan's Wake*—is the promise of a second comeback, a second coming. There is an ironic twist; despite Bush's rhetorical predilection for rear-subject positions, he is unable to come from behind and is beaten by the comeback kid. The uncanny echoes of this metaphysical "end" being behind us ("Finback") was displayed by vice presidential candidate Al Gore's quite literal insistence, at the 1992 convention, on a resuscitational ideology of the new Democratic party with an analogy to his son's "second" breath of life. Clinton addressed this as well with his pose as Reanimator—"revitalizing" the "brain-dead politics" with a second coming/new covenant. A Reanimator candidate as a response to an "Administration that will never have lived"?[38]

Clinton as Reanimator recalls (albeit not totally) Bush's self-stylization as the Terminator. In the New Hampshire primary, Arnold Schwarzenegger campaigned against Patrick Buchanan as Bush's stand-in. He evoked his *Terminator* persona (rather than that of *Kindergarten Cop*) against Buchanan with the movie tag line "Hasta la vista, Baby" and asked voters to "pump up the vote" (we will discuss the obvious phallic anxiety implicit in this last imperative in a later section). But what is noteworthy is that the Terminator is an odd paternal imago for a president to invoke. (The continued saliency of this figure is raised to a meta-strategic as well as meta-textual electoral principle in the 1993 Texas senatorial runoff campaign of Bob Kreuger.)[39] *The Terminator* has been read by Constance Penley as a subverted family romance, as an attempted *end*-run (my emphasis) around Oedipus as John Conner (J. C.) stages his own paternity, casting Kyle in the primal scene: "John Conner can identify with his father, can even be his father on the scene of paternal intercourse and also conveniently dispose of him in order to go off with his mother."[40] Jonathan Goldberg's reading of *The Terminator* concurs with Penley's in that it highlights the antipaternal (as well as conflicted and reversible) features in a play of cross-identifications: "The quasi-Oedipal plot in which the son kills the father is doubled by the exterminating anti-paternal Terminator; this doubling also is, in the present, a site of erotic identification as fully as in that future in which Reese is the worshipful follower of John Conner (this *reversal of father and son* serves, too, as a sign that the opposition of Reese and the Terminator may be read in *reverse*)"[41]—backwards.

Paternity is displaced by mirroring. Goldberg's variation is a more radical and disturbing one, recalling Ronell's metaphysical end of history—with Arnold Schwarzenegger as the cyborg end of the human at the limits of the drives. The post-Oedipal rewrite of *Terminator 2: Judgment Day* (where Arnold returns in Bush-era fashion as "kinder, gentler"—"no murderer now, just a maimer") reconstitutes the nuclear family in a way that should frighten Dan Quayle: "the father is a cyborg, the mother perhaps a lesbian and the kid is part juvenile delinquent, part computer hacker, a *bushy*tailed white version of the black computer technician the movie abjects" (italics mine).[42] *The Terminator* has also been read by Slavoj Zizek in apposite fashion to Ronell's *Finback*/death-drive emphasis. Zizek sees *The Terminator* as "the embodiment of the drive, devoid of desire," and as representing the connection between "the drive as uncontrolled demand and the domain between the two deaths."[43] Or, in Goldberg's words, "this father of the future is death-marked in every locus of his existence . . . it is difficult to say where or when he does exist." This "signals the death of the paternal even as it is being fulfilled."[44] There is something, however, overexposed, too legible and transparent in Schwarzenegger as Bush surrogate. Symptomatic readings here only contribute to a more radical and disturbing opacity, blocking analysis or interpretation.

Symptoms are both ontologically more and other than a compromise formation/coded message. In Lacan's last writings on "Joyce, the symptom," the symptom, for Lacan, is a "particular signifying formation which confers on the subject its very ontological consistency, enabling it to structure its basic constitutive relationship to enjoyment (*jouissance*)."[45] There is much at stake in these differing evaluations of the symptom, for, following the claims of the later Lacan, if the symptom is done away with, the subject disintegrates. In other words, we can read Bush's symptoms as a positive attempt at wish fulfillment (characteristic of hysteria). As a compromise formation, symptoms can also aim at fending off fulfillment. (An example of such a negative ascetic response of obsessional neurosis is Clinton's call to "sacrifice" in 1993.) Both the Freudian symptom and the Lacanian *sinthome* point to the mechanisms by which a president as master signifier (*m'être à moi-même*: mastering [*maître*] by being myself [*m'être*] to myself) comes to represent our libidinal desires in a process of symbolic exchange. However, each stands in a different relation to desire and calls for different readings. Symptoms can be read in the shelters of hermeneutics (a "secret" or "repressed" reading brought to interpretative light) or semiotics (the code between signifier and signified as in a dream rebus is cracked). As a ciphered message, the symptom yields under the pressure of a critical or analytic operation to meaning once the disguise or distortion is disclosed (in this way, it is a figure of ideological operation par excellence). At its most basic level, the symptom is a compromise formation, where the subject gets back (in distorted form) the truth he was unable to confront (or, as Lacan would have it, "the truth of his desire").

This level of analysis can be exemplified by the following exchange between President Bush and reporters during a predawn stroll at the Jefferson Memorial. Bush is discussing the necessity for term limits. An exchange about Peruvian military laws and Perot's candidacy ensues.[46]

Reporter: You're misinterpreting Jefferson [a reference to "with frequent changes laws and institutions must go hand in hand with the progress of the human mind"].
The President: No, I'm not.
Reporter: You ought to send this statement to Peru.
The President: Perot?
Reporter: Peru.
The President: Oh, sorry. I heard you.
Reporter: Perot, right. Is he on your mind?
The President: No, I think he's on yours.
Reporter: Not at all.
The President: This is a lovely memorial.

Here, the symptom (the lapsus underlining an apparent confusion between Perot and Peru) is a ciphered message in which the presidential subject/candidate Bush gets back his own message (a preoccupation with the Perot candidacy that can't be avowed) in reverse. Read simply, as symptom, it is a positive attempt at wish fulfillment (that Perot not exist as a threat, that Perot not be on his mind) characteristic of hysteria. We can laugh easily—both because of the Beckett-like staging: a moonlit, semideserted space and the predictable blank repetitive journalistic colloquy. The laughter engendered by a symptom is easy because the all-too-human lapsus is the point of shame and not the interpretation proffered, which is—relatively—easily accepted.

But there is something more disturbingly uncanny about this very example that as *sinthome* pulls us in by the signifier's idiotic homophonic glide from Perot/Peru (a, e, i, o, u). Phonic assonance covers psychic dissonance. Here the setting is spectral: a predawn stroll around a reflecting pool surrounded by a monument to a dead idealized president/father. The intriguing lapsus for a reading as *sinthome* is *why* Bush misinterprets Jefferson (about the mutability of law and institution) in the context of instituting a symbolic electoral death via term *limits*. What is threatening about the possible repeal of the ideal father's (Jefferson's) laws?[47] Framed by the instance of military rule (martial law) in Peru (raising diacritically the concept of nation), does Bush's lapsus enact the ever-present threat of totalitarian rule (of the primal or despotic father) if a law of limit (castration) is not maintained? In addition, does Perot as another electoral term also displace the usual election contest between imaginary rivals, triangulating it in a way that makes the Oedipal stakes even more apparent?

The stakes of this positioning implicate us. The lapsus of the *sinthome* embodies an idiotic *jouissance* that is difficult to laugh at. The *sinthome*, located in the uneasy crossfire of the real and the symbolic identification, precludes the comfortable (or comfortably uncomfortable) imaginary interpellative force of the symptom. Can Bush in 1992 still be read (transparently) as symptom, or does his electoral enactment (the insistence of his idiotic *jouissance*) call for a less interpretive and more transferential response? Let us suspend the answer to this question and look at the ways Bush uncannily evokes the Lacanian topoi of the drive and the barred subject, in other words, how Bush, like Lacan, is forced to incarnate gaps in the foundation of psychoanalytic theory, gaps that Alice Jardine has named: the female body, the male subject, oscillation.[48]

"Over My Dead Veto"

One possible reading of *The Terminator* stand-in thus ties it to the death drive and to the site of another telling rear-positionality parapraxis "Read My Hips," which for many underscored the true crime that deprived him of a second term. For if Twin Falls, Idaho, is Bush's primal scene, the budget crisis of 1990, which sets the stage for the Gulf War, is Bush's midterm (midlife) crisis. In Lacanian terms, it enacts his second or between the two deaths.[49] This refers to the address of some unconditional demand and incarnates pure drive without desire. Or there is something eerily akin to Lacan's "Subversion of the Subject" that is being played out in the Bush administration's showdown with Congress. Here the *topos* of masochism (in Tom Wicker's words, Bush's "self-inflicted political wounds") is tied to a reversal of sender and receiver ("defense turning to offense in the Middle East").[50] Another reading of the javelin thrower electing to receive (condensed in the figure of the javelin catcher) is the reversal of sender and receiver. Bush, in a talk to Detroit Republicans during the 1992 campaign, once again confused these two positions: "I'm getting sick and tired of being on the receiving line, ah, the receiving end of criticism."[51] Bush's aversion to the receiving line (on either side, as sender or receiver) asserted itself in the Gulf War, where Bush did not, according to Ronell, put in a call to Saddam Hussein at the "reception desk of international politics," as well as in Japan, where Bush begins to feel uncontrollably ill on the receiving line.[52]

This confusion of sender (agent) and receiver points to the dead center of presidential power[53] and is prefigured by Bush's lapsus during the budget showdown: "They're going to do it over my dead veto or live veto or something like that because it ain't going to happen." Bush's dead body—the "dead veto"—is projected onto the political stage in the context of "girding up my loins to go into battle to beat back [Bush is being beaten] the tax attempts I think are coming." And yet, none of Bush's "vetos" could be seen as a dead one. Bush had a perfect veto record (ten in 1989, twenty-one by the end of 1990, twenty-eight by May 1992). Congress was unable to override any of Bush's vetos, which effectively turned a defensive posture into an offensive threat. It was not a "purely negative *tool*," said members of Bush's administration. The "veto pen" filled the same function as the "tax axe."[54] And if Reagan threatened vetos that he rarely deployed, Bush in public laid out minimalist principles and then (in perfect passive-aggressive fashion) wielded a calibrated veto, leading Democrats to wonder if Bush's veto was the one part of him that couldn't be beaten.

The dead body is implicitly noted by Andrew Rosenthal of the *New York Times,* who titles his piece "With Eye on Voters, Bush Resurrects Anti-Tax Pledge." This resurrection recalls the earlier prosopoetic reanimation of "Read My Lips." Bush will not break what he has already broken. "Read My Hips" becomes here an attempt at a second reanimation. If Reagan was the dead father (who can still reassure), Bush exemplifies the fading father of Jane Gallop's reading of Lacan: neither wholly present nor the master of desire.[55] Bush's equivocation: "They're going to do it over my dead veto or my live veto or something like that. . . ." Doesn't Bush know if he is alive or dead? Is the third term: "something like that," Lacan's between the two deaths? Indeed, Bush does have trouble knowing if someone is dead or alive. On Lawrence Welk: "I'm all for Lawrence Welk. Lawrence Welk is a wonderful man. He used to be, or was, or wherever he is now, bless him." On Meir Kahane: "Look, look there's Kahane protesting on the boat. I thought this guy was kind of dead." It similarly subtends his electoral insistence on a "*stronger* death penalty." The death penalty provokes other discursive excesses besides this ably condensed figure. Instead of saying that he favored the death penalty for "drug kingpins," he said he wanted it for those "narked-up terrorist kinds of guys."[56]

Yet this liminality of death and life is a sign of the de-Oedipalization of the paternal metaphor. Bush exemplifies the differences between Freud and Lacan in the Oedipal drama. If for Freud Oedipus has the status of a universal myth, for Lacan Oedipus is a dream that demonstrates the relation between subjectivity and knowledge: "A dream reported by Freud . . . offers us, linked to the pathos which sustains the figure of a deceased father by being that of a ghost, the sentence: 'He did not know that he was dead.'" In place of the dead father, Lacan presents the unconscious one, unaware, not knowing too much. This unconscious father is unprotected, exposed (the dead father still protects the father, and, like Reagan, he can be profoundly reassuring). In Lacan's "Subversion of the Subject," the figure of the dead father returns as a ghost and a sentence: "He did not know that he was dead." "Over my dead veto or my live one or something like that. . . ." Bush, during the midterm budget crisis that sets the stage for Desert Storm, wears his unconscious on the outside, remaining ignorant of his own death. Bush is the subverted or barred subject. The barred subject is one who doesn't know that he is dead. Barring is the crossing out of something erroneous, something—like the phallic signifier of Hitchcock—that shouldn't be there. The barred subject, like the father in Freud's dream, is on his way to disappearing or fading. The Bush presidential subject is unaware of his own death, and figures of the *ghost* are omnipresent in Bush-era popular culture, in movies such as *Ghost, Jacob's Ladder, Reversal of Fortune* (narrated from the point of view of Sunny in a coma!), and *Total Recall* (alive or dreaming?). These ghosts are different from the "undead" of the Reagan yuppie-vampire movies, lost boys feeding on capitalist excess. The Bush era has produced another dubious genre: male masochism/amnesia films (*Shattered, The Doctor, Regarding Henry*) in which a yuppie protagonist is regressed to a pre-Oedipal linguistic stage (and becomes a better person). These heroes, like Poe's "Mr. Valdemar," hovering between death and life, sleeping and waking, memory and time, are emblems of a presidential subject, Bush, who (in Avital Ronell's words) can live neither "in time nor in introjection."[57] Bush can neither (like Mel Brooks's two-thousand-year-old man) "listen to his broccoli" (i.e., learn from experience) nor eat it!

De-Oedipalization of the paternal metaphor, the "javelin catcher" is a site of phallic anxiety. The javelin catcher valorizes the pleasure of *orifice* over that of integral organ, while not yet provoking the anxiety of candidates Bob Dole or Al Gore as Lacan's *lamella*.[58] One could read this lapsus as a meta-commentary linking second positionality with feminization. Bush's electoral and male anxiety about being second fiddle (figured as feminine receiving end) is turned around in the Saddamization of feminized territories or chiasmically, in the feminization of Manny Noriega.[59] In the domestic sphere, the 1992 State of the Union address revealed not just the priority of orifice over organ but the detachability and disputability of the phallus. "This will not stand." The State of the Union address recalls Lacan's "Signification of the Phallus" as Bush "unveils" his plan (the phallus "works" only if veiled), set against a background of "hard times": "Let me tell you right from the start and right from the heart: I know we're in hard times and I know something else: This will not stand." Bush speaks of *big* things, *big* changes, *big* promises. The *biggest* thing of all is the winning of the Cold War. The rhetorical insistence on the adjective "big" can be read as a "frenzy of filial distress," attempting to close the obvious gap between the symbolic and the actual father. It can also be read as part of a "hypermasculinity that fails in so far as it exceeds, to guarantee the gender category it means to serve."[60] Bush's address is figured on phallic ambivalence and oscillation: "falling on hard times"; "inflation, that thief, is down." The discussion of cuts in military hardware reads like an inventory of adjectives pertaining to phallic inadequacy/castration: shut down, cancel, stop, cease, eliminate, reduce, convert. Bush ends his speech with an appeal to a rising nation and in characteristic disavowal assures his fellow Americans that they will rise to the occasion: "We're going to lift this nation out of hard times inch by inch and those who would stop us had best step aside. Because I look at hard times and I make this vow: 'This will not stand.'"

Bar-Coda

Keep your snorkel above the water and do what you think is right. That's exactly what my mom told me when I was six. Do your best. Do your best. I'm trying hard. Stay calm.   —George H. W. Bush[61]

The 1992 State of the Union is a turning point, marking the last attempt to sustain the dominant fiction of penis = phallus = symbolic father. It marks the beginning of a radical cancellation of the normative Oedipal drama. The discourse on phallic ambivalence/divestiture is accompanied by a second leitmotif related to "Family Matters." However, this family is headed not by the paternal patriarch but by the maternal superego (i.e., Barbara Bush). The USS *Finback* is tied to "Bar," the name inscribed on the side of his TBM Avenger plane shot down in Japan. In a repetition, Bar Bush is given a second chance to avenge or "save" Bush, shot down/shut down in Japan.

Bush, during the budget talks, recalls his mother's injunction: "Keep your snorkel above the water. . . . Do your best. Do your best. I'm trying hard. Stay calm." Dorothy Walker Bush is described (by her son) as excessively energetic. "Mother was a first-rate athlete. She wasn't big, but she was a match for anyone in golf, tennis, basketball, baseball. For that matter, I don't recall a footrace Mother was ever in that she didn't come in first."[62]

The power of Dorothy Walker is belied by her appearance: "a slight brown-haired woman" reminiscent of Jessica Tandy in *The Birds*. (Is it coincidental that Tandy's film career has taken off during the Bush era?)

In the guise of either "Bar" or "Dorothy Walker Bush"/Jessica Tandy, this maternal superego is no less oppressive than the dead paternal one it displaces. Bush is framed by his mother (who shuns his use of the first-person pronoun and impels him to do his best) as well as Bar, whose name appears written on the side of his TBM Avenger plane shot down over Japan. It will be "Bar" Bush who avenges or saves Bush again shot down/shut down in Japan. The *New York Times* story read: "saved by the grace of Barbara Bush." Barbara Bush blames the Ambassador: "He and George played the emperor in tennis today and *they were badly beaten*. And we Bushes aren't used to that."[63] Bar, avenger/maternal superego, tells us that "Bush is being beaten." And if this message could not be clearer or more insistent, Bush frames his phallic oscillations in the State of the Union by a rhetorical appeal to the maternal superego/avenger Bar, paving the way for "Wives' Night" in Houston, during the convention. Wishing that Bar could give his overhyped address for him (as she saved him in Japan) and underscoring this with a winking nod to vomiting by commenting upon those readers of his lips seated safely *behind* him, the camera shoots up to view Bar looking down at him dismissively (effectively reversing and canceling the scopic economy of Nancy and Ronnie played out at the 1984 convention). Barbara Bush is appealed to in Step Nine (the last step) of his plan (to strengthen the family) ("Family Matters"): "When Barbara holds an AIDS baby in her arms and reads to children, she's saying to every person in this country 'Family Matters.'"

The State of the Union address, it should be noted, is framed by the electoral contest. Bush, in New Hampshire, self-identifies as a woman: "He tried to look on the bright side or as he put it, playing the role of "Mrs. Rose Scenario," searching for "the rainbow out there." He identifies with Evita Peron, telling a group of insurance workers in Dover, New Hampshire, "Don't cry for me, Argentina" (an unfortunate choice if one listens to the lyrics: "*I kept my promise*, don't keep your distance"). This is not the first time a contest/campaign situation has forced Bush to abandon the self-same gendered body. Defending his lack of charisma in 1988, he refused "to kind of suddenly try to get my hair colored, and dance up and down in a miniskirt or do something, you know. . . . I'm running for the President of the United States."[64]

A week after the State of the Union address, Bush visited the National Grocer's Association convention in Orlando, Florida. Reflecting on this much-reported-upon visit, analysts repeatedly commented upon how out of touch Bush was with the American people. Bush was fascinated by two things, suggestive of Lacanian theory. The first, the electronic pad used to detect check forgeries, revealed an anxiety over the name of the father: "If some guy came in and spelled George Bush differently, could you catch it?" (After being told yes, he shook his head in wonder.)[65] And there is the overly analyzed but profoundly misread incident of the electronic scanner. No, Bush was not so much out of touch as to be amazed by technology. He revealed something more profoundly disturbing. George was literally stupefied, mesmerized, *medusé,* as the French would have it, by a confrontation with the figure of the maternal superego, externalized in the form of the literalized *bar-code.*

Houston: Male Masochism and Presidential Abjection

Hit him again. Hit him again. Harder. Harder.
—Chant during Bush's acceptance speech

The phallic anxiety (of "This will not stand") is repeated throughout the 1992 campaign, whether in the fear of "wolves in the woods" or in the imperative to steer clear of a "Slippery When Wet Willie." If the 1992 State of the Union address was an attempt to sustain the dominant fiction, it also revealed in that very attempt an uneasy awareness of historical trauma denoted by Siegfried Kracauer as "ideological fatigue" ("a loss of belief in the adequacy of the male subject and small town life").[66] In a C-SPAN interview before the State of the Union, Bush reviewed the year with the following sentence: "It started with *trauma.*"[67] The use of the term "trauma" is highly significant. As Kaja Silverman notes, "the phallus is always the product of the dominant fiction and when this fiction proves incapable of mastering the stimulus of historical trauma, its male subject will no longer be able to find within himself its idealizing configuration." As with the heroes of the post–World War II movies Silverman describes (*The Best Years of Our Lives, It's a Wonderful Life*), Bush's inability to sustain the dominant fiction reveals a breakdown in the concomitant mechanisms of projection and disavowal that have traditionally underwritten presidential politics. The ideological fatigue of the 1992 State of the Union is repeated in "Wives' Night" in Houston with a difference. It is up to the wives to disavow male lack and to confer phallic sufficiency like Donna Reed in *It's a Wonderful*

Life. Barbara Bush attempted to reassure us about George Bush's health ("And, yes, the healthiest man I know"), as well as our own ("You did the right thing"). Marilyn Quayle played bad cop to Barbara Bush, chastising women who refuse to project and disavow—instilling guilt in all those who fail to recognize male sufficiency.[68] Yet Bush's arrival on the scene as paterfamilias was anticlimactic, reminding us that sexual differentiation is not about lack as much as it is about excess/superfluity. The final image of the convention was not of a triumphant Bush but of a *first couple being beaten* on the head by the largest balloon drop in convention history.[69]

The shift from father-son to mother-son in presidential politics relates to my last and perhaps most obvious reading of the "javelin catcher" figure. The "javelin catcher" becomes a symptom of *masochism*. Gilles Deleuze underscores the implicit paternal challenge within masochism. For what is beaten in masochism is not just the ego but rather the father in the male subject (*not* the male subject *as* the father).[70] Silverman is astute in underscoring that, for Deleuze, masochism is a mother-son pact to write the father out of his dominant position and to install the mother in his place. Bush in 1992 hoped to ride Barbara Bush's "Republican cloth coattails," an able condensation that gives her the phallus ("coattails") even as it diacritically distances her from a Venus in furs ('Republican cloth coat')—attempting to disavow that we are not on the terrain of Wanda and Severin.

Bush's rhetorical predilection for rear-subject positions can be seen as a symptom of what Freud calls *erotogenic masochism*. Here pleasure is derived from phallic divestiture (i.e., Bush's taunt at the 1992 convention: "I extended my hand to Congress and they bit it"). But is also can be seen in relation to Freudian *moral masochism,* where the ego provokes/enjoys the harshness of the superego. (Bush's parapraxis "standing *on* my conscience" is revealing in this sense.) The cheek that the moral masochist turns *is* his ego. The ego comes to take pleasure in the pain that the superego inflicts. Desire for punishment displaces fear of punishment as love is displaced by cruelty and discipline. To some extent, the moral masochist is "ordinary," or normatively congruent with masculinity as the Freudian male subject "oscillates between the mutually exclusive commands of the (male) ego ideal and the superego, wanting both to love the father and to be the father and prevented from doing either."[71] Silverman uses the term "sodomitical identification" for this aspect of moral masochism where "what one would like to be co-

incides with what one would like to possess."[72] In any of these interpretative recodings of the "javelin catcher," "going behind" maintains
the possibility of a "subject position at the intersection of the negative
and positive Oedipus complexes."[73] The political question, however, is
(paraphrasing Kaja Silverman): Under what conditions can masochism
sustain an aspiration to mastery and leadership?

One might juxtapose two male pathologies—hysteria and masochism
—onto the two Bush presidential campaigns (in contrast to the death-
driven symmetries of obsessional neurosis and moral masochism in the
1996 Clinton/Dole campaign). Bush's hysteria can be seen in his manic
1988 campaign insistence that "I'm one of you." (This rhetorical tick
exemplifies a crucial distinction between Bush and Clinton. Bush's identifications are heteropathic or centripetal—the subject identifies his own
self with the other: "I'm one of you." (Clinton's—"I feel your pain"—
are idiopathic/centrifugal; the subject identifies the other with or within
himself.)[74] This lack of self gave Bush the freedom to refuse any one
fixed identity; however, what is more significant for political leadership
is the way that hysteria attests to a "failed interpellation" or to the necessary failure within any interpellation. Bush's repetitive "I am one of
you" was, in effect, a reformulation of Lacan—"Why am I what you're
telling me that I am"—a refusal of a symbolic mandate. Slavoj Zizek
situates the hysterical question in this failure of the subject to assume
symbolic identification: "The hysterical question opens the gap of what
is in the subject more than the subject, of the object in subject that resists interpellation."[75] (Such resistance/refusal might be read in the debate performance of Perot's V.P. choice, Admiral Stockdale, a limit case
of abjection: "Who am I? Why am I here?")

Bush's hysteria corresponds to Freud's classical depiction of someone whose symptom stages a repressed desire. What marks Bush are his
eerily resonant stylizations of this *topos*. Bush literalizes or, rather, enacts the hysterical identification of "I'm one of you" sartorially. Bush
may not know who he is, but he clearly enjoys "being president." He is
the only White House officer who wears the presidential tie bar (literally, he is a barred subject), but he has turned the signature to the back
of the bar, placing the paternal metaphor behind. His closet in Kenne-
bunkport contains a collection of jackets embroidered with his name so
that everyone on deck can wear a jacket reading "George Bush,"[76] a
promiscuous dispersal of the name of the father. A tour of Air Force
One revealed a profusion of presidential seals: "on the dinner plates.

On the fuzzy gray slippers beneath Mr. Bush's bed. Even on the buckles of every seat in the forward compartments."[77] Perhaps the funniest enactment of hysterical demand takes place in the presidential limousine that transports local dignitaries to and from the airport. Bush, facing forward on the back seat of the armored Cadillac, seats his visitor on a facing jumpseat with a clear rear view:

> As the limousine moved through the streets, Bush would pick out someone from the crowd, usually an attractive woman or child, point, and wait until—pow!—eye contact and the victim realizes he's looking at me! That's when the target "lit up." Because the limo was facing forward, it fell to the guest facing aft to report to the president when he asked, "Did I get her? Did I light her up?" And then the game would begin again.[78]

Bush clearly enjoys parading the accoutrements of office and making himself seen as president (*se faire voir*). Duffy and Goodgame ably describe Bush's idiotic *jouissance*: "After taking the oath of office, Bush resembled nothing so much as a medieval boy king who woke up one morning, found himself atop the throne, and began tugging at the bell ropes for servants, ordering up royal carriages, and scheduling banquets and tournaments." Part of Bush's enjoyment no doubt derives from the keen surprise of finding himself there, forgetting that he had already been in the White House for eight years and metonymically attached to it for at least five more years before that, yet still displaying the arrested amnesiac quality Ronell and others have so aptly captured, acting "like a wide-eyed political maniac who has slipped away from a White House tour."[79] Yet there is a fine line between Bush's novice presidential disportments, which I have been describing as male hysteria, and the exhibitionist display and self-referentiality characteristic of Reikian moral masochism. The "shift" or turn I have been alluding to, from imaginary/hysterical appeals in 1988 to a symbolic masochistic one in 1992, may be a perspectival effect, an anamorphosis.

The hysteric (like Reik's masochist) "hastens through." He literally cannot bear to wait and rushes forward. He overtakes himself and misses the object of desire precisely because of this impatience. The object for the hysteric is not easily enjoyed: "à propos of every object, his experience is how 'this is not that,' which is why he hastens to reach, finally, the right object."[80] Or, as Bush himself put it, "I've got to run now and relax. The doctor told me to relax. The doctor told me to relax. He was the one. He said 'Relax.' "[81] The peripatetic Bush underscores the link between hysteria and mobility (described by Lynne Kirby as characteristic of early cinema).[82] Bush engaged in diplomatic decathlons. During his trip to Japan, he covered nineteen thousand miles in ten days, spanning four countries, transported by the hyperspeed of Air Force One at 560 miles per hour. On his arrival in Japan, Bush jogged, bicycled, played tennis with the Emperor, and bounced a ball on his head. (George W. repeated this frenetic pace in New Hampshire in 2000 under the benevolent gaze of his parents and Sununu.) Bush's penchant for perpetual motion was noted by Peggy Noonan, who found it easiest to engage Bush on Air Force One: "The fact that it is speeding through the air seems to relieve his need for movement. The car is good, too."[83]

Whether the hyperenergy is the result of an overactive thyroid or to "limitless ebullience," Bush wore out both his aides and pool reporters. Duffy and Goodgame report that, upon leaving church in Los Angeles in 1991, the president was in such a hurry to get onto the tennis court that the motorcade left behind a military aide carrying the briefcase with the nuclear strike launching codes. Bush's golf game is also consistent with hysterical hastening through. Bush, a *Golf Digest* writer noted, played more for speed than for score. Bush's golf game also literalizes the arbitrary nature of the drive: he is "a natural left hander who plays right handed."[84] Bush can but won't (or can't but will) swing both ways. Bush's hysterical hastening through—in golf or, in its French homonym, the Golfe—his drive points to the realization that any object can take the place of the thing (but on the condition that it is veiled). He appears to have transmitted this golfing style to his eldest son, who plays golf as if it were polo, wacking the ball without even teeing up.[85]

I repeat: the biggest shift between Bush's two campaigns was from an imaginary oriented around hysteria in 1988 to a masochistic imaginary in 1992. It should be acknowledged that Bush's abnegation and abjection did not start with his most recent campaign. Garry Wills described Bush as being forced to accept a UN job under Nixon rather than a desired Treasury post. Bush's "abject service to the Goldwater movement is punctuated with prissy little moments of regret." Bush is continually described as "passive" *and* "feminized" by Wills: "the famed thick resumé of Bush is less a record of achievement than the back and forth trajectory of a man used as a shuttle-cock by others."[86] Bush's 1988 pandering to the right, to evangelicals and Jerry Fallwell, and, above all, to his critic William Loeb's widow are duly noted as episodes worthy of Sacher-Masoch, that is, "licking the hands that cuff him." (In a somatic *en-abime*, Bush's presidential cuff links fall off during an electoral photo op with congressmen staged to show his drive.) And yet there is something qualitatively different about the excessive masochism (one might call it "masochistic ecstasy") of the 1992 campaign. I am tempted to wonder why Bush's hysteria in 1988 and in Desert Storm/"Desert Glands" (*Spy* magazine's apt term) was so popular. Was this because of its congruence with American popular culture—the hysterical male as figured by Bob Saget, Tommy Lasorda, Pete Rose, and Al "I'm in Charge" Haig? Moreover, was Bush's defeat in 1992 one of masochistic interpellation, or did Clinton's calls for sacrifice postcampaign (as well as Tsongas's during) somehow attenuate such an interpretation? Were the American people uneasy with such an obvious (i.e., literal) exhibition of suffering? Or did it expose precisely what disavowal aims at concealing?

Freud cautions us against the danger of underestimating masochism as a kinder, gentler perversion. Silverman resumes the stakes eloquently:

> What is it precisely that the male masochist displays and what are the consequences of this self-exposure? To begin with, he acts out in an insistent and exaggerated way the basic conditions of cultural subjectivity, conditions that are normally disavowed: he loudly proclaims that his meaning comes to him from the other, prostrates himself before the gaze even as he solicits it, exhibits his castration for all to see, and revels in the sacrificial basis of the social contract. The male masochist magnifies the losses and divisions upon which cultural identity is based, refusing to be sutured or recompensed. In short, he radiates a negativity inimical to the social order.[87]

This "negativity" is different from the willed subjective irony of Bush's self-referential (hysterical) "winks" at the presidency: doing imitations of Dana Carvey doing an imitation of Bush at his own press conferences, wearing a George Bush mask on Halloween 1988 and walking through the campaign plane reiterating "Read my lips! Read my lips," or parodying Reagan's threat: "Make my twenty-four-hour time period!" The targets of Bush's willed mockery are particular contingent postures of the contemporary presidency, whether it is the oblig-atory photo op (visiting the Acropolis in 1991: "You want your basic Parthenon shot?") or political ploys expected of a leader such as visiting preschools: "I learned an awful lot about bathtub toys."[88] At its most radical, this parodic performance merely highlights the necessary gap and the attendant absurdity between any contingent office/placeholder and his symbolic mandate ("the leader of the free world"). It in no way puts into question the symbolic alignment itself (and the force of its im-aginary appeal may well shore up the social order).

The parodic contestation of presidential identity profoundly differed from the structural negativity of masochism that was on display at the Houston convention. Indeed, Bush's 1992 performance reads as a com-pendium of male masochism. Bush's "wooing of those who humiliate him" with the "renewal fervor of desperation" is, for Wills, a sign of Bush's disintegration. Indeed, he compares Bush's acceptance of Pat Bu-chanan (after Buchanan's savage attacks on Bush's manhood) to a mas-ochist crying, "Hit me again! Hit me again!" Wills sees a groveling in-cumbent president who apologizes for his subordinates, reflective of Bush's inability to disavow the detumescence of the once "big tent," which has been reduced to a "radical right *fringe*": "The Republicans must beg people to come into this shrinking tent." Yet, as we have seen in chapter 2, Wills refuses to pursue the *theoretical* consequences of what he has seen. What do abasement, humiliation, and detumescence have to do with the degeneration of the Bush ego and the decomposi-tion of the Bush era? Bush in 1992 combines the exhibitionism of his body on display with an (erotic) aggression turned upon his own self. Exhibitionism, both denuding and parading, plays a major role in mas-ochism. Reik's depiction of masochistic warriors also reads as an apt de-piction of Bush: "closed, self-referential, exhibitionist, demonstrative, revolutionary fervor, suspense."[89] ("Stay tuned.") Bush embodies both sides of Reik's contradictory characterization of the masochist: he pro-longs preparatory detail at the expense of climax as end pleasure is linked in his mind with punishment (i.e., the Bush of "prudence"). But the masochist also is characterized by the flight forward to hasten pun-ishment, provoking his own ruin.

The Houston convention made the connection with masochism un-avoidable. As Bush received his nomination (in the context of a forced abjuration of his mistakes), the crowd chanted, "Hit him again, hit him again. Harder. Harder." What one witnessed was less a nomination than a flagellation during which the "javelin catcher" made an appeal to patriotism. Finback. Bush's discourse, and his body language, during his nomination acceptance speech activated a masochistic imaginary of biting to dissociate him from his opponent: "I bit the bullet. He bit his nails." (Yet, even here, Bush committed a parapraxis of mispronunciation in delivery, emphasizing the object—bullet—and not the subject of the enunciation—in other words, getting it backwards.) Throughout the campaign, Bush positioned himself as "being beaten back and bitten by Congress" (prompting the *New York Times* to note that Clinton "bites back fast at Bush advertising").[90]

In the C-SPAN interview that preceded the 1992 State of the Union address, Bush spoke of "beating back" bad legislation and of press access to the presidency as "lancing the sores that build up." He spoke cheerfully of his intention to "whip" the marines with the Bush Wallyball team. The emphasis on whipping and biting/lancing are consonant with a masochistic imaginary and reactivate an association between Bush and masochism, especially since Bush's relation to the utterance belies any univocal positioning. "Whipping" also was an important verb in his description of his leisure time activities, such as reading.

> I read. I read a bunch of books. I whipped it out for—a magazine asked me this the other day—and I whipped it out and I've read, oh, about, I think, 12 books since mid-March.

Whipping it out usually refers to something other than books, something—a phallus—that for Lacan has power only when veiled. Whipping is also a part of Bush's television ritual:

> Watch quite a bit. I watch the news and I don't like to tell you this because you'll think I'm into some weird TV freak here, but we—I have a set upstairs that has five screens on it and I can sit on my desk and whip —just punch a button if I see one off to the corner, that moves in the middle screen the other one goes to the side. Then I can run up and down the—up and down the dial.
>
> So, I—and you can record all four—four going at once, while you—when you're watching. I don't quite know how to do that yet. But I cite this because Barbara accuses me of being too much—not too much, but plugged into TV too often, put it that way. Love sports on TV.[91]

Obviously, Bush enjoys whipping/beating/biting. Yet any univocal authorial positioning is subverted by pronomial oscillation ("but we—I"; "So, I—and you"; "while you . . . I don't quite know"), as well as by the Barbara Bush maternal superego ("Barbara accuses . . ."). The C-SPAN interview attempts to position the president as master of his video desires (it takes place in the map room of the White House). On one level, we see an active Bush-subject zapping through the channels, rather than the more familiar image of him as a passive wireless remote. Yet. as Bush is whipping, Barbara is accusing the Bush excess of "being too much," of overcompensating. Bush's authoritative stance ("whipping," "beating") is belied by his syntagms. He is, in fact, dominated, overshadowed by his digressive, repetitive, degenerate discourse.

This pronomial oscillation is most characteristic of Bush's disavowals. When asked about whether the budget deal was worth the high price (of going back on his "Read My Lips" pledge), he is similarly difficult to position within his declaration:

> I'm not interested in talking about that. *I'm* interested in governing. But let me tell you this. I expect *others* will be talking about that. *Fine.* Take the heat. Take the hit. There have been changed times. It didn't work out the way I want. I don't have the horses in the Congress to do it exactly my way. So *you* have to govern. *You* have to lead. And that's what I'm going to do.[92]

Bush's opening use of the first person is in the negative ("I'm not . . .") and begins to drift after the invocation of the unnamed "others." Then come implied subjects, a metonymic phonic slide (heat-hit), and a passive construction (not: Times change). The "I" appears only to assert that it didn't get what it wanted or to express lack (like Richard III, he just was lacking requisite "horses"). The second person appears and underwrites the final use of "I." Even Bush's more successful utterances are ambiguous about his agency or passivity. In his highly regarded convention speech ("I am that man who can sit and take what comes across that big desk"), it is unclear whether this is a self-assertive utterance (he can stand up to whatever arises) or a harbinger of masochism ever ready to receive the blows of fortune. In any event, the "Big Desk" looms larger than the speaker himself.

Bush's attempts to situate himself as the subject-master of his enunciation misfired in what was (in my opinion) the most telling episode of the 1992 campaign. Addressing a conservative group in Colorado Springs prior to Houston, Bush told an anecdote that involved a gladiator who had killed every lion in town. The meanest lion is sent for, and the gladiator is buried in the sand with only his head sticking out. The lion charges: "making a deadly pass at the gladiator's head." Bush continued, "And as he did, the gladiator reached up and took a very ferocious bite in a very sensitive place in the lion's anatomy. And the lion howled in pain and ran for the exit. And the lead centurion ran out and attacked the gladiator, screaming: 'Fight fair, damn it, fight fair.'" (Fred Barnes noted that the audience members first looked at each other in disbelief, then laughed, then applauded.)[93] This identification, ostensibly with the Roman gladiator, is as illustrative in its way as the "javelin catcher." On the level of the manifest content of the anecdote, Bush clearly positions himself as the Roman gladiator biting the balls off his opponent, Clinton. (One might wonder just how presidential an identification this is.) But what is most problematic is that, in Bush's telling of the story, his own body language belies such a univocal position. For he clearly enjoys the contemplation of castration, the possibility that he, too, will be beaten/bitten, as he is also jubilant about taking his rebuke from the Centurion. The Roman gladiator, like the javelin catcher, is an identification that works fantasmatically (hence the applause). It works in part because of its masochistic appeal, which itself relies upon an identification with a masculine corporal image of strength and integrity (Roman gladiator, javelin *thrower*). The erotics of this masochistic ecstasy combine the joys of self-surrendering penetration (the figure of the javelin catcher) with an equally heady dissolution of identity.

Yet the Roman gladiator anecdote ups the fantasmatic ante of the masochistic imaginary and underscores how an initial (successful) heteropathic identification ("I'm one of you") can become a fatal (for a candidate) masochistic ecstasy. This has less to do with Bush's oscillating identification (first with the gladiator, next with the position of the victim) than with the way the Roman gladiator story *literally* enacts the theme of castration. This literalization makes the Roman gladiator story an identification that profoundly subverts the normative masculinity subtending any presidential subject (as paternal imago, father figure). In other words, in recounting this anecdote, Bush, like the gladiator, bites off more than he can (es)chew, in this case "the male subject's symbolic legacy."[94]

The theoretical stakes of the gladiator anecdote tie it to the other fantasmatic *locus classicus* of masochism, the Moloch fantasy recounted by Reik's patient:

> To an ancient barbaric idol like the Phoenician Moloch a number of vigorous young men are to be sacrificed at certain not too infrequent intervals. They are undressed and laid at the altar one by one. The rumble of drums is joined by the songs of the approaching temple choirs. The high priest followed by his suite approaches the altar and scrutinizes each of the victims with a critical eye. They must satisfy certain requirements of beauty and athletic appearance. The high priest takes the genital of each victim in his hand and carefully tests its weight and form. If he does not approve of the genital, the young man will be rejected as obnoxious to the god and unworthy of being sacrificed. The high priest gives the order for the execution and the ceremony continues. With a sharp cut the young man's genitals and the surrounding parts are cut away.[95]

The castration/dismemberment is only a prelude to the rest of the scenario, in which the victims are totally annihilated—suspended over a grate, singed, and then burned in a fire below. It is not an understatement to see this as a radically negative fantasy. But it is interesting as a backdrop to the Roman gladiator-Houston convention theme in two senses. There is an implicit identification with the victim by someone who watches, recounts, or stands second in line. Moreover, castration is only the beginning (foreplay) to an even more spectacular display of sufferings. There is the further feature of suspense: how much suffering can any victim stand before he "flees forward" into the fire?

Bush's surrogate Sununu emerged as the original Moloch figure (with a Texas-updated inflection) during the budget crisis, part of a triumvirate of pitbulls aptly called by their nicknames: Nick (Brady), Dick (Darman), and Prick (Sununu). Sununu taunted presidential allies with "I'm going to chain-saw your balls off" and repeated this threat to the EPA director, Bill Reilly: "*I've got nothing against you*, personally, Bill, but there are some members of your staff that I'd like to castrate with a chain-saw!" The National Wildlife Federation displayed a cartoon with Sununu wielding a Homelite. Sununu disavowed that he was in any way a scapegoat ("No. No. I'm probably as bad as they all say I am"), yet still claiming, "I'm just taking the spears for the president" (Sununu as the original javelin catcher).[96]

Sununu identified with the castrating Moloch; in his resignation letter he misspelled "pussy"—"in pit bull or pussey [*sic*] cat mode (your choice, as always), I am ready to help."[97] Bush's posture is ambivalent, aligning itself with the gladiator but wanting a fair fight. Bush as oil wildcatter distinguishes himself from the crisis-driven manager, "up to his ass in alligators," who forgets that "he's come to drain the swamp." Bush looks forward with relish to wrestling the reptiles and savoring the contest. The alligator provokes images of phallic divestiture; Bush's example foregrounds another source of end-pleasure. This is reiterated in his diary entry about the budget process; he relates his anxiety about Republican party loyalty: "I don't know if Republicans will stay with me. Some of them want to paint their asses white and run with the antelope, as Lyndon Johnson said. They want to do it right now. Isn't that a marvelous image? From a very tired George Bush."[98] (His next excerpted diary entry talks about the "pounding" he's taking on Panama and his surprise that he's feeling relatively tranquil and resigned about it. In other words, he doesn't mind being beaten in the Canal Zone or, at least, doesn't mind taking a "pounding").

I see Bush's Roman gladiator/castration imago as the first part of the Moloch fantasy, with Houston its counterpart. The Houston convention even included a prostate cancer screening booth, with only a thin blue curtain separating those being screened from fifty thousand Republicans beyond its veil. This scenario displaces the traditional view of Houston as a mere tactical mistake—allowing Pat Buchanan to speak, parading a damaged president forced to abjure his mistakes. I prefer to read the Republican convention less as an error than as a radical *mise en scène* of masochism, conforming to both Freud and Reik in three respects: the "structural necessity of an audience" for the humiliated body, the "centrality of this body on display" (even and especially if it is being whipped or beaten), and the presence of a "master tableau" or group fantasy behind these exhibitions: "What is being beaten is not so much the body as the 'flesh' and beyond that sin itself and the whole fallen world."[99] The Roman gladiator anecdote prefigures the theme of the "culture wars." It is its opening act. Bush does not so much abase himself before the radical right as the radical right is a fictive screen on which Bush can parade his masochism. While this display does have great psychoanalytic coherence, it is a dangerous one for any subject claiming to represent the symbolic order as the masochist (Freud and Reik concur) is pitted against society itself. Moreover, the 1992 convention, understood in this sense of an epicene masochism, was less an assault on Hillary Clinton than a full-fledged assault on normative masculinity (the masochist addresses himself to the Big Other/Symbolic Order, which is also why the 1992 convention was noteworthy for its religious revivalist furor). Hillary Clinton represented the identification with the mother (or the Winnicottian WOMAN), displacing Barbara Bush for a moment.[100] The media criticisms that Bush was not running for "First Lady" are symptoms of the implication of the mother/feminine within moral masochism, as well as its necessarily strategic disavowal.

In short, what the voters rejected in 1992 was the masochistic appeal put on display in Houston—its implicit threat to normative masculinity and heterosexuality. And heteropathic Bush could not have had a better opponent on the field of the fantasmatic than the idiopathic Bill Clinton. For the idiopath, according to Scheler, makes "narcissistic profit" out of the heteropath's "self-loss." The struggle between these two is figured in a language as suggestive in its way as that of the Roman gladiator anecdote: a squirrel jumping down the throat of a snake:

> Schopenhauer recounts the following observation made by an English
> officer on the Indian squirrel: A white squirrel, having met the gaze of a
> snake, hanging on a tree and showing every sign of a mighty appetite
> for its prey is so terrified by this that it gradually moves towards rather
> than away from the snake, and finally throws itself into the open jaws
> . . . plainly the squirrel's instinct for self-preservation has succumbed
> to an ecstatic participation in the object of the snake's own appeti
> tive nisus, namely, "swallowing." The squirrel identifies in feeling with
> the snake, and thereupon spontaneously establishes corporal "identity"
> with it, by disappearing down its throat.

This anecdote displays the shift from javelin catcher to Roman gladiator. For it is not pure passivity as such that gives pleasure to the masochist but rather, in Scheler's words, "his self-identifying participation in the dominance of the partner, i.e., a sympathetic attainment of power."[101]

Displacing orifice (anus to mouth) and positionality (receiving to biting), Bush in the Roman gladiator anecdote identifies with a power position. On election eve, Bush gets his wish (revealed in a stunning parapraxis where he *thanks* Clinton when he should be congratulating him). He has become the squirrel lodged in Clinton's throat.[102]

6

"Chicks with Dicks"
Transgendering the Presidency
(2005/1996)

FOR BARBARA HINCKLEY

> Execrated and idolized, Plath hovers between the furthest poles of
> positive and negative appraisal; she hovers in the space of what is
> most extreme, most violent about appraisal as such. Above all she
> stirs things up, she lays bare the forms of psychic investment which
> lie, barely concealed, behind the process through which a culture
> . . . evaluates and perpetuates itself.[1]

The description Jacqueline Rose gives in her introduction to
The Haunting of Sylvia Plath could serve equally well to account for the
intense passions aroused by Hillary Clinton, reduced to that enigmatic
question of femininity: What does she/Hillary really want?[2] And yet,
like (Rose's) Plath: "What she is asking for is never clear, although it
seems highly unlikely that she is asking for what she gets."[3] As in the
classic porn scenario, Hillary is both humiliated and manipulative, "ut-
terly done over and asking for it," violated and Oedipal.[4] And although
Hillary Clinton did not produce the literary archive of Plath, I will argue
that her performances (or enactments) of femininity as First Lady, designated listener, candidate, and senator have produced an image archive
as interpellative and extreme as Plath's in its interweaving of sexuality
and misogyny, domesticity and violence: "She's like a widow, a lioness,
a doormat and an Amazon all rolled into one. We are the audience staring and waiting. Will she weep? Or roar? Or ever stop pretending?"[5]

The Clinton marriage, like the Plath-Hughes one, compels with the
force of a dysfunctional family drama: asking for judgment, "to appor-
tion blame, to parcel out innocence and guilt."[6] And, like Plath, every-

thing about Hillary is "read without reserve."[7] This chapter is an analysis of a "reading effect"—how we feel implicated by Hillary; how Hillary "gets" to us. Theoretically, this countertransferential focus will also let us revisit the Freudian *topos* of femininity.

Let us pretend for a moment that someone in the future (or, alternatively, someone emerging from a media biosphere of sorts) were to be confronted with a Hillary archive containing articles, biographies, her autobiography and books, a Grammy award (for *It Takes a Village*), a Marc Jacobs fall 2004 collection tee shirt, assorted birthday cards with her image, tapes of late-night talk show appearances, a daytime tape of her singing the "Telephone Song" from *Bye Bye Birdie* with Rosie O'Donnell, and so on. After they had been properly reassured that this was not a fictional character from a William Gibson or J. G. Ballard novel and was indeed a late-twentieth-century political figure, they would be hard pressed to find some evaluative middle ground. Hillary had been subject to demonology (Christopher Anderson's *American Evita*, Edward Klein's *The Truth About Hillary*), as well as hagiography ("the most compelling sexual persona of our times" Tom Junod). There would not be many A-list political or cultural villains or martyrs to whom she had not been compared: Madam Mao, Lady Macbeth, Eva Peron, Winnie Mandela, Joan of Arc, Antigone, Coretta Scott King, both Borgias, and Marie Antoinette, not to mention the self-comparisons to Nelson Mandela and Elie Wiesel (as fellow "survivors").[8] In the recent spirit of *blondenfreude*, her name is metonymically linked to pop cultural icons of will and extreme makeover: Madonna and Martha Stewart.[9]

Hillary emerges from the archive as a polarizing figure of sacrificial humiliation (after the 1998 midterm elections) and preening entitlement (registering for post–White House "gifts"). Alternately, she is a "victim," an "enabler," and an "opportunist" (or, perhaps, a celebrity—someone, in Paul Virilio's terms, who is "accidented," rather than "exploited/exploiting").[10] And, like the protagonists of J. M. Coetzee's novel *Disgrace*, the political animus against her is decidedly personal.[11] Early in her Senate campaign, Rudy Giuliani's pollster recounted how much bad feeling there was that "defied reasoned analysis."[12] Joe Conason cites the adjectives used in focus groups: "cold and dishonest." She is dismissed with alliterative couplets: "abrasive and annoying, brash and bitter, calculating and scheming, distant and deceitful, polarizing and power-hungry."[13] Hillary is amazed at the level of hostility of people who have never met her. But she does not fare much better with the

Senate majority leader Trent Lott after she is elected senator: "I'll tell you one thing. When this Hillary gets to the Senate—*if she does*—*maybe lightening will strike her and she won't*—she'll be one Senator and we won't let her forget it." (Even the "neutral" descriptive passages that attempt to poke fun at Al Gore during Hillary's swearing-in Senate ceremony leave murderous attributions in their wake. Al Gore, always the gloomy prince of Tennessee, recalls that other prince "as if he were Hamlet and *Gertrude* were taking her seat at Court.")[14]

For Tom Junod, the hatred Hillary evokes in men is the "most salient and interesting fact" about her. He relates the following joke: "What's the Hillary Clinton KFC special? Two small breasts, two large thighs, and two left wings." This is told by a representative everyman in the middle commuter airline seat—a hearty, fifty-something engineer who is "too big for his seat and ate his allotted bag of snack mix with a kind of puzzled proprietary disappointment." (This raconteur, disappointed with Junod's response to his "joke," adds, "I'll bet you she has bigger balls than he does.")[15] I was reminded of Laura Kipnis's reading of the innumerable Linda Tripp jokes as ways of producing social knowledge. "Appearance jokes are like the imbecilic cousin of Kantian aesthetics, born of the same lineage, but not invited to sit at the big table when the family gets together."[16] Falling short of "normative" or "ideational" beauty ("large thighs," "small breasts") does not necessarily make one caricatural or undesirable, only, in Kipnis's astute words, "ordinary." The jokes evoked by Hillary's body are less physiognomic than inter-subjective and symptomatic. But what are they the symptom of?

Indeed, my original interest in Hillary Clinton during the early years of the first administration could be formulated as a simple question ad-dressed to any target of collective projection: "Why do people hate her more than they should?" Or, to cite two of Rose's formulations: "What is it about some figures that generates a psychotic criticism?" Just who becomes a figure of "retaliatory" criticism?[17] In the case of Hillary, this retaliation, as in the case of Marilyn Monroe, can accompany an in-tense resentment and even a denial that she is a woman.[18]

If I have extensively referenced Jacqueline Rose, it is because of her work on the role of fantasy and political identification. One of the features of psychotic criticism is the way it slides into "anticipatory re-taliation," better known as Kleinian "projective identification." How does one distinguish between "pure projection" and "ideological effect" when it comes to affects as intimately linked as adulation and denega-

"Pinning Down Hillary," *Vanity Fair*, June 1994.

tion? This has become an increasingly urgent question as "anticipated retaliation"/"projective identification" (i.e., "preemption") has become the trope of the Bush administration. Moreover, it may well prove to be the case that negative affect is not as severe a detriment (especially in light of the 2004 election results) if what is needed in a post-9/11 politics' administration of fear is strong affectivity combined with a potent mediatic presence.[19]

But another reason is that Rose's theoretical work has accompanied equally compelling readings of three iconic women: Margaret Thatcher, Lady Diana, and Plath.[20] In many ways, Plath, as the only American in the triad and a Smith girl, is an interesting companion to Clinton. Because many readers are probably most familiar with Plath as a feminist poet and author, and not as a presidential metonym or critic, I will describe in some detail a collage Plath made while at Smith College. It contains a picture of a smiling Eisenhower at his desk. Plath has placed in his hands a deck of cards; on the desk are the digestive aid Tums and a camera on which is a cut-out of a model in a swimsuit, bearing a slogan, "Every man wants his woman on a pedestal." A bomber is pointing at the woman's abdomen. In the corner, Nixon is making a speech (in a small photo insert). A couple is sleeping with eye shields, with the caption "It's his and her time all over America." In the top left corner is a small news item: "America's most famous preacher's revival touches millions in the U.S."[21]

Rose enumerates the precisely focused points of cultural contestation addressed in this petit chef d'oeuvre: Nixon, the religious right, clichés of sexual difference, consumerism, male fantasies, and war. The perfect pin-up is a war target.[22] One is struck by the prescience of both Plath's collage and Rose's reading of it; the replete political body (a complacent Eisenhower?) needs Tums as America suffers from an "undigested surfeit of itself." I am not suggesting that Hillary has produced anything remotely this critical, but she exacerbates these precise points of tension within the national body addressed by Plath/Rose without "resolution or dissipation of that tension."[23] This is part of her maddening appeal. And then there are those uncanny policy moments (such as when she suggests that military technological advances used in surveillance and bombing be targeted for breast cancer) where she seems to fulfill one's worst Kleinian fantasies.[24]

This chapter is the first of two on Hillary Clinton. It presents a "real-time" reading of Hillary during the first term of Bill Clinton's presidency. Written for a conference in the spring of 1996, it attempts to situate Hillary bashing as a cultural symptom of the transgendering of popular culture and its theorizations (both conscious, in the case of Butler and Garber, and unconscious, as we will see with Mary Tilotson of CNN). It might be difficult now to reimagine the affirmative force of Butler's *Gender Trouble* at the start of the 1990s theory bubble. Similarly, so many of the protagonists of the first part have disappeared or mutated. *George* is gone, along with its founder, John F. Kennedy Jr. Cindy Crawford is no longer with Richard Gere and is a celebrity mom. Barbra Streisand has evolved into the antagonist Babette Van Anka, who kills the president with an overdose of vaginally applied Viagra (the Secret Service taste his food, right?) in Chris Buckley's *No Way to Treat a First Lady*.[25] (But it is Hillary/Beth MacMann/"Lady Beth Mac" who is accused and goes on trial for his murder.) This is in a later moment of the second term of the Clinton presidency, when Hillary has left the terrain of desire and entered that of the drive, entering the dream spaces of others: Buckley, Peggy Noonan, Joe Eszterhas.[26] *Spy* magazine is gone, as well, and caricatures of popular figures are more likely to be viewed on a screen than on a satirical magazine cover. And, needless to say, Michael Jackson is now scandalous for things other than his music videos.

The first-term reading of Hillary is framed by a tension between Lacanian feminist theorists of the masquerade and fetishism (Parveen Adams, Emily Apter, Mary Ann Doane, Jacqueline Rose, Naomi Schor) and theorists of gender performativity (Judith Butler, Marjorie Garber, Judith Halberstam), who also draw on the work of Rivière on the masquerade but posit cross-dressing as a possible cultural/political subversion. This reading bears the traces of what was once seen as a cultural possibility and limit: a semiotic guerrilla strategy against the symbolic.[27] It might now, at this writing, in 2005, make more sense to wonder if feminine practices of masquerade and fetishism are misplaced and should be situated in relation to *male* leadership: either the overaccessorized flight suit and ranch attire of George W. Bush or the "feminized" political performances of Tony Blair.[28] What does it signify for gender performance if two pro-warrior leaders are not afraid to admit they cry, see men's souls (Putin's), or feel things deeply despite the facts?

The final chapter, "Hillary Regained," focuses on Hillary during the impeachment period, her Senate campaign, and her tenure as a senator who voted for the Iraq war. Attention moves from corporeal metonyms of hair and eyes to those of mouth and voice. The focus on different part objects is no less obsessive, and the problem of femininity is rephrased in relation to narcissism and sublimation. As mentioned briefly, Hillary now appears in the literary imaginations and dreams of others. She has entered the Real.

White House of Style (1996)[29]

Cover stories cover or mask what they make invisible with an alternative presence that redirects our attention, that covers or makes absent what has to remain unseen if the seen is to function as the scene for a different drama. Cover stories are faces for other texts, different texts; they are pretexts that obscure context, fade out subtexts, and protect the texts of the powerful.[30]

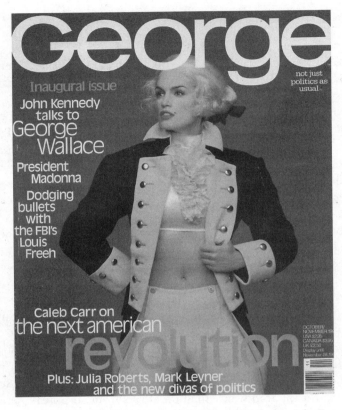

The inaugural issue of *George* magazine, started by the late John F. Kennedy, Jr., October/November 1995.

I was watching CNN and Company sometime during the O. J. trial when Mary Tilotson shifted the topic of conversation to a story about John F. Kennedy Jr.'s new magazine, *George,* as a counterpoint to the right-wing *Standard.* Mary Tilotson and her commentators watched a press conference clip during which the cover of the inaugural issue was unveiled. The cover showed the supermodel Cindy Crawford (cross)-dressed as George Washington. After a bit of uneasy laughter that signaled some degree of disbelief from even these jaded, cynical media analysts, Tilotson described this "Butler-esque" gender performance as "undrag," immediately upping the crossing/passing and otherwise gender-bending ante.[31] For "undrag" (like "undead") provided a *frisson* of epistemological pleasure about hopelessly blurred boundaries—*especially* in the context of presidential authority: power, subjectivity, and agency were (to this spectator) delightfully confounded.

Several weeks later, my October 1995 issue of *Spy* magazine arrived. Hillary was featured on the cover, not in her earlier dominatrix mode but now looking very *femme*—a partially transparent black cocktail dress, blond Evita/Madonna hair, and a skirt blown up to her waist, recalling the other *femme* icon Marilyn (*Seven-Year Itch*), as well as providing a sartorial-historiographic footnote to the suggestive eighteenth-century mode of "retroussé" crinolines.[32] Hillary's underwear was revealed to show her wearing men's briefs with a prominent phallus. The cover proclaimed "Hillary's Big Secret." Its manifest content was ostensibly about Whitewater, but its all too (b)latant message telegraphed a

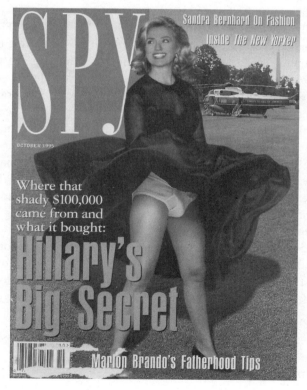

The October 1995 cover of *Spy* magazine.

more uncanny enigma—the type of open secrets offered up to mass delectation, like those of the *Crying Game.*

I scrambled to purchase a copy of *George* to compare these gender subversions as cover stories, indeed as *en-abimes* of cover stories as they addressed that "*bête noire* of feminist theory—the masquerade."[33] What precisely was masked in this defiant display of the masquerade? What did it disclose or occlude about the cultural anxieties now (re)cathected to the presidency (via its gendered metonym)? Eager to read more about the cover photo, I opened to the table of contents, where a miniature of the cover photo is conventionally displayed and titled.[34] But the cover photo had mutated in two overdetermined ways. "George" was now re-coded in the photo credits as "First Lady." Cindy Crawford/"George" was surrounded by her makeup artist, photographer, stylist, and hair stylist. (That is, it took a media village to make Cindy Crawford.) The change was not limited to a textual change of caption from "George" to "First Lady"; "George" was now in a different pose. This "First Lady" had her hands crossed over her crotch, and in her hand one could discern the handle of a sword. Whereas the body language of the cross-dressed George (of the cover) was one of exuberant display—a jacket opened to the navel revealing ambiguous underwear, part bra, part period ruffled shirt, the "First Lady-George" inside photo appeared to be one of concealment—hands crossed in front, shoulders hunched forward. With Crawford surrounded by her imagemakers and handlers, the inside photo underscored the artifactuality of this liminal George. Yet the eye was insistently drawn to the hands crossed over the crotch. Could I read this inside cover—as Marjorie Garber reads Madonna—as a "sartorial centaur" covering what she hasn't got? Is this a case of "empowered transvestism" or "empowered womanhood"? For there were obvious parallels with Garber's reading of the Madonna video "Express Yourself": "Madonna is a famous female star who is impersonating a famous male star celebrated for his androgynous looks. Why is it shocking when she does what Michael Jackson does, saying: "I'm not intact, he's not intact, I am intact, this is what intact is."[35]

But What About the Sword?

We have here two or more highly intertextual and overcoded crossings: a woman in a man's clothing and a rhetorical displacement from president to First Lady. And yet it is uncertain which crossing is more in the direction of phallic sufficiency or virile display. Moreover, Cindy Crawford is a complicated libidinal intertextual referent, having suggestively posed on the cover of *Vanity Fair* with the "out" lesbian singer k.d. lang in a makeup session. Cindy is also figured as a makeup spokesperson for Revlon in the first two-page ad after John F. Kennedy Jr.'s signed editor's letter. Here, Cindy is wearing a red dress, arms extended towards two pillars of ice on a red background. Across the pelvic area reads the following textual display: "Play With Fire. Skate on Thin Ice." As an ad for Revlon's perfume "Fire and Ice," it winks at the dangerous ambivalence of gender performance of masquerade. And it is not exactly as if Cindy and Hillary have nothing in common. Both are from suburban Illinois and share a belief in dress codes. The last page of the inaugural issue of *George* features—who else?—Madonna in a textual impersonation "If I were President: Madonna—A political virgin takes a romp through the White House."

A female supermodel in the clothes of the figure of all presidents
—*George*

A "femme" First Lady sporting men's briefs.

What if our Founding Father were really a cover girl? What if our First Lady could both have and be the phallus? This chapter (ad)dresses the gender-bending performances of the presidential masquerade.

The work of Marjorie Garber and Judith Butler has addressed the imbrication of cultural and gender anxieties in a way curiously apposite to the transgendering of the Clinton presidency. I would like to draw upon this contribution to offer yet another reading of Hillary Rodham Clinton by addressing the rhetorical unconscious that undergirds these pop cultural covers. But my interest is less in explaining the cultural phenomenon of "Hillary hating" than in questioning that particular symptom in ways that raise issues central to contemporary feminist theory. What does all the verbiage surrounding the Hillary factor/Hillary as cultural Rorschach tell us about the limitations and aporia of feminist conceptualizations? More specifically, to what extent is the phenomenon commonly referred to as "Hillary-hating" or "Hillary-bashing" less a resentment of Hillary (or Hillary bashers) than it is a referendum on the possibility of what Catherine Millot, Parveen Adams, and others designate as post-Oedipal feminine identification.[36] For Parveen Adams, the political stakes of these theoretical questions are clearly posed: Could unconscious representations be different? "Does the unconscious simply borrow whatever is most appropriate and ready to hand, in which case the bits of reality which are appropriated in a representation are but possible and predictable materializations of unconscious life?" For, if unconscious representations could be organized in a post-Oedipus-complex way, then "sexuality could be organized in a different relation to the phallus, that there could be new sexualities . . . divorced from gender positions."[37]

To answer these questions will require several detours and several outfits.

Jefferson in Vegas

The Clinton presidency might seem a peculiar site for transgendering. And yet, from the inauguration on, it has been the site of impersonations and gender transgressing. The two most visible female presences at the inaugural festivities were Hillary and Barbra Streisand. Barbra Streisand's performance singing at the inaugural was her first live one in many years. It thus figured as a comeback for both Bill Clinton and Streisand. Nor was this the only similarity. Clinton's inaugural began with a visit to Monticello, President Thomas Jefferson's home (Jefferson is Clinton's middle name). This initiated a major Jefferson revival, Joseph Ellis recounts, during which more people visited Jefferson's desk at the Smithsonian than went to Graceland.[38] (Clinton's secret service code name is Elvis.) Barbra Streisand's inaugural performance was a preview of her triumphant comeback in Las Vegas in a set design simulacrum of Monticello. "Jefferson" is restaged as Barbra descends a staircase dressed in a period outfit. Barbra dresses as a woman (in a black velvet and white satin empire-style dress), yet she is (post-Yentl) ambivalently figured *as* Jefferson.[39] Clinton's mother made a highly publicized appearance at the Las Vegas show, and it was the last event she attended before her death from breast cancer. I am not holding Barbra in any way responsible for her death but am showing the imbrication of Clinton/Streisand/Jeffersonian/(Elvis) associational patterns that facilitate transgendered leadership—celebrity impersonations also subject to parody in the comic film *My Fellow Americans.* Garber has subjected *Yentl* to an extended analysis in which Barbra's many transgressions (including orthographic) are gendered (i.e., Streisand as former UJA *Man* of the Year) and eerily reminiscent of Hillary's.[40] Both produce polarized affects. (One is not indifferent to either.) Both have been to "Monticello."

The presidency has figured in curiously gendered ways cinematically during the first years of the Clinton presidency. In many ways, it is decentered to accessorize a powerful female or domestic presence. In the female buddy serial-killer counterpart to *Seven, Copy Cat,*[41] the presidency, *qua* name of the father, is reduced to a mnemonic (similar to the naming of state capitals) remedy for a panic attack. Sigourney Weaver (a gender liminal figure, Ripley, in *Aliens*) recites the names of presidents from Washington to Van Buren before her tranquilizers kick in. *The American President,* in which the lead is modeled on Clinton, kills off the First Lady (Shepherd is a widower). His daughter (Chelsea stand-in) tries to marry him off to an aggressive lobbyist with the androgynous name of Sidney (although she does look very good dressed in the president's shirttails). Indeed, in *The American President,* the White House quickly dissolves from an icon in the opening shots to function as an obstacle-sign to desire. Walking around the White House, Shepherd/Clinton is a spectral figure, unable even to send flowers to his girlfriend. *The American President* (which presents a knowingly "Capra-esque," idealistic view of a boomer presidency and which serves as a template for *The West Wing*) marks an early moment of Hillary hating, which reaches a cinematic crescendo in *Independence Day,* where the First Lady/Hillary stand-in is punished for her careerism and dies a prolonged death from internal hemorrhaging.[42] If, as Baudrillard once remarked à propos of the hyperreal presidents Ford and Reagan—that they were entitled only to "simulated" or "puppet" assassinations— Clinton/Shepherd is so unpresidential (unconventionally phallic) that assassins shoot at the *House* itself!

What one witnesses in popular representations of Clinton-era presidential authority such as Oliver Stone's *Nixon* or PBS's *Truman* is a further uncoding of masculinity after the Bush presidency: an evacuation of principles of male leadership and a displacement toward the feminine (either domestic interiors, or, as in the case of Oliver Stone's *Nixon*, Pat Nixon).

Éperons: *Hillary's Styles*

> Fashion is both *too* serious and too frivolous at the same time, and it is
> this intentionally complementary interplay of excess that it finds a solu-
> tion to a fundamental contradiction which constantly threatens to de-
> stroy its fragile prestige. . . . Moreover, it is probable that the juxtaposi-
> tion of the excessively serious and the excessively frivolous, which is the
> basis for the rhetoric of fashion, merely reproduces, on the level of
> clothing, the mythic situation of Women in Western civilisation, at once
> sublime and childlike. —Roland Barthes[43]

> The problem with Mrs. Clinton is "she hasn't found her style. The way
> she changes her hair, changes the color she wears, changes her clothes:
> long suits, short suits, large and small, it's like she's a child who can't
> decide whether to take the train or the bus." —Sonia Rykiel[44]

It is rare to find an article about Hillary that does not take note of her
appearance.[45] The First Lady as an object of scopic fixation (and pleasure) is not in itself surprising. For First Ladies since Martha Washington have set a "presidential tone"[46] and have been conveyed by a lexical
shorthand that links social cause or public interest with some sort of
Barthesian "little real," biographeme, corporeal, or sartorial metonym:
Barbara Bush—campaign for literacy, white hair, fake Kenneth Jay Lane
pearls, and a penchant for blue; Nancy Reagan: "Just Say No," foster
grandparents, the color red; Betty Ford: ERA, breast cancer "candor";
Rosalyn Carter, the "steel magnolia" ("a Sherman tank in a field of
clover") who "bought off the rack" and championed mental health (no
causal relation). Other sartorial metonyms achieved epic ontological
or anthropomorphic proportions: Pat Nixon's "Republican cloth coat"
(did it really vote Republican?), Jackie Kennedy's pillbox hat—still the
standard. Earlier First Ladies were praised for their democratic style
(Dolley Madison), Euro-trashed as fashion victims (Elizabeth Monroe),
heralded for their successful mediation between upper-class and democratic style (Jackie Kennedy), or "murdered" by bad reviews (Rachel
Jackson). Julia Tyler was perhaps the most beautiful First Lady and received the best press. Collective accounts of First Ladies reveal both a
consistency of gossipy interest and an accommodation to a wide range
of styles and body morphologies.

Hillary's problem is somewhere else. There is something about the range and variability of her sartorial performances that is unsettling. Her inconsistency (a lack of sartorial secondary revision) can be read as an outward manifestation of her hypocrisy or deviousness. "She has contrition down pat . . . Hillary the Submissive, pretty in pink."[47] Or, it can be read in accordance with a logic of exaggerated disavowal: "Mrs. Clinton is such a bigger person than fashion. She's more fashionable than what she wears," Donna Karan states while Hillary is in full view wearing one of her (Karan's) suits! Ralph Lauren is awed: "She's sharp. She's bright. She's kind. She's"—the designer pauses, momentarily at a loss. "I think she's a wonderful woman. If she ran for president, I'd vote for her."[48] (These remarks were made at the White House reception honoring the fashion industry's concern for breast cancer.) The Parisians' reception ranged from unabashed hyperbole (i.e., "I think she's ravishing" [Christine Okrent]; "I think she looks absolutely wonderful. She has great style" [Anne-Elisabeth Moulet]); "She has solved the problem of power dressing") to a litotic preemptive strike of lowered expectations ("The president would be ill-advised to recycle the quip of John Kennedy in 1963 . . .") to banal disavowal ("What she wears is not very important"; "This visit was very solemn and official. We respected that.").[49]

However, in the wide variability of styles depicted, mostly caricatural (Vogue Vamp in black Donna Karan, Vestal Virtue as Saint Hillary of the Politics of Meaning, Contrite for the Pretty in Pink Press Conference), Mrs. Clinton's trajectory suggests less the vestimentary progress narrative than a failed contender for "realness" at a drag ball. Butler reminds us that "realness" has little to do with mimetic aping or other respects for the sartorial minutiae of a social role. Success is measured not by the verisimilitude of the representation but by interpellation, "an ability to compel belief, to produce a naturalized effect."[50] Hillary's performances never achieve the paradox of the Barthesian connoted signification—they are always read and not *received*.[51] For Hillary's variable array of performances contains a semiological consistency: a misreading of the ideology of fashion and its rhetorical signified that is neither implicit nor explicit but *latent*. Unable to "pass," Hillary has an appeal that is iconic. Rather than "realness," she produces the counter-effect, that of a "cover-girl"—the body of no one: "the cover girl represents a rare paradox: on the one hand, her body has the value of an abstract institution, and on the other hand, this body is individual, and between these two conditions there is no *drift*." The cover girl is a "structural

Cover story: "Hillary Rodham Clinton and the Politics of Virtue,"
by Michael Kelly, *New York Times Magazine*, May 23, 1993. Kelly
was later killed while covering the Iraq war.

paradox," presenting not a beautiful body but a "deformed body with a
view to achieving a certain formal generality."[52]

In short, for Hillary, the "subject" self-evacuates; the clothes take
over and wear her. Who has not been reminded of this in the myriad
photographs of Hillary possessed by her costumes—her inauguration
hat, gown, and cloak—becoming increasingly defamiliarized as media
rhetoric usurps the place of fashion editor and tries to contextualize
her into a scenario: the "pink press conference," her "St. John 'civvies'
in the Map Room"?[53] These performances never achieve the affirmative gender subversions of Madonna's rock videos and filmic personae.
And yet, they resist facile appropriation (they are "read" rather than
"received"). Less a commodity than Madonna, less "real" than Venus

X-travaganza, Hillary demonstrates a crucial double bind of Butler's performative model.

Let us return to Rykiel's rebuke: "it's like she's a child who can't decide whether to take *the train* or the bus." Who, after reading Lacan's "Insistence of the Letter," cannot read this as a taunt, an invitation to choose a gender assignment: train or bus? Ladies or gentlemen: a choice not of destination but its vehicle. (And who would not wish to stay caught on the rails?)

Rykiel suggests that the First Lady "stand in front of her mirror for one hour, two hours, one day, two days, eight days, *however long it takes*, until she finds who she really is."[54] Rykiel presents, as Butler herself has remarked, the most prevalent misreading of gender performativity as voluntarism—"choose": "For if I was to argue that genders are performative, that could mean that one woke in the morning, perused the closet for some more open space for the gender of choice, donned that gender for the day and then restored the garment to its place at night."[55] Overlooking Rykiel's substitution of "mirror" for "closet" (and the importance of narcissism for her "project"), Rykiel is precisely the "willful and instrumental subject" who can decide *on* a gender precisely because of her putative exemption from it.

I would like to read Hillary's "failed" transvestism (her inability to pass) affirmatively and suggest that part of the *resistance* to Hillary (countertransference is quite different from "hating," although it can take on forms rhetorically quite similar to "bashing"; it acknowledges its libidinal investments) is due to her successful masquerade. Like the patients of Joan Rivière,[56] both highly successful professional women (one compelled to speak in public, the other a professor of abstruse material), Hillary is compelled to repeat and "re-iterate a performance which both legitimates and delegitimates the realness norms by which it is produced."[57] Hillary "reworks" and works feminization—"and sometimes succeeds."[58]

Hillary Rodham Thatcher, Drag Queen?

For only if you are operating within a rationalist concept of fantasy will the dislike of Thatcher automatically dispense with the idea that *something about her image is at work* in the political process that returned her to power. What if Thatcher was re-elected *not despite* her

image but also in some sense because of it? *What if that force of iden-*
tity for which she is so severely castigated somewhere else also operates
as a type of pull? —Jacqueline Rose (italics mine)[59]

The voluntarist rendering of cross-dressing/drag meets the "rationalist" conception of fantasy in Camille Paglia's depiction of Hillary Clinton ("Ice Queen, Drag Queen: A Psychological Biography").[60] Banal yet provocative as psycho-biography, Paglia's account is most useful as a cultural symptom—as a sometimes quite perceptive misreading that, in missing the mark, offers a way to theoretically unpack the differences between transvestism and masquerade, as well as between affirmative and renormativizing conceptions of the masquerade. Butler poses the question succinctly: Are we to read masquerade as "performative production of a sexual ontology—an appearance that makes itself convincing as 'being'" or as "a denial of feminine desire that presupposes some prior ontological femininity regularly represented by the phallic economy"?[61] Each reading suggests a different political strategy. The first reading opens the masquerade to a performative, parodic deconstruction of gender ontology; the second leads to an "unmasking" in order to recover some putative originary feminine desire or essence. Paglia's article is inscribed within this second reading and its political trajectory. The cover of *The New Republic* issue that contains Paglia's article includes the teaser "Hillary unmasked," with the letters covering Hillary's eyes. We will see that the textual foregrounding of the second reading of masquerade (as a recovery of a lost feminine essence) inadvertently underscores Mary Anne Doane's contribution. Female transvestism allows for mastery over the image and the possibility of attaching the *gaze* to desire.[62]

I would like to spend a few moments rehearsing the differences between transvestism and the masquerade in order to differentiate a performative (Butler) from an "unmasking" (or otherwise critical) strategy and to suggest some of the stakes implicit in where one draws the radical social constructionist line. For Doane, Apter, and Butler, transvestism appropriates the artifactuality of femininity (its insignia, gestures, habits, rites), whereas masquerade provides a more radical critique of how (in Joan Rivière's terms) femininity itself is constructed as a mask, that is, as a defensive reaction formation against woman's transgendered identifications (Rivière). To cite Rivière's most radical formulation in full:

Womanliness therefore could be assumed and worn as a mask, both to hide the possession of masculinity and to avert the reprisals expected if she was found to possess it-much as a thief will turn out his pockets and ask to be searched to prove he has not the stolen goods. *The reader may now ask how I define womanliness or where I draw the line between genuine womanliness and the "masquerade." My suggestion is not, however, that there is any such difference; whether radical or superficial they are the same thing* (italics mine).[63]

Rivière's intellectual woman patients evince a hyperrationality and calculation that can be read à la Paglia as a brilliant, utilitarian, clear-cut cynicism. Rivière gives several examples from both clinical work and everyday life, including that of a capable housewife who is skilled at typically masculine crafts; yet, when "any builder or upholsterer is called in, she has a compulsion to hide all her technical knowledge from him and show deference to the workman, making her suggestions in an innocent and artless manner, as if they were 'lucky guesses.'" Her behavior does not vary even with the butcher and the baker, "whom she rules in reality with a *rod of iron*" (italics mine).[64] Rivière's other quotidian example concerns a university lecturer in a typically masculine "abstruse" subject, a wife and mother who wears inappropriately feminine clothing and acts in an unprofessionally flippant manner while giving public lectures to colleagues (but not to students). Rivière's American propagandist is her most elaborated clinical example. She tempers her performance anxiety after an impressive "highly impersonal and objective" (read masculine) public-speaking performance by seeking male sexual reassurance from selected father figures. Rivière analyzes her provocations as well as her highly charged racial childhood sexual phantasies to show how this particular reaction formation was a "compulsive reversal of her intellectual performance." She endeavored to "make sure of safety by masquerading as guiltless and innocent." Her racialized and theft phantasies were congruent with other parts of her dream life: "Before this dream she had had dreams of people putting masks on to avoid disaster. One of them was of a high tower on a hill being pushed over and falling down on the inhabitants below, but the people put on masks and escaped injury."[65]

There is something disturbing about these caricatures of hyperrationality (Rivière's examples, Thatcher, Rodham Clinton) in relation to the theatricality of sartorial self-presentation and the efficacious instrumentalization of gender roles. At times Paglia's description reads like a simple butch-to-femme progress narrative: "Hillary had discovered that the masks of femininity could be learned and appropriated to rise in the world. She had become a political drag queen, a master-mistress of gender roles." And, as with all progress narratives, there is a liberal recuperative moment: "Yet, with all that said, Hillary Clinton is now and is likely to remain, a leading role model for women throughout the world," representing a "Steiner/MacKinnon winning side of sixties feminism" (against the pro-porn, pro-pop culture losers of this culture war) that "overvalues the verbal realm and confuse good intentions with good effects."[66]

But what if masquerade's (and Hillary's) relation to femininity were more complex and ambiguous? What if masquerade addressed not so much any gender-specific content (e.g., "master-mistress of gender roles," "the butch substrate than can be seen in . . . Susan Thomases")[67] but rather the definition and regulation of the limits of the social itself? As Rose remarks with regard to Thatcher, "what might it be about a woman in power that brings us up against the *furthest and most perverse* extremities of the social bond?"[68] The masquerade, understood as a transgressive, performative ontology (think of how many of Rivière's examples involve public or social discursive situations) is a direct assault on the entire symbolic order (and not one's place within it). It does not avoid the interrelation of gender and image but questions the way symbolic identifications work in often contradictory or paradoxical fashion.

Thatcher could be an illustration of the very phantasmatic identifications Hillary now inhabits. Writing at the start of the Gulf War, Rose gives us a brilliant presentation of Thatcher's electoral appeal that shows how gender liminality and ambivalence work to secure a limit definition for state violence. Thatcher was a staunch supporter of capital punishment, launched the Falklands War, and, as we saw in the previous chapter, urged Bush to be a man and not "go wobbly" in Iraq. To get at the return reversals of such a paradoxical identification, Rose twins Thatcher with Ruth Ellis, the last woman executed in England (perhaps familiar to Americans as the subject of the film *Dance with a Stranger*). Rose contends that Ellis was executed because "her femininity didn't come into play at the right point."[69] In this way, Ellis is similar to Camus' character Meursault in *The Stranger*, as Meursault's putative humanity didn't come into play in the right place. (He didn't show emotion when his Mom died.) Thatcher is Ruth Ellis in reverse—a grotesque and ambivalent parody of femininity that stands for "super-rationality which writes violence into law instead of being executed for it."[70]

Thatcher has been presented as the iron lady, a black widow—a castrating mother and punitive superego—and as the political figure responsible for the reshaping of Great Britain in ways as fundamental as the realignment achieved by Reagan in the United States. Yet she has also been figured domestically as a woman who controls the "purse strings." Thatcher worked to both play to and mitigate her perceived "femininity." She trained for years with a vocal coach, worried that her voice was more shrill than that of the other Honourables, yet she still earned the name "Attila the Hen."[71] Once out of office, she bequeathed the speeches she gave to Parliament, along with the handbags she took them out of and that they had been associated with (but these were refused by the archivists).

Thatcher's phantasmatic resonance is precisely the "ambiguity of a femininity appealed to and denied, a masculinity parodied and inflated." Rose is quite astute in recognizing as well that the "scenario" Thatcher (and, I will argue, Hillary) embodies "goes way beyond her": "it is the worse of a phallic economy countered and thereby rendered permissible, by being presented as masquerade."[72] Reading Thatcher with Ellis underlines the tragic and violent (definitely *non*affirmative) performativity of the masquerade. But, what if Rose had twinned Thatcher not (tragically) with Ruth Ellis but (ludicly) with Dame Edna? And, while this latter doubling might seem preposterous, Rose reminds us that the twinning of any two women constitutes a fantasy in itself.

In Paglia's simple binary system, the transvestite adopts the sexuality of the other. Masquerade, on the other hand, involves a realignment of femininity—a recovery or simulation of a missing gap or distance.[73] Pop icons such as Madonna, Callas, and other divas demonstrate that what is key in the masquerade is the manufacture of a lack, an active distantiation between oneself and one's image.[74] In this way, the masquerade may appear to be a peculiarly antihysterical form in which the woman uses her own body as a disguise, as a separation between the object-cause of desire and herself. This is quite different from what Paglia reads as the simple sexual repression of the Mackinnon brand of feminism; it also differs from the presentation of Lady Di, who uses her body as a terrain.[75] I am aware that even this view of the masquerade can be seen as a voluntarism of sorts—a willful self-marking of a distance, again a "choice" of self-presentation. Yet I insist that this manufacture of a gap be read *not* according to a concept of representation but as interpellation—in this case, a negative interpellation that compels *dis*belief. It is as if, in the case of Hillary Clinton, Althusser's (or any other fashion) policeman's[76] call "Hey, you" would be answered by "You've got to be kidding."

"Men Don't Make Passes at Girls Who Wear Glasses" II

Both transvestite (Paglia) and masquerade readings of Hillary Clinton focus on the change in highly overdetermined sartorial and corporeal markers. They capitalize (and my presentation is no exception) on certain visual clichés. The disappearance (or confiscation, depending upon one's own identification with the symbolic order and/or eyesight) of Hillary's "coke-bottle thick" glasses is part of the cure: Bill's comeback is accompanied by the adoption of Bill's last name (de-Rodhamization), hair dye, and contact lenses. Indeed, it is rare to find such a high degree of conformity in all types of accounts (friendly or hostile, high or low culture, children's books, biographies of Bill Clinton or the First Lady). This repeated intertwining of Bill's political comeback and Hillary's fashion makeover almost reads like an elaborately crafted alibi. For the stories told in the different media are related in compellingly similar detail.

Let us begin with Doane on the trope of a woman with glasses as a condensed signifier. The primal scene of the Clinton-Rodham romance is recounted in a children's book, as it is presented in other noteworthy accounts such as Marraniss's biography of President Clinton and Elizabeth Drew's portrait of Clinton's first term:

> Bill Clinton was talking with a friend in the Yale Law School library when he was distracted. A young woman wearing a flannel shirt and thick glasses was sitting at the other end of the room reading. He couldn't stop staring at her. When she looked up from her book, she noticed him watching her and she stared back. Finally she shut her book, walked down to where Bill sat and said, "Look, if you're going to keep staring at me and I'm going to keep staring back, I think we should introduce ourselves. I'm Hillary Rodham. What's your name?"

Completely taken by surprise, Bill for a moment forgot his name. "I was embarrassed," he says now. "It turned out she knew who I was. But I was really surprised and we've been together, more or less, ever since."[77]

The *Vanity Fair* version of this story concludes: "I was *dumbstruck*. I couldn't think of my name:"[78] This often-repeated anecdote can be read as a hyperbolized reverse formation—a cross- or trans-gendered narrative of seduction. In the conventional format, the woman with glasses takes them off and is transformed from a repressed and undesirable person into a privileged libidinal object for male scopic consumption. "Glasses" (especially "thick" ones) represent sexual repression, as well as condensing "knowledge, visibility and vision, intellectuality and undesirability."[79] This scene of mutual staring is gender reversed. Hillary gives Bill her "best line"—she already knows his name. It is also an erotic cabinet scene, taking place in the Yale Law School Library (described as Gothic and cloistered). The seduction works as an instance of a woman's active looking. Hillary looks—unsurps the gaze as well as denaturalizes the sexual alignment of the scopic economy (seeing/being seen). Like Rivière's intellectual woman, she looks. Rather than being punished, however, Bill is literally *medusé* by her—struck dumb. He forgets his name. (We will return to the gaze of Medusa.)

Children's books have a particularly direct way of stating the instrumental terms of the makeover:

> In order to help her husband with the next election, Hillary allowed herself to be "made over." Ever since she was sixteen, Hillary had tried to wear contact lenses, but she couldn't get *hard* contact lenses to stay in her eyes. After Bill's 1980 defeat, Hillary got *soft* contact lenses to replace her thick glasses. She began using makeup, dyeing her hair blond, and wearing fashionable suits and dresses instead of the baggy sweaters she preferred. The biggest change, however, was giving up her maiden name. When Bill and Hillary were married, she kept the last name of her family—Rodham—rather than changing it to Clinton. Before the 1992 campaign, Hillary Rodham became Hillary Rodham Clinton.[80]

> With her thick glasses and shapeless sweaters and her refusal to wear makeup, she did not look like the First Lady of Arkansas. Worst of all, she had kept her family name—Rodham—rather than changing her name to Clinton when she married Bill.[81]

Glasses, hair, new clothes, and a change of names are linked, and all are necessary for the complete Rodhamization of Hillary. Rather than seeing the change of name as a submission, I would like to play on the phallic associations the media displays where "Rodham" comes to stand for the phallus itself. In an account of the First Lady's Symposium on Children of the Americas published in the *Washington Post*, Joel Achenbach describes the choreographed scene: "Mrs. Clinton carried papers with her. The other First Ladies, *incompletely Rodhamized*, had purses."[82] The phallic opposition between Hillary (who has it—both the papers/briefs and the Rodham) and the other First Ladies could not be clearer (purses, lack of papers). And yet, the completely Rodhamized Hillary is wearing a very femme outfit in pastel ("creme de menthe"), in contrast to the colorful power suits of the other First Ladies ("as boldly colorful as lifesavers"). Hillary's hair was also not obviously phallic/helmet hair. A Georgette Klinger spokesperson described it as "a very natural, soft, gentle cut, slightly underturned in the lower area" (in other words, a *page boy*). The dizzying juxtaposition of a femme Rodham, still sporting a page boy, suggests less a submissive successful "makeover" than a performance of powerful gender-fuck drag. It is the fully Rodhamized Hillary in her femme outfits that flaunt not just femininity as Rivière's patients did but parody masculinity and all gender assignments. This is why it does not work as successful "seduction" but induces an estrangement effect that in turn produces a verbal counteroffensive—the desire to "Rodhamize" her with her own name.

What makes Hillary's performances so interesting to me is that the cosmetic "makeover" is alluded to precisely in a context of a staged symposium—a surreal event "like make-believe governance, an exercise in the correct identification of the obvious." Here, Achenbach is describing the summit—not a drag performance—but the fact that this description could ably describe *both* drag ball and presidential performance is unsettling. It suggests that the range of the masquerade might not be restricted to the First Lady's hair and clothes, implying that politics should be read as or shares some affinities with costume drama. Commenting upon an earlier staged event involving a First Lady and an actress who plays Cleopatra ("America's two Queens: Jackie vs. Liz"), Wayne Koestenbaum suggests that this is indeed America's national fantasy. When Jackie Kennedy responded to her intense mediatization— "What does my hairstyle have to do with my husband's ability to be President?"—*Cleopatra* implies that the realms of "presidency" and "hairstyle" are not easily separated. (Think of JFK's constant haircuts, or Reagan's shiny, shoeblack cowlick.)" [83]

This long excursion on the name of the father—Rodham—and its link to other sites of visual cathexis (glasses, clothes, hair) is included to signal that we are dealing not with an instrumentalist-rational calculus but rather with an attack on the symbolic order itself. What we see with Hillary is not a realignment of political power, unsurping Al Gore's role as vice president (he gets REGO, she gets REDO), as much as it is a questioning of its gendered foundations. "The correct identification of the obvious" is missed both by those sympathetic to Hillary and by the bashers. But we should also note that the "correct identification of the obvious" is perhaps the most formidable task of politics and is peculiarly vulnerable to parodic subversion.

In more than one sense, Al Gore is a man who knows too much. In the context of the *Washington Post* article on the Baltimore Symposium, he asks: "What is she, *Madonna*? I don't think so. She doesn't have to *reinvent* herself after every album." Note the artifactuality of "What"— not the more conventional "who." This Hillary is a "what," an artifact like Madonna. Tipper Gore also warns an inquiring reporter about to do an article on Hillary not to "genderize." One should always listen very carefully to Tipper's "No"—for there is something symptomatic in her (and Al's) utterances. For Hillary has been "insufficiently gender-ized" by the media, which have read only part of her performance.

Let us reexamine some of the sites of press scopic fixation on Hillary to regenderize her (and Rodhamize them?).

Heads in hieroglyphic bonnets
Heads in turbans and black birettas
Heads in wigs and thousand other wretched, sweating heads of hair.

—Heine[84]

Comb my hair, oh!
Comb my hair, That will cure me;
. It must be combed. Look at my head
How I suffer and my hair hurts me so
(as though I were handling snakes).

—Guy de Maupassant[85]

Always look at the hairstyle when studying evanescence.

—Wayne Koestenbaum[86]

No reading of Hillary would be complete without a discussion of her hair. Hillary's hair, like Imelda's shoes, is a presumed site of obsession and fetishization. It appears to be the most obvious symptom (but of what and for whom?). Hillary's hair is the armature of a national cathexis, a part-object that attaches itself to social issues and is a chronicle of the first three years in office. Jim Borgman's cartoon for the *Cincinnati Enquirer* is an end-of-millennium rewrite of the eighteenth-century *coiffures parlantes* (speaking hairstyles).[87] Hairstylists in the eighteenth century were attuned to the symbolic (political as well as erotic) dimension of hair. Hair marked rites of passage (loss of loved ones), commemorated political events (*"la coiffure à l'insurgent"* heralded political revolution), and contested the phallic order (*"la coiffure à la Dauphine"* was a gender crossover of a female hairdo that resembled a peacock's tail). Chantal Thomas notes that hyperbolic hair fashions demanded an extensive vocabulary and that the hairstylist had to "combine the talent of an architect" with the ability of a journalist ("to show himself capable of chronicling the daily news"). Apter notes that in Benjamin's Arcades project (*Passagen-werk*), "enhanced" hair is given pride of place as an erotic fetish as well as a mediation between consumer culture and gender assignment.[88]

Wayne Koestenbaum describes Jackie Kennedy's hair in a language that resonates with both Rivière and the American exceptionalist mission: "They are excessive hairdos. In their artifice, they are nearly obscene; or their monumentality surpasses the 'proper' function of a hairdo. So large is the hair, it seems a mission." Jackie's "enhanced" hair also has names: "brioche," "slash bangs," "bouffant," "chignon." Such large, artificial, laminated, stiff hair, Koestenbaum writes, "contains" and "composes" her like a "turtle" or an "armadillo." (It reminds me of the astronaut's wives' hair in *The Right Stuff*.) This is hair as the ego's armature, hair as bunker; it is a defensive projection and is resolutely phallic: "It is the battle gear of a woman of means." It is Medusa hair, apoptropaic, crafting a "momentary dominatrix, putting opponents (photographers, public, husbands in their place)." Yet there is considerable instability in this figuration, at once battle gear (offensive) and defensive weaponry, defending Jackie and potentially deflecting an assassin's bullet in Dallas: "Her hairdos remind me of the bubbletop over the presidential convertible—the bubbletop that *should* have been lowered in Dallas."[89]

There is something about Jackie's hair that "eludes photographic rendering" (i.e., "a mini mushroom cloud that billows in excess of its source").[90] Yet Hillary's hair can be read, photographically, microscopically, under a loupe; it is overexposed. Hillary's hair is not just the object of comic/media parody but also one of the few sites of her own self-irony: "How many of you counted the different hairstyles in the slides? I go to nineteen and quit."[91] Rather than reread Hillary's hair as one more aspect of her makeover and Bill's comeback, some clue to her hypocrisy or cynicism, or as a metonym for political expediency, I will argue that Hillary's hair stands less for her own vacillations than for the latent instabilities of all gender identity, which is why it is so powerful as an object of scopic fascination. This is in contrast with Jackie's hair, which fixed her as the icon's frame, allowing worship. Jackie's hair partakes of the reactive defensive uses of the masquerade. Her performance is less affirmative but is compensatory and not threatening. Although its hyperbolic crafting does suggest that codes of femininity are not "natural," it results in an idealized iconicity. All ambivalence and sadism (the all-too-human correlates of idealization) get displaced or downloaded onto Pat Nixon, Lady Bird, or their offspring or second husbands/stepchildren. (Or perhaps Jackie works according to the logic of desire over identification?)

Hair in the Clinton administration has taken on epic—indeed, mythic —proportions. In Drew's chronicle of the travails of the first year in office, the president's haircut on (h)Air Force One occurs between Travelgate and Vince Foster's suicide.[92] National obsession with the presidential haircut is twinned with and metonymically linked to Hillary's traumas—the firings in the travel office and the alleged Whitewater coverup, as well as the suicide of her friend and colleague Vince Foster. But I would not like to reduce the Clinton presidency to a few bad-hair days. There is something uncanny at work here. For in Hillary's hair (together with her glasses/gaze) we can see the phallic nemesis of the Medusa.

> Thy gory locks at me
> Are you a man?
>   —*Macbeth*, Act 3, Scene 4

One of the more banal caricatures of powerful First Ladies such as Hillary is that they are "Lady Macbeth." Their French equivalents, Claude Pompidou (the original lamp-throwing lesbian) and Danielle Mitterrand, are "Andromaques of the Fifth Republic."[93] If I were stranded on a desert island with only one piece of Hillary bashing, the choice would be clear—Daniel Wattenberg's "Boy Clinton's Big Mama: The Lady Macbeth of Little Rock." This article, initially brought to my attention by Patricia Williams's reading of it in *The Rooster's Egg*, compelled me to reread *Macbeth* for the first time in years.[94] "Lady Macbeth," like "Machiavelli," is one of those cultural markers that, in Barthesian fashion, are more "received" than "read." The stereotype is of a conventional harpy—a phallic woman who nags her husband and hounds him into committing unspeakable acts, one characterized by "consuming ambition, inflexibility of purpose, domination of a pliable husband, and an unsettling lack of tender human feeling along with . . . contempt for traditional female roles."[95] The gender roles are stereotypic—"the power behind the throne"—and are unnuanced. Imagine my surprise when I actually reread the play in the context of Hillary and saw how apposite it was with Butler's (and Garber's) conceptions of gender identity. Rather than offer secure gender assignments for Lady Macbeth and her husband, the play raises questions of sexual indeterminacy: "Are you a man?," "Un-sex me here," and "to be not of woman born" are just a few of the memorable sound bites from this play. And this sexual limbo and boundary crossing are thoroughly implicated with hair:

You should be woman, and yet your beards forbid me to interpret that you are so.

Do I yield to that suggestion whose horrid image doth unfix my hair . . .

to hear a right shriek and my fall of hair . . .

Banquo's "gory locks" and severed body parts ("Here I have a pilot's thumb") suggest that the question of political power is both thoroughly gendered *and* undecidable. Garber's reading of *Macbeth* as a "male Medusa" figure is, for me, the clearest formulation of the tremendous anxiety Hillary provokes—not because she is a castrating, punitive superego but because of the imbrication of political power with gender undecidability. In Garber's words: "power in *Macbeth* is a function of neither male nor female, but of the suspicion of the undecidable. The phallus as a floating signifier is more powerful than when definitely assigned to any gender."[96]

Hair and eyes figure prominently in the Medusa story. In ways not incidental to the Medusa legend, the anecdote of Bill and Hillary's first meeting needs to be amended. For the encounter (Hillary's active return of Bill's gaze) was preceded by an earlier incident of hair smelling. Bill follows Hillary out of class, smells her hair, says to himself, "This is trouble," and stops. The smell of Hillary's hair stops Bill in his tracks, as her chilling glance will later devastate others.[97] "You need to take those two paragraphs out, *because Hillary will see them* and if she sees them you'll be dead."[98] Dick Morris echoes this sentiment after his post-Maraniss book ostracism: "There is no colder feeling on the planet."[99]

"To Be Not of Woman Born"

The masquerade, unlike tranvestism, is about the creation of a distance, the repudiation of the "nearness" and "realness" of gender assignment. Hillary's hair, like Jackie's, is both a hieroglyph and iconic. One can indeed read Hillary's hairdos allegorically (as Wayne Koestenbaum does for Jackie), as Stations of the Cross. Her hair functions as a fetish and has its rhetorical part to play in the construction of the "Medusa effect" in the media narrative. But what is for me the most pertinent aspect of Hillary's hair is its detachable quality—its artifice. And this artifice creates a gap precisely at those moments when there should be congruence or seamlessness. Hillary's body—a conventional metonym for her femininity—becomes "unmasked" as contrived when she presents her bona fides as a child and family advocate. There is a passage in *It Takes a Village* that is startling in how much it conveys the unnaturalness of Hillary's own body. It concerns what should be a moment of "nearness" of femininity: maternity.

> There I was lying in my hospital bed, trying desperately to figure out how to breast-feed. I had been trained to study everything forward, backward and upside down before reaching a conclusion. *It seemed to me I ought to be able to figure this out.* As I looked down in horror, Chelsea started to foam at the nose. I thought she was strangling or having convulsions. Frantically I pushed every buzzer there was to push. . . . Chelsea was taking in my milk but because of the awkward way I held her, she was breathing it out of her nose.[100]

Rather than revealing the maternal beatitude usually associated with the first moments of mother-daughter bonding, the hospital scene is decidedly not a Hallmark moment—a combination of *Alien* and *The Exorcist*. One's own body and that of one's spewing child are not part of one's corporeal integrity but appear as part of the unmasterable superhuman forces. This view of maternity as highly unnatural and horrific is reminiscent of Linda Zerilli's Kristevan reading of de Beauvoir's maternity chapter in *The Second Sex*.[101] It is a moment of profound abjection. Rather than "humanizing" Hillary by showing how she's just one of us, or demonstrating the inevitable invincibility of maternity over reason, this episode presents Hillary as Chelsea's *unnatural biological mother*.

Chelsea's birth is described in the opening moment of *It Takes a Village*. It provides both a guarantee of Hillary's expertise as a child advocate ("I have spent much of the past twenty-five years working to improve the lives of children") and an acknowledgment of the limit of the social ("Despite all the books I had read, all the children I had studied and advocated for, nothing prepared me for the sheer miracle of her being"). And yet there is something very unnatural about giving birth to one's own child: "For the first time, I understood the words of the writer Elizabeth Stone: 'Making the decision to have a child—it's wondrous. *It is to decide forever to have your heart go walking around outside your body.*'"[102] While many who have had protracted labor have wished for an "out-of-body" experience, this is certainly not a *normative* rendering of femininity. Ostensibly about the wonder of motherhood, the pages on Chelsea's birth underline how unnatural "femininity-motherhood" is for Hillary: "Think of a baby like a football and hold it tight." She goes into labor and free-associates about ice sucking and the *Titanic*: "I remembered what a woman reportedly said as she was helped over the railing of the Titanic: 'I rang for ice, but this is ridiculous!'"[103] Unfortunate associations with the Titanic include disaster, inadequate or unjust planning, shipwreck, loss of control, submersion, and hypothermia, none of which are synonymic with idealized or normative motherhood.

For a long time I wondered about why Hillary chose to share these moments with us in what is otherwise a policy book. They appear as aberrant textual moments but can perhaps be understood according to the logic of Rivière's patients, as a masquerade in reverse, a *Victor, Victoria* logic. Rivière's patients try to undo their "artificial" masculinity by putting on feminine behavior. Here, Hillary undoes the "natural" nearness of femininity to establish her policy bona fides. The cover of the book is very "femme" blue (which, Garber recounts, used to be the color for girls; pink was seen as a stronger, more aggressive color).[104] Hillary is sporting a 1950s shirtwaist, and her hair is in a blond feminine flip.

I think what is disturbing here is the way that Hillary plays on both sides of the ambivalence that Mary Anne Doane notes in her "Masquerade Reconsidered"; she appears to both show how femininity is constructed as a mask and also how it is a defensive reaction formation that reposes on a masculine logic. Hillary intrigues because she appears to suggest that both terms of masquerade's ambivalence can be instrumentalized when reversed (when there is a transgendered identification) if strategically disavowed (as in strategic passing). This might suggest, *contra* Doane, that the masquerade could be more than a compensatory gesture. But it is not insignificant that this legitimation of a masculine logic (in Doane's terms) does tend to work, as in the case of welfare reform, against those very mothers and children she would seem to be an advocate for.

The political question, to which we will return in chapter 9, is how we distinguish between exploitative appropriations of the masquerade and enabling identifications with it. Yet, due to the fundamental ambivalence of identification, even attempts at strategic appropriations, however well intentioned, may not fully yield the political possibilities (i.e., ethical or political alliances) envisioned.[105] Conversely, even if Hillary's enactments are ultimately judged as cynical or "imitative" gender masquerades, this should not serve as masquerade's ultimate referendum. Rejecting a certain enactment, practice, or author, in Gayle Wald's astute formulation, should not "leave us in the difficult position of also abjuring the very political possibilities associated with the transgression."[106]

7

"Honey, I Shrunk the President"

Psychoanalysis, Postmodernism, and the Clinton Presidency (1997/1998)

Bill Clinton burst into cackling laughter one day in 1982 as he related what a friend had told him a day or two before. "Bill, there's
just something about you that pisses people off." Clinton found it
funny. . . . He reacted with mostly egoistic self-entertainment, but
it seemed that a bit of introspection would have been appropriate
as well.
—John Brummett[1]

L'Intraitable: *The Unanalyzable One (1997)*

For the past five years I have not been able to watch President Clinton.
This unwatchability is tied to a peculiar lack of transference, which
I believe results not from the unpresidential-like stature of a fellow
boomer. Nor does this lack of transference result from the ambivalently
gendered Clintonian performance—that is, a postpaternal, post-Oedipal, postphallic presidency giving way to a regime of the brothers or, in
this case, Bubbas.[2] Rather, it is due to the profound mutation that Clinton has introduced into the presidential thing, a move parallel to the
epistemic rupture of the *virtual* characteristic of Baudrillard's most recent work, *The Perfect Crime*. The presidency of Bill Clinton represents
the next stage of Baudrillardian sign theory: the presidency as a pure or
fatal object that can successfully evade the attempts of analysts to snare
it. Exploring the methodological impasse of the president as fatal object
will necessitate many detours. For, although fatal objects cannot be
dominated and hence loved, one can, with a little work, learn to enjoy a
perverse esthetic *jouissance* with them. Here is one girl's story.

My reading of the late-twentieth-century presidents has been premised on a theoretical progress narrative in which presidents represent

different moments of Baudrillard's sign theory. Reagan as the *hyperreal* and Bush as the *trompe l'oeil* instantiate the difference between the image repertoire of simulation and the symbolic order of seduction. With Clinton, we move into the virtuality of the pure (presidential) object, its technical perfection. This move signals different political consequences and aesthetic modalities that I will briefly outline. For the Baudrillardean virtual introduces subtle permutations into postmodern communications theory, as the political spectacle is replaced by the reality show.[3] Reality shows abolish the distance between audience and screen/stage as we have "ingested our receivers." "Telepresence," as opposed to (critical) distance, is characteristic of the virtual as we live our disappearance in real time.[4] As reality shows bring us inside the screen, they transform spectatorship. No longer couch potatoes, we have become citizen extras in the virtual democratic community.

And yet all this is met not without a certain resistance. Paradoxically, our most "unanalyzable" president has been the subject of unparalleled psychobiographical, lay psychoanalytic explanations that have disturbed presidential personality experts such as Fred Greenstein.[5] The first symptom of Clinton's unanalyzability is this very profusion of clinical terminology and the pathological scripting of the presidential body. Depicting Clinton, as we will see, variously as "compulsive," "obsessive," "schizophrenic," "appetitive," "voraciously oral," a daytime TV vocabulary permeates the presentation of Clinton as an "enabler" and "codependent" and the survivor of a dysfunctional family.[6] A language of personality disorder more characteristic of the *Diagnostic and Statistical Manual,* fourth edition (DSM-IV), is metonymically tied to his administration and to his policy-making process ("group therapy").

Both this *will to analyze* and its particular insistent clinical rhetorical formation, I will argue, are signs of a "reality-show" president. Political pundits become televisual mental health experts; *après* O. J., we're all forensic pathologists. This "will to psychological interpretation" implicitly addresses the Clinton presidency as what Laplanche has called "an enigmatic signifier." An enigmatic signifier is a *signifier of,* as opposed to a *signifier to,* a signifier to a specific signified. One can know that something signifies (i.e., it is a signifier of something) without being able to locate or fix its precise meaning (i.e., a signifier *to* a referent). It would be comparable to Christopher Bollas's idea of the "unthought known."[7] This enigmatic quality is rendered even more tantalizing because of Clinton's compelling *telepresence*: his seeming transparency, the latency of his (omni)visibility. Elizabeth Drew notes the coextensivity of the Clinton presidency with the vernaculars of popular culture: "Clinton stepped into the culture, became part of it."[8] Other observers of Clinton's presidency note its figural congruence with virtual media of screen and interface. As Michael Kelly notes:

> The president's face is a *screen* upon which plays a loop of expressions that have been consistently familiar: the open mouth grin of joyous wonder, the scowl of righteous but controlled anger; the lip biting, eyes lowered glance of pondering humility, the near tears of a man who is not afraid to show that he feels. In an important sense, these expressions are entirely honest; Clinton's empathy is wholly real. But it exists only in the moment . . . everything is true for him when he says it, because he says it. Clinton means what he says when he says it, but tomorrow he will mean what he says when he says the opposite.[9]

Drew's and Kelly's depictions of Clinton's televisuality recall Baudrillard's existential query in *The Perfect Crime*: "What would we be in real time? We would be identified at each moment with ourselves. A torment equivalent to that of eternal daylight—an epilepsy of presence, an epilepsy of identity."[10] Unlike Reagan, another televisual president, Clinton is most at ease unscripted, without a teleprompter, perfectly enmeshed with his medium and his audience. If Reagan was the prepackaged soundbite, an easy- or passive-listening president, Clinton is more like jazz: improvisational, narratively episodic and experimental, demanding active (or interactive) listening.

Clinton is amazingly coextensive with the medium of television—at home with Larry King, seamless with Donahue and Oprah and when paying a guest visit to *Beavis and Butthead*. Drew wonders, "Did the American people want a Phil Donahue in the President?"[11] One can compare cinematic quotations from Reagan's oeuvre with Clinton's merging with the television age as all of the preferred programs of the boomer generation get recycled as movies ("the remake" as the hallmark of Clintonian cinema, as well as the "presidential adventure" film, where the boomer gets to cast himself in the primal scene as dad/president).[12] Clinton has used the alternative TV networks of CNN and especially MTV. Indeed, Elizabeth Drew's reading of Clinton's deliberate demystification of the presidency privileges an MTV primal scene: when Clinton answered the question about "boxers or briefs." "Telling a questioner on MTV that he wore briefs, he *wiped away* much of the mystique of the office, took risks with the authority of the office. In due course he was out there *without any protective wrapping*. Clinton had become an *undifferentiated* president" (emphasis mine).[13]

And, perversely, it is Bill Clinton's own televisual striptease, his evasion of the authority of office, that compels his onlookers to reclothe him in the vestments of psychoanalysis. For what is there left to say about a president who sartorially bares all—he wears briefs and then gives away his *used underwear* as a tax write-off?[14] Let us leave aside for the moment the obvious Lacanian question of whether the (presidential) phallus can work only if veiled (and not discursively de-briefed). It might be useful to recall the 1986 debriefing of the presidential penis incidental to Reagan's bladder (discussed in our previous reading of Iran-Contra). Larry Speakes, giving a medical update in the briefing room, used a precise denotative language: "under local anesthesia, an instrument is inserted into the penis and goes up the urinary tract." (This transparency of language contrasts with Speakes's obvious *jouissance* in recounting the incident: "Public discussion of the president's penis —yes, it happened in the Reagan White House—on my watch.")[15] Clinton's stripping off of the authority of office, however, becomes an *enigma*—that is, an object that offers itself up in total transparency but cannot be naturalized or absorbed by either critical or aesthetic discourse.

Or can it? Can psychoanalysis master (re-master) the virtual telepresent reality show president?

All the President's Analysts

I reiterate: one of the most pronounced symptoms of Clinton's unanalyzability (his resistance to both interpretation and transference) is the very proliferation of attempted analyses, a will to interpret whose rhetorical inflections are congruent with the daytime talk-show confessional, the hyperbole of the news magazine (*Dateline*), and the feigned intimacy of the television interview (Larry King, Barbara Walters). Let's look more closely at this discursive formation. For critics, fans, and ambivalent boomers (a pleonasm?), despite divergent political and normative assessments of the Clinton presidency, share discursive similarities, forming a body of work I call the presidential pathography. I will be focusing on the presidential biographies and the biographical feature story

(*The New Yorker, Vanity Fair* magazine, the *New York Times*).[16] The two most obvious rhetorical markers of Clintonian biography are the trope of *hyperbole* and the clinical assessment.

Presidential chronicling is a genre, like biography, prone to rhetorical overstatement and theatrical presentation. The stock-in-trade is the anecdote or Barthesian *biographeme*; the "little real" of realist narrative that all good journalists since Balzac strive for.[17] What is peculiar to the Clinton biographical presentation (as opposed to those of Reagan and Bush) is the clinical turn within this discourse—toward the pathogenic or, more properly speaking, the anomalous (that which escapes the jurisdiction of the norm/normative). Moreover, it seems to make little difference if the author of the account is an "objective" journalist like Elizabeth Drew (who practices a "middle-level journalism"; she catches events while they are still fresh "before they become . . . retouched in recollection" but also "offers some analysis")[18] or a former disgruntled staffer such as Jeffrey Birnbaum (*Madhouse*), a right-wing think-tank author (Dr. Fick), or a boomer seething with resentment such as David Maraniss (why him? out of all the people of my generation? Maraniss asks in *First in His Class*; the unspoken question is "Why him and not me?") All these different subject positions produce a coherent discursive block.

The titles of narrative accounts of Clinton's years in office are suggestive of this rhetorical turn: *Madhouse*, "A Fever in the White House," "It All Co-Depends," *High Wire* (with the first chapter entitled "A Real Life Psychodrama"), *On the Edge,* and, the *ne plus ultra* of the genre, Dr. Paul Fick's *The Dysfunctional President: Inside the Mind of Bill Clinton.* All of these titles suggest a pathogenic, out-of-control presidential subject—a Regis Philbin presidency. (Have we just moved from one Dana Carvey imitation—Bush—to another—Philbin, remaining within the *topos* of the hysterical male? No, for Carvey's Philbin is different—it entered the real! Carvey as Philbin actually replaced the on-vacation Philbin—in a hallucination of the real that perhaps only Baudrillard and Kathie Lee Gifford could appreciate.)

Not only the titles of narrative accounts but also adjectives and modifiers used to describe Clinton underscore his "excessive" nature. There is something obviously *démesuré* about him; he is "overeager," has an oversized index finger (Maraniss) and an "outsized need for reassurance" (Drew). He "overloads his agenda." In all accounts, Clinton is a voracious appetitive creature who "ate a lot, worked hard, talked a lot," a "food binger" (Peter Boyer) whose corporeal intransigence is further underscored by those "baggy Donna Karan suits that emphasize his bulk" (Drew) and by his Secret Service code name, Elvis (Allen and Portis). Everything about him is excessive: he has "platoons of friends" (Allen and Portis) and is someone who started his Rolodex in kindergarten; he has "volcanic self-pity" (Dowd) and "dizzying brain power, awesome policy command, disarming charm—virtually impossible to dislike in a personal meeting, a man of mind-boggling accomplishments" (Brummett) and is, for Maraniss, simply "the best politician of his generation."[19]

And yet it is just one metonymic slide from the hyperbole of the presidential hagiography to the clinical assessment: it's all too much. Allen and Portis's "voracious reader" who read more than three hundred books while at Oxford is labeled "compulsively overactive." Richard Cohen dubs Clinton's (over)eagerness "the president's compulsion." The hard work and endurance of the presidential progress narrative slide into masochism as Clinton's remarks on assuming the governorship ("I'll break my back to help my state"), his closing tirade in a *Rolling Stone* interview, and his performance at the 1988 Democratic Convention ("I fell on my sword") are evidence of a profound masochism. A man of large appetites with a penchant for large southern breakfasts is the "bulimic" of Peter Boyer's account. Clinton's charm is also, for Boyer, a manifestation of *don juanism*; he is "the greatest seducer who ever lived." Clinton's interest in Kennedy (and his identification with him) is called a "Kennedy *fixation*," with "Kennedy as a sexual compulsive role model."[20]

This discourse would appear more appropriate to the supermarket checkout line, yet, because of its omnipresence—on the op-ed pages of the *New York Times,* in the intellectual high-prestige pages of *The New Yorker* and *The Nation,* and from respectable journalists such as Drew and Maraniss—the tabloid turn in presidential depiction goes unmarked as symptom. It is difficult to remember the shock and outrage that attended Kitty Kelley's biography of Nancy Reagan. This tabloid rendering of the presidency is consumed by people who never watch daytime TV (only PBS) or never read the *Enquirer.* There's no longer any need to. I do not want this to read as one more cry of outrage about the desacralization of the presidency or a diatribe against tabloid consumer culture. I want merely to mark its specificity. For Nancy's astrologer was seen as an aberration, a moment of rupture in narrative accounts of Reagan's presidency in a way Hillary's channeling of Eleanor simply is not.[21] What interests me here is two developments in the rhetoric surrounding the presidency: the facility with which what were formerly restricted medical and clinical diagnoses are meted out *and* the foregrounding of our own libidinal investments in the presidency. The profound identification engendered by this telepresent president is best stated by Dowd's "We are the President," recalling the transgendered Flaubertian cry "I am Madame Bovary." With a peculiar twist in the hands of a Frank Rich, a John Brummett, or a David Maraniss: "His schizophrenia is ours." Or, as the *New York Times* states: "Even those who hate him love him."[22]

How has Clinton been diagnosed by his "analysts"?

(1) President Clinton suffers from "multiple presidency disorder." He suffers from profound *disassociation*. There are several Bill Clintons who are all genuine (Elizabeth Drew,[23] David Maraniss, John Brummett, Robert Reich, Dick Morris). There is the energetic Clinton, the populist Clinton, the highly connected Clinton, the wonk, the poor Southerner, the East Coast elitist—a man, in Frank Rich's words, of both "high ideals and narcissistic pragmatism."[24] Dowd asks: "Which Bill Clinton does one know and how long will that one be around?" If Bush and Reagan were constant, fixed points of identification, Clinton is the Mighty Morphing President: "Everything is synthesis, nothing is fixed." MPD (Multiple Presidency Disorder) is linked with schizophrenia and regression to adolescence: "The president as adolescent is good and bad, idealist, energetic, still learning *and* self-indulgent, lacking in discipline and has volcanic self pity."[25]

The typical day of the president is congruent with this depiction. In the morning, Clinton throws a juvenile temper tantrum; later on in the afternoon, he gives a wise, moving speech about race relations, then he is the "slack jawed celebrity groupie." He takes a defiant stand with Rushdie and apologizes to Muslims later on. He can change in midsentence, as in his April 20 photo op: "The U.S. should always seek an opportunity to stand up against—or at least speak out against—inhumanity" (quite a disparity within one sentence!).[26] MPD is the reason Clinton can't control his image, resulting in a "stature gap." Just when Clinton appears to be in control of his image, in September 1994, he appears in a blue windbreaker holding a football—"Are you ready for some football?" Or, after a solid presidential performance, giving a moving speech at Oklahoma City after the bombing, he can go on Larry

King and do a Marlon Brando imitation. Clinton is both capable of political shrewdness (Les Aspin's forced resignation) and terrible political misjudgment (Bobby Ray Inman's nomination) *over the same* political appointment.

Variation 1a (a subset of MPD): "a co-dependent enabler suffering from multiple presidency disorder who is so open to suggestion as to be practically an empath." Clinton does suffer from Multiple Presidency Disorder, but he can't do it alone. He needs former President Carter, a "classic Pacifist Aggressor." Each has become the other's enabler: Carter defuses crises, while Clinton allows himself to become ensnared in them, in the words of Joe Klein (*Primary Colors*), "carrying his personal shitstorm with him."[27] Like the characters in *Strange Days*,[28] or the character Empath on *Star Trek, The Next Generation*, Clinton as empath can literally feel your pain or at least morph into something that looks like he does.

Variation 1b (differential diagnosis): garden-variety "splitting." Clinton has two modes, politician "realist" and Boy Scout idealist. As "politician," he tries to win; as Boy Scout, he "enjoys." "When he needs to be a politician, he is, but he enjoys the Boy Scout role much more. And he constantly separates his idealist and politician modes, consciously keeping the purity of the one apart from the pragmatism of the other." In psychopedagogical fashion, Morris instructs us: "Psychiatrists call it splitting when someone fails to integrate good and bad in a unified coherent personality."[29] The alternation of "mind sets" accounts for his various comebacks: winning the governorship in 1982 (politician), assuming the Boy Scout mode in 1994 (a posture that persisted through the 1996 election).

(2) President Clinton suffers from *boundary confusion*, characteristic of a *borderline personality* who lacks identity integration and mature defenses. These boundary issues are evidenced in his relation with Hillary. John Brummett's introductory chapter to *High Wire: The Education of Bill Clinton* ("A Real-Life Psychodrama") gives several humorous examples of Clinton's boundary and identity confusions:

> This was the man who in 1988 drank the water from the glass that other leading Democrats in Arkansas had passed along the head table towards Lloyd Bentsen, who was speaking in Hot Springs. . . . Bentsen needed to clear his *throat, as everyone in the convention center except Clinton* had sensed. Then there was the time Clinton took his family

to Disneyworld. As he stood in line, he spotted a family whose attire promoted the University of Arkansas Razorbacks, his favorite team. Presuming the family members were from Arkansas, he went back to engage in the proper gubernatorial behavior and speak to them. He departed by telling them "Thank you for coming" as if he were Walt Disney himself.[30]

(3) Clinton is a premature adult who felt primal abandonment and used his rage to drive forward, mediating ever-higher levels of conflict. Clinton is presented as a garden-variety neurotic (who, like the rest of us, suffers from repetition compulsion and self-destructive tendencies). What is scarier still is the implied banality of it all; according to Paul Fick, "Clinton represents the group of Americans commonly seen in outpatient psychotherapy offices."[31] Before turning to Fick's remarkable study, *The Dysfunctional President: Inside the Mind of Bill Clinton*, I would like to offer Elizabeth Drew's "objective" presentation of both Gingrich and Clinton (in *Showdown*) as a more modulated example of this discursive regime:

> Both were bulky (Gingrich the bulkier), both came from middle class families and dysfunctional families including missing fathers, adoring mothers, problematic relationships with adoptive fathers and were examples of meritocracy; both were garrulous, both had to show off, both had deep flaws and histories of infidelity.[32]

It's a small world, after all! How is this pan-dysfunctionality constructed? Drew's depiction implicitly equates the middle-class family with dysfunction as the metonymic contagion between enumerated family members (missing fathers, adoring mothers, problematic adoptive fathers, and the people who love them) and the so-called normative American nuclear family. This is further underscored by the democratic values inherent in "examples of meritocracy." Drew has rewritten "nuclear family," allying it with dysfunction.

"I'd Rather Have a Bottle in Front of Me Than a Frontal Lobotomy" (Country-Western Song Title)

The slippage between clinical and biographical presentations of the president (as well as the House Speaker) de-authorizes and renormativizes Clinton in a most perverse and interesting way. Alexis de Tocqueville meets Michel Foucault: "We're all potentially twelve-steppers now." What both the clinical assessment and the biological/medical stigmatization ("Hillary is a *congenital* liar"; Clinton is a pathological one) address is the notion of a cure. Something is wrong with the president's body; the president needs treatment; the president can be helped. We witness the merging of the King's two bodies—and they both need treatment.

Fick's book *The Dysfunctional President* and the diagnosis of Clinton's cognitive disabilities by Edith Efron in "Can the President Think?" (published in *Reason* magazine) are extreme formulations of a clinical depiction of a sitting president. Efron sees the president as cognitively impaired because of an "obsessive compulsive" personality disorder and reads President Clinton's remarks in various interviews against the *Diagnostic and Statistical Manual of Mental Disorders* (DSM-IIIR), soon to be required reading for any presidential expert.

Efron sees Clinton's cognitive functioning as meeting five of the DSM-IIIR criteria, citing his "perfectionism, preoccupation with detail, inability to establish priorities, avoidance or postponement of decision making, poor time allocation, and an insistence that he be in control."[33] She believes that Clinton received the DSM-IIIR diagnosis of obsessive-compulsive personality disorder while undergoing family counseling after his brother's cocaine bust and that this is the reason Clinton's full medical records have never been released. Fick sees the president's problem as more properly "behavioral" than cognitive (i.e., the president can think; he's just emotionally disturbed). While these explicit and overt clinical readings are at times so laughable as to appear parodic (as in the collected essays "Oral Sadism and the Vegetarian Personality" with its essay on "Psychoanalysis of the Dead"),[34] they are not easily dismissed, as they merely condense in a more obvious form the rhetorical tendencies of the mainstream media.

Take, for example, Edith Efron's contention that Clinton's cognitive inability to think is "masked" "by the inclusion of Hillary in the decision making process." Hillary is a "prop" to the president's mind: "To an inordinate degree Hillary *thinks* for Bill Clinton." However, it is Bob Woodward (of the *Washington Post*) who said in a C-SPAN interview that "I'd go so far as to say she's [Hillary] a part of Bill Clinton's brain." Dick Morris, in a similar fashion, was seen by the editors of *Time* magazine to be lodged within the president's brain and figured as his mind. Morris, in turn, describes Hillary in neuronal, metabolic terms: "Throughout his life, Clinton has usually had a person close by to help him process information . . . not an advisor in the traditional sense of the term. He needs someone to enter his thinking process, and, like an *enzyme*, like *insulin*, assist in *the digestion* of the data and in its transformation into a decision. Hillary has usually helped him to see the larger picture and occasionally played this role as well" (emphasis mine).[35] In David Maraniss's imagistic language, Clinton is a "zigzag and Rodham is a straight line."[36] The most openly clinical presentations of Clinton thus depict him as either *unable to think* or *in need of treatment*.

Let's look at Fick's presentation. Paul Fick is a practicing clinician, so his reading is qualitatively different from those of journalists and biographers, since it is part of his day job—"based on my observation of Clinton from my professional experience as a clinical psychologist."[37] Moreover, he has frequent contact with those who suffer from the same syndrome as Clinton: ACOA (Adult Children of Alcoholics). The problem with Clinton is not that he is an ACOA or even an undiagnosed one (for he was diagnosed when in family therapy for his brother's cocaine problem): it is that he is *an untreated* ACOA. Moreover, *untreated* ACOAs tend to replicate unresolved issues in their work environment (e.g., Clinton's unresolved guilt over domestic and welfare policy).

It should be noted that Clinton is not the only American president to be an ACOA. Two other presidents have suffered the same dubious distinction: Franklin Pierce (1853–1857) and Ronald Reagan. Pierce, the son of an alcoholic, depressive mother, suffered a similar fate to hers and is described (according to his biographer Roy Franklin Nichols):

> Pierce was open, congenial and pleasant. He mixed readily and won friends easily. . . . Pierce found it hard to say no. He lacked a sustained feeling of self-confidence and was desirous of approbation, consequently he endeavored to be gracious and accommodating to all when they sought favors. His graciousness was interpreted by many to mean approval of their requests.[38]

Sound familiar? Like Clinton, Pierce is a typical ACOA in his construction of a seamless facade ("the imposter syndrome"), as well as what Drew (among other biographers) describes as his "virtual incapacity to say no."[39] Reagan was a "privileged ACOA" (i.e., he didn't need treatment because his father was not violent, as was Roger Clinton; most important, Nelle Reagan told the children in a forthright fashion that their father suffered from a *disease*).

The dysfunction in Clinton's first term is read in terms of his reliance on primary defenses such as denial. Lying, miscommunication, splitting, and self-inflicted chaos are all *learned behaviors* of the ACOA. The untreated ACOA excels at projecting a "false image" and lies automatically (because of a learned preference for appearance over truth—a Platonic invert?). He keeps others at a distance while appearing near. David Maraniss describes him as a man with hundreds of close friends but no best friend.[40] He is a type of simulacrum that *hurts*.

Why is this president a diagnostic subject? What are all the readings symptomatic of? And if I have chosen to conclude this part of the chapter with Fick, it is because of the felicity of the link between the word "treatment" and the French word for unanalyzability—*l'intraitable*. What can be a more fitting demonstration of the cultural anxieties attendant upon an "unanalyzable" president than a frenetic search for the proper hermeneutic-depth model of meaning—that is, conventional psychoanalysis? What could alleviate these fears more than the reassurance of the behaviorist that the unanalyzable president is eminently treatable (*traitable*)?

We recall Baudrillard's poetic formulations: "On pain of dread we have to decipher the world and therefore wipe out the initial illusoriness of the world. We can bear neither the void, nor the secret, nor pure appearance. And why should we decipher it instead of letting its illusions shine out as such, in all its glory? Well, the fact that we cannot bear its enigmatic character is also an enigma. It is part of the world that we cannot bear either the illusion of the world or pure appearance. We would be no better at coping with radical truth and transparency, if these existed."[41]

ER(R): The Presidency in a State of Emergency (1998)

In wound culture, the very notion of sociality is bound to the excitations of the torn and open body, the torn and exposed individual as public spectacle. To the very extent that private and public communicate in the opening of bodies and persons and in the gathering around the wound, one detects a radical mutation and relocation of the public sphere, now centered on the shared and reproducible spectacles of pathological public violence.[42]

The genesis of tabloid liberalism, or how the president has become a diagnostic subject, is a story that can be told in several ways.[43] On this side of the Atlantic, we like to orient our narrative around the idea of a public sphere and a national mythology. Lauren Berlant, in *The Queen of America Goes to Washington City,* tells an analogous tale about the post-Reagan construction of an incipient infantile citizen, who, with time, is further "downsized" to the personal, familial "volunteer." As the 1997 State of the Union address demonstrated, Clinton is now the "principal in chief"—appearing on *Mr. Rogers,* speaking out for curfews and school uniforms and against Joe Camel and heroin chic. At the same time, political identifications are deflected from the institution of the presidency and rerouted in familial norms, policed by an ever-vigilant scandal deterrence machine (Paula Jones, Chinese lobbyists, Filegate, military sex scandals). This all can be read, as indeed Berlant has done brilliantly, as shifting the definitional frame for citizenship ("The political is the personal") or, psychoanalytically, as signaling a commitment to sublimation.

What interests me here is the way Clinton, as a national icon, has lost one of the fundamental privileges of a masculine subject—his freedom to go unmarked. In Berlant's felicitous formulation:

> in mass mediated public spheres and in the spaces of everyday life, to have had a remarkable American body has meant that a person has become magical and symbolic, perhaps in an auspicious, iconic way, as for a powerful Queen *or* a president.[44]

The Clinton presidential body is a site of vulnerable corporeality. Again, the comparison with Reagan is significant in other ways. Iran-Contra (as we have seen in chapter 3) was figured as a cancer on the president's formerly intact body; the operative metaphor was one of parasite and host, foreign external agent and domestic re-agent. Reagan's cancers were site specific (colon, nose). Clinton's entire body is metastatic.

The reconfigured presidential icon (as a festering wound or as metastatic) can be seen as a metonym of what Mark Seltzer has called "wound culture" and Hal Foster has delineated as "the pathogenic public sphere." In this reading, the Clinton presidency becomes another atrocity exhibit, allied with abject art's Oedipal insolence and congruent with the popular fascination with O.J., Jon-Benet Ramsey, and Ennis Cosby, as well as with all other instances of violated subjecthood (the victims of the Oklahoma City bombing, serial killers, and random acts of urban violence such as the Empire State Building shooting). Indeed, the success of televised trials (as well as Court TV and CNN's *Burden of Proof*) attest to the possible citizen-subject positions available in wound culture as witness, survivor, plaintiff, or corpse (while displacing earlier forms such as "contestant").[45] Clinton is the most presidential when immersed in wounded attachments, feeling our pain, addressing the victims of burned churches, and eulogizing slain civil rights leaders, since he is also an absolute master of its media venues: talk television and the public-service announcement ("the more you know").

I would like to reorient my presentation of President Clinton away from what Susan Stewart calls the postmodern aesthetic "probing of the wound" and toward an exploration of the effects of repetition of the trauma—to read Clinton as a trauma *victim,* as a failed figure of masculinity. He figures ambivalently, as a transgression of the symbolic code as well as an absolute subject (as all trauma victims must be). The scandal-deterrence-tabloid effect of the Clinton presidency is part of the subversion of the institutional office, but not in the way it has been traditionally figured. For, if we look at this presidency as an *abject testing of the symbolic,* we can appreciate the way it stages the role of mimetic compulsion. We can read in Clinton's lapses (more effective than the challenges posted by Bush's seduction) a *provocation of the paternal law.*

> It always takes two traumas to make a trauma.
> —Jean Laplanche, *New Foundations*

How is this reading of Clinton as a trauma victim different from the pathological focus of "expert" discourse? Rather than situate the "traumatic" as an effect of biography—Clinton as son of a father he never knew, the victim of a crash; the stepson of an abusive alcoholic; the brother of a coke addict; the family "enabler" and "survivor" of family counseling—I locate the traumatic in his political behavior. Clinton resembles the traumatized victim in his mimetic compulsions, his repeated failed attempts in primary competitions (earning him the title of the Comeback Kid), and in the nomination process (who else, after Zoë

Baird, would have nominated Kimba Wood?) My focus in this chapter, as in the others, is the political unconscious, a place where things go wrong. For, as Lacan tells us, what trauma designates is a *missed encounter with the real*. And "abjection-envy" (or, in Foster's more felicitous phrasing, "conscientious abjecting"), testifies to our nostalgia for this missed encounter.[46]

What first appears as a Foucauldian rescripting—now locating the source of truth in a damaged body (seen, as well, in the debates concerning the FDR memorial)—might be less a re or transvaluation than something with more psychological resonance. As Zizek has argued, using the example of the election of Kurt Waldheim, and as we have witnessed with Thatcher in a previous chapter, traits of identification can be *failed* characteristics. Waldheim's appeal was precisely the way he repressed Nazi war trauma.[47] And, like Waldheim, Clinton's appeal is *not despite but the result of his status* as trauma victim. At the moment of writing this chapter (post–Paula Jones 1998 Supreme Court decision), Sunday talk-show pundits are speculating on the inadvisability of a trial and how a trial would compound the damage to the president (of lobbying disclosures, campaign finance, Whitewater, and so on), yet at the same time, saying that so far (for the past *five* years!) these disclosures about sex and money haven't hurt him in the polls. Whose disavowal is this? How does this disavowal operate? What makes it *work*? What precisely is being disavowed? What if the American electorate in 1996 was similar to those Austrians who in 1986 elected Waldheim, a man with a "dubious" past (possible war crimes) and an inability to work through Nazi traumas? Rather than deploying the ineffectual unmasking strategies of Clinton bashers (which bear an eerie reminiscence to those used by Austrian leftists in 1986), we will consider how Clinton's "failures" successfully disavow the rifts upon which American national identity is sutured: race, sexuality, and class. For Clinton's traumatic body functions as a *screen*, enabling him to dispose of the wound's utility (those rifts in the symbolic order) while occupying the site of the corpse's radical nihility (becoming Berlant's "dead citizen"-in-chief). We will also examine the relation between the breaching of the presidential body (in the parapraxis) and its relation to the gaze. If the Reagan presidential subject was *caught* in the gaze and the Bush-subject was invaded by it, the Clinton-subject is obliterated by it. (We see a shift from the *trompe l'oeil*, tricking of the eye, of Bush's ecstatic fakery to the Clintonian *dompte regard*, or taming of the gaze.)

> What is repeated, in fact, is always something that occurs . . . as if by
> chance.
> —Jacques Lacan[48]

One of the pleasures of Clinton watching is the way his mistakes appear accidental—that is, avoidable. Yet, at the same time, there is something comforting in their seemingly automatic, repetitive nature. Just as his presidency appears to get "on track"—usually in the midst of some compelling foreign policy or domestic achievement—a scandal "erupts." Media pundits call this "stepping on the story," and a complex televisual semiotics obtains: Paula Jones trumps Clinton-Yeltsin at the NATO summit; the O. J. Simpson civil trial verdict merits a split screen with the State of the Union address. At other times, a logic of highway car crashes prevails, a pileup of "accidents": Zoë Baird is followed by Kimba Wood and gays in the military. And, last, there is the *schizo* logic (as in the nomination of Ruth Ginsburg), where Clinton seems to take the path of *most* resistance.

Let us look at these missteps or "outtakes" of the Clinton presidency, what Freud designated in *The Psychopathology of Everyday Life* as *parapraxis* (*Fehlleistung*—faulty function or, in French, *acte manqué*). Laplanche and Pontalis resume the theory that "bungled actions turn out in fact—on another level—to be quite successful ones."[49] These "failures" fulfill unconscious wishes and can be read like symptoms, as compromise formations between conscious intent and disavowed (or repressed) desires. Bush's parapraxes were mostly slips of the tongue (*Versprechen*); Reagan's involved forgetting (*Vergessen*) and misreading (*Verlesen*). Clinton's concern bungled actions (*Vergreifen*) and symptomatic and chance action (*Zufalshandlugen*). Hillary's parapraxes include *verlieren*—mislaying. Although Freud divides these two faulty functions into separate chapters in *The Psychopathology,* he states that the distinction between the bungled act and the chance or symptomatic misstep is arbitrary. The division is less epistemological than descriptive. Bungled actions include drinking from Lloyd Bentsen's water glass, eating off others' plates (a highly parodied aspect of Clinton's behavior), and serving ham to survivors of the Holocaust at the opening of the Holocaust Museum.[50] Food and drink are, for Freud, highly overdetermined sites: "Anyone who cares to observe his fellow men while they are at table will be able to observe the most instructive of symptomatic acts."[51] Other nonprandial bungled actions, such as going overtime at the Dukakis nomination speech or falling and self-injury are seen by

Freud as displaced forms of self-criticism, the "mistake" representing a mistake committed elsewhere. Can we read Clinton's fall in the home of a golf pro as such a reproach to his ambitions—a warning not to exceed his drive? Bungled actions are sacrificial ones, and their success can be read in the relative composure and equanimity that one retains in the supposed accident. One's ability to accept the resultant damage with grace, for Freud, is comprehensible when we realize that one's unconscious desire has been attained.

This grace is in contrast to "that travel office *thing*" where Clinton felt like a "punching bag" or other reactions of vocalized self-pity after "Hairgate" (a narrative of disempowered masculinity, of failed Icarus/Samson tropes). Chance or symptomatic actions do not appear to have a conscious intention. Unobtrusive, they appear on their own account. They are unmarked, unsuspect; symptomatic acts "give expression to something which the agent himself does not suspect in them and which he does not as a rule intend to impart to other people, but to keep to himself."[52] These may occur habitually, like tics, regularly under certain conditions, or sporadically. I am particularly interested in those that occur regularly, of which Clinton remains unaware, clueless and without seeing the effects of his actions:

> There are a thousand unnoticed openings . . . which let a penetrating eye at once into a man's soul, and I maintain it. That a man of sense does not lay down his hat in coming into a room—or take it up in going out of it, *but something escapes, which discovers* him.[53]

Or, as a White House observer put it: "There's no brain watching these things."[54]

My reading of Clinton's parapraxes differs, however, from that of Freudian hermeneutics, which seeks to supply their meaning or purpose. It is an activist or diagnostic gambit, closer to Felix Guattari's formulation:

> Lapses, parapraxes and symptoms are like birds tapping at the window. It is not a matter of "interpreting" them, but *tracking their trajectory* to see if they can serve as indicators for new universes of reference susceptible of acquitting sufficient consistency to change direction of the situation.[55] (emphasis mine)

In other words, this symptomatic reading is looking for a way out.

Lost Honeymooners: The Bungling of the First Hundred Days

The first hundred days are usually a privileged presidential period where one accumulates and does not use up one's symbolic capital. Clinton's active and seemingly clueless squandering of it—the "misfires" of his initial "honeymoon" period—is fascinating (not the Republican *potlatch*, but another sacrificial logic). What multiple repressions and displacements are evinced in this "senseless expenditure"? How does this "squandering" reveal an "accursed share" (*la part maudite*)—that which cannot enter into a functionalist-rational exchange? Unlike Bush's verbal parapraxes which occurred (see chapters 4 and 5) in electoral or contest situations, Clinton's both appear self-generated *and* occur in a nomination process.[56] They appear as a result of his agency and decision making alone (not in a transferential space, such as electoral contests or State of the Union addresses, in which discourse is addressed to another).

The nomination of Zoë Baird first appeared within a calculated, deliberate, rational (*realpolitik*) frame. The nomination process (especially for cabinet positions) was predicated on a strategy of metaphor/resemblance: to have a "cabinet that *looks* like America." After promising a diverse cabinet, Clinton gave us one in which the Big Four positions (State, Justice, Treasury, Defense) all went to men. Not wishing to seem either a "willing hostage" to interest groups or defensive about complaints of a cabinet glass ceiling, in choosing his nominee for attorney general, he bypassed Brooksley Born (the leading contender, who had women's group backing) for Zoë Baird, an acquaintance from his Renaissance weekends. All of this would be quite banal were it not for the cluelessness with which Baird's legal improprieties were met.

> What seemed to be a *minor matter* turned up in the course of vetting Baird as she and her husband hired illegal immigrants as nanny and chauffeur in the summer of 1990. They were in the process of seeking legal advice. (emphasis mine)

> *No one* sitting around the table at the Governor's mansion thought it was a problem to support as *Attorney General someone who violated a law* that would be *under her jurisdiction*.[57] (emphasis mine)

Although the offense was trivialized as an "unpaid parking ticket," Joe Biden in his role as judicial reality principle supplied a more apt automotive metaphor: "No, it's more like a wreck on an L.A. freeway."[58] A pattern was established that we saw often during the nomination process: a clueless nomination ("oversight," "insufficient vetting") is followed by hyper media exposure (with its tagline "Nannygate"), characterized by a profusion of cover stories—exposés that effectively mask other stories, becoming a site of repression in turn. "Nannygate" demonstrated how the exposure of class and gender conflict (working/professional women) covers issues of immigrant labor. The media insisted that this was a problem of *working* mothers and not of insufficiently remunerated immigrant and domestic labor. After all, what else is a six-figure lawyer supposed to do?

The Nannygate debacle and the feminine gendered readings it provoked (the problems of professional/working mothers) became metonymically inscribed within other presidential decisions involving women's reproductive bodies and the imbrication of these bodies with state power. A series of executive orders followed the failed Baird nomination, lifting the ban on gays in the military, supporting sponsored research on fetal tissue, permitting U.S. military hospitals to perform privately funded abortions overseas, lifting the ban on the French abortion pill RU 486, and agreeing to pay for UN programs that offered abortion counseling. All of these were coded as women's issues and their euphemism, "social" issues, as the contagion with Nannygate reinscribes Clinton's concern with gender (and obscures issues of race or class). Moreover, at the same time (mid-January/early February 1993), this focus on women and social issues masked anxieties about sexuality and sexual orientation. The first executive act of this "Abraham Lincoln of homosexual civil rights" (David Mixner's characterization of Clinton) is to lift the ban against gays in the military. Yet this further threatens to expose the slippage between the categories of sex, race, class, and orientation.[59]

It is in this context that the Family Leave Act (his first legislative achievement) was passed. Kimba Wood (a federal district court judge) became Clinton's second nominee for attorney general. Wood and her husband, Michael Kramer, had an illegal babysitter (before the law made it illegal, and they did pay Social Security taxes for her). This parapraxis is again met with little apparent *affect*; it is seen as a problem of "insufficient vetting" and a defense of projection (i.e., the American people are too stupid to understand a fine legal distinction). After the withdrawal of Wood's nomination, minor gaffes follow, which turn on Clinton's overexposure and overaccessibility. Clinton has now been in office a mere three weeks and one day.[60]

The nomination of Lani Guinier reads at first like that of Baird and Wood, with two key differences: the position in question was a relatively minor one (an under secretary post, with no policy-making powers), and Clinton was disproportionately upset by the mistakes in vetting this nomination (calling it "felony stupid" and yelling at Vernon Jordan). Like Baird and Wood, Guinier had fine professional credentials: a law school professor at the University of Pennsylvania, a Yale law graduate and a friend of Bill and Hillary (who were guests at her wedding), a former voting rights litigator for the NAACP, and a legal specialist in voting rights cases. She also had previous political experience as a Carter appointee. The only fly in the ointment was the possible interpretation of her law review articles concerning the minority veto, supermajorities, and cumulative voting. There was a nuanced shift in the rhetoric surrounding this appointment; it was a case not of "oversight" but of "misjudgment" (not in relation to an economy of visibility but an ontology of *error*). Bernard Nussbaum stated the terms of the "misjudgment": "the misjudgment was that she would be judged on the basis of her overall career and that she wasn't a policy maker. We failed. The White House failed and the Justice Department failed."[61]

Guinier's case reads like a racialized confrontation with the law—not a colorized Bork rewrite but more a "textual one-drop theory" (as one part names the whole). Bork's writings displaced attention from his body to his text. In Guinier's case, her textuality reframed her corporeal eccentricity. Her writings were discussed amid fears that the public would not tolerate *her*: a mixed race (Jewish/black), strong woman with "an exotic name and weird hair." She was described physically in a way the other women nominees were not and in a caricatural way, almost as a blackface mask:

> A black woman with prominent eyes and hair combed back and bursting into puffs at the sides and with a strong name and radical sounding ideas was vulnerable. She was too different. The white males couldn't empathize with her.[62]

Given the order of her enumerated problems (weird eyes, hair, and name, then radical ideas), her legal writings appear the least of her problems, even while remaining their alibi and pretext.

Yet, interestingly, white males could empathize with (Attorney General) Janet Reno's "bluffness and breezy self-assurance" or even with San Francisco City Supervisor Roberta Actenberg, an avowed lesbian and a vocal critic of the Boy Scouts (she advocates the employment of gay Scoutmasters) who was nominated to be an assistant secretary of HUD. Actenberg was coded not as a radical but as a lesbian. "The word was coming back from the Senate floor—'I'm going to vote for the lesbian, but not the black radical.' "[63] (The fact that Reno's butch qualities reassured and that lesbianism, even when it takes on the Boy Scouts, could be domesticated is indicative of the complexity of race-gender performativity.)

I wish to stress the difference between this nomination and the other bungled ones. What makes this one symptomatic can be read in Clinton's *anger*: "How the hell did this happen again?" The president calls this relatively low-level appointment gone awry "felony stupid." The president yells at Vernon Jordan and calls him back from lunch: "Get the hell over here. Have you read these . . . this is some shit we're in, Jordan, get yourself over here."[64] The initial misjudgment is met with heightened affect, a painful nomination process is prolonged, and an inevitable decision is postponed. All of these suggest a symptomatic rather than a bungled action.

Anger is directed against a racialized agent of his administration, Jordan. Racial anxieties are transferred away from Guinier's body to the body of her law review articles in Clinton's anguished message announcing the withdrawal of this nomination. The shock of discovery of the racialized carapace (weird hair jutting out in puffs around the ears, bizarre name, protruding eyes), first displaced in the texts, is now located on the president's body as a site of failed introjection: he can't *stomach* the constitutional stands she takes: "This is about my center." He appears physically spent, vampirized ("little blood left"), depleted.[65]

Clinton's parapraxes concerning race and femininity function according to a logic of mask/cover—a procession of perspectival filters and frames that changes what eludes view. Parapraxes concerning sexuality and sexual orientation, in contrast, partake of a strategy of mimicry/doubling/*en-abime*. The last spectacular failure of the first year is twinned: the policy regarding gays in the military *and* the nomination of Bobby Ray Inman.

The Strange Case of Bobby Ray Inman

I fell on my sword. —Bill Clinton

The presidents we have been looking at have all had a relation to their swords. Ronald Reagan adapted an activist position: wood-chopping wielder of the tax axe (a wood-splitting, horse-riding emblem of normative masculinity). Bush I, as we have seen, displayed the exuberant posture of masochistic Moloch fantasies, as well as the erotic contemplation of "going behind—the "javelin catcher.". Clinton's rhetoric again appears equally deliberate—what we might call "willful impalement"—electing or choosing which policies or nominations are worthy of self-impalement. Self-impalement here is framed as *sacrifice* (a functional, symbolic exchange), not pleasure. After the Dukakis nomination speech debacle, *Governor* Clinton is jubilant: "I fell on my sword." Yet, on gays in the military: "You can't say, 'This is the sword I'll fall on when I didn't for the middle-class tax cut.' "[66]

That the figuration for "gays in the military" should be selective impalement is odd. Odder still, or perhaps more uncanny, is the mimicry or *en-abime* that surrounds the policy on gays in the military. Les Aspin flies to South Korea, intending to take the new policy with him. David Gergen asks Aspin not to bring the policy on gays aboard because of possible news *leaks*. This request of Gergen's is then leaked. Concerns with "leaks" meet up with a homophobic unconscious concerned with "fluids" as (on vacation) Clinton's waterplay in Hawaii (at the time of the news leak about not leaking the gays in the military policy . . .) misfires, juxtaposed with the floods in the Midwest. Fluids cannot be exchanged with fun and play (recreation); rather, fluids, as well as all types of "watersports," = death. This is the figural framing for "gays in the military" gaffes—a tropology that mimes or doubles the ambient fears of the American cultural imaginary concerning gay men (especially in submarines, where going down is equated with going under).[67]

Although Aspin had been marginally successful with the "gays in the military policy," the Mogadishu debacle set the stage for the nomination of Bobby Ray Inman to replace Les Aspin. The nomination of Inman, like the other nominations we have seen, is set up discursively as a quick and easy, "one-day 'vet' " in person. Since Inman already has sensitive (high-level) security clearance, there is little concern about the ambient rumors concerning his emotional makeup or suspect (homosexual) orientation. Indeed, it is only Inman's growing impatience with the nomination process that is the first sign of trouble. *Le cas* Inman, like those of Baird and Wood, is a case of "oversight," but one that lacks the legal finery of domestic employment complications, and is glaringly botched. Strange signs are overlooked: why is the secretary of state negotiating with the secretary of defense over an appointment? Why does Inman insist on announcing at a press conference that he voted for the other guy (Bush), yet could still work with Clinton, undoing much of the "feel-good spirit" of bipartisanship undergirding this appointment? Why won't Inman give up the (exclusive, all-male) Bohemian Grove Club membership, and why then does the secretary of state intervene, enabling an unprecedented deal that would allow Inman the top position on the waiting list for admission after his public service is over? Finally, why does Inman "out" himself, offering up rumors about his orientation on *Nightline* and in a hysterical op-ed diatribe against the press?[68] The whole Inman episode has the air of a negative therapeutic reaction: Inman exchanges his subject position with the president and then taunts him: "Try and understand me; I'll only get worse."

Having had enough of his self-inflicted wounding, on December 20, Inman *pulls out*: "It's not worth it." This is followed by state trooper's charges about Clinton's infidelities, the missing Vince Foster files, more revelations about Inman's failure to pay Social Security taxes for his housekeeper, and the arrest of Jocelyn Elder's son on drug charges. Inman externalizes the big other in his paranoid projections, and all the symbolic detritus of the first year is downloaded onto the president. Inman becomes the shadow figure of the president (*he* calls it quits, *he's* had enough, it's not worth it); his paranoia mirrors Clinton's masochism. The presidential body in "real life" is reduced increasingly to (in Zizek's words) an excremental remainder. The automatism of these last days of 1993 have the feel of a runaway train—giddy, exorbital, surreal, and out of control. The presidential language is both oneiric ("I can deal with only one nightmare at a time") and funereal ("The atmosphere was eerie as if someone had died" [i.e., the president]).[69]

One could see in this automatism of shadow events (as the phantoms of first-term events return) a move away from reality as an effect of representation (either imitation or illusion) to the Lacanian (traumatic) real. The interrogation of the presidential lapses (surrounding the nomination and policy processes of the first year) thus situates these moments when the political spectacle cracks (at the time—1993—when there was still a political spectacle), whether in the disruption of (racialized) maternal bodies of immigrant domestic labor; in Guinier's racialized confrontation with the law; or in the fetishes of hair, eyes, money-feces, or swords, or other eroticized/abject part objects: sex, drugs, and Joycelyn Elders. Situating the traumatic real as oppositional to simulation can explain the disposition to abject the presidency while simultaneously probing behind the president's body for the obscene gaze of the real. The focus on either cracks within the symbolic real (Guinier, Baird) or the abject testing of its limits (Inman) as revealed in the presidential *parapraxes,* moreover, designates a shift in our mode of identification with the president: no longer *symbolic* (we identify with him, in Zizek's formula, "at that point in which he is *intimitable*")[70] but imaginary ("we identify with him to the point at which he is *like us*").

The traumatic real can underscore the irony of how the *failure* of certain imitative/mimetic strategies (i.e., a "cabinet that looks like America") can produce the obsessional pleasure of a president who looks like us. We now are the president and can cast him in our fantasmatic scenes: Michael Douglas, Jack Nicholson, Bill Pullman, Gene Hackman, Harrison Ford, Cliff Robertson, or John Travolta (the "pulp president" of *Primary Colors*—who can, like Clinton, express his *jouissance* over a *Royale* with cheese). What the traumatic real is less apt at capturing, however is the sense of play with which we now live the interactivity of the presidency. Is the Clinton presidency a traumatic (Foster) or a fatal (Baudrillard) object?

8

Father, Can't You See
I'm Bombing?

A Bush Family Romance (2003–2004)

FOR MICHAEL ROGIN

> I must, however, commence my contribution to this psychological
> study . . . with the confession that the figure of the American Presi-
> dent, as it rose above the horizon of Europeans, was from the be-
> ginning unsympathetic to me, and that this aversion increased in
> the course of the years the more I learned about him and the more
> severely we suffered from the consequences of his intrusion into
> our destiny.[1]

An eminent psychoanalyst prefaces his psychological study
with a blunt statement of antipathy. He depicts a president who takes
religion literally and whose faith-inflected leadership is providentially
authorized: "God ordained that I should be the next President of the
United States" (*TWW*, xiii). This American president's disregard for
facts, "his alienation from the world of reality" (*TWW*, xv), matches the
intensity of his religious certainty. Indeed, the president's aversion to
facts (he "repeatedly declared that mere facts had no significance for
him, that he esteemed nothing but human motives and opinions") induced a natural disposition to deny any fact "in conflict with his hopes
and wishes." "He therefore lacked motive to reduce his ignorance by
learning facts" (*TWW*, xiv). The president's lack of geographic knowledge rivals his contempt for all Europeans except the British; this contempt reaches phobic proportions in response to France. Yet these defi-
cits do not deter him in his quest for global security and peace, for a
"new world order." The psychoanalyst is unsparing in his description of

his monumental hubris: "(h)e put himself in the deplorable position of the benefactor who wishes to restore the eyesight of a patient but does not know the construction of the eye and has neglected to learn the necessary methods of operation" (*TWW*, xiv). The president's characterological traits are succinctly stated: "insincerity, unreliability, and tendency to deny the truth" (*TWW*, xiv).

With uncanny prescience for contemporary America, Sigmund Freud thus described America's twenty-eighth president, Thomas Woodrow Wilson. Freud first developed an interest in Wilson when he discovered that they were both born in 1856. *Thomas Woodrow Wilson: A Psychological Study* was co-written (with William Bullitt) between 1931 and 1932 and published posthumously, in 1961, after Edith Wilson's death. It began as a distraction when Freud, convalescing in Berlin, was visited by his friend William Bullitt, who engaged him in conversation about the book he was writing on the Treaty of Versailles.[2] Bullitt recounts that Freud became quite lively at the mention of Wilson's name. A collaborative venture was agreed upon. Bullitt as protégé of Colonel House, and as an under secretary during Wilson's administration, supplied the necessary research. Bullitt and Freud considered the volume a counterpart to Freud's short studies of Leonardo and of Michelangelo's *Moses*. However, I will argue (along with Gérard Miller, Paul Laurent Assoun, and Michel Schneider)[3] that the resultant text comes closer than any other Freudian text, such as *Group Psychology and the Analysis of the Ego*, in addressing contemporary politics.

My focus here is on leadership, especially the wartime presidency, as an exemplary psychoanalytic object. It might first appear counterintuitive or perverse to compare Wilson, the idealist history professor and president of Princeton University, with the anti-intellectual and anti-academic George W. Bush. I am not principally concerned with the numerous superficial similarities. As we will see, Wilson was equally faith driven; he was indifferent to facts, and his ethnographic as well as geographic ignorance about Europe had disastrous consequences. Wilson believed there were no German speakers south of the Brenner Pass and gave the Tyrol to Italy (*TWW*, 186). An analogous ethnographic ignorance permitted him to cede Bohemia to Czechoslovakia. Wilson's Francophobia was so extreme as to motivate the petty gesture of leaving Jefferson out of an Encyclopedia of Illustrious Americans; Jefferson was too philosophically French and not Presbyterian enough (*TWW*, 137).

My return to Freud and Bullitt's study of Wilson is rather to reexamine the terrains of the father-son drama (as enacted textually in *Totem and Taboo*) and the relay between faith and ignorance (with reference to *The Future of an Illusion*) in the context of W-Bush's war. If I restage W-Bush as Wilson, it is to ask (à propos of leadership): What do the American people really want? What particular kind of father-function underwrites particular presidencies? Under what conditions is the ideal father of regulated enjoyment displaced by the primal father of obscene *jouissance*? What are the political possibilities and dangers of appeals to the surplus enjoyment of the Other? And it is also to ask a set of more disturbing and unanswerable questions about the status of national projects (a war for peace, a defensive shield, homeland security) and their propinquity to delusion. For it is but one (French) homophonic glide that separates the asylum/*l'asile* from the presidential palace/l'Elysée.[4] Freud concludes his introduction to the Wilson study by noting that "Fools, visionaries, sufferers from delusions, neurotics and lunatics have played great roles at all times in the history of mankind and not merely when the accident of birth had bequeathed them sovereignty" (*TWW*, xix). And Zizek has concurred that what separates a delusional paranoiac who thinks he is president from any fool who happens to actually occupy the office is less a distinction between those capable of direct identification and those who are not than it is a question of social recognition.[5]

Jacqueline Rose's brilliant reading of Thatcher echoes Freud's recognition of the profoundly contradictory and paradoxical logics of leadership (and the collective identifications and symbolic processes they condense). "What if Thatcher was reelected not despite the repugnance that many feel for her image, but also in some sense because of it? What if that force of identity for which she is so severely castigated *somewhere also* operates as a type of pull?" (emphasis mine).[6] Political leadership (whether that of Thatcher, Wilson, or Bush) is not amenable to a strictly instrumental or rational analysis. Because collective identifications and imaginaries operate in contradictory fashion, there is no (psychoanalytic) limit to the "potential range of their aberrant causes and effects."[7] Leadership is ultimately a story of continually improvised and failed attempts to secure or found the rationality of the social order. Within this frame, Rose addresses the interpellative process, the way the ego is deeply invested in precisely those political fantasies it is called on to avoid.[8] Avital Ronell's account of the first Gulf War restates this pertinent question: "Why was it possible for George Bush to be president? Why was it possible, at this particular moment in history, for Saddam Hussein to pose as Adolf Hitler? Whether or not you voted, protested, freaked out, or elected one or another mode of passivity, it is a question of our history."[9] Ronell reminds us that the continual appeal of leaders draws upon a metaphysical reserve: "The incredible fact that the Iraqi leader was prompted to pose as Hitler's double (Same), in other words as a by-product of the Western logos (it is grotesque to forget that Adolf Hitler was a *Western* production), in itself demonstrates the compulsive aspect of this war."[10]

Something About a Boy

Wilson's is the story of a boy who dreamed of winning glory by great speeches that would move people, parliaments and parties, of a boy with intimations of immortality, a boy who arranged to make his dreams come true. A rare boy. —John Morton Blum[11]

Thomas Woodrow Wilson: A Psychological Study is an account of the Oedipal drama between "little Tommy Wilson" and his adored father, the Reverend Joseph Ruggles Wilson. It is an object lesson of an intense father cathexis, as exemplary in its way as that of another (Senate) president, Judge Schreber. Wilson, however, is a "normal" neurotic or perhaps a borderline case.[12] The son, "little Tommy," identifies with his exalted father, identifies his father with God, and erects that (divine) father with a superego. The divine father is internalized ambivalently; on the one hand, he is reassuring (everything will be fine because God the father authorizes it), and, on the other, he is fearsome (this God-father is insatiable). This produces precisely the kind of superego that creates psychotics, neurotics and "a few great men" (*TWW*, 66).

The Freudian outline of a strong father cathexis is anchored in libido theory: It is difficult to find an outlet for such strong paternal feelings. "Little Tommy" (a virgin until he was twenty-eight years old) is extremely passive and cannot symbolize his femininity (*TWW*, 53). In Wilson's case, the quantity of libido becomes so great that he loses the ability to recognize the existence of facts in the world of reality. Even two happy marriages (to Ellen Axson Wilson and, later, to Edith Bolling Galt Wilson) do not help: "Satisfaction for the thin stream of his libido which was directed towards women could not compensate him for the lack of satisfaction for the great streams of libido which had been directed towards his father" (*TWW*, 217). This disappointment is on a world-historical scale: "In the winter and early spring of 1916, when he had been so happy, he had believed that he was about to lead the United States into the war and become *dictator of the peace*. We have seen that this project offered a magnificent outlet for all the currents of libido directed toward his father" (*TWW*, 217, emphasis mine). Unfortunately, the American people wanted their leader to keep them out of the war, thwarting his plans to dictate a peace and spoiling his chances for happiness: "He could no longer be happy unless he could believe that he was about to become the Saviour of the World. If he could not lead the United States into war as a crusade for peace, he did not much care whether he was President or not" (*TWW*, 218).

The religious tone of his foreign policy plans is interpreted (by Freud and Bullitt) as deriving from his Christ identification (as both father and son). Freud's general model takes on even greater acuity when we recall that, in Wilson's particular case, his own "incomparable father" is a Presbyterian minister. In other words, it does not require much imagination to transform this father into "a leader of the elect of God, the interpreter of God on earth" (*TWW*, 31). Bullitt and Freud emphasize the Reverend Wilson's daily subjection of his family to his voice, instantiating the word of God: "Five times a day the father prayed to God while his family listened. Twice a day he read the bible to his family and in the evening led his family in the singing of hymns" (*TWW*, 31). The Reverend Wilson, like Schreber's father, Dr. Daniel Gottlob Moritz Schreber, was an imposing figure, physically strong and handsome. This made the adoration of his weak, puny, somewhat learning-impaired son even more poignant. "Little Tommy" identified with the patronymic Wilson, but corporally he was a feminized Woodrow, with a feeble body, weak eyes, and timidity.

The devotional habits instilled in little Tommy Wilson's childhood were preserved for the rest of his adult and presidential life. Wilson prayed on his knees daily, said grace before every meal, and believed in the efficacy of prayer. "I do not see how anyone can sustain himself in any enterprise without prayer" (*TWW*, 32). These habits also insulated him from doubt; doubting would have meant doubting his father. Moreover, as his father was so closely associated in his day job with God, this certainty was underwritten by both father and divine providence: "I believe in divine Providence. If I did not I would go crazy." Bullitt concurs with an apt litotes: "That was perhaps true" (*TWW*, 92–93). Indeed, had he not been able to find an outlet in prayer, "he might have become not the occupant of the White House but the inmate of an asylum" (*TWW*, 92).

Bullitt's contribution ("Digest and Data on the Childhood and Youth of Thomas Woodrow Wilson") situates Wilson's father worship as a "dominant passion" and "the core of his emotional life" (*TWW*, 30). Tommy remained financially dependent upon his father well into adulthood and never made an important decision without his advice until he was forty (*TWW*, 91). Because of his many physical breakdowns, he spent three of the ten years between the ages of seventeen and twenty-seven being cared for at his father's house. Freud and Bullitt remind the reader that this is a period when men are in the "full vigor of their manhood . . . but he clung to the habits of his childhood and remained a virgin full of dyspepsia, nervousness, headaches and ideas" (*TWW*, 108). Wilson's numerous breakdowns, which occurred at least *fourteen points*[13] during his life, are interpreted in relation to the conflict between Wilson's femininity and filial passivity and his superego's demands that he be hypermasculine (*TWW*, 107–108). Even during the negotiations at the Paris summit for the Treaty of Versailles, Wilson refused to use masculine weapons of force, financial threat, or withdrawal from the conference but relied upon feminine means of persuasion: "appeals, supplications, submissions" (*TWW*, 269). Freud and Bullitt reiterate that Wilson "never had a fist fight in his life. All his fighting he had done with his mouth" (*TWW*, 245–246).

The Reverend Joseph Ruggles Wilson was not only the voice of God but also a tutelary figure. If Schreber's dad was, in Colin MacCabe's felicitous formulation, "the personal trainer from hell,"[14] the Reverend Wilson was his analogue in rhetoric (*TWW*, 28). Things had to be expressed in perfect English: "Pickwick, the prophets, Presbyterianism and phrases, words, synonyms, similes were driven into the son's head" (*TWW*, 32–33). It was under the tutelage of a seminary student, Frances Brook, that Wilson was born again and departed from the strict filial pattern. He was admitted into the Church in 1873 and from this point on felt himself in "direct communication with God" (*TWW*, 40). His relationship with Brook was a passionate attachment, a "*coup de foudre*," and the identification with Christ was heightened by the fact that Brook gave his theological seminars in the provisional housing of a *stable* (*TWW*, 106). Wilson now recoded his minister-father as a Christian statesman and decided upon a career in public life. His libido was evacuated into speech making, passionate male friendships, submission to God, and an identification with Christ (*TWW*, 143). This pattern continued throughout his tenure at Princeton and as president.

Wilson's presidency at Princeton might be retitled "leave no college student behind." The symbolic stakes of his tenure were manifest in a letter to a parent: "If I had to choose between your life or my life or anybody's life and the good of this college, I should choose the good of the college" (*TWW*, 160). Wilson increased the severity of the examination system, resisted the liberalization of mandatory chapel attendance, and reorganized the entire course of study. He overhauled the preceptorial system, added more than fifty tutors, and engaged in a long battle over the establishment of a graduate system and its placement on campus (*TWW*, 143–144). These projects were accompanied by the return of his physical ailments (habitual headaches, neuritis, digestive problems, hysterical blindness in his left eye), dysthemia, and a hernia. Wilson's final years at Princeton (1906–1910) centered on the battle to reorganize the university into a Quad system modeled on those at Oxford and Cambridge. It was an expensive proposal that met with a great deal of opposition from "the big dark men" who, while not exactly Fleschig (Schreber's asylum director and malign demigod figure), were nonetheless father representatives. (Wilson continued to dream that his opponent Dean West was president during the war.) Freud and Bullitt read Wilson's paranoia as a protective mechanism for his passivity. As Wilson never dared to oppose his father, he saw any opposition to his plan as an abject betrayal. Wilson's mental degeneration around the Quads project prefigures what happened later with the Treaty of Versailles in its apparent illogic and oversight: "His intellect at that moment was the tool of his unconscious desires and nothing else" (*TWW*, 157). In the Princeton Quad case, wishful metaleptic thinking substituted longed-for effect as cause. The Treaty of Versailles was a search for a rationalization that would allow for him to have it both ways—to surrender to the Allies and yet remain the Savior of the world.

In Freud and Bullitt's fused and repetitive narrative, the story of Wilson's disavowal of how the treaty abrogated the Fourteen Points is doubled by the tragic case study of an unresolved Oedipus complex. It moves between the intensely individual to the sociopolitical and relates how a narcissistic object choice (in this case, an overidealized father) fueled an ambitious idealist foreign policy. This yields two highly unsatisfactory outcomes: first, "Wilson came to betray the trust of the world as a matter of principle" (*TWW*, 304); second, "A considerable portion of the human race had to suffer for the overwhelming love which the Reverend Joseph Ruggles Wilson inspired in his son" (*TWW*, 133). This reading of tactical errors is circumscribed by the mythic frame of a failed Oedipus: an individual destiny inflicts world historical suffering on others as collateral damage. The limitation of Freud's mythic and paternalist framing of the political has been duly noted by others to the epistemological profit of a Lacanian revisiting of the question tersely stated in *Seminar IV*: "What does it mean to be a father?"[15] Indeed, Freud's case so directly translates into readily available Freudian analogues (e.g., the Reverend Ruggles Wilson is the grandfather of the League of Nations; the Fourteen Points are his father's sermons on a larger scale) that it is preferable to see this facile conversion as an invitation to read otherwise.

There is such an excess of textual and corporeal symptoms that Freud's emphasis on constitutional factors and biological stresses at first seems warranted. Wilson underwent a crisis of investiture analogous to that of Schreber. On inauguration day, he brought his stomach pump and a one-quart can of headache tablets along with him (*TWW*, 181).[16] In Paris, Wilson so deeply resented being used as Europe's tool that he suffered "high fever, profuse diarrhea, bloody urine, coughing, pain from a swollen prostate, neuritis in the shoulder and the left side of his brain twitching" (*TWW*, 286). Wilson's phallic relation to world leaders such as Clemenceau, Lloyd George (flaccidity), and Henry Cabot Lodge (rigidity) do recall a doubling of his father-son identification as a statesman whose aims are to be and to eat daddy: "to identify the incomparable father with the face of Gladstone and by a cannibalistic identification to destroy the old man" (*TWW*, 135). Wilson's fantasies—even his quite elaborate religious ones—can be read in relation to drives and instincts. His ego ideal was staged in familial and national terms.[17] The Allied powers were a fraternal assembly, a "band of brothers" who would receive the Fourteen Points as a Sermon on the Mount from Wilson. This fraternal ordering was underscored by Wilson's expressed desire that wives not be allowed to accompany their husbands to Paris. (This order was contravened by Colonel House's nephew Auchincloss, Wilson's proposed secretary, who referred to the president as "little Woody.")

Freud and Bullitt misread Wilson's self-sabotaging behavior (refusing to accept Auchincloss and going to the Treaty meetings without a secretary) and his increasing estrangement from Colonel House over the issue of nepotism. Nepotism is seen as the conscious screen for his animosity, with the God/Father fixation as the unconscious and "real" source. Here we see the deficiency of Freud's essentially object-relations approach. For it would be more accurate to read nepotism as a highly charged signifier within a symbolic order. Nepotism is a charge that threatens the orderly assembly of brothers (referencing etymologically sons of dubious legitimacy masquerading as nephews).[18] Derrida's allusion to Wilson in *Without Alibi* ("We now know how to analyze what Freud thought of the more or less legitimate father of the League of Nations, Woodrow Wilson")[19] attenuates the question of paternity as biological rather than social/symbolic construct. Derrida's aside suggests that Wilson's wartime presidency coheres less around the Oedipus myth than around a paternal metaphor or master signifier. In other texts, such as *Group Psychology and the Analysis of the Ego*, Freud does not directly name Wilson, referring to him as the object of a signifier ("The Fourteen Points of the American President").[20] Wilson as president is not an unequivocal father but is a (civil union) sort of father, a not-quite dad. The Fourteen Points are the Reverend's sermons on a larger scale; the League of Nations becomes the master signifier of the Fourteen Points, in John Morton Blum's words, "its crowning point."[21] The League of Nations is precipitated from the Fourteen Points and performs the symbolic role of guaranteeing in advance the Treaty of Versailles.

Freud and Bullitt place too little emphasis on textual symptoms that demand a symbolic framing. Wilson's primary interest in his chosen career of law and during his tenure as a wartime president was the drafting of constitutions, which he did (or attempted) at all the universities (Davidson College, Wesleyan, Johns Hopkins, the University of Virginia, Princeton) and governmental offices (the New Jersey State Constitution when he was governor) with which he was associated (*TWW*, 117). For Wilson, constitutions were, like words, "vehicles of life."[22] It is by way of the master signifier that one can account for the apparent paradox that Wilson, as author of *Congressional Government* (with its advocacy of checks and balances),[23] became the exponent and the prime example of an absolutist presidency in foreign affairs and in the suppression of domestic dissent (along with that other Presbyterian savior, President Richard Nixon).

The psychopathology of presidential neurosis obscures the stakes of the Wilson presidency as elegantly formulated by Michael Rogin. As supreme patriarch, "Wilson located in the presidency unprecedented power over life and death and due process of law."[24] The benefit of a Lacanian reframing of the Wilson text is in elaborating a context for parallels with the Bush presidency, both pre– and post–Patriot Act. On numerous aspects of policy and public concern—stem cell research, family policy, the presence of arsenic in the water supply, the availability of ephedra, the use of medical marijuana, partial-birth abortion, the successful renaming of the estate tax as the "death tax," intransigent support for the death penalty (even for the severely retarded and even when the accused had woefully inadequate counsel) to the treatment of Guantanamo detainees and the acceptability of preemptive war—the presidency of W-Bush occupies a resolutely symbolic terrain, as opposed to the imaginary aggressive father-son rivalry of popular media accounts. For in the symbolic order, it is the signifier that must remain inviolable. Freud and Bullitt cannot account for the preemptive logic of Wilson declaring that the League of Nations was the central fact of the peace process, which, in their eyes, meant that Wilson had given away his trump card. (Yet, in a symbolic game, what else is one to do with it?) Wilson's allegiance to the master signifier similarly accounts for his blindness to the Allies' secret agreements as one signifier "mandate" could plausibly substitute for another "annexation" (*TWW*, 248). (Or, closer to home, we could substitute "Saddam" for "weapons of mass destruction.") Zizek reminds us that (when it comes to the superego), $S2$ is the $S1$ of a chain of easily substitutable $S2$s, "the dimension of an unconditional injunction inherent in knowledge itself."[25] Zizek convincingly argues that our "War on Terror" (indeed, war itself) has ceased to remain the last stand of Master discourse but has been integrated into University discourse.[26] The terms of our present war similarly trace themselves to Wilson's "new world order."

John Morton Blum astutely remarks that Wilson's suppression of dissent was less about power per se than about empowering the anxiety of a people at war.[27] The repression of civil liberties under Wilson uncannily presages that of our own time. The Total Information Awareness program had its analog in the Committee on Public Information to

Mobilize Opinion (CPI) under George Creel. The Espionage Act of 1917 gave the government the power to punish "willful obstructionism" and was enforced by the Justice Department and the Post Office. Mail (the operant form of telematics) was closed to the public whose only "offense" was anti-British sentiment or a belief in socialism. Individuals who dared to criticize the YMCA, the Red Cross, or the financing of the war were prosecuted (and convicted), as were those men who "merely declared war contrary to the teachings of Christ."[28] Larger censorship powers fell under the Orwellian-sounding "Trading with the Enemy Act," which gave the Postmaster General virtually unlimited power over the foreign-language press. We are perhaps most familiar with the Sedition Act of May 1918, which authorized the federal government to punish "expressions of opinions which regardless of their probable consequences were 'disloyal,' profane, scurrilous, or abusive of the American form of government, flag or uniform."[29] These measures targeted populations as the effect of signifiers (mail, flags, uniforms) that threatened to detach themselves from the master signifier, "America." Blum and Rogin address the abdication of all three branches of government when it concerned free-speech protections. Yet it was the president, as head of the executive branch, who furthered the enforcement of this "arsenal against free speech."[30] The effects of this suppression were 1,500 arrests, only 10 of which were for alleged sabotage. It was not that Wilson "turned his back on civil liberties because he loved them less" but rather that, because of his attachment to the master signifier "peace," "he loved his vision of eventual peace more."[31]

Freud and Bullitt's preoccupation with the international effects of Wilson's father complex not only obscures the affinity of presidential absolutism for domestic policy but overlooks the implications of the ambivalent gendering of America. Like Wilson, the nation is attached to paternal authority and feminized by it. Little Tommy fled the European continent after his first visit to France, Germany, and Italy, in 1903, and he did not return until 1919 to redraw its map. (He came back on the felicitously named ship the *George Washington*.) "Europe" functions as a signifier that threatens the screen of rationalizations sustained by Wilson's parochialism. (This parochialism is also shared by W-Bush's generation and class atypical lack of foreign travel and curiosity.) "America" is an apotropaic signifier that shields American men from the recognition of their own feeble masculinity. Parochialism is a defensive (one might even say phobic) strategy, as one is not forced to face those conflicts within one's own nature that are inescapable in the "comparative freedom of European civilization" *(TWW,* 97) (Oh, those French!).

It is not surprising that Freud sees religion as explanation: "Wilson was fortunate to have been born in a nation that was protected from reality during the nineteenth century by inherited devotion to the ideals of Wyclif, Calvin and Wesley" *(TWW,* 98). The American male's ego ideal is unconflicted about community or family. This passivity toward the father is shored up, in turn, by a faith-driven ideology, as outlined in Freud's *The Future of an Illusion.* America's idea of itself is tied to the "historical beginnings of the idea of God." Here men "could recover the intimacy and intensity of the child's relation to his father." The "America" of pious Americans claims a "Chosen" status: "God's own Country." [32] And, as the original model of God is itself paternal, [33] alignment with the signifier "America" reassures "potency." The passivity that Wilson never has to think about in America, his successfully repressed inner conflicts, is challenged in the Paris conference, where Wilson is "appalled" at his deference to European leaders and his "torment" at being "femininely used" as Europe's "tool." (This is a marked departure from Schreber's enjoyment.) The negative therapeutic reaction of these American presidents, Wilson and Bush, in the context of international organizations (the League of Nations, the United Nations), and their spectacular failures, provides a cautionary tale regarding the enlisting of the paternal metaphor for export-only unilateralism and preemption. In contrast, a Lacanian emphasis on the neurotic's ability to generate master signifiers marks a time when the symbolic order could sustain aspirations toward leadership and diplomacy, in contrast to our present perverse politics, in which, as we shall see, the paternal metaphor is more closely aligned with the state of exception.

Behindsight: Bush in Retrospect

America sensed that they had elected a different sort of president when George Bush let it slip that he had showered with his dog. [34]

Wilson represented a classic Freudian Oedipus complex: a neurotic son identifying with an overidealized and severe father. George Herbert Walker Bush presents quite a contrast with the authoritative Reverend Joseph Ruggles Wilson. We have seen that Tommy Wilson had little trouble introjecting this paternal figure. W-Bush's failed introjections have provoked much humor, whether in the form of dangerous pretzels or in a campaign-speech lapsus: "I know how hard it is to put food on your families."[35] W-Bush's relation to the paternal metaphor—the father function—is perverse and not neurotic. (He has, in other words, achieved alienation but not separation.) Unlike Wilson, whose *jouissance* is phallic, W.'s is decidedly Other. W., I will argue, is divided between Bar (the Woman) and G.H.W. "Poppy" Bush (the *père jouissant*).

One George Bush at a time.[36]

There is apparent uniformity in the depictions in the journalistic and popular media of the second Bush presidency as an Oedipal drama, recasting Attic tragedy with all the pseudo-Freudian trappings we have come to expect since the Clinton dysfunctional-family reality show (for those who truly miss the Clintons, there's always the Osbornes on MTV). David Frum, W.'s speechwriter, who coined the term "axis of evil," presents the prodigal son in terms of the second topography: "Bush's 'id' was as powerful and destructive as the Clinton id. But sometime in Bush's middle years his id was captured, shackled, manacled and locked away."[37] (Perhaps it will be found in Gore's "lock box.") It is W.'s "id control" that enables him to triumph over his "fierce anger."

We have witnessed in previous chapters a revision of the King's two-body doctrine for postmodern presidents and how they either need treatment (Clinton) or are in recovery (Bush).[38] Yet, even here, as a reformed alcoholic ("You know . . . I had a drinking problem. Right now I should be in a bar in Texas, not the Oval Office"),[39] Bush frames his addiction in a very 1990s vernacular. In contrast with the domestically inflected, suburbanized object relations of 1950s addictions, here addiction is used "to bring the world of desire to an end."[40] It is concerned with the last things of desire (death/destiny). W. tells us that the only reason that he is not in that *bar* in Texas is that he found faith: "I found God." God replaces the signifier Bar, which is what Barbara Bush was named by her family.

Indeed, one of the more interesting resignifications of the past few years has been the press coverage of Barbara Bush, now the First Mother. In the first Bush presidency, she figured less as a wife than as a virtual grandmother to her husband's eternal boyishness. G.H.W. Bush always looked like the Beaver, and *Spy* magazine made this connection unavoidable. G.H.W. Bush may have achieved his Oedipal wish of marrying a cross-generational mother, but at the price of remaining frozen, arrested in time.[41] Bar, as First Lady, was a reassuring presence, in contrast to those harpies, Nancy (who was interested only in designer clothes and famous friends, that is, the paternal metaphors of others) and the narcissistically career-driven and castrating Hillary. Bar accepted her looks, promoted literacy, and even ventriloquized the First Pet, the dog Millie.

The few departures from this model (as when she referred to the Democratic vice presidential candidate Geraldine Ferraro as something that rhymed with witch) served only to all-too-humanize her. What a surprise, then, to read during the 2000 campaign, in *Talk* magazine, that she was the punishing disciplinarian who forced her eldest son to run ("If he doesn't run, I'll kill him") or who settled the question of who was the real owner of the name George Bush: "There is only one George Bush and it is W." George H. W., the father, is "Poppy."[42]

Bar emerges from the *Talk* magazine article as very butch and antimaternal, recalling another Barbara, Barbara Stanwyck of *The Big Valley,* who wore the chaps in the family and ruled the ranch, or, in the words of the Texas wildcatter and former W. drinking buddy Joe O'Neill, "furiously smoking Newports and otherwise embracing the macho universe and bad ass redneck nature of life in the oil patch." This Bar is not the domestic-goddess mix of "Betty Crocker and Betsy Ross" but is a "lacerating wit," "wickedly disciplined without projecting the same micro-managerial tightly coiled aura that Nancy Reagan exuded."[43] Frum also confides that he thinks George's problem lies more with his difficult, judgmental mother than with his dad. This depiction emerges in the account by Paul O'Neill (told to the author Ron Suskind). One of the things W. likes about Camp David is the "comfort food" they serve there. When O'Neill's wife asks what favorite foods Bar cooked for him, he answers, "My mother never cooked. The woman had frostbite on her fingers. Everything came out of the freezer."[44] The severity of this depiction of his mother ("the woman") who is not nourishing and nurturing but is cold as (dry) ice ("frostbite") is stunning, and it unsettles O'Neill's wife. (W., however, goes on blithely to wonder what comfort foods they will be serving for dinner.)

It is in reference to Bar that one accounts for his choice of wife. Laura is, in Frum's words, his antimother, "his mother antidote": "warm, not stern, shy not assertive, domestic not political."[45] It explains his relationships with "Bushwomen" who provide the screen for his radical policies. Of the "Bushwomen"[46] (Rice, Christine Todd Whitman, Gale Norton), his most intimate is Karen Hughes ("who even looks much as Barbara Bush did in her mid-forties, but who offered him the unqualified admiration she never did"). Karen Hughes is "his mother substitute" and wields more power than any other woman since Edith Wilson, "not excluding Nancy Reagan and Hillary Clinton."[47]

In the W. family romance, W. has not only two Mommies (Karen and Bar) but two daddies, split between the "light and benevolent" Poppy and the "dark and vengeful" Dick (Cheney).[48] W. needs to supplement his dad; even an X-president does not suffice.

When it comes to the other parts of the normative Oedipal drama, the W. story is, on the surface, fairly straightforward in all popular accounts. As a firstborn son, he runs on his father's name and assembles a team of his father's advisers and public relations men, such as Sig "They hired me after he bit the guy" Rogich, Mike Tyson's crisis manager and the maker of the "Dukakis in a tank" ad.[49] The son methodically renovates his dad's legacy and avenges his defeat by Bill Clinton. "The 2000 election was about time travel. Here was George W. Bush, so much like a younger and politically more agile version of his father that he might have been genetically engineered, running against Al Gore, which is to say against the entire BC era." The fact that Bush was "chosen"(or "selected" with the help of the family *consigliere,* James Baker) "put the whole BC era under a strange kind of erasure."[50]

Nicholas Lehman sees the W.'s presidency as one of settling scores to remove the tarnish from the family name, especially as it is linked to leaving Saddam Hussein in power.[51] Powell and Rice, from the previous Bush administration (even though they were on the wrong historical side of the breakup of the Soviet Union), assist Cheney and Rumsfeld, from even earlier political administrations. The press notes the anachronism of this going forward by going backward, as a "Back to the Future" cabinet.[52] W.'s peculiar reenactment of his dad's presidency will foreground not repeating his father's mistakes (most of all, not alienating the Radical Right, those who are most tied to the hegemony of the signifier "life"), correcting some past mistakes (ousting Saddam from power), and completing the unfinished spatial-military ambitions of going to the moon and to Mars (projects for which his father's administration had insufficient means).[53]

This highly functional, if reductive, account gives us time travel as Oedipal narrative with a twist. As in the film *Frequency*,[54] it is less a question of producing a rightful heir than it is a question of saving the father and keeping him alive at all costs. The film is split between a traumatized abused killer and the exemplary son, able to vanquish history, reanimate his dead parents, and found a normative, baseball-playing (Lexus-driving) nuclear family. Indeed, the time travel paradox can now be exploited for secondary gains (as if one needed to supplement the Oedipal payoff), as it affords new possibilities for profit-making in terms of the ultimate insider-trading position—the future!

Frequency at least successfully rescues dad and the normative family, apparently resolving the Oedipal conflict to the son's advantage. This is in marked contrast to other dysfunctional and resolutely anti-Oedipal artifacts of Boomer pop culture, such as *Six Feet Under* (dad's dead, mom's a whore, sis is on crack, and brother is fratricidal), or the m/Other problems of John Singleton's *Baby Boy* or Spielberg's confessional *AI*, which present developmentally arrested men (let's say about age twelve) who are barred from attaining adult responsibility. And it's all mom's fault—too much love (*Baby Boy*) or too little (*AI*).[55] (Spielberg's *AI* goes even further than Hitchcock in the Norman Bates option!) The Cold War may be over, but the antimaternal animus of its national security state (enshrined in texts such as Philip Wylie's *Generation of Vipers*) is still resonant. Fathers are dead, dead-beat, or otherwise ineffectual.[56]

W-Bush, as son, would reverse the Darwinian underpinnings of Freud's totemic myth. He is repeatedly represented as a simian version of his dad: "As George W. aged into his forties, he looked something like the monkey version of his father, with no unkindness meant to George W. or simians."[57] Here the alpha comes after the beta male. Both Maureen Dowd and the film critic Elvis Mitchell read Bush as Thade of Tim Burton's *Planet of the Apes* remake, America's "scariest reality show." W. is President Primate: "Extremism in the defense of apes is no vice."[58] Tim Roth's Thade is, like W., a "mercurial mixture of rage and disgust . . . a preening vindictive chimp with ambitions to rule and do away with the compacts governing chimp society."[59] Thade is disturbingly feral, treating "every situation as if he is marking his territory." Tucker Carlson described W.'s stance during the 2000 campaign: "When he meets someone Bush stands two paces back and stares. His eyes get beady. He doesn't seem eager or smile right away. When he talks it is sometimes in grunts and usually out of the side of his mouth, like a prelude to a bar fight or before a close friend tells an intimacy."[60] (Carlson's article is a positive appreciation. As such, it illustrates how "rage is rooted in the Republican psyche," along with "deeply ingrained apocalyptic fervor, vitriolic rhetoric." Or, in Gingrich's rephrasing of Clausewitz: "politics is war without blood.")[61] Tim Roth plays the simian leader Thade with the "flamboyant insouciance" emblematic of the immediate pre-9/11 period. This "menacing atmosphere of the monkey planet" climaxes in the last apocalyptic scene of a simian (W.?) standing in for Lincoln. Former congressman Tom Downey and the actor Craig Wroe studied Bush's mannerisms during the mock practice debates of the 2000 campaign: "We'd watch the tapes trying to figure out Bush's mind set. . . . There's always this *fear* in Bush's eyes, like Dan Quayle, but two notches down. And then there's the smugness he uses to cover it."[62] Wroe, the method actor, reaches a breakthrough: "Bush has this look as if something smelled really foul near him. . . . As an actor, I'd play him as if there were always something that stinks nearby." We will return to W.'s proximity to the "Thing," which does account for a style that is "at once intimate and fairly menacing, it's weirdly compelling."[63]

Le Père

What accounts for this revision, and how do such enactments in popular culture point to a shift toward a perverse and no longer neurotic relation to the father function? Or, if Bush is "not your Father's Republican" (and is especially not his father's or his grandfather's [Prescott Bush, a moderate senator from Connecticut] Republican), what is he?[64] At first glance, it might seem that Bush represents an attempt to supplement a less than fully virile paternal metaphor. One could read an embodiment of "toughness" in his extensive accessorizing: cowboy boots and Oval Office belt buckle, flight suit, pickup truck, and an entire ranch in Crawford (but, like little Hans, he appears to keep his distance from horses). This "butch" president (in Richard Goldstein's words) is now available as a poseable twelve-inch action figure. ("We wouldn't just make any president in a business suit.")[65] W. Bush gets to be (if not have) the phallus. Bill Clinton would represent a reformist attempt to alter the *nom du père* in order to accommodate some *jouissance* (i.e., as an object of his mother's desire). One might see the larger impeachment struggle as a response to Clinton's breaking of the social-symbolic contract of leadership, that is, as a response to his refusal to exchange a part of his enjoyment for the name of the father.

In what ways did Bush the Father require supplementation? G.H.W. Bush was not a conventionally masculine father. As we saw in chapter 5, he is described repeatedly as an eternal son not up to the job, a man who called his mother, Dorothy, every day from the White House. W. as his dad's campaign manager (described in reversal as the oracle of his father's desires) says his dad is a much better dad than candidate.[66] (The fact that Bush *père*'s lack can be named does save his son from psychosis.) It is interesting to note that Bush *père* was a more passive president than vice president. He legislated (reactively) by vetoing bills and was self-described as a "better fielder than hitter."[67] His responses to historical events were inappropriate. When the Berlin Wall came down, he did not (unlike his son's administration) jump at accepting acclaim but looked "as if he had just seen his dog run over by a truck."[68] He disliked confrontation. His presidential style was "waffle, retreat, blink and flip-flop." He met all his military commander's requests rather than decide: "It was as if Bush had taken his two top commanders [Powell and Schwartzkopf] out to dinner and had ordered all the entrees on the menu."[69]

It is more accurate to see George H. W. Bush's presidency, in Slavoj Zizek's postmodern recoding, as a part-object who has not been transubstantiated into a symbolic function.[70] The father is no longer sublated in his name or dead but is "alive," if anything overly proximate in his "obscene" dimension. We have seen that Bush's two campaigns played on imaginaries linked to feminine pathologies. The successful 1988 campaign was figured in terms of male hysteria ("I'm one of you all") whose moment of paradigmatic parapraxis came when he admitted (in Twin Falls, Iowa) to having had sex with Reagan: "For seven and a half years, I have worked alongside him and I am proud to be his partner. We've had triumphs, we've made mistakes, we have had sex." He then corrected his lapsus "sex," substituting "setbacks" and comparing himself to a "javelin thrower who won the coin toss and elected to receive."[71] This lapsus gave some presentiments of the masochistic display of the 1992 campaign, in which Bush eliminates the projective thrust of the javelin thrower and the agency of one who "elects" after "winning" and instead offers the condensation of the "javelin catcher" ("I'm not going to be the javelin catcher" for tired liberals in Congress"), exhibiting masochistic ecstasy as anal *jouissance*.[72]

This exhibition is pronounced in Bush's collection of letters, *All the Best, George Bush*. It should be noted that Bush edited these letters himself, choosing the ones for inclusion and also choosing which journal entries would supplement them and their ordering (mostly, chronological, with one notable exception). Some readers may recall Bush's broken tax pledge when he joked, to reporters who followed him on a run, "Read my hips," which was seen as an only slightly displaced way of saying "Kiss my ass."[73] At the time, I remembered Roland Barthes's formulation in *The Pleasure of the Text*; Barthes juxtaposes the person who speaks frontally from the place of the phallus with "that uninhibited person who shows his behind to the political father."[74] So I was not that surprised to read an entry in which Bush recounts breaking his tailbone and having to bring a rubber ring to the Oval Office, where he is to have lunch with Reagan. It turns out that Reagan was gracious about it, and, although Bush found Reagan difficult to read, "I feel uninhibited bringing things up to him."[75] At the time of the budget crisis, he again asserts (figurally) his pleasure in orifice over organ pleasure as he speaks of the Republicans who may not want to go along with him and quotes an expression of LBJ's: "Some of them want to paint their asses white and run with the antelopes. . . . Isn't that a marvelous image?"[76]

In his collection of letters, Bush revisits the sites of trauma in his life and his presidency. The signifier Japan is linked to the downing of his World War II TBM Avenger plane and to the trip where he throws up on the prime minister of Japan.[77] The trip to Japan occurred before the 1992 State of the Union as a kickoff event for the electoral campaign. Bush was accompanied on the trip by prominent CEOs who were intent upon establishing the United States as a power player—a corporate Pacific rim job to Singapore and Australia, as well as South Korea: "I just wanted access to the other guy's markets." Bush's nausea begins in advance of the dinner, when he is halfway through the receiving line for Prime Minister Miyazawa's dinner party. He is unable to eat or speak but breaks out in a profuse sweat: "water just pouring out of me, and the next thing I know literally, I was on the floor. I woke up and I had this euphoric feeling." This feeling is otherwise described as "out of body" and "one hundred per cent strange."[78] In the correspondence he shares with us upon his return to the White House, he uses every available pretext to bring this incident up again, whether as a jocular aside in a thank-you note to Ron Reagan Jr. or as a New Year's message to his nephew (and Fox newsman) John Ellis.[79] His message to his economic adviser Nicholas Brady links the vomiting episode to its fiscal-policy analogues (where many of the Bush presidential parapraxes are located). Vomiting is a symptom of stalled or frustrated anality: "Our Japan trip was productive, but 'throwing up' was the whole story. The Budget Compromise—that now infamous agreement that would have been *digested* if the economy had vigorously recovered" (emphasis mine).[80] The Japan episode is indicative of the way Bush points to, rather than deflecting our attention from, failure. It also represents a corporeal zone in relation to the *jouissance* of the budgetary process[81] different from Reagan's phallic "tax axe." (The bowels, as was argued in an earlier chapter, were the metaphorical site of Reagan's covert operations.)

Bush will return to "Japan" in 1997 (at age seventy-five) to make a parachute jump and to relive the earlier traumatic wartime crash. The narrative about his decision to jump is an extended journal entry with verbal reaction shots of his sons, Bar, and Colin Powell, punctuated by self-conscious soliloquy. In the midst of recounting a war experience, something happened: "An idea, sleeping like Rip Van Winkle, alive but not alive. Now it was quite clear. I want to make one more parachute jump. . . . 'Piece of cake,' thinks me."[82]

"Thinks me" is a typical Bush locution, situating him as the object of his enunciation. (This is even more peculiar as it is a thought that thinks him.) Socializing with an incredulous Colin Powell at a Desert Storm reunion party, Bush underlines his strong desire to make the jump: "I do not want to do anything dumb, but I must complete my mission." He wonders out loud: "Why has this now become an obsession? I have everything in life as God would have it. I have never been happier, but I want to do the jump." He is clearly elated and communicates this elation in what he terms a "ribald joke": "Don't give them the name of my laundryman." He then parodies Dana Carvey—"Shouldn'd dunnit, wasn't prudent, wasn't nice"—and explains (to the joke-obtuse) that the remark goes back to his Air Force carrier days; pilots would say, "Only my laundryman will ever know." The next association makes the link with end-pleasure stronger as he compares this jump with the earlier wartime jump into an endless sea: "I have a goal. I will achieve it."[83] In other words, he has an end in sight.

His son's responses are indicative of the way they erotically associate this jump. Jeb tells him it's fine but not to change his sexual preference, while W. admonishes him not to tell anyone about his eighteen-year-old girlfriend (just barely past the age of majority).[84] On jump day, he dons his Desert Storm boots and white Elvis suit with helmet and gloves ("The King would have approved").[85] His jump is recounted with an unbridled elation that exposes and textually reenacts a prohibited scene of fist and end pleasure that recalls Sedgwick's scene of Jamesian "queer tutelage" where "dense and highly charged associations concerning the anus did not cluster around images of the phallus. They clustered around the hand."[86] The "fisting image" as sexual phantasmatic negotiates between "allo- and auto-eroticism" and, more important for Bush the presidential subject, "between the polarities that a phallic economy defines as active and passive."[87] Rather than reading Bush's oscillations, either pronominal or *sportif* (in golf he's a "naturally right hander who plays left-handed"),[88] as some type of less than heteronormative "switch-hitting," it might be more productive to consider this handsome man an "anatomical double entendre."[89]

Hyped with the other jumpers, he describes an elaborate fisting ritual (fists on top of the other guy's fists, knocking the ends of his and their fists, and finally pointing index fingers). Now he reverses the traumatic crash where "tight fisted and knotted up" George Bush would take refuge in submersion and repression.[90] His only moment of fear comes when he nears the exit zone and is commanded to back up. Here "fear" connotes desire. It is expressed as a "twinge" and is disavowed as panic, "rather a halting feeling in the legs, groin and gut." Then he jumps in good Elvis position, shoulders arched, pelvis out, and is surprised by the jolt of the cord. He experiences an orgasmic little death: "I was at peace. Gone was the noise from the free fall. I was alone, floating gently towards earth, reveling in the freedom, enjoying the view. It was a marvelous sensation. . . . I had lived a dream."[91]

The last (unchronological) letter in the book is addressed to his kids, and, even following the Japan and parachuting entries, it is bizarre. It is about aging, taking Metamucil (for constipation), and his loss of balance and memory. Bush chronicles the long-term memories he still possesses in detail, starting with his mother's feet (to illustrate her fierce competitiveness, as exemplified in her tennis game with a much younger woman, Peaches Peltz). "Mother literally wore the skin off the bottom of her feet."[92] But she won. (Peaches is being beaten by my mother, whom I love.) His next association is to his uncle Johnny Walker, who told him in 1945 about a famous lawyer friend who "liked to stand in a cold shower and let icy water hit him in the crack of his buttocks." Yet he admits that he cannot recall what Gorbachev told him in 1991 or what Kohl "said when the wall came down in 1989."[93] The end of the Cold War bring us back to cold water and end pleasure as Bush insists that he doesn't share his uncle's friend's taste. "Warm water there— sure, but icy water no way." In other words, to paraphrase President Reagan, "Mr. Gorbachev, tear down that *stall* [shower]!" He next associates to the happy memories of all five of his children! The only "phallic" moment of the letter from dad is about his repeated exposure (having to be publicly reminded that his zipper was unzipped), referencing his own beloved quotation: "An old bird does not fall out of the nest." He then describes his "zipper recovery technique," which he learned from Italy's Prime Minister Andreotti: He turned around, pretending to admire the Gilbert Stuart portrait of Washington, "and then with no visible concern zipped his pants up."[94] What is "tragic" about this last example is that it no longer embarrasses him.

The Bush that emerges from these letters is less the symbolic authority than what Zizek has called the anal father who materializes "sprouts of enjoyment."[95] This anal father (a term he prefers to "primordial father") points to his obscene nature as a presymbolic partial object.[96] Yet this presymbolic father is a resolutely modern phenomenon—a result of the paternal metaphor's decline (modernism) or the excessive presence of a father who can't be reduced to the bearer of a symbolic function.[97]

Zizek returns to this figure in a recent reading of the film *Apocalypse Now: Redux*. Here the *père jouissant* (Kurtz) is a sign of state power's excess, which can be neutralized only by a secret operation.[98] Indeed, one way to read George W.'s obsession with secrecy, as well as his object choice of "bad guy du jour" (Taliban and bin Laden, Noriega in Panama, or Saddam and the Baathist regime), is precisely by means of this disavowed excess of state power that finds its complement in the CIA covert op. The elder Bush, as former head of the CIA is, like Kurtz, overidentified with the nonsymbolizable *objet a* of state power. The extreme care with maintaining secrecy and a foreign policy driven by the modern state's *objet a* are only two signs of a perverse presidential politics.

Ou Pire . . .

I will not use my office as a mirror to reflect public opinion.[99]

W-Bush asserts that his administration will not be situated in the imaginary register. Nor will we witness the abject testing of the symbolic that often characterized the Clinton era. Even before 9/11, W. was differently situated in relation to the symbolic and the real. W-Bush was selected into office by the Court's rejection of the *objet a*/hanging chads[100] and the electorate's near-rejection of an ideal father of regulated enjoyment (Gore). Neither candidate was able to sustain the imaginary identification of elected leadership. The first few months of the W-Bush presidency could be read as a tutelary regime, explained in part as indicative of a post-Cold War world of uncertainty where we are deprived of those phobic objects or signifiers (the USSR, "communism," or even rogue sovereign nation-states) that allowed us to respond to or to cover over the lack in the Other. More significantly, W.'s (and his selected agent of the law Ashcroft's) intransigence in allowing for any limit on the symbolic in relation to the real was particularly apparent in the administration's attachment to the production (and regulation) of signifiers of life. ("Life" here parallels Wilson's master signifiers "peace"/"absolute justice").

What John Kerry and others have deemed the most extreme administration is less an interest-driven pandering to the radical right (although it also is that) than an inability to permit any liberalization of social policy. (Even Senator Orrin Hatch differs with Bush's parsing of the stem cell issue, which restricts researchers to "previously killed" embryos.) Whether it is a question of "partial-birth abortion," the availability of abortion in the case of rape and incest, or the use of embryonic stem cells in medical research (one of the few policies that W. is reported to have cracked a briefing book about), "liberalization" in the W-Bush era is equated with the erosion of the signifier "life" and as such exposes us to the insufficiencies of the symbolic to totally protect us. Or worse: in the case of the successful referenda on doctor-assisted suicide and medical marijuana (which Ashcroft took time out to combat as a homeland security issue in the immediate aftermath of 9/11), the symbolic may actually desire our death (organ harvesting) or *jouissance*.

Could we read these "life issues" as a symptom of the refusal of any higher cause (coincident with the inability of the subject to identify with a master signifier)? Thus, in Zizek's words, "the ultimate purpose of our life is life itself."[101] Both intense support for and opposition to the death penalty similarly point to "death" as the ultimate traumatism of a politics of administered life. Deprived of a more resonant symbolic (that is, something worth dying for), life itself figures as an ultimate political horizon underwriting a military-industrial complex (that destroys life), a medical-industrial complex (that prolongs life), and, I would add to these two Zizekian examples, a prison-industrial complex (that warehouses life).

It is in this sense that I read the contribution of the Bushwomen differently from Laura Flanders. They are less (imaginary-driven) identity puppets concealing the "real" stakes of his policies than "women" who, as Lacan would have it, have less to lose when it comes to the symbolic. Their inconsistencies or equivocations in relation to the hegemony of the signifier "life" ("pro-choice," but, in the case of Christine Todd Whitman, "pro-arsenic"' in water and less concerned about the toxicity in lower Manhattan post-9/11) are not "hypocritical" (always the rational, "interest"-driven reason) but rather either less cathected to the master signifier or simply less traumatized by the spectacle of lack in the Other.

W-Bush's response to the Other's lack is perverse. When confronted with symbolic limitations, Wilson evinced neurotic symptoms. The repressed returned corporeally or in self-sabotaging repetition compulsions or in the production of a phobic object (the League of Nations). Wilson's pattern was antinomical:[102] one or the other, Lloyd George or Cabot Lodge, desire or law. His many hesitations and abrupt reversals during the Treaty process as detailed by Freud and Bullitt are so many neurotic complications of his unresolved father complex. W., the pervert, however, disavows what the neurotic perceives.[103] W. stages his disavowal of the father function, restricting the sphere of illusion to the medical/military/prison-industrial complex. In this sense, his "Top Gun" flight suit is less a media-motivated electoral photo op than a paternal "mission-ary (position) accomplished." This display threatens considerable exposure (and not just if the war casualties continue) of the reason for military intervention in the first place. (And since when has Tom Cruise represented unequivocal normative masculinity?)

Jean Clavreul and Joan Copjec underscore that it is not the question of object choice (appropriate or not) or a relation to a particular other (however normatively figured) that defines the pervert as much as it is his libidinal investments in the law and institutions that govern social relations, which are markedly different from those of the neurotic subject. Indeed, this "perverse" relation to the law was apparent from the beginning of the W-Bush administration—in the withdrawal from the Kyoto Treaty, the ABM treaty, the World Court, and Clinton's agreements in North Korea and in W.'s dismissive attitudes toward international organizations, such as the UN. These stances can be read as precursors to the policies of preemption or unilateralism, but I think they are more cogently situated as instantiations of a perverse foreign policy in which preemption is the master trope. Again, the comparisons with Wilson are illustrative. Whereas Wilson enjoyed the crafting of constitutions (as so many obsessive replays of repressed and unresolved father-as-Christian-statesman functions), W.'s provocative withdrawals are less about the law's revocation than the struggle to bring a law into being so as to make the Other exist. Elizabeth Kohlbert notes that George W. Bush "went into Iraq with the law behind him because it was the only way, in his mind, to reestablish the law."[104] She reads this as congruent with his "cowboy" image. Preemption or unilateralism can be read as a policy that forces some Other to pronounce the law (W. at the UN), indicating oneself the place of law (to achieve separation), or as an attempt to prop up the law so that limits can be set to *jouissance* (the Ridge-Ashcroft solution).

In other words, we should not read Bush's provocations aimed at established law (treaties, the charters of international organizations, diplomatic agreements) as neurotic transgressions. The pervert, unlike the neurotic, does not desire as a function of law, that is, doesn't desire what is prohibited. "Nor is the pervert's relation to the law characterized by neurotic hesitation, torn between trying to please figures of authority and to show proper respect on one hand while questioning their legitimacy and taking precautions against or making allowances for their fallibility on the other. *For, unsure of the Other's desires and unsure therefore if this particular representative isn't actually a fraud, the neurotic ends up wavering in her allegiance to particular laws. It is not that she doesn't want to obey the law—it is just that she is a little vague about what it is.*"[105]

The pervert replaces neurotic hesitation with clarity and certainty. Bob Woodward quotes the president in his hagiographic *Bush at War:* "I have not doubted. There is not one doubt in my mind we're doing the right thing. Not one doubt."[106] Paul O'Neill concurs that the "pres-

ident is showing conviction, but from what source? With his level of experience, I would not be able to support such a conviction." Bush is
"driven by a secular faith in his instincts," which are figured as a second
religion.[107] This contrasts with Wilson's alignment with the master signifier "God," or the God-derived "America."

W-Bush's ultimatums ("For us or against us") and his full-frontal
taunts ("Bring it on") are not polyvalent figures like his father's "line in
the sand" (whose implicit effacement, as Ronell has astutely noted, is
ripe for catachrestical metalepsis).[108] Copjec distinguishes the determined character of this perverse universe: "We are no longer in the presence of some indeterminate other consciousness of a public with which
we maintain a relation of 'uneasy determination' but of an infallible law
with which we maintain a relation that leaves little room for doubt."[109]
The pervert's Other is arbitrary, relative yet absolute. Unlike the neurotic, he does not try to "puzzle out" what it wants from him. This lack
of curiosity, this disengagement or passivity, is at times noted in the various insider accounts of O'Neill or Frum and would be more accurately
described as perverse apathy

Rigidity and contractual, rather than symbolic, relations obtain. Even
in the case of Bush's "relenting" on having Condi Rice testify before
Congress, there are a host of contractual conditions that must be arranged rather than the more fluid give-and-take of admitted all-too-
human fallibility and ambivalence. Indeed, "ambivalence" is a word
that W. could not mispronounce on cue, requiring numerous retakes for
his *Saturday Night Live* appearance.[110]

Jean Clavreul notes the impact of this rigidity in relation to knowledge; the pervert's "fixity" allows for no temporal bounds; there is no
"before" or "after," which makes it impossible to revise knowledge in
relation to facts.[111] This counterfactual strain in W.'s presidency has
resulted in a cottage industry of best-selling popular books that note
the symptom and name this (perverse) relation to knowledge as "lying."
(David Corn's and Al Franken's books are examples of this genre.)
What Clavreul insists upon, however, is that "this knowledge that is
given as truth" relates to the split-off part of the pervert that is not
(as with the neurotic) repressed but that has still not been adequately
subjectivized. What is missing in W. (which is the enigma pondered by
insider accounts and seen as transparent perfidy by popular critics) is
what Clavreul calls "the absence of the subjective root of not knowing . . . of the desire to know."[112] This is what (in one of the more

amusing moments of the Democratic debates) underscored the Reverend Al Sharpton's retort that if Bush didn't know he was lying, it was *worse*" (*Ou pire . . .*). The pervert's knowledge "refuses to recognize its insertion in a 'not knowing' which precedes it. . . . It is a knowledge given as truth."[113]

Bush's knowledge is obdurate and resolutely literal. Lacking any *fantaisie,* his field of illusion persists in the fetish. The necessity of a self-sustaining illusion is lodged in the WMD or in Saddam/regime change or perhaps (in October) in Osama or in any other ready-to-hand pedestrian other. What is key here is the tenacity this fetish has on him/us as it is "doubly derived from contrary ideas."

Père Sévère

One of the more intriguing of Bush's lapses occurred during the 2000 campaign. The setting was doubly significant; it happened in New Hampshire (a return to what passes for the Bush ancestral home) and in an elementary school—an eminently tutelary setting. We have seen how New Hampshire was the site of a prior Bush electoral lapsus in 1992 when Bush *père* was literally stupefied (*medusé*) by his confrontation with the supermarket scanner—the m/Other literalized as the *bar*-code.

The son's lapsus is equally telling and similarly situated in relation to the m/Other. W-Bush was invited to the Fairgrounds Elementary School in Nashua, New Hampshire, to speak during Perseverance Month. Perseverance, however, proved to be a word he couldn't say, transforming it into "preservation." "This is Preservation Month. I appreciate preservation. It's what you do when you run for president. You gotta preserve."

Recently, Zizek read this as just another undifferentiated proto-Heideggerian "art of generating deep insights from tautological reversals," translating it as follows: "The essence of preservation has nothing to do with the ontic preservation of our physical resources. The essence of preservation is the preservation of the essence of our society itself—and this is what the president of the USA has to do, even if, at the vulgar ontic level, he allows the destruction of more natural resources than in the entire previous history of the USA."[114] For Zizek, there is, surprisingly, nothing particular or contingent about the phoneme "preservation" or the site of its locution. Any analogous chiasmically structured tautologous utterance (indeed, many similarly structured ones from the first President Bush or from Dan Quayle would fit) that would meet the Heideggerian formula "das Wesen der Warheit ist die Wahrheit des Wesens" [the essence of truth is the truth of essence] would do, and he gives us other compelling philosophical examples from Donald Rumsfeld: "There are known knowns. These are things we know that we know. There are known unknowns. That is to say, there are things that we know that we don't know. But there are also unknown unknowns. There are things we don't know we don't know."[115] Zizek goes on to point out the fourth *combinatoire* omitted by the great sage: the "unknown knowns," or what Bollas called "the unthought known," or, as Zizek renders it, "the disavowed beliefs and suppositions we are not even aware of adhering to ourselves." Let us look more closely, then, at "preservation."

This lapsus is telling in what Bush says and cannot say. Running for president would seem to be about perseverance, a long-distance or marathon process in which endurance is key. Yet "preservation" is an apt condensation for the pervert president who does "preserve" the certainty of the law's truth, in Joan Copjec's elegant formulation, and who would replace "the autonomy of the citizen-subject with a determination to carry out the duty spelled out by a heteronomous edict."[116]

Preservation is also suggestive of the secrecy of Clavreul's perverse contract, which must be *preserved*. Preservation connotes a form of death in life, as in the case of preserved meats or fruits, something that retards spoilage. It also connotes a desire to keep something intact or unimpaired (a wildlife preserve) or the state of keeping something in such a condition. This integrity or intactness is precisely what is at issue. Permanence is something the pervert cannot supply when it comes to propping up a deficient paternal metaphor. Preserve contains serve; the pervert serves as the *objet a* and is preserved as the *objet a*, the bearer of an anxiety-producing *jouissance*: "Let the other get off on me!" ("Bring it on!").

Perseverance contains *severance*, a synonym for the separation that the pervert has not achieved, perhaps expressing a wish for the father as symbolic separator, a father who would be able to bar the m/other (in this case, abyssal: to bar "Bar"). It contains *severe*, as in the desired anxiety or anguish produced by the sadistic pervert as well as his characteristic severity, that is, the unsparing rigidity and moralism that stage the pervert's will to *jouissance*.

But the substitution of preservation for perseverance (as a word he can not say) most literally points to the *père sévère,* the anal, obscene father who haunts the idealized father function and moves, like the presidencies of Bush *père* and *fils,* from the symptom of the father to the father itself as symptom.[117]

On Zizek and Consequences

> The name of the father is no longer the symptom/*sinthome* that holds together the social link. The political consequences of this insight are capital.[118]

Zizek reminds us that, for Lacan, the Oedipus complex was just one more symptom to be interpreted. "The Father" was the symbolization of a deadlock (i.e., the enigma of the m/Other's desire), and as such it worked as a compromise formation, alleviating the "anxiety of confronting the void of the Other's desire." Michel Schneider and Eric Laurent, writing after the trauma of the 2002 French elections, concur in the effects of the desymbolization of the political subject: the deinstitutionalization of the social bond, the decline of the paternal function, the infantilization of citizens, and the fantasy of a politics freed from conflict.[119] It might prove interesting to compare their diagnosis with Lacan's explicit political pronouncements.

From his earliest writings, *Les Complexes Familiales* (1938), Lacan links the decline of paternal authority with dire consequences: the concentration of economic capital and political catastrophe.[120] Today's economic argument is less about the redistribution of surplus value than it is about the violent allocation of work and nonwork, between "nonwork remunerated by the labor of others" and work as the biopolitical threshold of social inclusion.[121]

But it is Lacan's elliptical reference to racism and his genial neologism "humanhysterianism" ("*humanitairerie*") that must be read against the reminder that perversion is not only a relation to law but also an attitude to the Other's *jouissance.* Lacan warns, in *Television* (1973): "With our *jouissance* going off the track, only the Other is able to mark its position, but only in so far as we are separated from this Other."

The pervert, however, is incapable of "leaving this Other to his own mode of *jouissance,* that would be possible by not imposing our own on him. . . ."[122] He follows a policy of "zero tolerance" for the Other's *jouissance*. Racism is not a rejection of the Other; it is an anxiety-ridden defense against the proximity of his imagined enjoyment.

Perverse politics can not do without the alibi of humanitarianism, which Lacan situates in relation to surplus enjoyment (*plus de jouir*). "Given the precariousness of our own mode, which from now on takes its bearings from the ideal of an over-coming (*plus de jouir*), which is in fact no longer expressed in any other way, how can we hope that the empty forms of humanhysterianism (*humanitairerie*) disguising our extortions continue to last."[123] For Zizek as well, humanitarianism is a fetish: "Charity is, today, part of the game as a humanitarian mask hiding the underlying exploitation." It is a "superegotic blackmail"[124] in which the rich nations and their international organizations (the IMF, the World Bank) "help" the poor ones with aid, credits, and possibly debt forgiveness and thereby "overlook" the paradoxical relation between First-World "profit" and what Marx called "immiseration" of the Third World. But Zizek's castigation of the humanitarian gesture is less a reformulation of Marxist ideology critique than a shift to the biopolitical stakes of humanitarianism, which replaces the antimony of class struggle with a splitting of two (paired) excluded *homo sacer:* on the one side terrorists and "enemy combatants" and on the other refugees and clandestine immigrants (*sans papiers*).[125] Moreover, today's humanitarianism, as Zizek correctly notes, can't be dissociated from war, for it is the belligerent nation states (the United States, Britain) that take over the caritative functions of international organizations such as the Red Cross and the United Nations.

Humanitarian gestures can no longer be easily differentiated from military tactics. In 1967, Lacan referenced to Daniel Cohn-Bendit in his assertion that "cobblestones (*pavés*) and tear gas canisters performed the function of *objet a*."[126] This apportioning of *objet a* pairs those of the students (*pavés*) with those of the repressive police (tear gas). Today's *objet a* (WMD or anthrax) admits of no such tidy discrimination; the perverse logic is best exemplified by the *objets a* of bombs and snacks/food parcels in the Afghanistan war.

Homo sacer as university discourse is tied to the inability to assume a symbolic mandate.[127] This displacement of the master signifier can be seen in diverse manifestations of contemporary politics and their attendant theorizations: communitarianism as a nostalgia for the *nom du père*; the celebration of the "Not All" of "multiplicity" misrecognized as Deleuzian by Hardt and Negri; the pathetic search for a guarantee somewhere else—in world financial markets, in the secular faith in Alan Greenspan, in the accountability of audits. Our new fantasies are symptomatic of a symbolic/paternal metaphor that is no longer operative. We live in a perpetual present tense of politics that is strictly opposed to the temporality of symbolic castration. We long for the maternalization of authority, a shift from the Big Brother who sees to a mother who listens.[128] This last feature might seem counterintuitive in light of W-Bush's hypermale parody and his relentless rollback of New Deal welfare-state provisions. Yet the maternal is at work whenever it is the appeal to security and protection that is at issue.

Eric Laurent notes the profound effect of this desymbolization within contemporary subjectivity, describing the search for the presence of the Other in us as evinced in pastimes of risk (sexual and war tourisms, dangerous sports, amateur astronauts), as well as by the suicide bomber. Both the fantasy of neototalitarian repression and the suicidal bacchanal (in his terms, the "generalized overdose") share the same *jouissance* and the same failure to rise to the democratic challenge: "How to tolerate the inconsistency of the Other without ceding to the injunction of the superego to enjoy."[129]

Election 2004

This year's presidential campaign appears to be centered on perverse politics—on the one side is the incumbent, W. Yet the Democrat's strategy is no less perverse. For what underwrites "electability" if it is not the certainty of knowing where the Other's *jouissance* is located and the willingness to make oneself the *objet a* for the "surplus enjoyment" of the Other? We would do well to recall Lacan's analysis of deGaulle's appeal in 1958 as the man who said "No" on June 18: "The share of the signifier in politics—the signifier "No" when everyone slips into unspeakable consent—has yet to be studied."[130]

9

Hillary Regained (2005)

The Xena of mid-life career changes.

—Gail Collins[1]

Sixty-two counties, sixteen months, three debates, two opponents, and six black pants suits later . . . —Hillary Clinton[2]

It is perhaps a testament to the paradoxical workings of femininity and fantasy that I begin with the obvious: Hillary is still here and thriving. For who would have predicted after the health-care debacle (blamed for the Democrats' midterm congressional losses), which earned her the dubious distinction of being the rare First Lady to achieve a poll number lower than her husband (40 percent favorable for Hillary compared with 44 percent for her husband in 1994),[3] that she would triumph as the remaining star of the Clinton administration and a leading 2008 presidential contender? At this time, Hillary is being touted by Nicholas Kristof[4] on the editorial pages as the one Democrat who "gets the values" issue (read life and religion) and is the fodder for odd-couple/new-best-friend stories with none other than Newt Gingrich, who agrees with her on the need for a strong defense. She has successfully downloaded both patronyms—Rodham and Clinton—in her Senate campaign to emerge, diva-style, as "Hillary" (like Cher, who, as of this writing, *has* finally "left the building," and Liza, with even more embarrassing marital problems). Indeed, in the language of celebrity journalism, she now "owns" New York. "New York senator" is itself evocative of Lacanian femininity, as it represents *no One*; the state's voters often elect luminaries, like Robert F. Kennedy, who never really lived in the state or who transcend narrow considerations of local interest.

On one level, this development might not be so surprising, for it is a good narrative, read either as a Fay Weldon revenge fantasy of major payback (now it is her turn) or as cost-effective redemption: something or someone must be redeemed from the Clinton presidency (or, in Joe Klein's words, at least not voted off the island).[5] Hillary's story resonates with our wish that these be narratives of self-discovery, emancipation, and progress. Gail Sheehy's account, *Hillary's Choice,* presents the senator on the cusp of "the Flaming Fifties," an exciting and vibrant new life stage of postmenopausal women who are "brainy careerists."[6] Joan Acocella's review neatly resumes its contours as applied to Hillary's life story: "Sexually unconfident gal marries sex maniac guy, is rendered further sexually unsure by his sexual misdeeds, finds upon his culminating sexual defection that she is finally liberated into—sexuality."[7] She even manages to come up with a consistent look, a pageboy turned "bob" ("immaculate blond bob") and dark pantsuit with note of color, immortalized in her Senate acceptance speech remarks that serve as an epigraph to this chapter ("Sixty-two counties . . . six black pantsuits later"), as well as a decorative motif in her senatorial headquarters in New York's garment district. Harpaz describes an office filled with campaign photos of Hillary (contrasted with the stark, mostly photo-free headquarters of Rudy Giuliani): "Hillary holding a baby, Hillary talking to black women, Hillary meeting old people. *It was like an anteroom for some sort of religious cult worshipping a blond lady with blue eyes and a big smile whose holy garments consisted of black pantsuits*" (italics mine).[8]

As with the masquerade that we saw in the previous chapter, Hillary's political trajectory is staged as a series of what one might call "clothes encounters." Her sartorial and political progress narratives are still read together and off each other, with several nuanced differences. As her fashion choices are redeemed, so too is her political capital. These choices are also more self-consciously staged and overtly sexualized (i.e., her dress for the NEA awards had a "flattering plunging neckline revealing the 'first bosom'"). Former fashion and spousal victimhoods are transmogrified into celebrity iconicity unthinkable in the early years of the Clinton presidency (i.e., the 1996 "Hillary is a babe" tee shirt).[9]

This willful self-presentation revisits former sites of visual cathexes such as her hair, but now this must be ironically signified verbally, since she has achieved a consistent look ("growing older and blonder"). In her Yale commencement speech, she recounts the lessons she has learned about the importance of hair: "The most important thing I have to say to you is that hair matters. . . . Your hair will send significant messages to those around you. Whatever hopes and dreams you have for the world, but more what hopes and dreams you have for your hair. Pay attention to your hair because everyone else will."[10] In her autobiography, described by Joe Klein as "part love poem, policy paper, travelogue and campaign memo," she is self-deprecating about her hair and its vicissitudes: "Her hairstyles reflected a search for identity as she became an increasingly public figure." These "everchanging hairstyles are a running gag in the book."[11]

What I want to emphasize at this point is not so much the redemption as the crossing in this narrative. For Hillary has successfully crossed over—from First Lady to senator, from unelected wife to public, elected official, from domestic sphere to world stage—in a way that raises the stakes for the theoretical questioning of femininity. Hillary as First Lady/wife did play a role on the world stage—in her speeches at Beijing or Davos or her trips to Africa with Chelsea—and these trips were often read as having a hidden agenda, that is, as a way for her to recover political capital (after the health-care debacle) or as public cover for private humiliation (post-Monica). Yet I argue that this crossing over does allow for a different instrumentalization of femininity. As we have noted in chapter 6, Rose's point à propos of Thatcher is that femininity functions to secure the limits of what society will or will not recognize about itself. Like insanity, she writes, it is a type of mitigating circumstance.[12] The question of whether femininity comes into play at the right point for my purposes here is whether it works in securing a limit definition of state violence while respecting existing conceptual categories—how a successful masquerade may, in other words, help to legitimate acts of state-sanctioned violence—how Thatcher's femininity "let her get away with murder."[13]

To return again to Thatcher, Alan Hollinghurst's (2004 Booker Prize–winning) *The Line of Beauty* conveys both sides of her appeal:

"She showed them in the Falklands, didn't she?"

"You mean she's a hideous old battleaxe," muttered Catherine.

"She's certainly a manxome foe," said Gerald. Sir Maurice looked blank. "One wouldn't want to be on the wrong side of her."

"Indeed" said Sir Maurice.

Wani . . . said, "People say that but you know, I've always seen a very different side of her. An immensely kind woman . . ."; he let them see him searching for a kind of heart-warming anecdote, but then said discreetly, "She takes such extraordinary pains to help those she . . . cares about."

Maurice Tipper expressed both respect and resentment in a dark throat clearing, and Gerald said,

"Of course you know her as a family friend. . . ."

"I love her!" exclaimed Sally Tipper, hoping perhaps they would take love to include friendship, as well as surpassing it.

"I know," said Gerald. "It's those blue eyes. Don't you just want to swim in them—what?"

Sir Maurice didn't seem ready to go quite that far, and Rachel said, "Not everyone's as infatuated as my husband," lightly but meaningly.[14]

If I have quoted this dialogue extensively, it is because it condenses the range of emotions Hillary also provokes, beginning with fearsome masculine feats of prowess—"manxome foe"/"one wouldn't want to be on the wrong side of her." Congressman Jim McDermott used an analogous military metaphor for Hillary: "If I were going to war, I'd want her covering my rear. She's never going to run from a fight."[15] (And he is a psychiatrist!) But then follows the more heartwarming, conventionally feminine, empathic anecdote (here even rendered with ellipses in a dependent clause: "she . . . cares") that has to be alluded to or searched for or that is archived as evidence of one's own "private Hillary" (or, in this case, Thatcher). And the final coup de grace is the fetishization of some corporeal metonym—"those blue eyes you could just swim in."

It is important to underline here, in my story about Hillary's crossing, how Thatcher functions in the dialogue just quoted as both fantasy and authority: "For anything that might be said about the power which she concretely exerts . . . starts to join in and be complicit with the forms of projection which—precisely because of that strange and unique position she occupies as a woman—she provokes."[16] At a time when it may well be that the most viable candidates for 2008 are Condoleezza Rice and Hillary, Kristeva's "Women's Time" should once again become required reading.[17] While recent national poll figures may equivocate about whether Hillary is a more divisive figure as senator than as First Lady, they do show her as a "strong" leader who would deal effectively with terrorism if elected president—a strength where Kerry was seen to be weak. (This same poll saw Condoleezza Rice ranked among the top three Republican candidates, even though she was the only one report-edly not interested in the job.)[18]

Kristeva presents two antagonists: an excluded woman terrorist who takes up arms against the state and, more pertinent to our analysis, "a woman who identifies with and consolidates power because she brings to it the weight of the investment consequent on her struggle to achieve it."[19] Hillary's position, I will argue, is, like Thatcher's, a "hybrid":

> a consolidation of power which is also a violence, not of counter-invest-ment, but the violence which underpins power as such. Blatantly draw-ing on this violence, Thatcher legitimated it and encodes it (the real risk of fascism) but she also lays bare the presence of violence at the heart of the socio-symbolic order. *Certainly because she is a woman, she appears to do both of these things . . . separately and together, in the form of an extreme.*[20] (emphasis mine)

It is interesting to note that Rose locates this ability of Thatcher's in part in a paradox of right-wing ideology that she was able to exploit and embody. Nicholas Kristof appears to concur when, speaking of a possi-ble Hillary candidacy, he says that Thatcher could not have been elected prime minister if she'd been in the Labor Party.[21] But this only under-scores the saliency of Rose's point about femininity coming into play at a precise point, relying as it does on Laplanche's notion of fantasy, which is always linked to a determinate place or site or *mise en scène.*

In 2005, Labor's place may well include quite "feminine" postures of Prime Minister Blair posing semi- or "torse"-nude on page three of the *Sun* tabloid prior to Election Day (enabling him to "get away with" neoliberal economic policies and an unpopular pro-war stand on Iraq). This is a pinup spot that will only a short time later be replaced by pho-tos of Saddam in his underwear. Again, it is interesting to compare the feminization of Blair with Thatcher. Not only are his "makeup" ex-penses duly reported as a part of the national budget, but offhand re-marks in the popular media reveal a likeness to Thatcher in other acces-sory ways, as well. While writing this chapter, in the south of France, I listened to an expatriate British radio station (Riviera Radio) discuss Blair's struggle with Chirac over European agricultural subsidies and the "check" Britain receives from the EU. Rob, the morning d.j., com-mented that Blair may have to go out and get a purse to threaten Chirac with, perfectly expressing as a joke what Blair had become: *Thatcher—* her liberal economic policies, her support of the Iraq war, Bush's loyal buddy—*without the purse!*[22]

While Blair's gender crossing may prove Rose's point about the ability to put on "femininity" in a precise place (Labor, not Tory: these strategies would have made a John Major only look weaker, like an ersatz Dennis Thatcher parody of the Bond films of that era), one could argue that "femininity" didn't come into play in such a facilitative way with the first woman secretary of state. Madeleine Albright's "domestic" details (from her use of networking among private-school alumni to the "distracting" accounts of the bathrobe she wore while waiting for that all-important phone call from Clinton to the plain and simple fact that she would have never had a career if her husband had not dumped her) seemingly detract from her legitimacy to underwrite and further authorize state-sanctioned violence. Her memoirs, *Madam Secretary,* are touted as a great Mother's Day present.[23] And no doubt many readers will more easily identify with her to-do list than with Colin Powell's: "1. Call Senator Helms; 2. Call King Hussein; 3. Call Foreign Minister Moussa; 4. Make other Congressional Calls; 5. Prepare for China meeting; 6. Buy nonfat yogurt."[24] While Albright's narrative captures her powerful ambitions—she details how hard she campaigned for the post of secretary of state—it also portrays her insecurity, ambivalence, and desire both to please and to have fun—attributes missing from "the super-rational" feminine. Actually, it would be interesting to compare Sciolino's opening anecdote of Albright, as UN ambassador, landing on an aircraft carrier,[25] emerging with a huge grin, orange life vest, and matching lipstick, as well as protective goggles, and squealing, "That was fantastic" with President Bush's aircraft-carrier moment as its transgendered send-up. But, of course, her landing was a real, not a staged, event, and the Navy did not allow her in the cockpit.

Hillary shares with Condoleezza Rice a strategic deployment of femininity. Both are seen as enigmatic or opaque presences, not given to much improvised self-disclosure, and are self-contained. In Sarah Kofman's words, "the enigmatic woman neither speaks nor 'betrays herself' through any of her pores."[26] French as well as American journalists describe "the calculated emptiness" of her campaign rhetoric as well as the overall lack of spontaneity of a campaign where the sight of any unguarded moment, even a yawn, is the subject of disproportionate excitement.[27] For all the books, articles, and media stories written about Hillary, she remains an enigma. I will argue, following Kofman, that her appeal is linked to the *topos* of the narcissistic woman. In contrast to her husband, Bill, Hillary is "opaque": "You can't read Hillary Clinton from a distance."[28] Articles that cover Hillary's campaign reiterate the tedium and frustration of Hillary's lack of disclosure, warmth, accessibility, of natural—as opposed to cultivated—empathy (qualities that her husband seems to possess in abundance). And yet they also recount that there is the presence of a palpable seduction, a star quality. Stephanie Chayret describes an event with Mayor Dinkins in Brooklyn—an Antillaise parade—where Hillary dances to calypso music before a "spell-bound audience" (*"une assistance medusée"*).[29] Could it be that these very qualities that Hillary purportedly lacks are part of the fascination she exerts?

While pursuing clippings of Hillary during the many humiliations of the Lewinsky affair, I came across the following, in many ways typical, utterance: "She may dread the impending Starr investigation, but she's not showing it. *Showing it is not in her nature.* Not a hint of aggrievement or anger creases her face. No open wound to probe. Just a smiling, waving, poised diva is all we see" (emphasis mine).[30] I recalled Joan Smith's formula for late-twentieth-century female iconicity: "beauty, silence and suffering."[31] There are myriad references to Hillary as "the Mona Lisa of long suffering housewives who will never tell."[32] And it is this "never telling," as much as her suffering, that is the lure, fascinating as it also terrifies. What Hillary represents is less phallic authority than the self-sufficiency (*Selbstgenugsamkeit*) and inaccessibility (*Unzuganglichkeit*) of "certain animals, who seem unconcerned with us, such as cats and large beasts of prey."[33] Sarah Kofman, reading Freud through Nietzsche, locates a place and a text ("On Narcissism") where woman is seen not as suffering from lack (penis envy) or hysteria but rather from an unassailable libidinal position of still retaining a part of that originary narcissism of childhood, found in humorists and in great criminals as depicted in literature, in addition to the aforementioned cats, children, and birds of prey. While still not as fully affirmative as Nietzsche's "Dionysian" subject, she does not suffer from *ressentiment* and appears to have little need for male desire in order to please or desire herself.[34]

One can see a similar phenomenon in the press accounts of Condoleezza Rice. Rice, an adviser to both President Bushes, is portrayed as an enigma, an ideological puzzle: "She is a kind of mystery in matters of foreign policy . . . Iron Lady or Teflon."[35] We should recall that both terms refer to leaders in a transgendered way: Thatcher is the Iron Lady and Ronald Reagan is the "Teflon" president. Both senator and secretary of state strategically deploy gender and, as Flanders has argued in the case of Rice's Birmingham backstory, race.[36]

The phrase "charm offensive" denotes the appropriation of the masquerade and is used in connection with both women. For Hillary, its recent usage includes her offering to run out and get coffee to prove to her fellow senators that she is not above doing freshman grunt work; for Condoleezza, it is to show a more genial face abroad, especially in Europe, to soften America's posture of unilateralism/preemption. One might even argue that Hillary's "mix" of woman's support of defense and the Iraq war and capital punishment and her post-9/11 discourse, inflected with its dark tutelary Foucauldian resonances of "governmentality" ("security, territory, population")—indeed, her insistent advocacy of governmentality and its sites of regulation (children's rights—but not necessarily Iraqi children; health care; education, including testing for teachers in Arkansas; her seat on the Senate Armed Services Committee)—throughout her career position her as the only Democratic female grotesque with the right degree of proximity between terror(ism), death, and femininity to go up against the "Bushwomen."[37]

Our cinematic unconscious is already wise to this in the hilarious election-year remake of *The Manchurian Candidate,* with Meryl Streep in an ice-cube-crunching, castrating channeling of Hillary, lamenting, "Where are the men?" (But was it Kerry's fault if the power he exerted —nil—could not meet up with the projections—Vietnam—he provoked?) This was not the first time Meryl Streep was a star substitute for a woman leader like Hillary. In 1999, David Foster was developing *Madame President,* about a vice president, ousted in a scandal, who is replaced by the president's old law school friend, Senator Diane Bradley. She becomes president after the president has a stroke and "slaps around sexist Arab leaders and takes revenge on a sexist water polluting billionaire." Suggested actresses were Emma Thompson (who did play Hillary in *Primary Colors)* but without the accent, or Meryl Streep as she was in *The River Wild.* What was called for was "a man in a dress. A Margaret Thatcher type, without the accent."[38] Gender trouble was similarly on display in Paul Rudnick's remake of *The Stepford Wives,* whose plot, he presciently argued (in light of the 2004 election), has only grown more resonant: "men have grown more anxious about gender issues and begrudge having their hegemony shredded by women, gays and minorities. Straight white males act like the new endangered minority." It is the remake's perverse twist that women turn themselves into Stepford wives! "Hillary Clinton, once so angry about tea and cookies, is now so eerily glazed and good natured that she could be the Senator from Stepford." (Martha Stewart is a "haywire fembot with a team of lawyers.")[39]

In Rose's schema, Condi represents the part of Thatcher, designated as "a super-rationality that writes violence into law," playing the role of global-power punitive superego; Hillary presents the "kinder, gentler" tutelary power of governmentality's darker side or, in Peggy Noonan's more hostile appraisal, "a prison matron's need for government to discipline people."[40] Both, like Thatcher, construct themselves as "personae" or masks that are ambiguously gendered: "The paranoid structure which I am describing here no doubt thrives on this *ambiguity of a femininity appealed to and denied, a masculinity parodied and inflated*" (italics mine).[41]

Rice's "buddy-ism" with Bush, her athleticism, competitiveness, discipline, ambition, and attention to detail are all coded as masculine ("For her discipline trumps patience") and works with and against her elegance—groomed within an inch of her life ("*tirée à quatre épingles*,"[42] in the *Libération* closeup. "She is always impeccably dressed, usually in a classic suit with a modest hemline, comfortable pumps and conservative jewelry")[43] like Hillary and is described with similar adjectives. Rice "keeps two mirrors on her desk, apparently to check the back as well as the front."[44] Both have life stories of sublimation and hard work; witness Rice's training as a concert pianist and competitive ice skater; she is up at 5 a.m. to do her treadmill, is at her office by 7 a.m. and in bed by 10 p.m., and she still often packs her lunch! (Hillary mentions a similar "frugality" in her autobiography when she speaks of still wrapping up a small piece of cheese and an uneaten olive.) Even Rice's choice of music is indicative of her will: Brahms, and not Liszt or those romantic Russians, as Brahms is "structured" and "restrained" and "has a sense of tension that never resolves." Indeed, it would be interesting to imagine if either Hillary or Condoleezza Rice could have gotten away with the unempowered performance that Colin Powell gave at the UN (or confess, as Bush did in the 2000 campaign, that, although he was weak on foreign policy experience, he did know whom to ask).[45]

Hillary's calculation emerges at noteworthy points in her own *Living*

History—in her explanation of why she supported the welfare reform bill and in her urging of the bombing of Kosovo ("I urged him to bomb").[46] This demonstrates a doubly strategic masquerade, as these decisions (like the favoring of capital punishment) are presented as rational ones, with moral certainty and knowable villains. (In the case of welfare reform, the villains were the Republicans and how the Democrats would run against them if they didn't get this bill passed.) The rationality or calculation behind Hillary's decisions does two crucial things. Like Thatcher in the Falklands or during the miner's strike (or her allowing American aircraft to use British bases during the U.S. bombing of Libya in 1986), it shows phallic resolve, conferring coherence and logic upon an ambivalent and socially chaotic world. It empties these issues of their social and moral complexity (i.e., We will fix welfare reform next term; it is better to pass the flawed bill now). Moreover, this moral certainty and foregrounding of knowable limits has a profoundly dissuasive effect, "concealing or displacing fantasies of vengeance and retribution."[47] (I think of this each time I see Hillary vaunting some bipartisan piece of legislation that she is working on with one of her former nemeses, such as Lindsay Graham or Newt Gingrich, people directly responsible for her husband's impeachment and her global shaming. I think that what compels in these stories is less the pull of the conversion narrative than the good old tug of not-so-repressed or displaced sadism.)

But the Kosovo bombing decision does not repose only on an instrumentalization of phallic leadership. For it also draws upon the considerable gendered resources of "femininity" by reinscribing that decision as part of the larger family melodrama. In other words, policy brings a personal story into the picture as it provides a moment of post-Monica confessional "healing." This, in turn, is chronicled (as in chapter 6) by the outfits she wears: in Belfast, she chooses a "long military greatcoat," her eyes hidden behind sunglasses (and a "cold voice"); these give way to a more cheerful look (a bright yellow slicker in Limerick) as a successful peace initiative is brokered.[48] Both Hillary and Condoleezza Rice share with Thatcher and Blair (all successful practitioners of the political masquerade) a potent combination of pragmatic uses of normative gender and paradoxical image repertoires (in Condi's case, the civil-rights-era girl from Birmingham with a Chevron tanker named after her) as effective covers for quite violent state policies. To cite just one more dissonant image from Hillary's biography, she recounts the horrors of the violence at Columbine at the same time that she depicts a coy marital scene (Bill and she were cutting up their morning grapefruit when . . .).[49] And it is this slippage from domestic bliss in Chappaqua to another, simultaneous suburban scene of explosive violence, this "domestic glue," both the grapefruit and the policy talk (school violence), that keeps this marriage together, eroticizing and containing both. Moreover, this apparent openness, like Blair's "openness" and "ordinariness," shows how, "even in private, the screens are up."[50]

From Crossing to Gender Crossing: Revisiting Drag

> It is important for me to concede however that the performance of gender subversion can indicate nothing about sexuality or sexual practice.
> —Judith Butler[51]

> Sex does not budge.   —Joan Copjec[52]

I will now acknowledge another obvious fact: drag's celebratory moment—in theory and in high het cultural entertainment—is now over. Our gendered reading of the presidency and its metonym Hillary, no longer as First Lady but now as senator-presidential contender, still references Butler, who, in recent works, such as *Undoing Gender* and the preface to the tenth anniversary edition of *Gender Trouble,* has presented a more sober assessment of the claims and uses of "drag": "The point of this text is not to celebrate drag as the expression of a true and model gender (even as it is important to resist the belittling of drag that sometimes takes place) but to show that the naturalized knowledge of gender operates as a preemptive and violent circumscription of reality."[53] But before we travel the cultural distance between 1996 and 2005 appropriations of drag to read Hillary, I would like to reinscribe an alternative vision of what could have been a different "Hillary regained," a different "Hillary diva" or "queer Hillary," projected from chapter 6's more affirmative reading of drag.

We start with a question: What would it have meant had Hillary become post-transsexual? We continue with the affirmative reading of the masquerade and add to it some of the axioms of Eve Kosofsky Sedgwick's *Epistemology of the Closet* (which subtend her "genealogy of the unknown," since, for Sedgwick, "knowing" assumes the place "recognition" has for Butler). Let us start with Axiom 1: "People are different from each other." Hillary becomes, in this reading, another postmodern body, like Halberstam's po-mo lesbian, fragmented by theory/representation, uncontainable by categories (wearing a chador in *Talk* magazine, "standing by her man, Bill," and arguing for a Palestinian state, spouting Oprah and Rabin), and dispersed into the "making and unmaking and remaking and redissolution of hundreds of old and new categorical meanings concerning all the kinds it may take to make up a world."[54]

This is the affirmative "It takes all kinds of nonce taxonomies to make a village." Halberstam's reading of Sedgwick attests to the pluralization of possible identities and post-Oedipal pleasures ("guys with pussies, dykes with dicks, queer butches, aggressive femmes, F2Ms, lesbians who like men, daddy boys, gender queens, drag kings, pomo Afro homos, bulldaggers, women who fuck boys, women who fuck like boys, dyke mommies, transsexual lesbians, male lesbians").[55] Halberstam is aware that this enumeration at once threatens to overgeneralize the concept of sexual identity (and the transsexual in particular) and (paradoxically) marks the "terrifying precision" of desire: "Wanting a man with a vagina or wanting to be a woman transformed into a man having sex with other men are fairly precise and readable desires," even if they are incapable of being mapped by "extant conceptual categories."[56]

The movie example Halberstam subjects to analysis here is *Vera*, whose eponymous hero/ine coins a term, "gender phobia," to denote how a gender community is often "Othered" by the gay community: "Gender phobia is my term. I made it up because there is a clone movement in the non-heterosexual movement to make everybody look just like heterosexuals who sleep with each other. *The fact is that there is a whole large section of the gay community who is going to vote Republican*" (emphasis mine). Placed in this context, voting Republican becomes another "perverse" behavior, metonymically associated with other precise and locatable desires like "wanting a man with a vagina." This is obviously not the point Halberstam is explicitly making, but if one looks at the next sentence, voting Republican is linked or contained within all sorts of gender trouble: "Gender phobia, as Vern suggests, indicates all kinds of gender trouble in the mainstream gay and lesbian community. Furthermore, the increasing numbers of female to male transsexuals (f to m's) appearing in metropolitan or urban lesbian communities has given rise to interesting and sometimes volatile debates."[57]

The point of an affirmative recuperation of drag would be to re-create gender as fiction and learn to "read" post-transsexual embodied fictions as places of productive disruption and pleasure (as in Sandy Stone's Manifesto)[58] and to begin to see the "strangeness of all gendered bodies, not only the trans-sexualized ones, and that we rewrite the fiction that divides a sex from a transsex, a gender from a transgender. All gender should be transgender, all desire is transgendered, movement is all."[59] Who knows? Straight bodies voting Republican may begin to be seen as the "queer" and "perverse" activity it is.

And if I have indulged a Hillary-as-post-transsexual scenario, it is also because it exposes some of the theoretical assumptions attendant on the utopian or affirmative or postsymbolic imaginings in the romance of "gender outlaws." Another way of framing this is to ask to what extent the celebratory emphasis on movement conflicts with the Lacanian assessment that "sex does not budge." For even Halberstam's article raised some vexed queries about whether anatomy is dis- or re-placed into a signifying chain that stabilizes into something like an identity.[60] Halberstam is aware that her reading is predicated on Butler's definition of sex as a "performatively enacted signification . . . that . . . can occasion the parodic proliferation and subversive play of gendered meaning."[61] As Copjec reads this passage, she clearly states what Butlerian assumptions are operative in Halberstam's text: "All kinds of practices construct masculinity and femininity as discrete entities, and there is no denying the effectiveness, the reality of this construction; . . . but if sex is something that is 'made up,' it can also be unmade. *What's done, after all, can always be undone*—in the order of signification at least" (emphasis mine). [62]

Is the critical practice, then, one of deconstructing gender fictions? Or is the sole problem concerning the gender outlaw one of subcultural recognition or survival? Is this sexual subject the subject of a signifier or, rather, "sexually subjectified" precisely where signification fails? Or, to the extent that drag and performativity appear to address sexual difference (and possible alternative resolutions of the Oedipus complex), it might be prudent to recall Parveen Adams: "Desire is a problem precisely because sexuality is linked to gender."[63] What is necessary is not so much gender's undoing but rather its *separation* from sexuality. As I argue in our last section, "imaginary" categories of gender (figuring binary or normative heterosexual difference) are not useful in explaining Hillary's continued appeal. We will see that this appeal is best understood by situating sexual difference (in Zizek's terms) as "the Real of an antagonism, not the symbolic of a differential opposition."[64]

To return from this "golden age" of drag to the somber realities of our increasingly homophobic and maritally normative present, it might be helpful to reframe some of the more modest claims for drag not as an election 2005 "morning after" or as an after-9/11 theory backlash but as read against Butler's own reframing in her 1999 preface to *Gender Trouble*. Here we are told that the discussion of drag is not meant as a "paradigm of subversive action, or indeed, as a model for political agency." Although it "offers to explain the constructed and performative dimension of gender," it is "not precisely *an example* of subversion" (*GT*, xxii, emphasis hers). Neither paradigm nor example, it is rather on the order of a bad simile, which "naturalizes knowledge" and is linked to the possibility of category questioning and failure. As this is such an important point, I will quote her paragraph extensively:

> If one thinks that one sees a man dressed as a woman or a woman dressed as a man, then one takes the first term of each of those perceptions as the "reality" of gender: the gender that is produced through the simile lacks "reality," and is taken to constitute an illusory appearance. In such perceptions in which an ostensible reality is coupled with an unreality, we think we know what the reality is, and take the secondary appearance of gender to be mere artifice, play, falsehood, and illusion. But what is the sense of "gender reality" that founds the perception in this way? Perhaps we think we know what the anatomy of the person is. . . . Or we derive that knowledge from the clothes that the person wears, or how the clothes are worn. This is naturalized knowledge, even though it is based on a series of cultural inferences, some of which are highly erroneous. Indeed, if we shift the example from drag to transsexuality, then it is no longer possible to derive a judgment about stable anatomy from the clothes that cover and articulate the body. That body may be preoperative, transitional, or postoperative; even "seeing" the body may not answer the question: for *what are the categories through which one sees?* The moment in which one's staid and usual cultural perceptions fail, when one can not with surety read the body that one sees is precisely the moment when one is no longer sure whether the body encountered is that of a man or a woman. The vacillation between the categories itself constitutes the experience of the body in question. (*GT*, xxii–xxiii)

Butler is quite explicit here about just what is at stake here: "When such categories come into question, the *reality* of gender is also put into crisis: it becomes unclear how to distinguish the real from the unreal"(*GT*, xxiii). This insight—that what we take to be "real" is in fact already "naturalized" and therefore "changeable and revisable"—gives rise to claims for drag that appear more modulated: "Call it subversive or call it something else." (What else?) Butler's preface does seem to be stating that semiotic guerrilla strategies are somehow politically necessary but insufficient: "Although this insight does not in itself constitute a political revolution, no political revolution is possible without a radical shift in one's notion of the possible and the real" (*GT*, xxiii).

Indeed, in "The Question of Social Transformation," Butler says this explicitly, using the examples of "compassionate" and "national" to resignify "conservatism" and "socialism," respectively: "So it seems clear that resignification alone is not a politics, is not sufficient for a politics, is not enough." Drag is a type of practice that could provoke such a shift; "certain kinds of practices precede their explicit theorization."[65] (Or, as Marx says, "here the content goes beyond the phrase.") Yet drag is given a crucial role to play in what Butler reveals is *Gender Trouble*'s "positive normative task," which is "to insist upon the extension of this legitimacy to bodies that have been regarded as false, unreal, and unintelligible." Drag is an example that is meant to establish that "reality" is not as fixed as we generally assume it to be. Exposure of the "tenuousness of gender reality" should "counter the violence performed by gender norms" (*GT*, xxiv).

"The Question of Social Transformation" further elaborates on the political stakes of drag, in relation to Foucauldian power/knowledge: "The question of who and what is considered real and true is apparently a question of knowledge. . . . Having or bearing 'truth' and 'reality' is an enormously powerful prerogative within the social world, one way in which power dissimulates as ontology" (*Undoing Gender*, 215). But it is also a way that transgender enters the political field. Drag continues to be pertinent for my reading of Hillary here in this second dimension: as an exemplification of "the cultural life of fantasy" and its impact on "the material conditions of life": survivability, violence, beauty, pathos. "The turn to drag performance was, in part, a way to think not only about how gender is performed, but how it is resignified through collective terms" (*UG*, 216). So while drag is no longer celebrated unequivocally (as subversive of gender norms), it still has a critical role to play in delimiting the ontological presuppositions at work in "received notions of reality," as well as in one's embodied experience. "And what drag can *point out* is that (1) this set of ontological presuppositions is at work, and (2) that it is open to rearticulation" (*UG,* 214) (my emphasis).

The possibilities of such a "rearticulation" can be seen in relation to the workings of fantasy, which, like "drag," is indexical: "Fantasy is what allows us to imagine ourselves and others otherwise. Fantasy is what establishes the possible in excess of the real; *it points* elsewhere, and when it is embodied, it brings the elsewhere home" (*UG,* 29, emphasis mine, repeated on 216–217). Does the figure of indexicality— "pointing to" itself—indicate a confusion of the real with reference, as Tim Dean has argued is symptomatic of rhetoricalist accounts?[66]

It is in the context of the discussion of drag in *Undoing Gender* that Butler's concept of fantasy is most clearly enunciated, and I will give another example of how it assists her project of extending or constructing norms that could sustain viable or flourishing life. "Fantasy is not simply a cognitive exercise, an internal film that we project inside the interior theatre of the mind. Fantasy structures relationality, and it comes into play in the stylization of embodiment itself" (*UG,* 217). The introduction to *Undoing Gender* provides further specification. Fantasy is not reality's obverse: "it is what reality forecloses, and as a result, it defines the limits of reality, constituting it as its constitutive outside. The critical promise of fantasy, when and where it exists to challenge the contingent limits of what will and will not be called reality" (*UG,* 29). "Fantasy is part of the articulation of the possible; it moves us beyond what is merely actual and present into a realm of possibility, the not yet actualized or the not actualizable" (*UG,* 28).

It is clear that this concept of fantasy differs in significant ways from Lacanian-derived ones that inform the work of Rose's readings. For Rose, fantasy also has an important role to play in the necessarily "vexed and complex" relation between feminism and psychoanalysis, but its role is far more ambivalent. One the one hand, for Rose there is a more fraught interrelation between idealization and sadism/horror. This necessarily complicates how the unforeclosing of fantasy acts to "produce sustaining bonds of community." Why, in other words, should what exceeds reality–what is excessive in nature—be seen as benign and without its own forms of intrinsic violence, abjection, and morbidity? There are moments—Rose's inspired reading of Plath's "Daddy" is just one of these—when questions of sexual difference further complicate matters. Rose queries, à propos of works such as "Daddy" (or Duras's wartime diary, *La Douleur*), whether "it is a woman who is most likely to articulate the power—perverse, recalcitrant, persistent—of fantasy as such. Nor would such an insight be in any way incompatible with woman's legitimate protest against a patriarchal world."[67] (This binary construction—fantasy/legitimate protest—appears to break down the fantasy/reality opposition. Or, as Jean Baudrillard reminds us, "The reality principle is never anything other than the *imaginary* of the other term.")[68]

Binaries are also symptoms indicating that we are on the terrain of the imaginary—ego construction and its aggressive rivalry. Butler's "constitutive outside," Dean avers, is useful in thinking about ego and collective ego formation, which he carefully distinguishes (as does Rose) from subjectivity and the unconscious. Dean resumes the problems I have with the usefulness of Butler's notion of fantasy in understanding Hillary's appeal succinctly: "To conceptualize subjectivity in terms of exclusion and the regulation of inside/outside or human/abject borders is to think subjectivity imaginarily, to remain caught in binary categories."[69]

Moreover, fantasy can be further qualified as undoing precisely those theories of interpellation and identification upon which Butler's performative depends. Rose questions whether fantasy has become so overgeneralized that "the implied ease of self recognition gives way to something that belongs to the order of impossibility or shock to a point where the language or model of interpellation through which we thought we could understand collective identification is no longer adequate."[70] Rose then goes on to discuss the death drive's link to symbolic and real violence and "its stubborn refusal to be located." Hillary's appearance before Congress (after Vince Foster's death) is revealing in how it precisely references this uneasy terrain. After Dick Armey says, "We welcome you here," she quips, "Yes, like Dr. Kevorkian." Doctor-assisted suicide is not an incidental place for a joke, hinting that the symbolic order (the doctor as paternal stand-in and guarantee) just might want our death. Hillary's own term for self-disclosure is no less suggestive of forms of symbolic death: "open kimono."

These theoretical disagreements might be reframed otherwise by asking whether, for Butler, her idea of fantasy is still predicated upon a reading of Lacan that sees the symbolic more or less as an extension of the imaginary and less in terms of the "nonrhetorical logic" of the Lacanian Real, subjects of the signifier but not subjects of desire.

For heuristic purposes, I find Tim Dean's schema suggestive: the ego as an effect of the imaginary order, the subject as an effect of the symbolic order, and sexuality as an effect of the real order.[71] This enables us to resituate Hillary away from the terrain of gender, where her sexuality is unreadable, to that of *jouissance,* where, like that of W, it is daily more apparent.

Thus, this long theoretical excursus on Butler's revision of drag is less about a critique of Butler per se than it is a way of reframing the question of sexuality away from drag, impersonation, and fantasy as linked to the imaginary. What can be more helpful in articulating Hillary's appeal at the present moment is to punctuate it with the stakes of a different reading of sexuality, in line with the later Lacan of the Real, the *objet a,* and "that point of greatest theoretical and political difficulty," the death drive.[72] But, my presentation also does tell us a story about how even our avant-garde cultural theories find themselves resonant within a particular political context. As theories themselves are heterogeneous, Butler's writings in *Undoing Gender* still provide powerful concepts for understanding the content of Hillary's appeal and the shift in her political rhetoric (in a post-Schiavo-Gitmo-W-Bush-era world), when she increasingly brings out the concept of "life," "flourishing," sustainable life, and its obverse, precarity and bare life, which undergird "realness" norms.[73] For the moment I will consider Hillary's successful transition, her near-impossible "second act" in politics, and suggest that if Hillary has become a body that matters politically, it is only because she has first become a "body that mutters."

A Body That Mutters: Resexing Hillary

She has a sexy mouth, I think. That slight palatial overbite—it gets to me. She seems expert at marshaling her mouth's resources, at inspiring its ingenuity. She can fold her lips into an origami of fleeting smiles. Her basic smile is sort of chipmunky and schoolmarmish, but sometimes, when she is pouncing on the possibility of an idea, her lips extend their reach into her cheeks and carve out a wolfish, carnal line, as though nothing could please her more than her own hunger. Her mouth is enigmatic in its capacity for adjustment—it seems both the origin and the repository of her secrets. Sure, when she is under duress, it can appear small, pinched, grudging, harsh, unforgiving, and grimly determined—

nippy—but when she is at ease, free to discuss, you know, the *issues* . . . well, then her mouth becomes the very instrument of her freedom, and her laugh rings the bell of her throat. Her laugh is the sexiest thing about her, in fact; it packs a lewd wallop because it seems to take her by surprise. There's a wickedness about her laugh, in its offhand suggestion that she is willing to be entertained, to be *pleased*. It's quick and sudden, an unabashed, throaty gargle, and it seems to put dazzle in her eyes from below, like footlights.

She has pretty eyes, I think. They are direct, almost imperiously so, but not cold. They seem shy—shy beneath the veneer of command. They are almost almond shaped, slightly catty, set high in the broad planes of her mighty cheekbones. . . . Of course, her hair is bright and fixed, but sometimes a tendril of it will come loose and fall into her face and she will seem open to the intrigue of dishevelment. . . . She shows very little skin other than her throat and hands, but her throat is clean and delicate and alive, and her hands are small and vivid, organs of attack and exclamation and instruction and delight. . . . She wears expensive pantsuits, drapey around the legs, and flat shoes. She projects an aura of power but not of invincibility. . . . She still looks like the smartest girl at the dance, waiting, the girl smart enough not to escape her vulnerability or ambitious enough to escape her longing, and now like a woman of incipient bloom; I imagine it would be easy to make her blush. I imagine her easily courted and easily seduced by a certain stripe of practiced seducer, and if you were to ask—as all men eventually do, when the subject is Hillary Rodham Clinton—that terrible question, "Would you . . . ?" I would have to say, yes, I would. Sure I would. Of course I would. Hell *yes* I would. I would do it . . . in a New York minute.[74]

I do not know which is most surprising in this description of Hillary Clinton as a new senatorial candidate and (still) First Lady: whether it is the openly pleasurable fantasy scenarios that would have been unthinkable even eighteen months earlier, the transvaluations of sites of previous castration anxiety (eyes, hair, mouth, even this Medusa's "laugh") into imaginative moments of blissful reverie, or the easy displacement between voting for and "sexually having/doing" Hillary, which is of course what Tom Junod is contemplating: "I would vote for her in a New York minute." This is not to say that the former view of a castrating Hillary has disappeared entirely: her mouth can be "nippy," her hands are still "organs of attack," her eyes, while not cold, are "catty" and, well, we all know about felines. While once Hillary had been just a calculated manipulator—Hillary of the crude hand job—now her hands join in: exclaim, instruct, and delight. Her hair is fixed phallic armature, the corporate hair of a successful editor, lawyer, or Wall Street executive,[75] but it now can appear open to the possibility of being undone. Yet a tendril could unleash, if one is not too cautious, a head of snakes just like that of the Medusa. Her infamous *Talk* interview similarly alludes to a possible "bedhead," a glimpse through the open door of the still-rumpled blue sheets in her private quarters, as if she had almost been dragged from bed: "The imprint of her pillow is still on her cheek."[76] And, while her clothing still plays with gender indeterminacy, it now mixes conventional power dressing with a feminine fluidity: "expensive suits, drapey around her legs."

Even less affirmative responses to Hillary's candidacy (those who might hesitate before saying "yes" in a New York minute or, um . . . pulling a lever) still evaluate the candidate in sexualized terms. Chris Buckley's *No Way to Treat a First Lady* depicts its protagonist, Beth MacMann (Lady Bethmac), in many familiar ways: "wearing a black pantsuit," a "shoving" (if not lamp-throwing), misunderstood First Lady who tried to "push through initiatives on child care, prescription drugs for the elderly, the environment."[77] She sees herself as a "transitional" figure, as the first professional woman who is a First Lady and who harbors hopes of a future Senate race. But it also portrays her as someone who likes sex a lot, has frequent fantasies about her defense attorney, and wears fur-lined panties after hearing about them in court. The jury consultant discovers that, in addition to her popularity with gays and hardcore lesbians, she scores high with a key demographic group: "males twenty-five to forty-nine," who want to have oral sex with her. Catherine Zeta-Jones is "desperate" to play her in the movie that *Vanity Fair* thinks only Natalie Wood could do full justice to: "That limpid sexuality, the steel hidden beneath the puddly dark eyes, the tragic glamour."

Not surprisingly, Buckley's framing descriptions begin with her voice, presenting her as very much the *femme fatale*:

Her voice was all business. Cool as a martini, no more emotion than a flight attendant telling the passengers to put the seats in the upright position. He'd have preferred a little more raw emotion, frankly even a stifled gasp or sob. Some clients, even burly men . . . broke down the first time they spoke to him. . . . But even now, placing a call that must have humiliated her, Beth was in her own upright position, not a trace of begging or desperation in her voice.[78]

The next part-object targeted is her hands:[79]

With that she sat down and began pulling off her gloves. . . . Boyce couldn't help himself watching her take them off finger by finger in an incredibly sexy Barbara Stanwyck let's-get-down-to-business way. He couldn't take his eyes off her. Men are men and fools to a man, but it amazed Boyce, seeing her this close, that Ken MacMann had needed to screw all those other women when he had this waiting for him at home, warm in his own bed. . . . Her eyes looked at you in an evaluating but not unfriendly way. . . . If she had been an actress, she would have gotten the part of the take-charge businesswoman who turns out to be an absolute panther in the sack. He remembered how every time he walked behind her and saw the lovely sexy sway of her bottom, his mouth went dry and his heart soared with possession.[80]

Nor is this sexualization limited to male readers. Lucinda Franks "orientalizes" Hillary:

Hillary Clinton, head covered in a flowing chador of golden silk, stands barefoot outside the Citadel of Cairo. The chants of the Muslim call to prayer echo through the winding streets. Quietly declining the slippers set aside for privileged visitors, she walks barefoot into the ancient mosque like a common Egyptian woman, her head bowed, her face turned away from the reporters and photographers. . . . On the day before she leaves Egypt, an antiquities expert talks her through the ruins of the Temple of Queen Hatshepsut, Egypt's only known female pharaoh, pointing out that the queen's nephew erased her name from every edifice after her death.[81]

Maureen Dowd, in "Blonde on Blonde," metonymically links Hillary's interview in *Talk* magazine with Marilyn's auction at Christie's. Both Marilyn and Hillary are blond icons, known by their first names alone. In the type of easy simile that Americans make effortlessly (myself included): "Both paired off in rocky romances with sex addled young presidents. And both were painted variously as stubborn, accomplished and self-defeating, smart and dumb. Misfits both, neither quite believable as a Yankees fan or wannabe Jewish girl."[82] Although the "wannabe Jewish girl" supposedly refers to Marilyn as the wife of Arthur Miller, it could definitely apply to Hillary, who hired a coach for Yiddish pronunciations, only to sound sometimes like a poor parody of Sally Field's Norma Rae: "Ka-vetch, ka-vetch, ka-vetch."[83] The point for Dowd is that Hillary's Senate bid would be unthinkable without her status as "celebrity victim," which is a "cocktail Marilyn would have understood perfectly." To what extent are Hillary's "troubles" or, in Marilyn's vernacular, "getting stuck with the short end of the lollipop," necessary for a political crossover from First Lady to senator, and what does this portend for a presidential campaign for a female candidate? I am concerned here with the way iconic women operate as fetishes, as well as with how they serve as the recipient of popular (national) identifications. For the moment, we will consider how a posthumiliation, celebrity Hillary functions as a transitional object.

All accounts of Hillary's candidacy concur that she was far more popular "as an injured party than she ever was as an equal party." *Talk* magazine states the terms bluntly: "though she hates playing the victim, public sympathy has transmuted her from a scary political termagent into a woman widely admired for her courage. Her ordeal has given her a certain glamour, almost a regal look."[84] Or, in Sheehy's hyperbolic formulation, she is "the world's most publicly degraded wife, she levitates far above her husband."[85] Even a reader as prudent as Garry Wills describes the postimpeachment-ordeal Hillary reverently, her comportment equivalent to Jackie's dignified grief after the assassination, which moves her to a "new level of public authority in her own right." What makes this a more important question than just the more crass one of Hillary "cashing" in her victim chips (in Wills's words: "She was a woman whose public world was now an oyster full of pearls")[86] is the larger role that shame plays in our celebrity-driven culture and more general questions about the politics of affect *tout court*. Jacqueline Rose queries, à propos of Diana, whether there can be celebrity without public humiliation. "Could it be then that celebrity is indeed our guilty secret, a veiled way of putting into private circulation certain things that do not admit to easy acknowledgment? Hence the pull and the paradox, why it is so exciting and demeaning at the same time."[87] Rose reminds us in her probing that "the pleasure we take in celebrities, the contract we strike with them is more complex and perverse—crueller than at first glance." She also astutely notes that, "in the cult of celebrity, the potential for failure may be the key to success."[88] This means that we must look at places overlooked as sites of potential by conventional political analysts, sites of failure, blame/shame, and humiliation, and, especially, those failures that resist easy symbolization. Moreover, if as Rose argues, "the cult of celebrity always harbors a political subtext,"[89] celebrity should be seriously interrogated as more than trivial escapism/displaced political "realism." In particular, we could recognize the peculiarly potent mix of violence and sadism, the murderous relation to celebrity that could well serve as an alternative (or a supplemental) appeal/interpellation to that of war.

So, part of Hillary's availability to being "resexed" does have to do with her "shaming" and public humiliation. Her public suffering is not incidental but is an integral part of her transformation. And, as such, it restages the putting of sexuality into speech (and its dangers). Here it might be interesting to recall again Chris Buckley's depiction of Hillary as a *femme fatale*. The *femme fatale* is noteworthy as an embodiment of transparent deceit, as a "sort of proto-illusionist element in noir's illusionist field,"[90] which I believe can be more helpful in articulating Hillary's appeal at the present moment. "Rather than screening *jouissance*, she hoards it."

Oral Sex in an Age of Deconstruction

It might be less surprising that Hillary's resexing will proceed via an intense visual and verbal cathexsis on her mouth if we recall that it is her husband's alleged perjury about oral sex with an intern, incidents of phone sex, rimming, and cigar sex play (and endless cigar jokes) that is the exciting cause for Hillary's public resignification: "She wouldn't be running if it weren't for Monica." As we have seen, she would not have been "electable" without first becoming a celebrity-icon, and she needed to pass through the national "shame-fest" of humiliation, chastening, feminization, desexualization, and emasculation to satisfy public cravings. But that only leaves you like G.H.W. Bush in Houston or Bob Dole doing Viagra ads. In other words it is necessary but not sufficient.

Monica does make her the "Mona Lisa of long-suffering wives who will never tell," which recalls another enigmatic smile. But she also supplies Hillary with oral metaphors/drives, "a hunger for power and a thirst for revenge." It is these drives that fuel her "run." For Junod, Hillary will not be electable unless "readable" in her own sexual light, once again implicitly referencing the epistemological links among knowledge, visibility, and sexuality. How does this happen? "By being resexed by the words in her own mouth."[91]

Hillary's campaign is crafted as a sexual/political progress narrative, starting from its opening scene, an assignation in Senator Patrick Moynihan's one-room schoolhouse in Pindar's Corners. She is given a courtly introduction that concludes with Moynihan saying, "I hope she will go all the way."[92] The not-yet candidacy (which will be announced, months later, in Purchase, New York) of the political novice starts with a listening tour. Hillary presents herself as a blank slate and mute. Analysts are quick to see this as a sharp strategic move, as either "Orwellian political theater" or, more simply, a "response to constraints that any ordinary person would have found paralyzing."[93] It inverts the typical political campaign; instead of the candidate presenting her views, she solicits ideas from the voters. This contributes to an imitative electoral masquerade: "an elaborate show of humility to the citizens of New York." It is doubly strategic, as it also eliminates any of Hillary's views that might be objectionable and that are part of her "controversectomy."[94] This does immediately draw attention to her physical presence as she listens: "Boy could she listen. She was an indefatigable listener, insatiable. She listened to panels of selected guests, then to general audiences."[95] It draws attention to her eyes ("I remember being struck by the intensity of her gaze")[96] as it evokes favorable comparisons to her empathic husband: "It must be said she was Clintonesque: No story was too trivial, no nugget of wonkery too arcane, no concern too parochial for Hillary to *make eye contact* with the speaker" (emphasis mine).[97] This recalls the Bill Clinton of the opening pages of *Primary Colors*, who "had his big ears on," noteworthy for listening in its hyperbolic state: "the most aggressive listening the world has ever known: aerobic listening . . . when he gives you full ear . . . his listening becomes the central fact of the conversation."[98]

It also draws considerable attention to her mouth, voice, and laugh when she does speak. I was struck by how many news magazine covers or accompanying story photos focus on her mouth—in *Esquire,* a red-

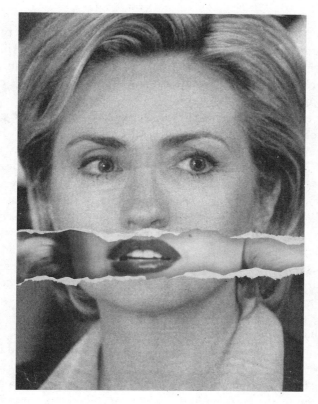

Tom Junod, "Hillary as you've never seen her before," *Esquire*, October 1999.

lipsticked mouth seemingly torn from a color photo is placed over a black and white photo of the rest of her face; the March 1, 1999, *Newsweek* cover has an open-mouthed, pink-lipsticked Hillary. The *Talk* cover shows a laughing Hillary. It now appears that, with her hair and clothes reduced to a minimum look that "works," Hillary's mouth becomes the way we are to read her. Sheehy concurs in very Kleinian terms: "It's her mouth that signals which Hillary you are getting. A mouth that can turn on like the Christmas lights at Rockefeller Center or bite your tongue out. She is soft and feminine—all smiles now."[99] Tom Junod, in our opening quotation for this section, sees her mouth as an emblem of wolfish carnality, sexy when it is ready to pounce on an idea and metonymically linked to her "wolfish carnality"—as "though nothing could please her more than her own hunger." (Klein and her daughter Melita Schmideberg could also tell us a thing or two about object and reality relating, eating and its discontents.)[100] This "wolf-ishness" is a somewhat dangerous attribute for a politician; although wolves are seductive and do like to play dress-up (in sheep's clothing), they are marginal, outlaw figures.

But it is Hillary's laugh that has received the most media attention. It is the part of her biography that is selected to "humanize" Hillary in reviews and excerpted as well as paraphrased with a frequency not un-like that of the Bill-Hillary encounter in the Yale library discussed in chapter 6. And, while this appears to be a similar gendered reversal of a woman's active looking, this particular subversion begins at the symbolic and takes us to the Real of Hillary's appeal. The description of Hillary's laugh is to be found in the paragraph where she first describes her father, Hugh Rodham, the son of Hugh Rodham Sr. and Hannah Jones, descendant of blackhaired Welsh coal miners. "Like Hannah he was often gruff, but when he laughed the sound came from deep inside and seemed to engage every part of his body. *I inherited his laugh, the same big rolling guffaw that can turn heads in a restaurant and send cats running from the room*" (emphasis mine).[101]

Joe Conason similarly describes the effect of this laugh and its spread to her eyes and voice: "Hillary has a full throated laugh and a habit of widening her huge, expressive eyes when she wants to make a point. . . . Get the candidate speaking about what she calls the partisan attack on her and her husband and audible passion returns to her voice."[102]

This laugh, you will recall from Junod, is "the sexiest thing about her, in fact it packs a lewd wallop because it seems to take her by sur-prise. . . . It's quick and sudden, an unabashed, throaty gargle, and it seems to put dazzle in her eyes from below, like footlights." Garry Wills recounts being in the presence of such a laugh—here called a "loud guffaw"—which he contrasts to the book's general lack of vibrancy. It cannot capture her "voice," especially those parts that detail stories he heard live as dinner party stories, where Hillary discussed her pro bono legal cases in Arkansas, slipping into a "southern drawl." "When she went to see the black woman in the jail where she was being held, she imitated her. Ms. Clinton is a natural mimic and raconteur, who auto-matically 'does the voices' when telling a story."[103] This is what gets her into trouble, and Wills gives the *Sixty Minutes* example of Hillary speak-ing of "standing by her man" in a Tammy Wynette accent. Wills says it is her capacity for mimicry and not the content of the utterance that goes awry, and I do agree with Wills, but not exactly for the reasons he states.

Hillary's voice is described by Junod as having a "clarion call": "it is a sexy voice, a pliable and professional voice, clarion and piping, verging towards the range of alto." Hillary is in control of her voice, can "tighten its timbre" just as Wills's examples show that she can reign in her spontaneity, vibrancy, and natural mimicry. Junod concurs that she "tightens its timbre" in order to "express a wish for a neutered sort of popularity."[104] Her vocal range and ambition are congruent with the ideas expressed in Anne Carson's magisterial essay, "The Gender of Sound," in two pertinent ways. The first addresses the anxiety of women in public life that their voices are "too high or too light or too shrill." We have previously mentioned Margaret Thatcher's vocal coaching and her "Attila the hen" nickname, which was also bestowed upon Nancy Astor, the first female member of the House of Commons: "She rushes about like a decapitated hen."[105] Junod's own assessment, despite the positive attributions "professional," "alto," and "tightening . . . timbre," does hint at the shrill; both "clarion" and "piping" suggest "shrill," as well as (in the case of "piping") hissing, sizzling, wailing, and whistling.

The second way Carson informs my reading reframes the listening tour entirely. For she recontextualizes it within a larger politics of sound, which, since antiquity, has associated female speech with "madness, witchery, bestiality." Carson reminds us of just how many mythic figures, whom she calls "female celebrities," "make themselves objectionable by the way they use their voice." The very name "Gorgon" is etymologically derived from the Sanskrit word for a guttural howl. And who can forget the furies, the sirens, Helen's "dangerous ventriloquism," Cassandra's "babbling," Artemis's "fearsome hullabaloo"? Indeed, so many of Carson's examples are less those of language (*logos*) than sound—growls, babbles, high-pitched or horrendous voices, shrieks—or vocal accessories, such as Aphrodite's belt ornament, to be worn or loaned to other women. "In general the women of classical literature are given over to disorderly and uncontrolled outflow of sound—to shrieking and wailing, sobbing, shrill lament, loud laughter, screams of pain or of pleasure and eruptions of raw emotion."[106]

It is not just in classical mythology but also in Hollywood where this is at work. Liz Taylor's *Cleopatra,* for Wayne Koestenbaum, is an important point of convergence for Jackie Kennedy and Liz Taylor, as well as a well-funded (an at-the-time unprecedented $1 million) "misogynist fantasy of what happens when a woman rules." Both the film and the diva-queen who plays the lead role are subject to scathing criticism. As *Time*'s film critic wrote, "When she played Cleopatra as a political animal, she screeches like a ward healer's wife at a block party." (Jackie would be the "refined," that is, "screechless" ward-heeler's wife.)[107] Hillary's deeply guttural laugh—sending cats racing out of the room—has a resonant pedigree.

It appears that the listening tour or primary presentation of a political spouse is part of the crafting of civic virtue as moderation (*soprosyne*) that in men resides in dissociation from emotions and control over the production of sound.[108] In other words, bad sound is a political disease (*nosos*), and female noise in particular must be regulated. Women's sound can be bad to hear either because of its vocal qualities (shrill, screeching, uncontained emotion) or because of what the speaker may say. It has usually been man's civic responsibility to control women's sound. Last year's electoral campaign was a case in point. "Whenever Teresa Heinz Kerry stepped before a lectern . . . her husband's aides collectively held their breath . . . if he can't rein in his wife, how can he run the country?"[109] (Interestingly, this quotation is from a story about the Hillary-Jeanine Pirro senatorial race in New York and the candidates' husband problems.)

Men usually control women's sound in politics, but part of Hillary's crossing (both gender and political) is that she is self-policing, deciding on the proper circumstances for her speech (when the listening tour will end) and just how much women's speech (laughter, wailing, yawning, eating) she will allow. Part of the appeal of the listening tour, to appropriate Carson here, is that Hillary has "put a door on the female mouth" and thus linked the closed mouth with uterine health and sexual and verbal continence.[110] The one exception—which proves the rule and then some—is her laugh. But it is foregrounded narratively, rerouted through the *logos* of hers and others' texts. Laughter is indicative of the separation between language and sound that is at the crux of both Carson's and my argument, and it is crucial in understanding how the listening tour worked, the libidinal forces it targeted, to turn Hillary into a desirable (thus electable) "body that mutters."

Hillary stated that when her normally gruff father laughed, "the sound came from deep inside and appeared to engage every part of his body." In other words, his laugh (and hers as a direct inheritance) is, to paraphrase Carson, a direct translation of what should be formulated indirectly by the *logos*. "Woman is that creature who puts the inside on the outside. By projections and leakages of all kinds—somatic, vocal, emotional, sexual—females expose or expend what should be kept in."[111] Carson recounts that Alexander Graham Bell did not want his deaf wife to learn sign language because of his deep mistrust of bypassing the *logos* and direct corporeal inscription. Again, what was objectionable about sign language was the perception of a "direct continuity between inside and outside." Moderation (*soprosyne*) dictates a dissociation of surface from what goes on inside, a separation of public decorum from private messiness. (Indeed, one of the most often mentioned —and disbelieved—examples of Hillary's improbable behavior during the impeachment debacle is how she "cleaned closets."[112] She speaks about how she also likes to do this in her Senate down time. And I have to say, after spending so much time with textualized versions of her, that I find it deeply congruent and do believe her.)

Every sound that issues from the body is a private datum, Carson asserts, a little bit or piece of autobiography, combining a private interior with a public trajectory.[113] Lacan denotes this as "respiratory erotogeneity": "Speech comes out of our very mouths, connecting our insides to our outsides."[114] It is precisely this distinction between sound and language that is (unconsciously) addressed by the masterstroke of the listening tour. I would be so bold as to see it as the tactical correlative to Clinton's "war room." In many ways, it surpasses it, as Clinton's war room targeted the manifest content of messages; it practiced state-of-the-art communications. For Clinton did not have any electoral problems with a Real that kept threatening to erupt—like some badly programmed snooze alarm. His electoral difficulty was one of the imaginary/symbolic, to construct him as the subject of *signifiers* (either "the man from Hope," or subject to a sentence, "It's the economy, stupid.") The war room functioned to continually resuture Clinton to signification. It was a campaign that produced a "suave" electoral body—easily a textbook case for rhetorical analysis or documentary interest.

Hillary emerges from the listening tour as a subject of *desire*. And this does not have to do with what Maureen Dowd would call her "resexing," relying on Junod's article in her op-ed piece "Sure I Would," which would read Hillary along the lines of an "extreme" makeover as well as question why voting for Hillary would necessarily imply "doing" her.

Extreme makeovers do repose upon an imaginary logic to the extent that they see the subject as a cultural Rorschach or mirror, reflecting an ideal (role model). This would attach a signification to Hillary—give her a fully textualized, inscribed sexuality that we could then decipher. Hillary would have found her signifier as easily as she found her signature look—the black pantsuit and her hairdo, the blond bob.

But the extreme-makeover analogy is not entirely this straightforward, as any observer of reality shows such as *The Swan, I Want a Famous Face, Nip/Tuck,* or *Extreme Makeover,* which work on the outer limits of the drive, would know. For Lacan, "desire" and *jouissance* take the gaze, the voice, the phoneme, as its object, but also those cuts and rims and places of corporeal edges, such as the slits of the eyelids, "the lips, 'the enclosure of the teeth,' . . . not to mention the hollow of the ear." These are objects that cannot be grasped imaginarily: "It is to this object that can not be grasped in the mirror that the specular image lends its clothes. A substance caught in the net of shadow, and which robbed of its shadow-swelling volume, holds out once again the tired lure of the shadow as if it were substance."[115]

The listening tour deflects attention from signification-rhetorical "mattering"—to what Tim Dean calls "muttering": "a form of signification which condenses and carries with it *jouissance* in a way ordinary language can not since *jouissance* and language conventionally are conceived as antithetical."[116] Hillary's campaign worked brilliantly in large part because its opening gesture allowed Hillary to be set free of the signifier; her desire has not yet found its signifier but rather evinces *jouissance,* in J. A. Miller's words, "a secret satisfaction which . . . attaches the subject to his sickness." We witness this in her radiance and in her intractable opacity.

I think the people covering Hillary's campaign have understood and articulated, in indirect and oblique ways, the truth of Lacan's claim that it is gaze, voice, and phoneme that connect our bodies to the sociocultural. Harpaz describes the tedium and frustration of a campaign where nothing seems to happen that isn't scripted, so she locates drama in other things: seeing Hillary swallow or shed a tear, catching her eating or even yawning: "It was a normal thing to do, but it was so shocking to me to actually see her yawn."[117] I was struck by how consistently and insistently these stories return to those places that mark a cut, those apertures or borders of the body: again, the mouth, eyelids, throat, involved in eating, tearing up, yawning, with perhaps only a hint of sound (the phoneme). These accounts do construct a body that mutters, linking language, the body, *jouissance*, and the *objet a*.

Junod's story is, like Sheehy's ("Flaming Fifties"), an empowerment fable, where empowerment is all about sexualization. Like Camille Paglia's article discussed in the earlier Hillary chapter, it almost gets it in a symptomatic way. Junod does locate his critical moment of "getting" Hillary (deciding to scuttle adjudication between "good" and "bad" Hillarys) to a microphone scene, a repeat of an earlier listening-tour panel performance where he witnesses Hillary being "resexed by the words in her own mouth." (I prefer to see this as Hillary enacting different ways of inhabiting desire.) There are several differences between this scene and earlier ones: she is now speaking instead of listening, but yet not quite speaking: "nobody could hear her because of a problem with her microphone. At least, the television men couldn't hear her, and they made themselves known. They had primacy so they started yelling at her. Finally someone on her staff scooted up and adjusted the microphone on the lapel of her flowing blue pantsuit. 'Is that okay?' Hillary said it was okay—*her voice was now amplified into its deep clarion call. 'Well,' she said as she crossed and recrossed her legs, 'I've been waiting for someone to turn me on.'* " Hillary receives a big laugh apparently due to her perfect timing and also because "suddenly the first Lady was . . . saucy. One could imagine her talking dirty, heck, she *was* talking dirty, sort of."[118]

This is highly suggestive, but less in the straightforward functionalist manner of Junod's analysis. For the scene does differently distribute "the gender of sound": the male technicians ("having primacy") are "yelling"; the microphone is displaced to a part of a garment, sartorially exiled to a flowing pantsuit's lapel; the pantsuit and her legs receive as much textual attention ("as she crossed and uncrossed her legs") as the "sort of dirty" words in her mouth: "I've been waiting for someone to turn me on." The message is that Hillary had in fact turned herself on—with the words in her own mouth. This mouth, now free to discuss the issues, "becomes the instrument of her freedom and her laugh rings the bell of her throat."

I would like to conclude by contrasting this textual image of Hillary with another, equally nonperspectival one—a 1989 installation by Geneviève Cadieux titled "Hear Me with Your Eyes." The piece consists of three large photographs. One is a black-and-white one of a woman with her eyes shut and with slightly parted lips. On an opposing wall is a color photograph with greater tension in the lips and head, which is simultaneously presented in full face and in three-quarter profile. The third and last wall has a black-and-white photo of a highly enlarged pair of slightly parted lips. Parveen Adams describes the spectatorial response to the artwork—usually, a self-conscious sensation about one's own "sightedness." This comes from the continual interruption by "that other spectator," that is, the pair of lips, which are "*in* the picture." These lips recall our canonical art example from the organizational note, that of Holbein's *Ambassadors*: "They function as the eye that flies in the foreground. . . . The lips serve the function of detaching the gaze so that the spectator's relation to the image is described. The detachment constitutes the object as an object of loss, a loss that is the very function of representation to deny."[119]

I should mention that the campaign photos accompanying the highly focalized mouth often are paired with other photos of Hillary in large black sunglasses, which make it impossible to see her eyes. Her eyes are literally blacked out, and her head is often presented in the same three-quarter and full-face juxtaposition, with these glasses on. The lips are, like Cadieux's, slightly parted; she is usually not smiling in these accompanying photos. These photos are, of course, given the obvious post-Lewinsky functionalist reading: to hide puffiness from crying or other signs of anger. But one would be remiss not to see how they function like the tains of mirrors in Francis Bacon's "Head" paintings: "the surface of the mirror which is repressed by the operation of its reflection."

The art critic Ernst van Alphen describes the qualities of a Bacon painting that recall the appeal of Hillary and of reality television: "Our gaze at the figure is repeated. It is not mirrored. Looking itself, not the object in the mirror, is reflected."[120] What can be said about the stories that focus on Hillary—biography, polemic, campaign account, journalistic profile, novelistic portraiture, hagiography, or hatchet job—is that they are not the same semiotic readings as we discussed in our earlier chapter 6. For these stories, which are ostensibly about her resexing or finding a campaign voice (or how the improbable happens to work out), turn out not to be about the redefinitions of a gender(ed) ego ideal (although on the surface they may read like them). They tell another story that is far more important for politics, briefly glimpsed during the first *trompe l'oeil* presidency of George H. W. Bush. For they are, above all, about "the detachment of the object gaze." The fixation on Hillary's mouth similarly invites us to "hear with our eyes"—an *en-abime* of her

"The Intimate Hillary," Lucinda Frank, *Talk,* September 1999.

electoral opening gesture (the listening campaign). Her dark, nonreflecting glasses solicit us to enjoy with our eyes. Or the dark glasses could reference blindness—turning a blind eye, as Hillary was often accused of: How could someone so smart not see what was going on under her eyes? Like the mirror's tain, they point to an absence behind identity.

I have been arguing that this Hillary "regained" who emerges refuses "imaginary capture." We do not receive a new feminine ego ideal in a positive sense, or in a dystopic ("gender decoy," "Bushwomen") form— something to identify or disidentify with. In this way, she is like the pervert W-Bush, who also does not provide a perspective from which we can see ourselves as satisfactory or lovable. Rather, what we see here is an image pushed to its limit (like W. on his mountain bike at the limit of the drive) and the empty place of the object given at that limit. With Hillary and W., we witness a shift from signifier to something radically heterogeneous to it—desire (in the case of W., a variant of fascist desire). Despite the loquaciousness of her textuality, it is Hillary's silence —the awesome silent *jouissance* of her body—that positions her as the ideal celebrity candidate and presumptive 2008 Democratic frontrunner. And this allows desire to emerge in the subject-electorate.

Hillary as an abject lesson leads me to two conjectures. First, traditional or progressive Democrats who spend time worrying about effective signification ("message") will continue to lose elections if they do not figure out ways to inhabit or mobilize desire. Karl Rove is less the master of the simplistic targeted message than he is an *agent provocateur* of *jouissance* in the form of hatred and the *objet a* that can be unleashed: homophobia, class, race, and gender war. Second point: the wager of feminist and, to some extent, much psychoanalytic theory (in the humanities at least) throughout the optimistic 1990s was that, in Parveen Adams's words, "The empty place of the object will come to be *occupied* by new things, among which may be the work of art itself" (emphasis mine).[121] I think this is still the hope of theorists such as Baudrillard (a poetic last singular stand against both the revenge of the mirror people and the cynical art conspirators). But we would be in considerable denial if we were to overlook the more recurrent and obvious sense of occupation; the "empty place of the object" could be occupied by war and death. That (W-Bush's) perversion and (Hillary's) *jouissance* remain two poles of presidential plausibility gives this subject of desire pause.

Epilogue: The Laugh of the Medusa

> And the eating theme was repeated in the jelly-fish shape in the left, *the jelly fish being a spineless creature that is almost nothing but an enveloping mouth.*   —M. Milner[122]

While writing this chapter, in Cap d'Antibes, I was reading Marion Milner's *On Not Being Able to Paint*. She was describing a painting of hers and its connection to eating themes and the mouth and the recurrent motif of the jellyfish. On a note of synchronicity, there had been many reports of an unprecedented number of jellyfish along the Riviera, and warnings had been posted in local newspapers and most area beaches. Although I had read Hélène Cixous's hilarious and provocative "The Laugh of the Medusa," I had never before connected the jellyfish with its French name, which is "*méduse.*"

At the same time, I was reading an account of the new fall television shows. It appears that Geena Davis will be starring as a vice president who becomes president (after the president dies) and refuses to step down and let the Speaker of the House assume the more gender-appropriate role of an aggressive "war president." But what got the most commentary was not the details of the actual show but the fact that Ms. Davis "had work done" on her mouth and that her "lips" preceded her entry into the Oval Office. I do not know if this show will displace 24 or early *West Wing* episodes.

All I can say is that they are onto something.[123]

Notes

1. On "Robo Clinton" or the animatronic Clinton, see Jon Wiener, "Disney Imagineers a President," *The Nation* 81, no. 4 (December 1987): 1381–1382. The example of the best-selling Nixon gift shop souvenir is based on a personal communication during my visit to the Nixon Birthplace and Library, January 1996.

2. Lauren Berlant, *The Queen of America Goes to Washington City: Essays on Sex and Citizenship* (Durham: Duke University Press, 1997), 44–45. Her brilliant reading of the "Mr. Lisa" episode appears in chapter 1, "The Theory of Infantile Citizenship," 37–49. For Berlant, Clinton's appearances in youth-culture venues such as MTV or on *Mr. Roger's Neighborhood* are part of a "construction of a patriotic youth culture . . . coded here as a postmodern nationalist mode of production" (49).

3. Ibid., 180–185. On *Forrest Gump* see the insightful reading of Joseba Gabilondo, "Morphing Saint Sebastian: Masochism and Masculinity in *Forrest Gump*," in Vivian Sobchack, ed., *Metamorphing: Visual Transformation and the Culture of Quick Change* (Minneapolis: University of Minnesota Press, 2000). Gabilondo's article is noteworthy in its attempt to displace technical discussions of morphing into the arena of the construction of determinate forms of subjectivity (in this case masculine): "My contention is that throughout the 1990's, morphing becomes instrumental in articulating a new masculinity that is masochist, lacks agency, and yet is capable of reappropriating and reproducing difference for its own legitimation" (183). A recent use of the Lincoln Memorial as an ad is its appearance in a promotion for a new TV series, *The Court*, starring Sally Field (by the producers behind *ER* and *The West Wing*). After seeing the Lincoln Memorial as a visual backdrop for the voiceover of JFK ("Ask not what your country can do for you . . .") and Martin Luther King ("I have a dream . . ."), there is a closeup of Sally Field in what looks to be the process of taking an oath prior to giving testimony in a confirmation hearing.

4. Rebecca Schneider, presentations of her "forefather" project, Cornell University colloquia. Other performance pieces include Anna Deveare Smith's "House Arrest," as well as her narrative account of the 1996 campaign, "Talk

to Me." On Lincoln in the context of the New Deal blackface films (of which *Holiday Inn* is an exemplar), see Michael Rogin's definitive study: *Blackface, White Noise: Jewish Immigrants in the Hollywood Melting Pot* (Berkeley: University of California Press, 1996), 177–198.

5. Patricia Cohen, "Sadder and Wiser," *New York Times Book Review*, October 23, 2005, 14. Other reviews of Shenk's *Lincoln's Melancholy* (New York: Houghton Mifflin, 2005) include Caleb Crain, "Rail Splitting," *The New Yorker*, November 7, 2005. The same year also saw the success of Doris Kearns Goodwin's *Team of Rivals: The Political Genius of Abraham Lincoln* (New York: Simon and Schuster, 2005).

6. Michael Rogin, *Independence Day: or How I Learned to Stop Worrying and Love the Enola Gay* (London: British Film Institute, 1998).

7. Frank Rich, *The Greatest Story Ever Sold: The Decline and Fall of Truth from 9/11 to Katrina* (New York: Penguin, 2006), 89.

8. Murray Edelman, *Constructing the Political Spectacle* (Chicago: University of Chicago Press, 1988); Jeffrey Tulis *The Rhetorical Presidency* (Princeton: Princeton University Press, 1987); Anne Norton, *The Republic of Signs: Liberal Theory and American Popular Culture* (Chicago: University of Chicago Press, 1998); Barbara Hinckley, *The Symbolic Presidency: How Presidents Portray Themselves* (New York: Routledge, 1990).

9. Gilles Deleuze and Felix Guattari, "Introduction: Rhizome," in *A Thousand Plateaus: Capitalism and Schizophrenia*, trans. Brian Massumi (Minneapolis: University of Minnesota Press, 1987), 3–25. The rhizome is informed by principles of connection and heterogeneity: "Any point of a rhizome can be connected to anything other and must be. This is very different from the tree or root, which plots a point, fixes an order. The linguistic tree or the Chomsky model still begins at a point S and proceeds by dichotomizing. On the contrary, not every trait in a rhizome is necessarily linked to a linguistic feature; semiotic chains of every nature are connected to very diverse models of coding (biological, political, economic, etc.) that bring into play not only different regimes of signs, but also states of things of differing status." The rhizome is a "collective assemblage of enunciation: a rhizome ceaselessly establishes connections between semiotic chains, organizations of power, and circumstances relative to the arts, sciences, and social struggles. A semiotic chain is like a tuber agglomerating very diverse acts, *not only linguistic, but also perceptive, mimetic, gestural and cognitive*" (7) (italics mine). "Unlike trees or their roots, the rhizome connects any point to any other point" (21). See Brian Massumi's excellent *A User's Guide to Capitalism and Schizophrenia: Deviations from Deleuze and Guattari* (Cambridge, MA: MIT Press, 1992).

10. Christopher Bollas, *The Shadow of the Object: Psychoanalysis and the Unthought Known* (New York: Columbia University Press, 1987), 13–29, 277–283; D. W. Winnicott, *Psychoanalytic Explorations,* ed. Clare Winnicott, Ray

Shepard, and Madeline Davis (Cambridge, MA: Harvard University Press, 1989). See especially "The Fate of the Transitional Object," 218–246. One of the best expository treatments of Winicott's transitional object and transitional phenomena is Adam Philips, *Winnicott* (Cambridge, MA: Harvard University Press, 1988): 113–126, 143–144.

11. Jan Abrams, *The Language of Winnicott: A Dictionary and Guide to Understanding His Work* (Northvale, NJ: Jason Aronson, 1997) 311–312.

12. Ibid., 312.

13. Ibid., 316–317.

14. Ibid., 319.

15. D. W. Winniccott, "The Place Where We Live," cited in ibid., 321–322.

16. Norton, *The Republic of Signs*; Lauren Berlant, *The Anatomy of National Fantasy: Hawthorne, Utopia and Everyday Life* (Chicago: University of Chicago Press, 1991), 27, 21. Berlant's focus in her Hawthorne book, like its companion volume on Reagan's America, *The Queen of America Goes to Washington City,* is on national culture as citizens ordinarily experience it— through periodic "patriotic" returns to the National Symbolic. What Berlant is situating as the "uniqueness" of America is its "utopian" dimension: "What is specific to America is the way it has politically exploited its privileged relation to utopian discourse: the contradiction between the 'nowhere' of utopia and the 'everywhere' of the nation dissolved by the American recasting of the 'political' into the terms of providential ideality, 'one nation under God' " (31). I am refiguring this potential space between "nowhere" and "everywhere" in Winnicott's "transitional phenomena." Berlant's notion of national fantasy and the National Symbolic is indebted to the work of Benedict Anderson, *Imagined Communities* (London: Verso, 1991), and of Anne Norton, *Alternative Americas: A Reading of Antebellum Political Culture* (Chicago: University of Chicago Press, 1986), as well as her *Reflections on Political Identity* (Baltimore: Johns Hopkins University Press, 1988).

17. Winnicott, "Place Where We Live," quoted in Abrams, *The Language of Winnicott,* 321–322.

18. Ibid., 322

19. Winnicott, "The Capacity to Be Alone," quoted in Abrams, *The Language of Winnicott,* 323.

20. Christopher Bollas, *Focus of Destiny,* quoted in Abrams, *The Language of Winnicott,* 323.

21. D. W. Winnicott, "Transitional Objects and Transitional Phenomena," cited in Abrams, *The Language of Winnicott,* 326. See also D. W. Winnicott, *Psychoanalytic Explorations,* "The Fate of the Transitional Object," 218–246.

22. For DeLillo, the JFK assassination was "seven seconds that broke the back of the American century." Like 9/11, it was an "apocalyptic event profound in its impact and uncertain in its ultimate meaning." Both Ruby's murder

of Oswald and the funeral were worldwide televisual events, and Oswald was a proleptically postmodern figure: self-referentially watching himself perform and evincing a notion of character in which the self isn't fixed but is open to continual revision/self-invention. See the *South Atlantic Quarterly* 89, no. 2 (Spring 1990), a special issue on "The Fiction of Don DeLillo," edited by Frank Lentricchia. The quotation is from an interview in that issue by Anthony De Curtis, "An Outsider in This Society: An Interview with Don DeLillo," 281–304. It is De Curtis's opening question (285). See also John Johnston, "Superlinear Fiction or Historical Diagram: Don DeLillo's *Libra*," *Modern Fiction Studies* 40, no. 2 (Summer 1994): 319–342.

23. Mark Crispin Miller, "The Madness of King George," *The Bush Dyslexicon: Observations on a National Disorder* (New York: Norton, 2001), 77–78.

24. See Edelman, *Constructing the Political Spectacle*, chapter 3, esp. 37–40.

25. Shoshana Felman, "Psychoanalysis and Education: Teaching, Terminable and Interminable," *Yale French Studies* 63 (1982): 33.

26. Jean Baudrillard, *The Perfect Crime*, trans. Chris Turner (London, Verso, 1996), 101.

27. William Merrin, *Baudrillard and the Media* (Cambridge: Polity, 2005), 28.

28. Ron Suskind, in a *New York Times Sunday Magazine* story published shortly before the 2004 election, quotes someone in the White House as stating that "a judicious study of discernible reality is not the way the world really works anymore." "We're an empire, and when we act, we create our reality." See Rich, *The Greatest Story Ever Sold*, 3–4.

29. Merrin, *Baudrillard and the Media*, 31.

30. Jean Baudrillard, *For a Critique of the Political Economy of the Sign*, trans. Charles Levin (St. Louis, MO: Telos, 1981), 155.

31. Charles Levin, *Jean Baudrillard: A Study in Cultural Metaphysics* (London, Prentice Hall, 1996), 128; and Merrin, *Baudrillard and the Media*, 38.

32. Laura Kipnis, *Against Love: A Polemic* (New York: Pantheon Books, 2003). See chapter 4, "And the Pursuit of Happiness," on adultery and the Clinton impeachment process.

33. Jean Baudrillard, *Seduction*, trans. Brian Singer (translation modified) (New York: St. Martin's Press, 1990), 30. Gore Vidal situates the Puritan legacy as backdrop for the Clinton impeachment in *Sexually Speaking: Collected Sex Writings* (San Francisco: Cleis Press, 1999); he suggests that the Puritans left Holland for North America not because they were religiously persecuted there but because they could not persecute others for their beliefs. "Only North America was left. Here, as lords of the wilderness, they were free to create the sort of quasi-theocratic society they dreamed of. *Rigorously persecuting one another for religious heresies, witchcraft, sexual misbehavior, they formed that ugly polity whose descendants we are*" (16–17) (emphasis mine).

34. Baudrillard, *Seduction,* 32.

35. Ibid., 31.

36. Joan Copjec, "The Teflon Totem," in *Read My Desire, Lacan Against the Historicists* (Cambridge, MA: MIT Press, 1995); Kurt Andersen, Graydon Carter, George Kalogerakis, eds., *SPY: The Funny Years* (New York: Miramax Books, 2006), 82. Mark O'Donnell was the author of this cartoon, which appeared in February 1989.

37. Baudrillard, *Perfect Crime,* 46.

38. Baudrillard, *The Intelligence of Evil or the Lucidity Pact* (Oxford: Berg, 2005), 31.

39. Jean Baudrillard, *The Impossible Exchange,* trans. Chris Turner (London: Verso, 2001), 73.

40. Ibid., 127.

41. Ibid., 5.

42. Ibid., 22.

43. Ibid., 129.

44. Ibid., 133.

45. Justin A. Frank, M.D., *Bush on the Couch: Inside the Mind of the President* (New York: Regan, 2004), 211.

46. Mark Crispin Miller, *Cruel and Unusual: Bush/Cheney's New World Order* (New York: Norton, 2004), 106.

47. For a good analysis of this see Paul Verhaeghe, "Enjoyment and Impossibility: Lacan's Revision of the Oedipus Complex," in Justin Clemens and Russell Grigg, eds., *Jacques Lacan and the Other Side of Psycho-analysis: Reflections on Seminar XVII sic 6* (Durham: Duke University Press, 2006), 34–35.

48. Slavoj Zizek, *The Sublime Object of Ideology* (London: Verso, 1989), 105. See also 107–110.

49. Russell Grigg, "Beyond the Oedipus Complex," in Clemens and Grigg, *Jacques Lacan and the Other Side of Psycho-analysis,* 65.

50. Rich, *The Greatest Story Ever Sold,* 76, 200.

51. Jacques Lacan, *Séminaire XVII: L'Envers de la psychanalyse* (Paris: Seuil, 1991), 205.

52. Alenka Zupancic, "When Surplus Enjoyment Meets Surplus Value," in Clemens and Grigg, *Jacques Lacan and the Other Side of Psycho-analysis,* 155.

53. *Séminaire XVII,* 90: "Ces rappels sont tout à fait essentials à faire au moment où, à parler de l'envers de la psychanalyse, la question se pose de la place de la psychanalyse dans la politique." Further along on this page he elaborates: "L'intrusion dans le politique ne peut se faire qu'à reconnaître qu'il n'y a pas de discours, et pas seulement l'analytique, *que de la jouissance*" (emphasis mine).

54. Parveen Adams, "Father Can't You See I'm Filming?" in Adams, *The Emptiness of the Image: Psychoanalysis and Sexual Differences* (London: Routledge, 1996), 92.

55. Verhaeghe, "Enjoyment and Impossibility," in Clemens and Grigg, *Jacques Lacan and the Other Side of Psycho-analysis*, 31.

56. Miller, *Cruel and Unusual*, 52–53, 279.

57. Ibid., 52–53, 279.

58. Verhaeghe, "Enjoyment and Impossibility," 31.

59. Eric Laurent, "Symptom and Discourse" in Clemens and Grigg, *Jacques Lacan and the Other Side of Psycho-analysis*, 250–251.

NOTES TO CHAPTER 2

1. Michael Rogin, *Ronald Reagan, the Movie and Other Episodes in Political Demonology* (Berkeley: University of California Press, 1987); Garry Wills, *Reagan's America* (New York: Penguin, 1988); Jeffrey Tulis, *The Rhetorical Presidency* (Princeton: Princeton University Press, 1987); Anne Norton, "The President as Sign," in Norton, *The Republic of Signs: Liberal Theory and American Popular Culture* (Chicago: University of Chicago Press, 1993); Richard Schickel, "Here's the Rest of Him," *Film Comment* 23: 3 (May–June 1987). On presidential leadership and rhetoric, see also Murray Edelman, *Constructing the Political Spectacle* (Chicago: University of Chicago Press, 1988), and Barbara Hinckley, *The Symbolic Presidency: How Presidents Portray Themselves* (New York: Routledge, 1990). For a view grounded in speech act theory, see Roderick Hart, *The Sound of Leadership: Presidential Communication in the Modern Age* (Chicago: University of Chicago Press, 1987).

As it turned out, Reagan's continental contemporary François Mitterrand was also deploying a similar sign theory. The astrologist Elisabeth Teissier claimed that astrological predictions played a role in the formation of the Cresson government, the Moscow "putsch," the selection of the date for the referendum on the Maastricht treaty, and the decision on best time to intervene during the Gulf War. "L'astrologue de Mitterrand dévoile ses confidences," *Libération*, June 26, 2000, 16.

2. Richard Hubler (with Ronald Reagan), *Where's the Rest of Me?* (New York: Duell, Gloan and Pearce, 1965); Lou Cannon, *President Reagan: The Role of a Lifetime* (New York: Simon and Schuster, 1982); Lawrence Leamer, *Make Believe: The Story of Nancy and Ronald Reagan* (New York: Dell, 1983).

3. Rogin, *Ronald Reagan, the Movie and Other Episodes in Political Demonology*, 7.

4. Ibid., 12.

5. Ibid., 3.

6. Ibid., 11.

7. Fredric Jameson, "Postmodernism or the Cultural Logic of Late Capitalism," *New Left Review* 146 (July–August 1984): 66–67. An earlier version,

"Postmodernism and Consumer Society," is available in Hal Foster, ed., *The Anti-Aesthetic* (Port Townsend, MA: Bay Press, 1987).

8. Paul de Man, *The Resistance to Theory* (Minneapolis: University of Minnesota Press, 1986), 10.

9. Jean Baudrillard, "The Structural Law of Value and the Order of Simulacra," in John Fekete, ed., *The Structural Allegory* (Minneapolis: University of Minnesota Press, 1984), 70.

10. Mark Poster, ed., *Jean Baudrillard: Selected Writings* (Stanford: Stanford University Press, 1988), 166. Jean Baudrillard, *Simulacra and Simulation*, trans. Sheila Faria Glaser (Ann Arbor: University of Michigan Press, 1994), 1 (originally published as *Simulacres et Simulation* [Paris: Galilée, 1981], 10).

11. Jean Baudrillard, *Amérique* (Paris: Grasset, 1986), 56; Baudrillard, *America*, trans. Chris Turner (London: Verso, 1988), 28.

12. Charles Matton, Palais de Tokyo, 1987, ATUS Gentilly, Centre National de la Photographie. See also *International Herald Tribune*, June 20–21, 1987, 7.

13. Wills, *Reagan's America*, 212. Lou Cannon's landmark biography, *President Reagan: The Role of a Lifetime* (New York: Simon and Schuster, 1991), is the definitive depiction of this fusion of presidential role and filmic persona. An updated reedition for campaign 2000 supplements Cannon's previous analysis of Iran-Contra and addresses conservative reappraisals of Reagan and how the 1994 Contract with America was informed by Reagan's 1985 State of the Union. More important, Cannon's revision (Re-Ron) powerfully concludes with the same wonderful temporal paradoxes that inaugurated his biography's opening chapter ("Back to the Future"). "Politically Reaganism was a time bomb with a delayed fuse" (756); "Mark Twain liked to say that Wagner's music was better than it sounded, and it can now be said that Reagan's economic policy was better than it looked when he left office" (758). But the darkest ironies are perhaps reserved for Cannon's treatment of Reagan's Alzheimer's disclosure (which he compares to Magic Johnson's announcement that he is HIV-positive as incidents of public service). Yet the theme of heightened public awareness (implicit in these popular disclosures) collides poignantly with the issue of (presidential) memory in the case of Alzheimer's. After Reagan can no longer ride his horses safely, his Rancho del Cielo is sold to a conservative foundation that has promised to preserve it in his memory. "But Reagan himself has no memory. And although Alzheimer's disease prevents Reagan from knowing it, he has made headway even with the experts" (x–xi). And yet the question of presidential cognition and memory had always been an open question (see Cannon, *President Reagan*, 703, 707, 727–728). More recent reviews, from 2003 and therefore published prior to Reagan's death, in 2004, of Cannon's earlier biography *Governor Reagan* are seen as previews of a revision in the evaluation of Reagan's achievements as president and his management style as governor of California. The book is also read as prefiguring Arnold's incumbency as governor.

14. Gilles Deleuze, "Plato and the Simulacrum," *October* 27 (Winter 1983): 54.

15. Norton, "The President as Sign," 93.

16. Wills, *Reagan's America,* 1; Rogin, *Ronald Reagan, the Movie and Other Episodes in Political Demonology,* 9. This point is mentioned in Fred Greenstein's review of Wills in the December 1987 *American Political Science Review* 81, no. 4 (December 1987): 1381–1382.

17. Hayden White, *Metahistory* (Baltimore: Johns Hopkins University Press, 1973), 35. White discusses four master tropes: metaphor (object-object relations; a representational figure), metonymy (part-part relations, either cause-effect or agent-act; a reductive mechanistic, extrinsic figure), synecdoche (part-whole; integrative, organicist, intrinsic figure), and irony (trope of negation). See also Hayden White, *Tropics of Discourse* (Baltimore: Johns Hopkins University Press, 1978).

18. Rogin, *Ronald Reagan, the Movie and Other Episodes in Political Demonology,* 108. For a different take on presidential sodometries and the anal-sadistic Nixon, see Tom Dumm's discussion of Bush, Nixon, and Norman Mailer in "George Bush, or Sex in the Superior Position," in his *united states* (Ithaca: Cornell University Press, 1984).

19. Stephen Melville, *Philosophy Beside Itself* (Minneapolis: University of Minnesota Press, 1986), 96.

20. Rogin, *Ronald Reagan, the Movie and Other Episodes in Political Demonology,* 82.

21. Ibid., 109.

22. Gérard Genette, *Figures III* (Paris: Seuil, 1972), 27.

23. Wills, *Reagan's America,* 476.

24. Norton, "The President as Sign," 100.

25. In his afterword, "Innocents Abroad," Wills gives a reading of the Iceland summit consonant with Bataille and Baudrillard's theories of symbolic exchange. Frances FitzGerald's recent *Way Out There in the Blue* is a brilliantly dark comic account of Reagan's attempt to build and rhetorically sell the Star Wars Shield (SDI). Her account of the Reykjavik summit's (October 1986) surrealistic slide amplifies the presentations of Wills and Rogin addressed in this chapter. FitzGerald, *Way Out There in the Blue: Reagan, Star Wars and the End of the Cold War* (New York: Simon and Schuster, 2000).

26. Norton, "The President as Sign," 105.

27. Mark Green and Gail MacColl, *Ronald Reagan's Reign of Error* (New York: Pantheon, 1987), 9.

28. Poster, *Jean Baudrillard,* 177; Baudrillard, *Simulacra,* 19. The centrality of the assassination attempt can be read against its multiple restagings in the Reagan presidential museum and library. It is part of the initial photographic presentation, plays a role in the film version of the Reagan story, and is also a

major part of Nancy's narrative (in the First Lady's section). The Reagan library's fixation on the attempted assassination (and Reagan's amusing retorts) corresponds neatly to Baudrillard's analysis of the deterrence effect of scenarios of scandal and death, an attempt "to regenerate a moribund principle through simulated scandal, phantasm and murder—a sort of hormonal treatment through negativity and crisis." "Scenarios of deterrence" like Disneyland and Watergate (and impeachment?) evince a perverse epistemological logic; they attempt to prove the real through imposition of an imaginary framing. Assassination *attempts* conceal the fact that these leaders—Johnson, Ford, Nixon, Reagan—are "no longer everything but mannequins of power. . . . To seek new blood in its own death, to renew the cycle through the mirror of crisis, negativity and antipower: this is the only solution—alibi of every power, of every institution attempting to break the vicious circle of its irresponsibility and its fundamental non-existence, of its already seen and of its already dead" (*Simulacram,* 19). For an analogous Baudrillardian reading of a presidential library, see Ralph Rugoff's delightful "A Conspiracy of Vitrines: The Richard Nixon Library and Birthplace," *Circus Americanus* (London: Verso 1995), 87–91. The paraphernalia related to Nixon and Elvis are reputed bestsellers in the gift shop (author's consultation with library curators, Yorba Linda, January 1998; visit to Reagan presidential museum and library, January 1998).

29. Rogin, *Ronald Reagan, the Movie and Other Episodes in Political Demonology,* 3–4.

30. Wills, *Reagan's* America, 177–191.

31. Rogin, *Ronald Reagan, the Movie and Other Episodes in Political Demonology,* 26; Schickel, "Here's the Rest of Him," 15.

32. Norton, "The President as Sign," 94.

33. George Bataille, *La part maudite* (Paris: Minuit, 1967). Bataille's "The Notion of Expenditure" is translated by Alan Stoekl in Stoekl, ed., *Visions of Excess* (Minneapolis: University of Minnesota Press, 1985).

34. Stoekl, *Visions of Excess,* 118, 137–138.

35. We might also note that against Baudrillard's and Bataille's disembodied or enucleated eye, Norton presents the embodied ear. For Reagan is also an aural compulsive. No one since FDR has used radio so effectively. Both radio and the embodied ear speak to oral traditions, corporality, collective experiences, what we call "speech" or phonocentrism. The embodied ear is to the point in the recent attempt to float Reagan's nose and ear over Mt. Rushmore. On the disembodied eye, see Arthur Kroker's "The Disembodied Eye: Ideology and Power in the Age of Nihilism," *Canadian Journal of Political and Social Theory* 2, no. 1–2 (Winter–Spring 1983).

36. Rogin, *Ronald Reagan, the Movie and Other Episodes in Political Demonology,* 19, 23, 26, 33.

37. Ibid., 35–36.

38. Fekete, *The Structural Allegory*, 62.

39. Rogin, *Ronald Reagan, the Movie and Other Episodes in Political Demonology*, 9. See also Edelman, *Constructing the Political Spectacle*, 11.

40. Rogin, *Ronald Reagan, the Movie and Other Episodes in Political Demonology*, 265.

41. Fekete, *The Structural Allegory*, 54.

42. Ibid., 57.

43. Roland Barthes, *Mythologies* (New York: Hill and Wang, 1972).

44. Schickel, "Here's the Rest of Him," 12. See also Rogin, *Ronald Reagan, the Movie and Other Episodes in Political Demonology*, 7.

45. Anders Stephanson, "Regarding Postmodernism—A Conversation with Fredric Jameson," *Social Text* (Fall 1987): 29–54.

46. Ibid., 38.

47. Roland Barthes, "Third Meaning," in his *Image, Music, Text* (New York: Hill and Wang, 1977).

48. Edelman, *Constructing the Political Spectacle*, 128.

49. Barthes, "Third Meaning," 58.

50. Foster, *The Anti-Aesthetic*, 114–115.

51. Barthes, "Third Meaning," 61.

52. Melville, *Philosophy Beside Itself*, 96.

53. Wills, *Reagan's America*, 450.

54. Umberto Eco, *Travels in Hyperreality* (New York: Harcourt, Brace, Jovanovich, 1983), 6–7.

55. Baudrillard, *Amériques*, 67; *America*, 33.

56. Deleuze, "Plato and the Simulacrum," 46–47.

57. Wills, *Reagan's America*, 189.

58. Ibid., 192–197, 201.

59. Ibid., 218–219.

60. Ibid., 334. Although GE figured as an emblem for Disneyland and the hyperreal simulacrum characteristic of Reaganism in this initial chapter, these signs have mutated in ways symptomatic of virtual reality. In a more recent analysis, "Disneyworld Company," Baudrillard details the salient differences in a regime of the virtual simulacrum that we will see is characteristic of Clintonism (see chapter 7); Baudrillard, *Écran Total* (April 3, 1996): 169–173; Baudrillard, *Screened Out* (2002): 150–154. Whereas, in the earlier episteme, the imaginary "policed" or served as an alibi for referential reality, here it functions as a "simulacrum to the second power," with far more generalized ambitions: "Disney, the precursor, the grand initiator of the imaginary as virtual reality, is now in the process of capturing all the real world to integrate it in his synthetic universe, under the form of a vast 'reality show' where the real becomes a theme park." No longer an *imaginary* alibi, it is now "the hallucination of the real in its ideal and simplified version." The virtual colonizes the real "as it appears"

and instantly recycles it. There are concomitant shifts in perspective. We are no longer spectators but "extras," "interactive performers in the reality show we call our lives." We live spectrality, and *if* we have imaginary fantasies we can always go to the movies and experience the virtual reality of death (*Sixth Sense, Stigmata, Stir of Echoes, Dogma*). Indeed, for Baudrillard, "The New World Order is in a Disney mode." The virtual is a generalized and metastatic (viral) form, no longer a "spectacular logic of alienation but a spectral logic of disincarnation . . . an enterprise of radical deterrence of the world from the inside and no longer from the outside. . . ." Temporality changes—we have entered homogeneous empty time. The virtual erases the real by turning it into a three-dimensional image with no depth, but it also synchronizes all periodicity "lapse or collapse of time: that's . . . what the twilight zone (the fourth dimension) is about." No longer Rod Serling, but MSNBC! "Disneyworld Company" also exists in a translation by François Debrix, *C/Theory* (March 1996).

61. Eco, *Travels in Hyperreality,* 43. See also Scott Bukatmin, "There's Always Tomorrowland: Disney and the Hypercinematic Experience," *October* 57 (Summer 1991): 55–78, especially his descriptions of the dataist and the terminal eras. (The dataist would correspond to Baudrillardian fatalism in its autonomy/independent existence from direct human experience or control.) Bukatmin's article is useful in supplementing Louis Marin, *Utopiques: jeux d'espaces* (Paris: Minuit, 1973) by reinscribing Disney's utopia along with other urbanists such as Le Corbusier's Radiant City and also linking Reagan in direct (Reagan was present at the opening ceremonies [67]) and more oblique ways (how Disneyland/mall/world cultures mutually reinforce "the implosive reality of television" [68]).

62. Eco, *Travels in Hyperreality,* 47.

63. Mark Crispin Miller, *Boxed In: The Culture of TV* (Evanston, IL: Northwestern University Press, 1988), 299–300.

64. Poster, *Jean Baudrillard,* 171–172; Baudrillard, *Simulacres,* 24–26; *Simulations,* 12–14.

65. *International Herald Tribune,* May 16, 1987, 15; *Village Voice,* January 5, 1988.

66. *Le Monde,* March 20–21, 1988, 17. *Tanner* came back in election 2004: *Tanner on Tanner,* which included scenes from the "real" Democratic National Convention. However, a reality show, *American Candidate,* envisioned for Showtime/F/X in 2004 with simulated presidential politics as well as a proven producer (R. J. Cutler, acclaimed for the documentary *The War Room* as well as for *The Real Roseann Show*) did not capture the popular imagination. Jim Rutenberg, "Reality TV's Ultimate Jungle: Simulated Presidential Politics," *New York Times,* January 9, 2004, E3.

67. Holly Brubach, "Ralph Lauren's Achievement," *The Atlantic,* August 1987, 72.

68. David Johnson, "Press Secretaries: Who's Putting Words in Oval Office Mouths," *International Herald Tribune*, April 12, 1988, 8.

69. *International Herald Tribune*, September 26–27, 1987, 18.

70. Brubach, "Ralph Lauren's Achievement," 73.

71. Steve Lohr, "Made in Japan or Not? That Is the Question," *International Herald Tribune*, April 2–3, 1988, 7.

72. Barthes, "Third Meaning," 64.

73. Ibid., 58.

74. Ibid., 58.

75. Ibid., 62.

76. Miller, *Boxed In: The Culture of TV*, 81.

77. Barthes, "Third Meaning," 61.

NOTES TO CHAPTER 3

1. Lacan's "little object *a*" or "*petit objet autre*" is a surplus object, a leftover of the Real that eludes symbolization, yet *partially* represents the function that produces it. See Slavoj Zizek's *The Sublime Object of Ideology* (London: Verso, 1989), as well as Bice Benvenuto and Roger Kennedy, *The Works of Jacques Lacan* (New York: St. Martin's Press, 1986) for a further elaboration.

2. "Overdue mail," the "*lettre en souffrance*," is a trope of Derrida in "The Purveyor of Truth," in John P. Muller and William J. Richardson, eds., *The Purloined Poe* (Baltimore: Johns Hopkins University Press, 1988).

3. Stanley Fish, "Withholding the Missing Portion: Psychoanalysis and Rhetoric," in his *Doing What Comes Naturally* (Durham: Duke University Press, 1989), 540.

4. See in particular James Der Derian's "Arms, Hostages and the Importance of Shredding in Earnest (II)," *Social Text* 22 (1989): 79–91, for this aspect of North/"off-the-shelf entity" as simulacrum.

5. J. Lapanche and J.-B. Portalis, *The Language of Psychoanalysis*, trans. Donald Nicholson-Smith (New York: Norton, 1973), 281–282.

6. Ibid., 282.

7. For another treatment of the covert operation read as a signifier, see my "Hate Boat: Greenpeace, National Identity and Nuclear Criticism," in James Der Derian and Michael J. Shapiro, eds., *International/Intertextual Relations: Postmodern Readings of World Politics* (Lexington, MA: Lexington Books, 1989).

8. John Muller, "Negation in 'The Purloined Letter': Hegel, Poe, and Lacan," in John P. Muller and William J. Richardson, eds., *The Purloined Poe* (Baltimore: Johns Hopkins University Press, 1988), 363.

9. Richard Klein and William B. Weaver, "Nuclear Coincidence and the Korean Airline Disaster," *Diacritics* 16 (Spring 1986): 5–6.

10. Michael P. Rogin, " 'Make My Day': Spectacle as Amnesia in Imperial Politics," *Representations* 29 (Winter 1990): 105.

11. Frederick M. Dolan, "Representing the Political System: American Political Science in the Age of the World Picture," *Diacritics* 20, no. 3 (1990): 107.

12. Rogin, "Make My Day," 103.

13. Der Derian, "Arms, Hostages, and the Importance of Shredding in Earnest (II)," 79–91.

14. Oliver North, *Taking the Stand* (New York: Pocket Books, 1987), 554.

15. Der Derian, "Arms, Hostages, and the Importance of Shredding in Earnest (II)," 81.

16. North, *Taking the Stand,* 521.

17. Der Derian, "Arms, Hostages, and the Importance of Shredding in Earnest (II)," 80.

18. Ibid., 80–81.

19. Ibid.

20. Bakhtin, cited in Murray Edelman, *Constructing the Political Spectacle* (Chicago: University of Chicago Press, 1987), 128.

21. "Leaks" are addressed in another way relevant to Iran-Contra in Plato's *Gorgias* (493–494): "In the same way, he labels fools 'uninitiated' (or 'leaky') and that part of their soul which contains the appetites, which is intemperate and as it were the reverse of water tight, he represents as a pitcher with holes in it, because it cannot be filled up. . . . The sieve . . . he uses as an image of the soul and his motive for comparing the souls of fools to sieves is that they are leaky and unable to retain their contents on account of their fickle and forgetful nature." This image of the souls of fools as a leaky vessel could be read against Reagan's testimony (total "non"recall) as well. Plato, *Gorgias* (London: Penguin, 1960), 92.

22. Donald Regan, *For the Record: From Wall Street to Washington* (New York: St. Martin's Press, 1988), 285.

23. Ibid., 282.

24. Ibid., p. 283.

25. Larry Speakes with Robert Pack, *Speaking Out: The Reagan Presidency From Inside the White House* (New York: Avon, 1988), 332.

26. Arthur Kroker and Marilouise Kroker, "Panic Sex in America," in Kroker and Kroker, eds., *Body Invaders* (New York: St. Martin's Press, 1987), 11.

27. Speakes, *Speaking Out,* 101.

28. Other onamastically felicitous examples include "Armacost," "Secord" (a compromise formation combining secret and record), "Hall" (as a conduit between McFarland and North via her mother, Wilma Hall, McFarland's secretary), and "Cave" (the Iranian translator indispensable to our cryptic analysis). One also notes the difference of a letter—"a"—between Regan and Reagan, which Rogin discusses in " 'Make My Day.' "

29. Ben Bradlee, *Guns and Glory: The Rise and Fall of Oliver North* (New York: Donald Fine, 1988), 548.

30. Nicholas Abraham and Maria Torok, *The Wolf Man's Magic Word,* trans. Nicholas Rand (Minneapolis: University of Minnesota Press, 1986), 50–51.

31. For a full discussion of the implications of this doctrine for the increasing identification of personal with body politic see Michael Rogin, *Ronald Reagan, the Movie and Other Episodes in Political Demonology* (Berkeley: University of California Press, 1987), chapter 3, "The King's Two Bodies: Lincoln, Wilson, Nixon, and Presidential Self-Sacrifice."

32. The argument for hysterical somatization (a form of miming?) might be read in the recent medical history of President Bush. Bush, who has self-announced problems with "the vision thing," develops glaucoma!

33. Regan, *For the Record,* 3.

34. Ibid., 11.

35. Ibid., 25.

36. Speakes, *Speaking Out,* 1.

37. Ibid., 230.

38. This symptomatic reading reveals an interesting moment of blindness. Speakes expresses a petulant disbelief that the press corps see him as a "mouthpiece"!

39. Speakes, *Speaking Out,* 237.

40. Ibid., 238.

41. Regan, *For the Record,* 17.

42. Speakes, *Speaking Out,* 243–244.

43. Ibid., 245.

44. "The problem confronting all inscriptive readers and semiocritical writers of this story is how are we, armed with the resurrected data, excessively to reinscribe this story of arms, hostages and terrorism without overwriting the disorder which gave rise to it?" Der Derian, "Arms, Hostages, and the Importance of Shredding in Earnest (II)," 81. I will suggest another analogy that Derrida addressed at length in "Fors: The Anglish Words of Nicholas Abraham and Maria Torok," namely "the possibility of writing upon a crypt."

45. Tom Conley, "A Trace of Style," in Mark Krupnick, ed., *Displacement: Derrida and After* (Bloomington: Indiana University Press, 1983), 82.

46. Abraham and Torok, *The Wolf Man's Magic Word,* 117.

47. Jacques Derrida, "Fors: The Anglish Words of Nicholas Abraham and Maria Torok," trans. Barbara Johnson, Introduction to Abraham and Torok, *The Wolf Man's Magic Word.*

48. For a discussion of these figures see "Tayacán," *Psychological Operations in Guerrilla Warfare: The CIA's Nicaragua Manual,* ed. Joanne Omang and Aryeh Neier (New York: Vintage, 1985); "Some Literary Resources," 94–98.

Imprecation expresses "a sentiment in view of the just or homeless"; *conmination* is a similar figure expressing a "bad wish for the rest." *Apostrophe* "consists of addressing oneself towards something supernatural or inanimate as if it were a living being: 'Mountains of Nicaragua, makes the seeds of freedom grow,'" while *interrogation* consists of asking a question of yourself to underline rhetorically what is being said (97). North's testimony makes use of logic figures such as preterition, litotes, and rhetorical questions, as well as the plaintive figures of speech (e.g., imprecation, depreciation, just described).

49. "Alloseme" refers to word usage.

50. Derrida, "Fors," xiii.

51. Lila Kalinich, "Where Is Thy Sting? Some Reflections on the Wolf-man," in Ellie Ragland and Marc Brachler, eds., *Lacan and the Subject of Language* (New York: Routledge, 1991), 175–177.

52. Fish, "*Withholding*," 542.

53. Derrida, "Fors," xl.

54. Noonan also concurs in this assessment of McFarland in a few hilarious passages in *What I Saw at the Revolution*: he would say not "Pass the butter" but "The stationary oleaginous object that is now not within my grasp or the grasp of others within this administration would be desirable, though not necessary, within my sphere and on my muffin" (224). This of course is Noonan's parody. The "real" speeches quoted are actually funnier (223–224).

55. Speakes, *Speaking Out*, 334.

56. Ibid., 114.

57. Ibid., 247.

58. Ibid., 249–250.

59. Jacques Derrida, "The Purveyor of Truth," in Muller and Richardson, *The Purloined Poe*, 176. See the editor's note concerning the original French version in *Poétique*, "le trop d'évidence—où le manque a sa place," which we translate as "the surplus of evidence—where lack has *its* place." The Alan Bass translation is "the surplus of evidence or the lack *in* its place" (italics mine).

60. A fuller discussion of the parallels between Iran-Contra and "The Purloined Letter" could, for example, include the following: parallels between the staging of secrecy and revelation; narrative disclosure as a form of seduction in North's testimony; the veiling of truth as woman and the letter as pure signifier of negation. In short, a full reading of Iran-Contra as purloined letter would situate it in relation to the critical debate exemplified by the essays in Muller and Richardson, *The Purloined Poe*.

61. Bradlee, *Guns and Glory*, 183.

62. Ibid., 175.

63. Speakes, *Speaking Out*, 345.

64. Ibid., 364.

65. The question of whether or not a letter reaches its destination is at issue

in the debate between Derrida and Lacan (see Lacan, Derrida, and Johnson in Muller and Richardson, *The Purloined Poe*).

66. Another word that North does not like to say is "profit" (Bradlee, *Guns and Glory,* 500).

67. Conley, "A Trace of Style," 82.

68. Bradlee, *Guns and Glory,* 501.

69. Ibid., 538.

70. Fish, "Withholding," 539.

71. North, *Taking the Stand,* 342.

72. Speakes, *Speaking Out,* 358.

73. Bradlee, *Guns and Glory,* 517.

74. Fish's thesis in "Withholding the Missing Portion" also alludes to this wish: ". . . a report by the Wolf Man of what he thought to himself shortly after he met Freud for the first time: 'this man is a Jewish swindler, he wants to use me from behind and shit on my head.' This paper is dedicated to the proposition that the Wolf Man got it right" (526). The context of this remark within North's testimony is reminiscent of Fish's focus on the scatological: a discussion of money is linked to the "clean-up" (*TS*, 341). The discussion of "sitting on his head" occurs within North's assertion that if the Commander in Chief were to dismiss him, he would proudly salute and say, "Thank you for the opportunity to have served." "And I am not going to criticise his decision, *no matter how he relieves me,* sir" (*TS* 342, emphasis mine).

75. Bradlee, *Guts and Glory,* 517.

76. The position of the purloined letter has been read as an anatomical chart of the female body: "upon a trumpery filigree card-rack of pasteboard, that hung dangling by a dirty blue ribbon, from a little brass knob just beneath the middle of the mantlepiece." For differing interpretations of this female anatomy/textuality question see the essays by Marie Bonaparte, Jacques Lacan, Jacques Derrida, Barbara Johnson, and Norman Holland in Muller and Ricardson, *The Purloined Poe* (Bonaparte, 130; Lacan, 48 and 45; Derrida, 189; Johnson, 237–239; Holland, 311).

77. On the hysterical male, see Arthur Kroker and Marilouise Kroker, eds., *The Hysterical Male: New Feminist Theory* (New York: St. Martin's Press, 1990).

78. Herman Rapaport, "Staging Mt. Blanc," in Krupnick, ed., *Displacement,* 62.

79. Paul Mandelbaum, "Kinkmeister," *New York Times Magazine,* April 7, 1991, 38.

80. Derrida, "Fors," xi.

81. Ibid., xiii.

82. Derrida, "Fors," xiv. Derrida plays on the new configurations of inner and outer: "The inside as outside of the outside or inside; the outside as inside

of inside" (xix). This new topography occurs on the frontier between introjection and incorporation and is, as such, part of a much larger discussion of the critical possibilities in Abraham and Torok's work.

83. Ibid., xiv.

84. Bradlee, *Guns and Glory,* 497.

85. Derrida, "Fors," xix.

NOTES TO CHAPTER 4

1. Jean Baudrillard, *Seduction,* trans. Brian Singer (translation modified), (New York: St. Martin's Press 1990), 64. All references to *Seduction* appear in the body of the text and refer to the Singer translation as *S.*

2. *Spy,* August 1988, 98. Cited in Ken Brady and Jeremy Solomon, eds., *The Wit and Wisdom of George Bush* (New York: St. Martin's Press, 1989), 27.

3. *Spy,* November 1988, 128. The full quotation runs as follows: "The holocaust was an obscene period in our nation's history. I mean this century's history. But we all lived in this century. I didn't live in this century." See also Brady and Solomon, *Wit and Wisdom,* 17.

4. Umberto Eco, *Travels in Hyperreality* (New York: Harcourt, Brace, Jovanovich, 1983), 6–7.

5. Brady and Solomon, *Wit and Wisdom,* 75.

6. Bice Benvenuto and Roger Kennedy, *The Works of Jacques Lacan* (New York: St. Martin's Press, 1986), 166.

7. Mark Poster, *Jean Baudrillard: Selected Writings* (Stanford: Stanford University Press, 1988), 188.

8. Mark Crispin Miller, *Boxed In: The Culture of TV* (Evanston, IL: Northwestern University Press, 1988), 80.

9. Richard Goldstein, "The New Wasp Hegemony in the Wake of Bush," *Enclitic* 11, no. 2 (Issue 22) (1989), 8–14.

10. Mark Green and Gail MacColl, *Ronald Reagan's Reign of Error* (New York: Pantheon, 1987), 9.

11. Bernard Weinraub, "Campaign Trail: Bushspeak Fans, Bend Us Your Ears," *New York Times,* November 4, 1988, 14.

12. I am indebted to Scott Bukatman's brilliant reading of Jerry Lewis: "Paralysis in Motion, Jerry Lewis's Life as a Man," *Camera Obscura* 17 (May 1988): 194–205.

13. Maureen Dowd, "Bush-Speak. Not Pretty. Catching On," *New York Times,* March 9, 1990, B1.

14. Kaja Silverman, "Historical Trauma and Male Subjectivity," in E. Ann Kaplan, ed., *Psychoanalysis and Cinema* (New York: Routledge 1990), 111. (The reference is to Jacques Lacan, *Seminaire XVII,* 4.)

15. *Spy,* August 1988, 98, cited in Brady and Solomon, *Wit and Wisdom,* 57.

16. Baudrillard, *Seduction,* 65–66.

17. Brady and Solomon, *Wit and Wisdom,* 13–14.

18. Lynne Kirby, "Male Hysteria and Early Cinema," *Camera Obscura* 17 (May 1988): 126.

19. Bukatman, "Paralysis in Motion," 195.

20. Maureen Dowd and Thomas Friedman, "Those Fabulous Bush and Baker Boys," *New York Times,* May 6, 1990, 58.

21. Roland Barthes, *Sade, Fourier, Loyola* (New York: Hill and Wang, 1976), 107–109.

22. Brady and Solomon, *Wit and Wisdom,* p. 44.

23. Maureen Dowd, "Bushspeak," *New York Times,* March 9, 1990, B1.

24. Dowd and Friedman, "Those Fabulous Bush and Baker Boys," 62.

25. On this topic of "Let's Pretend" (as well as the way Poppy Bush continually pops up), Bush recalls Pee-Wee Herman. See the article by Constance Penley, "The Cabinet of Dr. Pee-Wee: Consumerism and Sexual Terror," *Camera Obscura* 17 (May 1988), for implicit comparisons between Bush and Pee-Wee on playing house: "I know you are but what am I?" and especially: "No! None of that stuff! Game's over," 133–135. Penley's article is also excellent for a treatment of the *unheimlich* in both Pee-Wee's and Bush's playhouses.

26. Richard L. Berke, "Bush's Drug Deal: The D.E.A. Meets the Keystone Cops," *New York Times,* December 16, 1989, 10. See also Richard Baker "Let's Pretend," *New York Times,* September 27, 1989, 37.

27. Maureen Dowd, "Presidential Decree: No More Broccoli," *New York Times,* March 23, 1990, B1, Bush recalled the broccoli incident in his collected letters (wedged between the March 15, 1990, letter to Peggy Say, the sister of Terry Anderson, who was being held hostage in Iran, and a March 22 letter to a mother who had lost her only surviving son on Pan Am Flight 103): "The broccoli war is heating up. On March 21st, the Broccoli Association announces they're sending a couple of tons of the stuff, but I'm sticking with my position that I hate broccoli. I think I'll get Barbara, who likes broccoli, to go out and greet the broccoli caravan. I refuse to give an inch on this, and I so advised the press. I can't stand the stuff; it smells up everything; and I'm against it." George Bush, *All the Best, George Bush: My Life in Letters and Other Writings* (New York: Scribner's, 1999), 463.

28. Brady and Solomon, *Wit and Wisdom,* 26.

29. Steven V. Roberts, review of Peter Goldman and Tom Matthews, *The Quest for the Presidency 1988, New York Times Book Review,* December 10, 1989, 38.

30. Brady and Solomon, "Turning Inward," 25–26.

31. Ibid., p. 26.

32. Slavoj Zizek, *The Sublime Object of Ideology* (London: Verso, 1989), 113.

33. Brady and Solomon, *Wit and Wisdom,* 38.
34. Ibid., 36 (see also 38 for a similar formulation).
35. *New York Times,* September 26, 1988, A17.
36. Brady and Solomon, *Wit and Wisdom,* 19.
37. Warren Weaver Jr. and E. J. Dionne Jr., "Campaign Trail," *International Herald Tribune,* May 13, 1988, 3; *New York Times,* May 12, 1988, A32.
38. Molly Ivins, "Texas George," *Ms.* magazine, May 1988, 24.
39. *New York Times,* May 19, 1980, B13.
40. Brady and Solomon, *Wit and Wisdom,* 37–38.
41. Ibid., 24.
42. *Wall Street Journal,* September 18, 1988, 1.
43. Gerald F. Seib, "Paradonnez-Moi, Mr. Bush: In French You Make No Sense," *Wall Street Journal,* June 18, 1989, 1.
44. Michel Foucault, *This Is Not a Pipe,* trans. James Harkness (Berkeley: University of California Press, 1982), 22–25.
45. Bice Benvenuto and Roger Kennedy, *The Works of Jacques Lacan: An Introduction* (New York: St. Martin's Press, 1986), 167.
46. Bice and Benvenuto, *The Works of Jacques Lacan,* 173.
47. Brady and Solomon, *Wit and Wisdom,* 35 (citing Mary McGrory, "The Babbling Bush," *Washington Post,* September 29, 1988, A2).
48. Brady and Solomon, *Wit and Wisdom,* 36–37. Here is how Mark Crispin Miller reads this: "This Bush's gaffes were often striking for their sheer inanity, their metaphorical confusion and their trivializing stream of consciousness" (73). "Often Bush's utterances turned comic at the end, as he would topple from the sentimental heights into an anticlimax that revealed the calculation underneath it all. Speaking in Ohio, Bush reminisced about his close call as the Navy's youngest flyer in World War II. . . . Not yet taught to feign the sort of piety that would attract the Christian right, Bush was evidently worried that his references to 'my faith' might sound unconstitutional, so he tossed in that last term" (80–81). Mark Crispin Miller's attentive and often hilarious reading of Bush père ("The Madness of King George," *The Bush Dyslexicon: Observations on a National Disorder* [New York: Norton, 2001], 77–96) is astute in distinguishing the "wacky lyricism" of Poppy Bush, a "weird patois: the pidgin English of an old preppy on acid" (77–78), from his son's malapropisms. My argument with Miller's reading is that it proposes a far too neat correspondence between the lapsus and the strategic interest his misspeaking serves, thereby eliminating the ambivalence and equivocations of unconscious formations.
49. Bice and Benvenuto, *The Works of Jacques Lacan,* 173.
50. Bice and Benvenuto, *The Works of Jacques Lacan,* p. 169. For everything that you ever wanted to know about stupidity's ruses but were too afraid to ask (for fear of seeming stupid), see Avital Ronell's most recent tour de force,

Stupidity (Urbana: University of Illinois Press, 2002). (On Barthes, see esp. 10–11, as well as the genial chapter "The Question of Stupidity: Why We Remain in the Provinces" [37–60]).

51. Brady and Solomon, *Wit and Wisdom*, 20, 23.

52. For more examples see ibid., chapter 7, "That 'Thing' Thing," 73–77. See also Ronell, *Stupidity*, 11, on the relation between obsession with/fear of stupidity and the dreaded Lacanian thing. On "thingification" in Bush's discourse, Ronell offers a pertinent reading in "Support Our Tropes: Reading Desert Storm," in Frederick M. Dolan and Thomas L. Dumm, eds., *Rhetorical Republic: Governing Representations in American Politics* (Amherst: University of Massachusetts Press, 1993), 13–37. We will return to Ronell's reading in chapter 5.

53. Bice and Benvenuto, *The Works of Jacques Lacan*, 177–181.

54. Maureen Dowd, "The President's Tastes, Down Home to Less So," *New York Times*, May 1, 1990, B1. It appears that both Bush *père* and *fils* have difficulty with introjects. Bush's refusal to eat broccoli (read by Ronell as a sign of the "decline of the superegoistic function for him"—as president he could "externalize the law without remorse"), as well as his inability to keep his meal down in Japan (see chapter 5), might mark the inaugural as well as declining moments of his presidency. W's campaign lapsus (in apparent sympathy with Michigan working families)—"I know how hard it is for you to put food *on* your families"—as well as the pretzel episode (restaging Oedipal refusal and submission: I should have listened to my Mother and chewed my food!) repeat, albeit in displaced fashion, Freudian *topoi*. Ronell, "Support Our Tropes," 37, footnote 6.

55. See Kaja Silverman's reading of "The Best Years of Our Lives" in Kaplan, *Psychoanalysis and Cinema.*

56. Peggy Noonan, *What I Saw at the Revolution* (New York: Random House, 1990), 307.

NOTES TO CHAPTER 5

1. Roland Barthes, "The Third Meaning," *Image, Music, Text* (New York: Hill and Wang, 1977); Jean Baudrillard, *Seduction* (New York: St. Martin's Press, 1990), 54. This reading of presidential semiotic excess is not restricted to Republicans, but, as Clinton's folic/phallic *coupure* on (h)Air Force One suggests, the process of supplementation/abjection is constitutive of the postmodern American presidency. Could we also read John Edwards's $400 haircut in an analogous fashion?

2. Slavoj Zizek, *Looking Awry: An Introduction to Jacques Lacan Through Popular Culture* (Cambridge, MA: MIT Press, 1991), 88.

3. Jane Gallop, *Reading Lacan* (Ithaca: Cornell University Press, 1985).

4. Kaja Silverman, *Male Subjectivities at the Margins* (New York: Routledge, 1992), 1. My theoretical debt to Kaja Silverman's work is enormous. I am thinking here of her brilliant reworking of Freudian masochism and her theoretical contribution of the twin concepts of masochistic ecstasy and ruination of masculinity. These notions are not restricted to literary or cinematic texts but subtend any understanding of the reconfiguration of the American institution of the presidency as postphallic, de-Oedipalized, and postpaternal. My reading is also theoretically grounded in the male trouble issue of *Camera Obscura* 17 (May 1988). More recently, I have benefited from more sobering reflections on male masochism in Suzanne R. Stewart's *Sublime Surrender: Male Masochism at the Fin de Siecle* (Ithaca: Cornell University Press, 1998), especially her chapter "Saving Love: Is Sigmund Freud's Leader a Man?"

5. Thomas DiPiero, "The Patriarch Is Not (Just) a Man," *Camera Obscura* 25–26: 103.

6. Ibid., 104.

7. Silverman, *Male Subjectivities*, 255.

8. Jonathan Goldberg, "Recalling Totalities: The Mirrored Stages of Arnold Schwarzenegger," *differences* 4, no. 1 (1992): 184. Also crucial in my reinscription of "gender trouble" in Bush is Goldberg's restatement (181) of Teresa de Lauretis's insight in *Technologies of Gender* that "bodies . . . made by ideology will never exhaust or fully coincide with them." Like Goldberg (and de Lauretis), I am resisting the move to read Bush/The Terminator as simply "regressive of the phallus" (181). I am concerned with the postmodern presidency as the site of an enacted postphallic power.

9. Di Piero, "The Patriarch Is Not (Just) a Man," 107. Di Piero uses this term to depict the alternative phallic economics of Silverman and Kirby.

10. Bice Benvenuto and Roger Kennedy, *The Works of Jacques Lacan* (New York: St. Martin's Press, 1986), 166.

11. Zizek, *Looking Awry*, 91.

12. Ibid., 44.

13. Jacques Lacan, *Seminar III: The Psychoses 1955–1956 (Seminar of Jacques Lacan)*, trans. Jacque-Alain Miller and Russell Grigg (repr. ed., New York: Norton, 1997).

14. Slavoj Zizek, *The Sublime Object of Ideology* (London: Verso, 1989), 46; Sigmund Freud and W. Bullitt, *Le Président T. W. Wilson*, trans. Marie Tadié, preface by Gerard Miller (Paris: Payot, 1990).

15. Zizek, *Sublime Object*, 32–33. See Tom Keenan's brilliant rereading, *Fables of Responsibility: Aberrations and Predicaments in Ethics and Politics* (Stanford: Stanford University Press, 1997), 178–189.

16. Ivins, "Texas George," 24.

17. Elizabeth Mitchell, *W: Revenge of the Bush Dynasty* (New York: Hyperion, 1999), 224.

18. Michael Duffy and Dan Goodgame, *Marching in Place: The Status Quo Presidency of George Bush* (New York: Simon and Schuster, 1992), 223.

19. Ibid., 224.

20. Ibid., 59.

21. See the hilarious recontextualization of the inaugural address in Lydia Millet, *George Bush, Dark Prince of Love: A Presidential Romance* (New York: Simon and Schuster, 2000), 13–21; Duffy and Goodgame, *Marching in Place,* 223.

22. Joan Copjec, *Read My Desire: Lacan Against the Historicists* (Cambridge, MA: MIT Press, 1995), 149–150.

23. On the trope of "bringing out," see D. A. Miller's perspicacious reading, *Bringing Out Roland Barthes* (Berkeley: University of California Press, 1992). This "bringing out" is not reduced to an intrapsychic ("knowing oneself") process linked to an individual's "repressed" but rather addresses a "staged imaginary relation" between subjects: "between us and of us both, fashioned within the practices and relations, real and phantasmatic . . . across the inflections given . . . by nation and generations" (6–7).

24. Warren Weaver Jr. and E. J. Dionne Jr., "Campaign Trail," *New York Times,* May 17, 1988, A32.

25. "Notebook," *New Republic,* August 5, 1991, 6.

26. Brady and Solomon, *Wit and Wisdom,* 86. Compare this with Silverman on Henry James (173): "I never 'go behind' Miriam, only poor Sherringham goes, a great deal, and Nick Dormer goes a little, and the author, while they so waste wonderment, goes behind *them.*"

27. Roland Barthes, *S/Z* (New York: Hill and Wang), 36: "contaminated by the castration she has just been told about, the Marquise impels the narrator into it."

28. Roland Barthes, *The Pleasure of the Text* (New York: Hill and Wang, 1975), 53.

29. Baudrillard, *Seduction,* 48–49.

30. Silverman, *Male Subjectivities,* 179–180.

31. Duffy and Goodgame, *Marching in Place,* 109. Vic Gold was Bush's biographer and former speechwriter.

32. Avital Ronell, "Support Our Tropes (Reading Desert Storm)," in Thomas Dumm and Frederick Dolan, ed., *The Rhetorical Republic* (Amherst: University of Massachusetts Press, 1993).

33. Ibid.

34. Ibid., 17.

35. Ibid., 17; Millet, *George Bush, Dark Prince of Love,* 33.

36. Ronell, "Support Our Tropes," 17.

37. Ibid., 19.

38. Ibid., 21.

39. This runoff contest was much parodied on *Saturday Night Live* for its competitive insistence on just who was tougher on the death penalty.

40. Constance Penley, "Time Travel, Primal Scene and Dystopia," in her *The Future of an Illusion: Film, Feminism, and Psychoanalysis* (New York: Routledge, 1989), 129. Penley notes: "A film like *The Terminator* could be called a critical dystopia inasmuch as it tends to suggest causes rather than merely reveal symptoms."

41. Goldberg, "Recalling Totalities," 182.

42. Ibid., 195, 196.

43. Zizek, *Looking Awry*, 22.

44. Goldberg, "Recalling Totalities," 195, 196.

45. Slavoj Zizek, *Enjoy Your Symptom: Jacques Lacan in Hollywood and Out* (New York: Routledge, 1992), 155.

46. Andrew Rosenthal, "Accused of Drift, Bush Steers into Gentler Seas for a Day," *New York Times*, April 9, 1992, A9. The tidal basin is not just the *topos* of the idealized Jefferson of *Born Yesterday* but the site of the lethal doubling of *Strangers on a Train* and, by extension, to parricide.

47. Joseph Ellis describes the momentary "Jeffersonian surge" in 1992–1993 in relation to the other "possible contenders" who occupy "sacred space on the Mall in the nation's capital, the American version of Mount Olympus." In contrast to George Washington's "distance" and "silence" ("the Delphic oracle who never spoke, more like an old testament Jehovah") and Lincoln, who was relatively "accessible and had also spoken magic words" ("But Lincoln's magic was more somber and burdened . . ."), Jefferson's iconic appeal was wholly positive: "light, inspiring, optimistic." Lincoln may have been "more respected but Jefferson was more loved" (3–5) It is in this sense that Jeffersonian associations are eminently idealized ones. Joseph J. Elllis, *American Sphinx: The Character of Thomas Jefferson* (New York: Knopf, 1997).

48. Alice A. Jardine, *Gynesis: Configurations of Woman and Modernity* (Ithaca: Cornell University Press, 1985), 160.

49. Slavoj Zizek, "You Only Die Twice," in Zizek, *Sublime Object*, 131–149. See also Zizek, *Looking Awry*, 21–22.

50. Tom Wicker, "Bush's Midterm Crisis," *New York Times*, November 21, 1990, A15.

51. Ann Devroy, "Besieged, Battered and Bewildered: Bush Gropes to Make Sense of a 'Weird Year,'" *Washington Post*, July 1, 1992, A1.

52. Ronell, "Support Our Tropes," 13; George Bush, *All the Best, My Life in Letters and Other Writing* (New York: Scribner's, 1999), 545: "Last night I went to the dinner given by Miyazawa, and half way through the receiving line, I began to feel very faint and broke out in a big sweat. I knew I was going to throw up. I asked to be excused from the receiving line and this caused a lot of consternation, so I went into the bathroom, threw up in there, came back,

finished the line, and I felt very, very weak" (letter of January 9, 1992). For other references to this event, see also the letter to Ron Reagan Jr. of January 11: "when I got back from throwing up on our friend P. M. Miyazawa, I found that large, lovely picture of the five of us." (This refers to a photo taken at the dedication of the Reagan library.) Bush also rhetorically situates his "throwing up" on Miyazawa with other "gifts" in his letter to his nephew, John Ellis, on January 12, 1992: "Just got back from barfing on Miyazawa (bad news) to find your good letter of December 26 (good news.) Thanks for the coffee machine" (546–547).

53. Arthur Kroker refers to this aspect of contemporary power in his book *The Possessed Individual* (New York: St. Martin's Press, 1992), 74. "The resuccitutional ideology of the simulacrum where power restages its own death in order to recharge its flagging energies." The "dead veto" remark is reported in an article by Andrew Rosenthal with the apt title "With Eye on Election Outcome, Bush Resurrects Anti-Tax Pledge," *New York Times*, November 11, 1990, A1, 19.

54. On Bush's perfect veto record, see Duffy and Goodgame, *Marching in Place*, 78, and, more generally, the entire section entitled "Red Lines," 77–82. The veto strategy is part of a larger Sununu program of "talking points" to counter the broken tax pledge: "the battles we fight focus on preventing things from taking place. Let me suggest the following. There's not another single piece of legislation that needs to be passed in the next two years for this president." These are Sununu's words. Duffy and Goodgame comment: "At this, the *lions* of American conservation, *ready to devour Sununu* only moments earlier, applauded" (82) (italics mine). We will return to the figure of the devouring lions in the last section of this chapter.

55. Gallop, "The Dream of the Dead Author," in Gallop, *Reading Lacan* 157–185.

56. Andrew Rosenthal, "The 1992 Campaign: Republicans: Economy Shadows Bush's Campaign." On Lawrence Welk, see *New York Times*, February 17, 1992, A9; on Kahane, "Notebook," *The New Republic*, August 31, 1992, A10; Mitchell, *W*, 226.

57. Edgar Allan Poe, "The Facts in the Case of M. Valdemar," in Philip Van Doren Stern, ed., *The Portable Poe: Tales and Poems* (New York: Viking, 1945).

58. The *lamella* denotes, for Lacan, the "undead organ without body" that, along with its metastasis "the Manlet" (*l'hommelette*), refigures libido as image and myth. "My lamella represents here the part of a living being that is lost when that being is produced through the straits of sex" ("par les voies du sexe": *Voies* is *homonymic* for *voix/voies*). Jacques Lacan, "Position of the Unconscious," in Richard Feldstein, Bruce Fink, Maire Joanus, ed., *Reading Seminar XI* (Albany: SUNY Press, 1995), 273–274. See also Jacques Lacan, "Seminar

XI," in *The Four Fundamental Concepts of Psychoanalysis,* trans. Alan Sheridan (New York: Norton, 1998) chapter 15, 187–200 (esp. 196–197).

59. See Jonathan Goldberg's introduction to *Sodometries* (Stanford: Stanford University Press, 1992), 1–5; Cynthia Weber, "Something's Missing: Male Hysteria and the U.S. Invasion of Panama," in her *Faking It* (Minneapolis: University of Minnesota Press, 1999).

60. Goldberg, "Recalling Totalities," 179.

61. Maureen Dowd, "Bush, Trying to Quell Tax Debate, Insists Budget Talks Will Be Open," *New York Times,* May 12, 1990, A1.

62. Ibid. On Dorothy Walker Bush, see Zachary Kent, *Encyclopedia of Presidents: George Bush* (Chicago: Children's Press, 1989), chapter 2, "Poppy Bush," 13–15. In a campaign 2000 interview for an article in *Talk,* Barbara Bush calls Dorothy Walker Bush the most competitive person she ever knew. George Bush, in *All the Best,* recalls his mother's competitive instincts in a letter to his children (September 23, 1998): "I can vividly remember the bottom of my mother's feet. Yes, she played a much younger woman named Peaches Peltz in tennis back in 1935 or so and Peaches was smooth. Mum was tenacious. Mother literally wore the skin off the bottom of her feet."

63. Maureen Dowd, "The 1992 Campaign: Republicans; Immersing Himself in Nitty Gritty Bush Barnstorms New Hampshire," *New York Times,* January 16, 1992, A1.

64. Linda Lee, "Arts and Politics/Popular Culture: Sound Bites: Testing, Testing," *New York Times,* October 25, 1992, 2:29.

65. Andrew Rosenthal, "Bush Encounters the Supermarket, Amazed," *New York Times,* February 5, 1992, A1.

66. Silverman, *Male Subjectivities,* 54.

67. "Interview with President Bush in Map Room," C-SPAN, December 22, 1992.

68. "Wives Night in Houston," *New York Times,* August 21, 1992, A8.

69. Elizabeth Kohlbert, "The 1992 Campaign: Campaign Watch; View from the Booth: A Faulty Speech," *New York Times,* August 22, 1992, A8.

70. Gilles Deleuze, *Masochism: An Interpretation of Coldness and Cruelty,* trans. Jean McNeil (New York: George Braziller, 1971). Silverman discusses Deleuzean masochism in *Male Subjectivities,* 210–213.

71. Kaja Silverman, "Masochism and Male Subjectivity" *Camera Obscura* 17 (May 1988): 41.

72. Silverman, *Male Subjectivities,* 179–181. See also Leo Bersani, "The Freudian Body: Psychoanalysis and Art" (New York: Columbia University Press, 1986), and Bersani, "Is the Rectum a Grave?" in Douglas Crimp, ed., *AIDS: Cultural Analysis/Cultural Activism* (Cambridge, MA: MIT Press, 1989), esp. 222, 212.

73. Silverman, *Male Subjectivities,* 173.

74. J. Laplanche and J. B. Pontalis, *The Language of Psychoanalysis* (New York: Norton, 1975), 206.

75. Zizek, *Sublime Object,* 113.

76. Maureen Dowd, "They're So Vain," *New York Times Men's Fashions of the Times,* Fall 1990.

77. Andrew Rosenthal, "Air Force One Journal: 200,000 Miles Later, the President Gets His Wings," *New York Times,* September 7, 1990, 1:26.

78. Duffy and Goodgame, *Marching in Place,* 49–50.

79. Ibid., 49.

80. Zizek, *Sublime Object,* 113.

81. *Bushisms,* compiled by Jonathan Bines, the editors of the *New Republic* Corporate Author (New York: Workman, May 1992), 17.

82. Lynne Kirby, "Male Hysteria and Early Cinema," *Camera Obscura* 17 (May 1988): 126.

83. Peggy Noonan, *What I Saw at the Revolution* (New York: Random House, 1990), 302.

84. Dan Jenkins, "Golf with the Boss," *Golf Digest,* September 1990.

85. Mitchell, *W: Revenge,* 170.

86. Garry Wills "The Hostage," *New York Times,* August 13, 1992, 21–27. See also Garry Wills, "George Bush, Prisoner of the Crazies," *New York Times,* August 16, 1992, E7.

87. Silverman, *Male Subjectivities,* 206.

88. Duffy and Goodgame, *Marching in Place,* 41.

89. Silverman, *Male Subjectivities,* 189; Theodore Reik, "Masochism in Modern Man," in his *Of Law and Lust: On the Psychoanalysis of Romantic and Sexual Emotions* (New York: Farrar, Straus, and Giroux, 1949), 195–366. See in particular 235, 259, 265, 295–297.

90. Michael Wines, "The 1992 Campaign: The Ad Campaign: Clinton: The Swift Counterattack," *New York Times,* October 3, 1992, A8.

91. C-SPAN interview, December 22, 1992. The "javelin" does share a commonality with "whipping." Fatima Whitbread, Olympic javelin gold medal winner, recounts: "what I didn't know then was that bowling in cricket has a lot in common with throwing a javelin. There is much the same whiplash motion." Fatima Whitbread with Adrianna Blue, *Fatima: The Autobiography of Fatima Whitbread* (London: Pelham Books, 1988), 59.

92. Duffy and Goodgame, *Marching in Place,* 237.

93. Fred Barnes, "Just Fine," *New Republic,* August 31, 1992, 16; Andrew Rosenthal, "Bush Says Rival Would 'Pull a Fast One' Over Texas," *New York Times,* August 7, 1992, A10.

94. Silverman, *Male Subjectivities,* 206.

95. Ibid. See also Reik, "Masochism in Modern Man," 204–205, 218.

96. Sununu is figured on both sides of the Moloch fantasy. The National Wildlife Federation's newsletter ran a regular feature entitled "Sununu's," which sported the chief of staff wielding a Homelite! And yet even this javelin catcher refused to take certain spears. Although George Bush told Sununu he could say that the lowering of interest rates on credit cards was Bush's idea and not Sununu's (even if it was Sununu's), Sununu went too far in claiming that President Bush had only ad-libbed the credit card remark. The result was a ten-point stock market plunge. The 1992 finale of the Sununu story is interestingly framed around phallic reversals. Sununu is likened to "a guard dog who starts attacking houseguests." Bush's inability to pull his polls out is compared to "a baseball team in a slump—the batters aren't hitting, *the fielders are letting balls roll between their legs*." George W. Bush, now manager of the Texas Rangers, fires the presidential "baseball team manager": "you're out!" The son, George W., must cut the "umbilical cord" of his dad's hatchet man. Duffy and Goodgame, *Marching in Place*, 122–128.

97. Sununu writes a four-page resignation letter on Air Force One, which ends with the valedictory lapsus "I assure you that in pitbull mode or pussey [*sic*] cat mode (your choice, as always), I am ready to help." Duffy and Goodgame, *Marching in Place*, 130.

98. Bush, *All the Best*, 480.

99. Silverman, *Male Subjectivities*, 197.

100. D. W. Winnicott, "This Feminism," *Home Is Where We Start From: Essays by a Psychoanalyst* (New York: Norton, 1986), 183–194. Winnicott, speaking about sexual difference to the Progressive League in 1964, distinguishes between men and women in terms uncannily apposite to our concerns in this chapter: "There is a difference between men and women which is more important than being at the sending or the receiving end in feeding or in sex. It is this: there is no getting around the fact that each man and woman *came out of a woman*. . . . However, every man and woman grew in a womb and was born, even if by caesarian section. The more this is examined the more it becomes necessary to have a term WOMAN that makes possible a comparison of men and women." The key aspect is the acknowledgement of dependency: "at the very beginning everyone was *dependent* on a woman. It is necessary to say that at first everyone was *absolutely* dependent on a woman, and then relatively dependent. . . . Now it is very difficult indeed for a man or a woman to reach to the true acceptance in so far as it applies to the actual man or woman. . . . WOMAN is the unacknowledged mother of the first stages of the life of every man and woman" (191–192). Here Winnicott echoes work of the later Melanie Klein: hatred of this dependency must be transformed in gratitude. The 1992 women's rights movement must disavow this aggression and dependency by projecting it as Hillary bashing. What must be denied is that it takes WOMAN to make a village.

101. Silverman, *Male Subjectivities,* 266.

102. The relation of the presidential phallus to the throat could be analyzed through (what Tom Conley felicitously calls) an "interfellation" of the Lewinsky affair. One can find no better example of Reik's slogan for masochism than "Victory Through Defeat." Reik, "Masochism in Modern Man," 362.

NOTES TO CHAPTER 6

1. Jacqueline Rose, *The Haunting of Sylvia Plath* (Cambridge, MA: Harvard University Press, 1991), 1.

2. The question surrounding Hillary, revealed in press coverage of her autobiography, *Living History* (New York: Simon and Schuster, 2003), can be condensed into three questions: (1) What's really with her and Bill?, (2) Does she want to be president?, (3) Is she really a liberal or an opportunist?

3. Rose, *Plath,* 1.

4. Ibid., 13.

5. Beth J. Harpaz, *The Girls in the Van: Covering Hillary* (New York: St. Martin's Press, 2001), 1.

6. Rose, *Plath,* 105.

7. Ibid., 92–93.

8. An extensive Hillary citational index would go beyond the scope of this chapter. Many sources for the information in this paragraph are cited in full in other notes. See the articles and books by Gail Sheehy, Dick Morris, Gail Collins, Tom Junod, Barbara Olson (1999), Christopher Andersen, and Peggy Noonan; *The New Yorker,* May 30, 1994. Chris Matthews, on *Hardball* (January 11, 1999) referred to Hillary's "Coretta Scott King–style grandeur."

9. "Blondenfreude" is the felicitous term coined by the *New York Times* critic Alessandra Stanley. It is discussed in Maureen Dowd's review of *Living History*; Dowd, "The Real Hillary," *New York Times Book Review,* June 2003.

10. Paul Virilio, *L'accident original* (Paris: Galilée, 2005).

11. For an extended reading of Coetze on this point see Jacqueline Rose, "Apathy and Accountability: The Challenge of South Africa's Truth and Reconciliation Commission to the Intellectual in the Modern World," 231–235, as well as "Introduction: Shame," 3, both in her *On Not Being Able to Sleep: Psychoanalysis and the Modern World* (Princeton: Princeton University Press, 2003).

12. Elizabeth Kohlbert, "Running on Empathy," *The New Yorker,* February 7, 2000, 36–42. This issue sports a cover that shows Hillary wearing the superimposed baseball caps of two teams.

13. Joe Conason, "Hillary on Her Own," *Talk,* October 2001.

14. Robert Sullivan, "Hillary's Turn," *Vogue,* March 2001.

15. Tom Junod, "You'll Never Look at Hillary Clinton the Same Again,"

Esquire, October 1999. See Maureen Dowd's perspicacious reading: "Sure I Would," *New York Times,* September 12, 1999 19.

16. Laura Kipnis, "The Face That Launched a Thousand Jokes," in Laurent Berlant and Lisa Duggan, eds., *Our Monica, Ourselves: The Clinton Affair and the National Interest* (New York: New York University Press, 2001), 58.

17. Rose, *Plath,* 96.

18. Dean MacCannell, "Marilyn Monroe Is Not a Man," *Diacritics* 17, no. 2 (Summer1987): 114–127. MacCannell's review of Mailer and Steinem, among others, traces the "reactive solidarity of these biographies and painting and images in the face of the emergence of the feminine as a separate gender" (124). Marilyn is seen as a double gender outlaw, against both men and women. She possessed sexuality despite the fact that she was not a man.

19. Virilio, *Accident,* 38–41.

20. Rose's other articles are discussed at length later in the chapter, as well as in chapter 9. On Thatcher see Rose, "Margaret Thatcher and Ruth Ellis," *new formations* 6 (Winter 1988): 3–29; reprinted in Jacqueline Rose, *Why War?* (Oxford: Blackwell, 1993), 41–86.

21. Rose, *Plath,* 9.

22. The pinup war target could be read as complement to Cold War sexual fantasy of mother as bomb. See Michael Rogin on the Enola Gay in "Kiss Me Deadly," in *Ronald Reagan, the Movie and Other Episodes in Political Demonology* (Berkeley: University of California Press, 1987), 243–244.

23. Rose, *Plath,* 9.

24. Gail Sheehy, *Hillary's Choice* (New York: Random House, 1999), 263. Hillary lobbied the Department of Defense for $20 million to "enlist military technology" used in the Gulf War in the "battle against invasions of the breast."

25. Christopher Buckley, *No Way to Treat a First Lady* (New York: Random House, 2002).

26. Peggy Noonan, *The Case Against Hillary Clinton* (New York: Harper Collins, 2000; Joe Eszterhas, *American Rhapsody* (New York, Knopf, 2000).

27. For a critique of Butler in relation to her reading of Lacan's symbolic, see Tim Dean, *Beyond Sexuality* (Chicago: University of Chicago Press, 2001), 68–93.

28. Heather Nunn, "Violence and the Sacred: The Iron Lady, the Princess and the People's PM," *new formations* 36 (1999): 92–110. This article was written prior to Blair's 2005 reelection campaign, which was replete with "feminized" Oprah-style events in which "disappointed women" expressed their dissatisfaction to Blair.

29. *House of Style* was a popular MTV fashion show hosted by Cindy Crawford during the early 1990s.

30. Wahneema Lubiano, "Black Ladies, Welfare Queens and State Minstrels: Ideological War by Narrative Means," in Toni Morrison, ed., *Race-ing Justice,*

Engendering Power: Essays on Anita Hill, Clarence Thomas, and the Construction of Social Reality (New York: Pantheon, 1992), 324.

31. Judith Butler, *Gender Trouble* (New York: Routledge, 1989).

32. Emily Apter, *Feminizing the Fetish: Psychoanalysis and Narrative Obsession in Turn of the Century France* (Ithaca: Cornell University Press, 1991), 73. It would be interesting to examine Hillary's sartorial *Verkleidungstrieb* (will to dress—Copjec in Apter, 65) in relation to the codes of eighteenth-century fashion, which calls attention to the "charade of femininity by highlighting its structural supports" (25), the exhaustive classification system for hairstyles (*coiffures parlantes*), the exaggerated—indeed, hyperbolic—quality of these hairdos, and the complicated semiotics of hats. Does Hillary's blue-saucer inaugural hat with upturned brim recall the eighteenth-century *capote* (a bonnet with crinoline, notable for the eroticism of its turned-up quality)? If women's headgear such as "enhanced heads of hair" suggests possibilities "beyond the simple symbolization of sexual organs" (73), could we read the inaugural *capote* as a "safe hat"? The eighteenth-century vestimentary mode is a challenge to conventional domesticity, Apter argues, as its overexposed "constructedness" carries a concomitant risk of exposing masculine vulnerability. As Lacan reminds us in "the Signification of the Phallus" (and as is apparent to anyone who recalls the spectacle of Dukakis in a tank or Clinton reviewing the D-Day troops): "the fact that femininity takes refuge in this mask, because of the *Verdrangung* inherent to the phallic mode of desire, has the strange consequence that, in the human being, virile display itself appears as feminine."

33. See Emily Apter, "Masquerade," in Elizabeth Wright, ed., *Feminism and Psychoanalysis: A Critical Dictionary* (Oxford: Blackwell, 1992), 242–243.

34. A look at the second issue cover of *George* highlights certain differences. DeNiro is *George* #2. DeNiro is known for his abilities at disguise and perhaps demonstrates a national cultural crossing (immigrant culture *as* George). The inside miniature with photo credits shows a smiling George, holding a royal flush (of spades) in hands whose fingers alone protrude from effeminate cuffs. The sword that on the cover (a head shot with spear) is piercing the ace of spades is one of five exact replicas of George Washington's sword, right down to the "worn spot on the ivory grip." (The original, we are told, is in the Smithsonian.) This replica of George's sword belongs to John F. Kennedy Jr.'s *sister*, Caroline.

The *George* cover has, of course, been parodied by *Spy*—here, the *George* of Cindy Crawford is "colorized." O. J. Simpson stands in as George. The caption reads "By George, He's Guilty." The inside photo shows O. J., still dressed as George, giving the finger (as in his courtroom performance).

These covers address how "George" as the site of "the presidency" can be transgendered by manipulating the signs of gender, race, or national culture.

35. Marjorie Garber, *Vested Interests: Cross Dressing and Cultural Anxiety* (New York: Routledge, 1992), 126–127.

36. Catherine Millot, "The Feminine Superego," in Parveen Adams and Elizabeth Cowie, eds., *The Woman in Question M/F* (Cambridge, MA: MIT Press, 1990; Parveen Adams, "Of Female Bondage," in Teresa Brennan, ed., *Between Feminism and Psychoanalysis* (London: Routledge, 1989); reprinted in Parveen Adams, *The Emptiness of the Image: Psychoanalysis and Sexual Differences* (London: Routledge, 1996). Both Adams and Millot trace out the resolution of the Oedipus complex, seen as the moment of sexual differentiation into masculinity and femininity. Adams's article is a response to Millot's (Lacanian orthodox) position that there is no ideal exit for women from the Oedipus complex. Millot frames the choice as an either/or: either staying within the Oedipus complex and not acceding to desire (masculinity complex) or a problematic exit (femininity/having a baby) or paternal phallic identification. Adams sees another alternative in the perversions and in the structural differences between lesbian sadomasochism and clinical (Reikian) masochism. She questions whether lesbian sadomasochism is a practice that has detached itself from the paternal phallus as the magnetic north of sexual reference. In other words, Adams asserts, "Desire is a problem when sexuality is linked to gender." Adams asks an intriguing question whose ramifications cannot be fully explored here but that takes on added urgency in the W-Bush administration: whether the disavowal of the truth of sexual difference at the heart of all perversions always has the same consequences? See also Michèle Montrelay, "Inquiry into Femininity," in Adams and Cowie, *The Woman in Question M/F* 37; Adams, *The Emptiness of the Image*, 31.

38. Joseph Ellis, *American Sphinx: The Character of Thomas Jefferson* (New York: Knopf, 1997). See especially "Jeffersonian Surge: America 1992–93" (3–23); the comparative figures for visits to Graceland and to Jefferson's desk at the Smithsonian are found on page 14.

39. "Barbra: le retour," *Le Monde*, January 5, 1994, 12.

40. Garber, *Vested Interests*, 80. Barbra Streisand is an overdetermined *topos* for both gender and national (ethnic) crossing. In her reading of *Yentl*, Garber notes that "The transvestite is a sign of category crisis of the immigrant, between nations, forced out of one role that no longer fits and into another role, that of a stranger in a strange land. . . . As a Jewish woman in a star category usually occupied by gentiles (*despite—or because of*—the fact that many male movie moguls were Jews) she is Yentl/Anshel in another sense as well, 'masquerading' as a regular movie star when in fact she differs from them in an important way" (73). Barbra/Yentl is a "transvestite vehicle" (74) and is metonymically linked, for Garber, to other category crises. Two further points in Garber's analysis inform my reading of Hillary: (1) in both cases, Barbra/Hillary, the "disruption" of the transvestite performance is resignified as a (liberal) progress narrative; (2) in both instances, "Medusa" curls (81)—indeed the entire Medusa trope—is crucial (need we forget Streisand's longtime and very

public romance with her hairdresser?). Garber situates transvestism on a continuum with transsexualism. A Lacanian reading would radically distinguish between the two. In transvestism, what is at stake is the phallus itself, attributed to everyone without exception. Absence of the phallus is not admitted or tolerated; it is foreclosed as possibility. In this way, transvestism differs from perversion, which universalizes the phallus and in so doing affirms the possibility of its lacking. Transsexualism does not contest the *general* phallic distribution. What is involved is the place assigned to him/her. Perhaps the most interesting distinction between transvestism and transgender is in relation to fantasy. Transvestism is often a ludic display, demonstrating the imposition of the form of one's particular and contingent fantasy on the real. In Safouan's neat formulation: *The transvestite . . . makes the real imaginary. . . . The transsexual realizes the imaginary as his demand makes evident."* Moustapha Safouan, "Contribution to the Psychoanalysis of Transsexualism," in Stuart Schneiderman, ed., *How Lacan's Ideas Are Used in Clinical Practice* (Northvale, NJ: Jason Aronson, 1993), 197.

41. Ramon Soto characterizes Copy Cat as a "virtual narrative"—a "mimetic inflection" that recalls Hitchcock's filmic imaginary of *Psycho*, the psychotic referent—seriality of the phantasmagoric rantings of matricide." We could also add transvestism to his matricidal impulse.

42. Michael Rogin reads *ID4* against Clinton's multiculturalist politics in *Independence Day: Or How I Learned to Stop Worrying and Love the Enola Gay* (London: British Film Institute, 1998), esp. 41–53.

43. Roland Barthes, *The Fashion System*, trans. Mathew Ward and Richard Howard (Berkeley: University of California Press, 1990), 242.

44. Dana Thomas, "Taking Paris Hillary Style: French Find First Lady's Fashions *Formidable*," *Washington Post*, June 8, 1994, C2.

45. Henry Louis Gates's sympathetic article on Hillary in *The New Yorker* ("Hating Hillary," February 26 and March 6, 1996) is notable, for he too begins with Hillary's appearance: her "nearly flawless skin"; "She's in what you might call her 'civvies': she's wearing a purple turtleneck and a blue St. John knit suit: 'It's great to travel in, you can crumple it and it doesn't show wrinkles'" (87). His depiction is curious in several respects: Why does a sympathetic observer of Hillary evince the same sartorial repetition compulsion as her trashers? Why does Gates's depiction, although motivated differently from Paglia's, still underscore the artifactuality of Hillary—her uniform ("civvies") and its unnatural-ahistorical fabric (it won't show wrinkles).

In many ways, Gates repeats the normative HRC story line: there is a gap between being and appearance, however improbable ("She looks younger than her photos"), that is demonized as cynical manipulation or given the revisionist disavowal "She's so much nicer, funnier, prettier, softer, warmer than she appears." Kathie Lee Gifford's introduction to Hillary's appearance on *Live with Regis and Kathie Lee* was an outstanding exemplar of this type of disavowal, which always provides the requisite anecdote of an unpublicized (until now) gesture of human kindness on Hillary's part (a phone call, a letter, a visit to a sick friend) but which has the effect of denaturalizing Hillary and making the "human" moment seem all the more exceptional. In Gates's resignification, it takes the form of "girling": "She's the one who'll lend you jewelry for that special date. . . . Hillary's the sort of friend who'd undo an extra button on your blouse when you are about to go on a date. She wants to know who you're going out with. She's a real girl." Mandy Grunwald says: "There's a part of her that is constantly commenting on whether you got your hair cut, how it looks, your clothes" (125). This Hillary "more den-mother than martinet" intrigues Gates: "Besides, would Harold Ickes . . . ever help you preen for a date? *I'm struck, somehow* by that detail of the unbuttoned blouse." So am I, but perhaps for different reasons from Gates, who reads it in binary fashion as a countermyth or stereotype, a reversal of sorts. What underlines the two types of Hillary resignification—both demonization and girling—is the fixation on the assignment of social *roles*. Neither addresses the question of what is *uncanny* about the Clinton-Rodham relationship, which is not simply role reversal (she's the head/he's the heart) but the question of perversity/the perverse couple. (Fidelity/infidelity is less of an issue, perhaps, than the ability to keep a secret.)

46. Margaret Truman, *First Ladies* (New York: Random House, 1995), 146. See also Carl Sferrazza Anthony, *First Ladies: The Sage of the President's Wives and Their Power 1789–1961* (New York: William Morrow, 1990); Paul F. Boller Jr., *Presidential Wives* (New York: Oxford University Press, 1988); and Betty Boyd Caroli, *First Ladies* (New York: Oxford University Press, 1987).

47. Leslie Bennetts, "Pinning Down Hillary," *Vanity Fair,* June 1994.

48. Julie Reed, "The First Lady," *Vogue,* February 1993.

49. The quotations come from Thomas, "Taking Paris Hillary Style."

50. Judith Butler, *Bodies That Matter: On the Discursive Limits of Sex* (New York: Routledge, 1993), 129.

51. Barthes, *The Fashion System,* 232.

52. Ibid., 259.

53. Henry Louis Gates Jr., "Hillary Hating," *The New Yorker,* February 26 and March 4, 1996.

54. Thomas, "Taking Paris Hillary Style."

55. Butler, *Bodies,* x.

56. Joan Rivière, "Womanliness as a Masquerade," *International Journal of Psychoanalysis* 10 (1929): 303–313.

57. Butler, *Bodies,* 131.

58. Ibid., 137.

59. Rose, "Thatcher," 5.

60. Camille Paglia, "Ice Queen, Drag Queen: A Psychological Biography," *The New Republic,* March 4, 1996, 124–126.

61. Butler, *Gender Trouble,* 47.

62. Mary Anne Doane, *Femmes Fatales: Feminism, Film Theory, Psychoanalysis* (New York: Routledge, 1991), 22–23.

63. Rivière, "Womanliness as a Masquerade," 306.

64. Ibid., 307.

65. Ibid., 304–306.

66. Paglia, "Ice Queen, Drag Queen," 26. On MacKinnon, see the insightful essay by Parveen Adams and Marc Cousins, "The Assault on Truth," in Adams, *The Emptiness of the Image,* 57–69.

67. Ibid.

68. Rose, "Thatcher," 8.

69. Ibid., 10.

70. Ibid., 25.

71. Anne Carson, "The Gender of Sound," in her *Glass, Irony and God* (New York: New Directions, 1992), 120.

72. Rose, "Thatcher," 22.

73. Doane, *Femmes Fatales,* 28.

74. Ibid., 32.

75. Simon Shama's article on Diana, "Lady Di: Royal Flesh," appeared in the same *New Yorker* issue as Gates's article on Hillary. Although "flesh" is not a word associated with Hillary but rather is linked to her husband, Hillary's narrative trajectory does share some affinities with Diana's in its postimpeachment, sacrificial, celebrity moments. In Shama's article, written prior to Diana's death, her political trajectory is read as a "make-over" in which a "molting swan" becomes a "bird of prey." (You may recall that "birds of prey" are but one figure Freud uses, along with comics, criminals, cats, and children, to describe femininity's enigma.) Shama connects "hats" to "constitutional bodies" as formal figures of authority. The body and its part-objects thus constitute a weapon and a battlefield for the transformation of victim to conqueror (paralleling the doubling Rose outlines in her article of executioner and victim). In Shama's presentation, Lady Di's body is a site of "regurgitation, transgression, consolidation," where the entire body becomes a fetish. (In this sense, it would be possible to read Shama's precrash Lady Di as a Baudrillardian transsexual. For more on Baudrillard's notion of transsexuality, see his "A World Without Women," in Baudrillard, *The Perfect Crime,* trans. Chris Turner [London: Verso, 1996], 111–114).

76. One wonders about the perverse synchronicity and appeal of the fashion police's interpellation in popular (2003–2005) reality shows where style mavens descend upon hapless souls in swat-team mock urgency (*Queer Eye*) or other forms of disciplinary pedagogy (Style's *Fashion Police, The Look for Less,* or *How Do I Look?*) at precisely the moment Hillary seems to have found a "convincing" look.

77. Joyce Milton, *The Story of Hillary Rodham Clinton: First Lady of the United States* (a Yearling Book) (New York: Parachute Press, 1999), 39.

78. Gail Sheehy, "What Hillary Wants," *Vanity Fair,* May 1992, 214.

79. Doane, *Femmes Fatales,* 27.

80. Milton, *The Story of Hillary Rodham Clinton,* 8–9.

81. Ibid., 49.

82. Joel Achenbach, *Washington Post,* December 14, 1994.

83. Wayne Koestenbaum, *Jackie Under My Skin: Interpreting an Icon* (New York: Plume Books, 1996), 78.

84. Cited in Sigmund Freud, "Femininity," in James Strachey, ed., *The Standard Edition of the Complete Psychological Works of Sigmund Freud* (London: Hogarth, 1964), 22:113.

85. "Apparition," in *Collected Novels and Stories of Guy de Maupassant,* trans. Ernest Boyd (New York: Knopf, 1928), 105.

86. In *Jackie Under My Skin: Interpreting an Icon* (New York, Plume, 1995), 81.

87. Jim Borman's cartoon can be accessed at http://borgman.enquirer.com/img/toons/colorhillary600.gif.

88. Apter, *Feminizing the Fetish,* 72–73.

89. Koestenbaum, *Jackie,* 53–55.

90. Ibid., 56.

91. Joel Achebach, "The First Lady's Mission Impossible," *Washington Post,* December 14, 1994, 1.

92. Elizabeth Drew, *On the Edge: The Clinton Presidency* (New York: Simon and Schuster, 1994).

93. Danielle Mitterrand was also a published author. See her *En toutes libertés* (Paris: Ramsay, 1996). Readers of Hillary Clinton's autobiography may be surprised to discover that the European First Lady Hillary felt the most affinity with was not Cherie Blair but Bernadette Chirac. See Clinton, *Living History,* 339: "She was the only presidential spouse I knew who had been elected on her own. I was fascinated by the independent role she had carved out for herself and her stories of walking and driving herself from house to house, asking for votes . . . in May 1998 I spent a wonderful day touring Correze with her, meeting the people she represented."

94. Daniel Wattenberg, "Boy Clinton's Big Mama: The Lady Macbeth of Little Rock," *American Spectator* 25, no. 8 (August 1992): 25–32. Patricia Williams, *The Rooster's Egg: On the Persistence of Prejudice* (Cambridge, MA: Harvard University Press, 1995).

Wattenberg's article begins with an amazing passage: "Hillary Clinton has been likened to Eva Perón but it's a bad analogy. Evita was worshiped by the 'shirtless ones,' the working class while Hillary's charms elude most outside of an elite cohort of left-liberal baby-boom feminists—the type who thought Anita

Hill should be canonized and *Thelma and Louise* was the best movie since *Easy Rider*. Hillary reckons herself the next Eleanor Roosevelt. But standing well to the left of her husband and enjoying an independent power base within its coalition, Hillary is best thought of as the Winnie Mandela of American Politics."

Of all Hillary's many overdetermined and overcoded posturings, the racial freighting of Hillary as Bill's "Big Mama" is at least as central to her construction as an object of retaliatory criticism as the sexual associations I address in this chapter. Places one might begin include the disavowed miscegenation/Mandingo scene involving Susan Stanton/Hillary Clinton in the novel *Primary Colors*, and indeed the disavowal that sees the narrator's colorization—an ethnic Stephanopoulos?—as he becomes a "blackened" civil rights hero's mulatto grandchild, Henry Burton, a change that is seen as a purely "instrumental" narrative device. (Michael J. Fox was even considered for the screen role, which was played by a non-American actor of color.) But it also includes Toni Morrison's compelling reading of Bill Clinton as our first "black" president (as well as the responses to it, such as that of Micki McElya, "Trashing the Presidency: Race, Class and the Clinton/Lewinsky Affair," in Berlant and Duggan, *Our Monica, Ourselves*, 156–174). For, as Michael Rogin has argued, this too exemplifies a logic that "colors black the bearer of the identifying wound." Rogin, *Blackface, White Noise: Jewish Immigrants in the Hollywood Melting Pot* (Berkeley: University of California Press, 1996), 241. The use of race ("Big Mama," a "blackened Stephanopoulos") to "humiliate" or "injure" bodies while it simultaneously is evacuated as a critical category for analysis may prove an unsettling harbinger of transition between the Clinton and the W-Bush administrations.

95. Wattenberg, "Boy Clinton's Big Mama," 26.

96. Marjorie Garber, "Macbeth: The Male Medusa," in *Shakespeare's Ghost Writers: Literature as Uncanny Causality* (New York: Methuen, 1987), 110.

97. John Brummett, *High Wire: From the Backwoods to the Beltway, the Education of Bill Clinton* (New York: Hyperion Press, 1994), 113–114.

98. Wattenberg, "Boy Clinton's Big Mama," 91.

99. Dick Morris, *Behind the Oval Office: Winning the Presidency in the Nineties* (New York: Random House, 1997).

100. Hillary Rodham Clinton, *It Takes a Village and Other Lessons Children Teach Us* (New York: Simon and Schuster, 1996), 69.

101. Linda Zerilli, "A Process Without a Subject: Simone de Beauvoir and Julia Kristeva on Maternity," *Signs: Journal of Women in Culture and Society* 18, no. 1 (Autumn 1992): 1–23.

102. Clinton, *Village*, 7–8.

103. Ibid., 1–3.

104. Garber, *Vested Interests*, 1.

105. Kobena Mercer, "Skin Head Sex Thing," in Bad Object Choices, ed., *How Do I Look? Queer Film and Video* (Seattle: Bay Press, 1991), 207–208.

106. Gayle Wald, *Crossing the Line: Racial Passing in Twentieth Century U.S. Literature and Culture* (Durham: Duke University Press, 2000), 78. Wald is referencing racial masquerades involved in "voluntary Negro" passing, but her discussion is especially pertinent to gender masquerades. At the moment of this revision (2006), Hillary has just marked Martin Luther King Day with a much-commented-on racial masquerade, referring to Congress as a "plantation."

NOTES TO CHAPTER 7

1. John Brummett, *High Wire: From the Backwoods to the Beltway: The Education of Bill Clinton* (New York: Hyperion Press, 1994), 3.

2. See Juliet Flower MacCannell, *The Regime of the Brothers: Beyond the Patriarchy* (New York: Routledge, 1991).

3. On the Baudrillardean "virtual": *The Perfect Crime,* trans. Chris Turner (London: Verso 1996); *Fragments: Cool Memories III 1991–1995* (Paris: Galilée, 1995); *Paroxysm: Interviews with Philippe Petit,* trans. Chris Turner (London: Verso, 1998); *Ecran total* (Paris: Galilée, 1997). Philippe Quéau's *Le virtuel: Vertus et vertiges* (Paris: Editions Champ Vallon, 1993) shares many affinities with the Baudrillardean "virtual." Parenthetical citations will be given in the text.

4. Baudrillard, *Fragments: Cool Memories III 1991–1995,* 108, 150.

5. Fred Greenstein, "There He Goes Again: The Alternating Political Style of Bill Clinton," *P.S. Political Science and Politics* 31, no. 2 (June 1998): 179–181.

6. This chapter was written before the now infamous *Talk* interview with Hillary Clinton in which she speculated on Bill's childhood abuse (being caught in the conflict between his mother and his grandmother) and its role in Bill's risk taking and other self-defeating behaviors. See Lucinda Franks, "The Intimate Hillary," *Talk* (September 1999): 174.

7. Jean Laplanche, *New Foundations of Psychoanalysis,* trans. David Macey (London: Blackwell, 1989); Christopher Bollas, *The Shadow of the Object: Psychoanalysis of the Unthought Known* (New York: Columbia University Press, 1987), esp. 277–283 ("At the very core of the concept of the unthought known, therefore, is Winnicott's theory of the true self and Freud's idea of the primary repressed unconscious." Bollas's view differs a bit from that of Melanie Klein: "Phantasy, however, does not constitute the true self, it represents it. . . . Phantasy is the first representative of the unthought known in mental life. It is a way of thinking which is there" (278–270), as well as Bollas's introductory remarks: "The object casts its shadow without a child being able to process this relation through mental representations of language. . . . While we do know something of the character of the object which affects us, we may not have thought it yet" (3).

8. Elizabeth Drew, *On the Edge: The Clinton Presidency* (New York: Simon and Schuster, 1994) 95.

9. Michael Kelly, "The President's Past," *New York Times Magazine*, July 3, 1994, 45.

10. Baudrillard, *Perfect Crime*, 53.

11. Drew, *On the Edge*, 95.

12. The canon of presidential adventure films during the Clinton years includes *Air Force One, Shadow Conspiracy, Escape from L.A., Independence Day, Mars Attacks, Absolute Power,* and *Murder at 1600;* this could be further extended to include comedic adventure (political satire) with *Dave, My Fellow Americans, Primary Colors, Wag the Dog,* and *First Kid.* In Robert Zemakis's *Contact,* President Clinton makes a cameo appearance, as he does in the animated *Beavis and Butthead Do America,* which ends up in the Oval Office. The disaster-comet films *Armageddon* and *Deep Impact,* films of the second term, displace the focus from the office and agency of the presidency to a state of emergency itself.

13. Drew, *On the Edge*, 420.

14. Paul Fick, *The Dysfunctional President: Inside the Mind of Bill Clinton* (New York: Citadel Press, 1996), 205.

15. Larry Speakes with Robert Pack, *Speaking Out: The Reagan Presidency from Inside the White House* (New York: Avon, 1988), 249–250.

16. Among the voluminous writings contemporaneous with Clinton's first term, the following are useful: Charles F. Allen and Jonathan Portis, *The Comeback Kid: The Life and Career of Bill Clinton* (New York: Birch Lane Books, 1992), and Gene Martin and Aaron Boyd, *Bill Clinton: President from Arkansas* (Greensboro, NC: Tudor, 1993), provide two of the earliest biographical accounts. David Maraniss's *First in His Class: A Biography of Bill Clinton* (New York: Simon and Schuster, 1995) is the Pulitzer Prize winner of Clintonian biography, and Drew, *On the Edge,* provides a superb narrative account of the early years. Drew's later volume *Showdown: The Struggle Between the Gingrich Congress and the Clinton White House* (New York: Simon and Schuster, 1996) continues this narrative through the initial success of the Contract with America and the government shutdown. Bob Woodward's *The Agenda* (New York: Simon and Schuster, 1994) and *The Choice* (New York: Simon and Schuster, 1996) attempt a more contentious view of the Clinton presidency throughout the period also addressed by Drew and are, in their emphasis on electoral tactics over policy, similar to Dick Morris's insider book *Behind the Oval Office* (New York: Random House, 1997). Brummett's *High Wire* shares this chapter's focus on the first year and is the work of an Arkansas reporter. Peter Boyer's *New Yorker* pieces, especially "A Fever in the White House" (April 15, 1996); the journalism of Jeffrey H. Birnbaum, *Madhouse: The Private Turmoil of Working*

for the President (New York: Random House, 1996); Richard Cohen, "Despite the Hoopla, Clinton's No Nixon" (reprinted in the *International Herald Tribune,* June 14, 1996; Nina Burleigh's piece on the presidential speech writers ("All the President's Pens," *George,* June–July 1996); Jessica Lipnack and Jeffrey Stamps, "Networking the World: People, Corporations, Communities and Nations," *The Futurist* 37, no. 4 (July–August 1993); Sidney Blumenthal's *New Yorker* pieces (especially "Rendez-vous with Destiny," March 8, 1993), and two articles by Michael Kelly ("It All Codepends," *The New Yorker,* October 3, 1994; "The President's Past," *New York Times Magazine,* January 23, 1994) all contributed to my discursive construction of Clinton "pathography." Joe Klein's *Primary Colors* (New York: Random House, 1996) in my opinion presents the definitive Clinton portrait.

17. Roland Barthes, *Sade, Fourier, Loyola,* trans. Richard Miller (New York: Hill and Wang), 1976, 9. See also Barthes, "The Reality Effect," in Barthes, *The Rustle of Language,* trans. Richard Howard (New York: Hill and Wang, 1986), 141–148.

18. Drew, "Author's Note," *On the Edge,* 439.

19. Page references refer to books listed in footnote 16: Drew, *On the Edge,* 17–18, Maraniss, *First in His Class,* 390; Drew, *On the Edge,* 67; Boyer, "A Fever in the White House," 58; Drew, *On the Edge,* 151, 223.

20. Page references refer to books listed in footnote 16: Allen and Portis, *The Comeback Kid,* 31; Cohen, "Despite the Hoopla, Clinton's No Nixon," A17; Boyer, "A Fever in the White House," 57, 58.

21. Another difference between Nancy and Hillary is irony. While Nancy did perform a self-mocking "Second Hand Clothes" at a Gridiron dinner, Hillary's joking about her hair, her outfits (even on her Senate victory night: "and six black pantsuits later") is seen as more idiomatic: Dick Morris recounts that when he informed Hillary about poll data on her "sessions" with Eleanor, she asked, "'By the way, Dick, is there anyone I can call for you? I thought maybe you'd like to speak with Machiavelli or someone?' I asked if she would tell Metternich to help me. 'No problem,' she said." Morris, *Behind the Oval Office,* 287.

22. Maureen Dowd, "We Are the President," *New York Times,* January 23, 1994, 6:18.

23. Drew, *On the Edge,* 71.

24. Frank Rich, "The Two Way Mirror," *New York Times,* March 27, 1994, 4:17.

25. According to Brummett, Clinton is a self-styled synthesizer of many presidents: part JFK, part LBJ (gregarious, appetitive), part FDR (synthesizer, ambitious agenda), part Ronald Reagan (advocate of positive spin; a somewhat effective communicator; especially his "combination of obliviousness and warmth"):

Brummett, *High Wire,* 24–25. According to Drew, however, these competing aspects of self and presidential performance were not unusual in other presidents, including JFK and FDR, where they were manifested in the characters of different personnel. What marked Bill Clinton's particularity was the existence of dissociated "separate cells" (Drew, *Showdown,* 194).

26. Drew, *On the Edge,* 153.

27. Kelly, "It All Codepends," 80.

28. Thomas Friedman, "Clinton's Range: Doing More than Bush, Less than Advertised," , February 14, 1993, E1, 3. The character Empath is one of a race of people who have the capacity both to empathize with and to absorb the feelings of others. The film *Strange Days* starred Ray Liotta as the protagonist in a sci-fi film (similar to the *Dead Zone* genre) who could see and experience the past traumas (including violence against women) of others.

29. Dick Morris, *Behind the Oval Office,* 14.

30. Brummett, *High Wire,* 3. (For other pertinent examples, see 3–8 as well as Brummett's primal scene, "Unveto Man," 10–30.)

31. Paul Fick, *The Dysfunctional President: Inside the Mind of Bill Clinton* (New York: Citadel Press, 1996), 136. The analogous book for George W. Bush appears to be Justin A. Frank, M.D., *Bush on the Couch: Inside the Mind of the President* (New York: Regan Books, 2004). Dr. Frank is concerned with the many discrepancies and inconsistencies within our current president: how he can promise to protect the environment and allow increased arsenic in the public water supply; how he "can sound so confused and act so decisively." The importance of Bush's dead sibling is a key to his analysis.

32. Drew, *Showdown,* 50.

33. Edith Efron, quoted in Fick, *Dysfunctional President,* 197.

34. Glenn C. Ellenbogen, Ph.D., *Oral Sadism and the Vegetarian Personality: Readings from the Journal of Polymorphous Perversity* (New York: Ballantine Books, 1986).

35. Morris, *Behind the Oval Office,* 164.

36. Maraniss, *First in His* Class, 368. Maraniss specifies that the one area where Hillary departs from this (where he is "deceptive" and she is "blunt") is money matters.

37. "The consternation I felt [about candidate Clinton] was based on my observation of Clinton from my professional experience as a clinical psychologist. It alarmed me that his significant behavioral characteristics mirrored so closely a particular clinical population which frequented my practice since I began serving as a psychotherapist in 1983. The more I observed Clinton, the more confident I became that my diagnosis was correct." Fick, *Dysfunctional President,* 7. Fick's book begins dramatically: "The President of the United States, William Jefferson Clinton, is in trouble" (3). And it attempts to elaborate on the *Reader's Digest* condensed versions of Robert J. Samuelson's *Washington Post* story,

"Please Tell the Truth, Mr. President" (June 9, 1993) and Michael Kelly's *New York Times Magazine* piece (July 31, 1994), "Why the President Is in Trouble."

38. Fick's discussion of Pierce relies on the biography by Roy Franklin Nichols, and his discussion of Reagan relies on *Where's the Rest of Me?* as well as on the work of Anne Edwards, *Early Reagan: The Rise to Power* (New York: Morrow, 1988); Ronald Reagan, *An American Life: Ronald Reagan, the Autobiography* (New York: Simon and Schuster, 1990); Fick, *Dysfunctional President*, 34–35.

39. Drew, *On the Edge*, 241.

40. Maraniss, *First in His* Class, 345.

41. Baudrillard, *Perfect Crime*, 2–3.

42. Mark Seltzer, "Wound Culture: Trauma in the Pathological Public Sphere," *October* 80 (Spring 1997): 3–26.

43. My theoretical readings in the second part of this chapter are indebted to the works of Lauren Berlant, *The Queen of America Goes to Washington City: Essays on Sex and Citizenship* (Durham: Duke University Press, 1997); Seltzer, "Wound Culture," 3–26; and Hal Foster, *The Return of the Real* (Cambridge, MA: MIT Press, 1996).

44. Berlant, *Queen of America*, 88.

45. For an analogous reading of Lady Di's death see my "That's the Way the Mercedes Benz: Di, Wound Culture and Fatal Fetishism," *theory and event* 1, no. 4 (1997).

46. See Hal Foster's discussion of Lacan's theoretical model in his *The Return of the Real: The Avant-Garde at the End of the Century* (Cambridge, MA: MIT Press, 1998), 132–136.

47. Slavoj Zizek, *The Sublime Object of Ideology* (London: Verso, 1989), 105.

48. In *The Four Fundamental Concepts of Psychoanalysis*, trans. Alan Sheridan (New York: Norton, 1998), 54.

49. J. Laplanche and J.-B. Pontalis, *The Language of Psychoanalysis*, trans. Donald Nicholson-Smith (New York: Norton, 1973), 300–301: "It is worth noting that before Freud these marginal phenomena of everyday life had never been seen as connected or brought together under one heading—witness the lack of a generic concept for them. It was Freud's theory which gave birth to the concept of the parapraxis, and as the editors of the Standard Edition point out, the English term had to be coined especially to render Freud's *Fehlleistung*" (301).

50. Brummett, *High* Wire, 3, on Bentsen's water glass; Drew, *On the Edge*, 134, on the serving of ham.

51. Sigmund Freud, *The Psychopathology of Everyday Life* (New York: Norton, 1965), 200–201, 166–167.

52. Ibid., 191.

53. Ibid., 213.

54. Drew, *On the Edge*, 181.

55. Felix Guattari, "So What?" in Sylvère Lotringer, ed., *Chaosophy* trans. Chet Wiener (New York: Semiotexte, 1995), 10.

56. The lapsus made in the *nomination* process points to the importance of the symbolic and the paternal metaphor in relation to the Real. Lacan's Symbolic/Real axis proves increasingly pertinent to the second Clinton term (impeachment), as it will to the election of George W. Bush in 2000.

57. Drew, *On the Edge*, 37–41.

58. Ibid., 41.

59. The displacement of race onto Lincoln continues in the ending of the remake of *Planet of the Apes* (dir. Tim Burton, 2001).

60. Drew, *On the Edge*, 53–54.

61. Ibid., 200. The Lani Guinier debacle is covered in the chapter "Civil Rights: 'A Ground I Could Not Defend" (198–211).

62. Ibid., 201.

63. Ibid., 203.

64. Ibid., 206.

65. Ibid., 211, 209.

66. Ibid., 250. This statement took place in an exchange with Gore: "If you want me to die on my sword on this one, you tell me why I shouldn't have done it on my middle class tax cut."

67. Ibid., 246.

68. Ibid., 369–372.

69. Ibid., 385.

70. Zizek, *The Sublime Object of Ideology*, 105.

NOTES TO CHAPTER 8

A shortened version of this chapter, "Father, Can't You See I'm Bombing?" appeared in *UMBR(a): A Journal of the Unconscious War* (2004): 143–158.

1. Sigmund Freud and William C. Bullitt, *Thomas Woodrow Wilson: A Psychological Study* (New York: Avon Books, 1968). Further references to this book will be indicated by parenthetical notations (*TWW*) in the text, along with page citations.

2. "Forward," William C. Bullitt, in ibid., v–ix. Gérard Miller gives a fuller account of Bullitt's life (as Colonel House's disciple, as adviser to both Wilson and FDR, as ambassador to Paris and Moscow, and as husband to Louise Bryant, John Reed's widow). It was as ambassador to Paris that Bullitt, along with Marie Bonaparte, greeted Freud at the Gare St. Lazare in 1938. Bullitt, the French singer Yvonne Guilbert, and H. G. Wells were the only people to address Freud by his last name without any preliminary title. Miller also situates the

peculiarities of this volume's publishing history. The original manuscript has never been found; Bullitt alone establishes the final text; it is not included in *The Standard Edition*. See Miller's introduction to the French translation of Freud's book, *Le Président Thomas Woodrow Wilson: Portrait Psychologique,* trans. Marie Tadié (Paris: Payot, 1990), i–xx.

3. Paul-Laurent Assoun, "De Freud à Lacan: Le sujet du politique," 15–24, and Michel Schneider, "L'Etat comme semblant," 43–54, in *Cités: Philosophie, Politique, Histoire* 16 (2003). This issue includes a special dossier "Psychanalyse et Politique." Assoun mentions Freud's earlier interest in other political leaders, including Lincoln and Alexander the Great.

4. Gérard Miller, *Le Président Wilson,* compares Wilson with one of his paranoid schizophrenic patients (Georges) who is in direct communication with God. xviii–xx.

5. Slavoj Zizek, *The Sublime Object of Ideology* (London: Verso, 1989), 25: "How can one not remind oneself here of the famous Lacanian affirmation that a madman who believes himself to be a king is no more mad than a king who believes himself to be a king—who, that is, identifies immediately with the mandate 'king'?" See also Zizek, *For They Know Not What They Do: Enjoyment as a Political Factor* (London: Verso, 1991), 254–256: "with the king we cannot simply distinguish the empirical person from his symbolic mandate—the more we isolate the person, the more this remainder remains a king" (255).

6. Jacqueline Rose, "Margaret Thatcher and Ruth Ellis," in Rose, *Why War? Psychoanalysis, Politics, and the Return to Melanie Klein* (Oxford: Blackwell, 1993), 46.

7. Ibid.

8. Ibid., 68.

9. Avital Ronell, "Support Our Tropes: Reading Desert Storm," in Frederick M. Dolan and Thomas L. Dumm, eds., *Rhetorical Republic: Governing Representations in American Politics* (Amherst: University of Massachusetts Press, 1993), 22.

10. Ibid., 17.

11. John Morton Blum, *Woodrow Wilson and the Politics of Morality* (Boston: Little Brown, 1956), 5: "in his father's presence, even as a Princeton professor, he was still a pupil" (7).

12. Miller, *Le Président Wilson,* xx. Even John Morton Blum's intended hagiography notes Wilson's compulsions: "Wilson was a troubled man whose compulsiveness helped him lead a nation" (5). Wilson's "political behavior suffered from his lack of joy" (111). Blum's depiction (published before Freud and Bullitt) concurs on several key points. Wilson's scholarship was molded as much by desire as by facts. He precipitated his own troubles at Princeton and as president was inflexible and incapable of tolerating disagreement on issues of policy or the division of authority.

13. The fourteen collapses or "breakdowns" occurred (1) June 1874 to October 1875, (2) December 1880 to June 1882, (3) November 1883 to March 1884, (4) October 1887 to June 1888, (5) November 1895 to August 1896, (6) June 1899 to August 1899, (7) the summer of 1903, (8) January 1905 to March 1905, (9) May 1906 to October 1906, (10) January 1907 to February 1907, (11) September 1907 to September 1908, (12) February 1910 to March 1910, (13) August 1914 to February 1915 (as president), (14) April 1919 (as president). *TWW,* 107–108.

14. Colin MacCabe, "Introduction," to Sigmund Freud, *The Schreber Case,* trans. Andrew Webber (London: Penguin, 2002), xiv.

15. Jacques Lacan, *Le séminaire, Livre IV: La relation d'objet* (Paris: Le Seuil 1994), 372.

16. Robert Dallek's highly publicized biography, *An Unfinished Life: John F. Kennedy 1917–1963* (New York: Little, Brown, 2003), addresses the question of presidential illness. Like Wilson, JFK was elected as a "sick man," and during the Cuban missile crisis, for example, he took his usual medications: antispasmodics (for colitis) and antibiotics (urinary tract and sinus infections), salt tablets, testosterone, hydrocortisone (Addison's disease), and a .1 milligram/day dose (twice daily) of Stelazine (576). In August 1961 he had recurrent "gut" problems, acute diarrhea, and back pain, for which he was medicated with codeine sulfate and procaine injections, penicillin, cortisone, Bentyl, Lomotil, Transentine, paregoric (colitis), testosterone, and Ritalin, in addition to "wine and those damned daiquiris" (471–472).

17. Sigmund Freud, *The Future of an Illusion,* trans. W. D. Robson-Scott, rev. James Strachey (Garden City, NY: Anchor Books, 1964), 27.

18. Nepotism (from Italian *nepote*: nephew). Historically, it designated excessive favoritism accorded by popes to their nephews and relatives in matters of church administration. Sometimes these "nephews" were their illegitimate sons.

19. Jacques Derrida, "Psychoanalysis Searches the States of Its Soul: The Impossible Beyond of a Sovereign Cruelty," address to the States General of Psychoanalysis, in Peggy Kamuf, ed. and trans., *Without Alibi* (Stanford: Stanford University Press, 2002), 250.

20. Sigmund Freud, *Group Psychology and the Analysis of the Ego,* trans. James Strachey (New York: Norton, 1959), 35.

21. Blum, *Woodrow Wilson,* 148. The entire Fourteen Points are elaborated on 147–148.

22. Michael Paul Rogin, "The King's Two Bodies: Lincoln, Wilson, Nixon, and Presidential Self-Sacrifice," in Rogin, *Ronald Reagan, the Movie and Other Episodes in Political Demonology* (Berkeley: University of California Press, 1987), 92.

23. John Morton Blum, *Woodrow Wilson,* 19, describes Wilson's scholarship (that produced *Congressional Government*) as "unimpressive, often shallow or

derivative"; in terms analogous to Freud and Bullitt, "Desire as much as scholarship molded Wilson's book" (18).

24. Rogin, *Ronald Reagan, the Movie and Other Episodes in Political Demonology*, 91.

25. Slavoj Zizek, "*L'Homo sacer,* comme objet du discours de l'université," *Cités* 16 (2003): 39.

26. Ibid., 38.

27. Blum, *Woodrow Wilson*, 141.

28. Ibid., 143.

29. Ibid., 144.

30. Ibid.

31. Ibid.

32. Sigmund Freud, *The Future of an Illusion* (Garden City, NY: Anchor Doubleday, 1964), 27.

33. Ibid., 69.

34. Michael Duffy and Dan Goodgame, *Marching in Place: The Status Quo Presidency of George Bush* (New York: Simon and Schuster, 1992), 32.

35. Stated on January 27, 2000; quoted in Molly Ivins and Lou Dubose, *Bushwacked: Life in George Bush's America* (New York: Random House, 2003), 50. See also Mark Crispin Miller, *The Bush Dyslexicon: Observations on a National Disorder* (New York: Norton, 2001),14. We might also recall Bush *père*'s refused introjects such as broccoli and the plastic Thanksgiving turkey W-Bush served up (photogenically) in Iraq.

36. Elizabeth Mitchell, *W : Revenge of the Bush Dynasty* (New York: Hyperion, 2000), 231.

37. David Frum, *The Right Man: The Surprise Presidency of George W. Bush* (New York: Random House, 2003), 55.

38. See chapter 8.

39. Frum, *The Right Man*, 283.

40. Parveen Adams, "Cars and Scars," *new formations,* no. 35 (Autumn 1998): 72.

41. Ronell, "Support Our Tropes," 17; Lydia Millet, *George Bush, Dark Prince of Love: A Presidential Romance* (New York: Simon and Schuster, 2000), 33. Or the Bushes might be the site of a queer Sedgwickian couple: "tutelary figures engaged in non-heterosexual and non dyadic relations." Eve Kosofsky Sedgwick, "Is the Rectum Straight: Identification and Identity in *The Wings of the Dove*," *Tendencies* (Durham: Duke University Press, 1993), 95. Ronell similarly sees the Bush couple as "disjointed" (18).

42. Bill Minutaglio, "George W.'s Secret Weapon," *Talk* (March 2000): 151.

43. Ibid., 152.

44. Ron Suskind, *The Price of Loyalty: George W. Bush, the White House and the Education of Paul O'Neill* (New York: Simon and Schuster, 2004), 189.

45. Frum, *The Right Man*, 41.

46. "Bushwomen" is Laura Flander's felicitous formulation: *Bushwomen: Tales of a Cynical Species* (London: Verso, 2004).

47. Frum, *The Right Man*, 40.

48. Maureen Dowd, "A Tale of Two Fathers," *New York Times*, October 12, 2003, 4:11.

49. Richard L. Berke, "Younger Bush Looks to Father's Image Burnisher," *New York Times*, March 26, 2000, A28.

50. Philip Baruth, *The X-President* (New York: Bantam, 2003), 218–219.

51. Nicholas Lehman, "The Iraq Factor," *The New Yorker*, January 22, 2001, 34–38.

52. David Ignatius, "A Familiar Crew Will Face Unfamiliar Problems," *International Herald Tribune*, January 12, 2001, 6.

53. See also Maureen Dowd's "His Magnificent Obsession," *New York Times*, September 5, 2001, A19.

54. *Frequency*, dir. Gregory Hoblet, 2000. In addition to Dennis Quaid as the father, the film stars Jim Caviezel, Mel Gibson's "Jesus," as the son. The mother's place is not fixed or secure, either. The "good" mother, who must be rescued from the serial killer, is doubled by the abusive bad mother, who created the serial killer in the first place.

55. In the fall of 2001, only 11 percent of the recurrent primetime characters on the six broadcast networks had parents of any kind, and only 61 percent of those parents were still married. Julie Saloman, "Staticky Reception for Nuclear Families on Prime Time TV," *New York Times*, July 30, 2001, E1. See also David Kehr, "Mother Love, Too Little or Too Much," *New York Times*, July 29, 2001, Arts 9.

56. The definitive reading of Wylie and "momism" in the national security state remains Michael Rogin's "Kiss Me Deadly: Communism, Motherhood and Cold War Movies" in *Ronald Reagan, the Movie and Other Episodes in Political Demonology*, 240–246.

57. Mitchell, W., 213.

58. Maureen Dowd, "Apetown, My Hometown," *New York Times*, July 29, 2001, 4:15.

59. Elvis Mitchell, "Get Your Hands Off, You Big Gorilla," *New York Times*, July 27, 2001, E1.

60. Tucker Carlson, "Devil May Care," *Talk*, September 1999, 103.

61. David Brock, "Fire on the Right," *Talk*, February 2001, 57–59.

62. Jane Mayer, "The Actor's Studio: Being George W. Bush," *The New Yorker*, October 2, 2001, 57–58.

63. Carlson, "Devil May Care."

64. Frank Bruni, "Bush the Baby Boomer Will Be His Party's First," *New York Times*, March 27, 2000, A19.

65. Jeff Stryker, "Go Play with Your Arnold," *New York Times*, September 21, 2003, A8. See also Tanya Barreatos, "Citizens, They've Shrunk the President," *New York Times*, August 30, 2003, E1, 5. The action figure is a 1:6 scale reproduction selling for $39.99.

66. Duffy and Goodgame, *Marching in Place*, 224.

67. Ibid.

68. Ibid., 189.

69. Ibid.

70. Slavoj Zizek, *Enjoy Your Symptom! Jacques Lacan in Hollywood and Out* (New York: Routledge, 1992), 124.

71. See chapter 4.

72. See chapter 5.

73. Duffy and Goodgame, *Marching in Place*, 237–238.

74. Roland Barthes, *The Pleasure of the Text*, trans. Richard Miller (New York: Hill and Wang, 1975), 53.

75. George Bush, *All the Best, George Bush: My Life in Letters and Other Writings* (New York: Scribner's, 1999), 321.

76. Ibid., 480.

77. Ronell, "Support Our Tropes," 36.

78. Bush, *All the Best*, 545.

79. Ibid., 546–547.

80. Ibid., 582.

81. See chapter 4.

82. Bush, *All the Best*, 598.

83. Ibid., 600.

84. Ibid., 601.

85. Ibid. Elvis is far from an unambivalently gender-neutral identification. See Marjorie Garber, *Vested Interests* (New York: Routledge, 1996), 363–374. It should be noted that Bush's identification with the "white suited" King further feminizes him as it is associated with the "fat" Elvis (368).

86. Sedgwick, "Is the Rectum Straight," 99. "Full fathom five thy fatherless" —"Fathom" is a term that also references water.

87. Ibid., 101.

88. See chapter 5. See also Dan Jenkins, "Golf with the Boss," *Golf Digest*, September 1990, 65–80.

89. Sedgwick, "Is the Rectum Straight," 103.

90. Ronell, "Support Our Tropes," 25.

91. Bush, *All the Best*, 602.

92. Ibid., 623.

93. Ibid.

94. Ibid., 624.

95. Zizek, *Enjoy Your Symptom!* 124.

96. Ibid., 144 fn. 22.

97. Slavoj Zizek, *For They Know Not What They Do: Enjoyment as a Political Factor* (London: Verso, 1991), 139–140, fns. 25, 26.

98. Zizek, "*L'Homo sacer,*" 35.

99. Carlson, "Devil May Care," *Talk,* September 1999, 104.

100. Linda Greenhouse, "Bush Prevails as Justices, 5–4, End Recounting," *New York Times,* December 13, 2000, A1.

101. Zizek, "*L'Homo sacer,*" 39.

102. Joan Copjec, *Imagine There's No Woman: Ethics and Sublimation* (Cambridge, MA: MIT Press, 2003). I am indebted to Copjec's lucid discussion of perversion in her chapter "What Zapruder Saw."

103. Ibid., 227.

104. *The New Yorker,* October 6, 2003, 44.

105. Copjec, *Imagine There's No Woman,* 224.

106. Bob Woodward, *Bush at War* (New York: Simon and Schuster, 2002), 256.

107. Suskind, *The Price of Loyalty,* 325.

108. Ronell, "Support Our Tropes," 26.

109. Copjec, *Imagine There's No Woman,* 231.

110. Alison Mitchell, "All Joking Aside, Bush Faces Letterman," *New York Times,* October 20, 2000, A12.

111. Jean Clavreul, "The Perverse Couple," in Stuart Schneiderman, ed., *How Lacan's Ideas Are Used in Clinical Practice* (Northvale, NJ: Jason Aronson, 1993), 223.

112. Ibid., 224.

113. Ibid.

114. Slavoj Zizek, *Organs Without Bodies: On Deleuze and Consequences* (New York, Routledge, 2004), 79–80.

115. Ibid., 95. In a private conversation with Zizek (at Hobart and William Smith College, Geneva, NY, in April 2004), I learned from Zizek that he was unaware of the context of the "preservation" lapsus.

116. Copjec, *Imagine There's No Woman,* 230.

117. Zizek, *Enjoy Your Symptom,* 125.

118. Zizek, *Organs Without Bodies,* 101; Jacques Lacan, *Le séminaire, Livre XVII: L'envers de la psychanalyse,* 159.

119. Michel Schneider, "L'Etat comme semblant," *Cités* 16 (Paris: PUF, 2003), 43–54; Eric Laurent, "Le nom-du-père: psychanalyse et démocratie," *Cités* 16 (2003): 55–62.

120. Jacques Lacan, *Les complexes familiaux dans la formation de l'individu* (Paris: Editions Navarin, 1984), 72.

121. Schneider, "L'Etat comme semblant," 54. See also my article, Diane

Rubenstein, "Did You Pack Your Bags Yourself? Governmentality After 9/11," *New Centennial Review* 3, no. 2 (Summer 2003): 326.

122. Jacques Lacan, *Television,* trans. Jeffrey Mehlman, *October* 40 (Spring 1987): 36 (originally published as *Télévision* [Paris: Editions du Seuil, 1974], 53).

123. Ibid., 37 (54 in the French edition).

124. Zizek, *Organs,* 178–179 (see also his discussion of the proposed uses of Benjamin Libet's experiment and engineered rat brains for humanitarian and antiterrorist purposes, 17–18.)

125. Zizek "*L'Homo sacer,*" 37–38.

126. Elisabeth Roudinesco, *Jacques Lacan,* trans. Barbara Bray (New York: Columbia University Press, 1997), 336.

127. Drawing upon Eric Santner's reading of Schreber, Zizek links the rise of university discourse with a crisis of investiture. Zizek, "*Homo Sacer,*" 27; Eric Santner, *My Own Private Germany: Daniel Paul Schreber's Secret History of Modernity* (Princeton: Princeton University Press, 1966).

128. Laurent, "Le nom-du-père," 59–61.

129. Schneider, "L'Etat comme semblant," 50.

130. Ibid., 61.

NOTES TO CHAPTER 9

1. Gail Collins, "Hillary Gets a Rewrite," *New York Times,* August 10, 2005, A27.

2. Beth Harpaz, *The Girls in the Van* (New York: St. Martin's Press, 2001), 250. The full quotation runs as follows: "We started this great effort on a sunny July morning in Pindar's Corners on Pat and Liz Moynihan's beautiful farm. And sixty-two counties, sixteen months, three debates, two opponents and six black pantsuits later, because of you, here we are."

3. Elizabeth Drew, *Showdown: The Struggle Between the Gingrich Congress and the Clinton White House* (New York: Simon and Schuster, 1996).

4. Nicholas D. Kristof, "Who Gets It? Hillary?" *New York Times,* March 16, 2005. See also Matt Bai, "Mrs. Triangulation," *New York Times Magazine,* October 2, 2005, 62–67.

5. Joe Klein, "The Humanity of Hillary," *Time,* June 16, 2003, 40.

6. Gail Sheehy, *Hillary's Choice* (New York: Random House, 1999).

7. Joan Acocella, "Shrink to Fit," *The New Yorker,* December 13, 1999, 99.

8. Harpaz, *The Girls in the Van,* 108–109.

9. These and (too) many more examples are found in Sheehy. Acociella selects a few of these and, in her review, she questions Sheehy's fixation on Hillary's secondary sexual characteristics throughout the biography.

10. Kate Zernike, "At Yale, Mrs. Clinton Ponders Her Hair and Her Politics," *New York Times,* May 21, 2001, B4. In the interest of full (hair) disclosure, the author admits that she has had her hair cut by two stylists who have also cut Hillary's hair.

11. Klein, "The Humanity of Hillary," 40.

12. The question of mitigation or mitigating circumstances brings us back to the (overworked) *topos* of Freudian femininity described by Sarah Kofman, "The Narcissistic Woman: Freud and Girard," in Toril Moi, ed., *French Feminist Thought: A Reader* (London: Basil Blackwell, 1987), 210–226. See especially the distinction between the criminal and the hysteric and the model of the enigma (222–224). For, although Freud does compare the narcissist woman to the criminal, comedian/humorist, cats, children, and birds of prey (210–211), for the most part, she is modeled on the order of the hysteric and not of the (great) criminal, who, according to Freud, in "Psychoanalysis and the Establishment of Facts in Legal Proceedings," in Freud, *The Standard Edition,* vol. 9, 103–114, does not comply with the law, as that would be working against his ego. The question for Kofman in this part of her essay is whether in Freud's inquiry into the enigma of femininity, Freud sees the woman as "knowing her secret" (the model of the criminal) or as not unaware of it (the hysteric).

13. Jacqueline Rose, "Margaret Thatcher and Ruth Ellis," *new formations* 6 (Winter 1988): 23.

14. Alan Hollinghurst, *The Line of Beauty* (London: Picador, 2004), 318–319.

15. Sheehy, *Hillary's Choice.*

16. Rose, "Thatcher," 22.

17. Julia Kristeva, "Women's Time," in Toril Moi, ed., *The Kristeva Reader* (New York: Columbia University Press, 1986), 187–213. See the especially relevant section "The Terror of Power and the Power of Terrorism," 201–205.

18. John Machacek, "Poll: Hillary a Leader but Divisive," *Ithaca Journal,* August 9, 2005, 1A. At this time, Hillary's support eclipses the combined support of her closest competitors for 2008 among registered voters: Kerry, Edwards, and Biden.

19. Rose, "Thatcher," 19. Kristeva, "Women's Time," discusses these antagonists to state power, both liberal democratic and totalitarian, on 203 and 201, respectively. Kristeva is especially prescient about the ways that liberal democratic societies are to become targets of terror.

20. Rose, "Thatcher," 21. Kristof, "Who Gets It? Hillary?" 22. For the iconicity of Thatcher's purse and (Hillary's lack of one), see chapter 6. Thatcher was known for the handbags in which she carried her speeches to such an extent that she asked that they be archived together. (The archivists refused the gift of the bags.)

23. Madeleine Albright (with Bill Woodward), *Madam Secretary: A Memoir* (New York: Miramax Books, 2003). Elaine Sciolino's review, "Prepare for China Meeting. Buy Nonfat Yogurt," in the *New York Times Book Review*, Sunday, October 12, 2003, 12, heralds it as "the perfect Mother's Day gift." The reviewer for *The Economist* (December 20, 2003) titled the review "Diplomat in a Flannel Nightgown."

24. Albright, *Madam Secretary*, 302 n. 4; Sciolino, "Prepare for China Meeting."

25. Sciolino, "Prepare for China Meeting."

26. Sarah Kofman, *The Enigma of Woman: Woman in Freud's Writings* (Ithaca: Cornell University Press, 1985).

27. On the French coverage of Hillary, one can begin with the veteran journalist Christine Ockrent, who has known Mrs. Clinton since the 1970s: Christine Ockrent, *La double vie de Hillary Clinton* (Paris: Robert Laffont, 2001). See also Stephanie Chayret, "Hillary, présidente en l'an 2000" and "L'Impénétrable Mrs. Clinton," both published in the French edition of *Elle* 2852 (2000): 77–83. Beth Harpaz's account in *The Girls in the Van* remains a highly readable portrait that is congruent with the journalistic reports of the *New York Times* reporters Adam Nagourney and Joyce Purnick and commentators, such as Gail Collins.

28. Joel Achenbach, "The First Lady's Mission Impossible," *Washington Post*, December 14, 1994, C1.

29. Chayret, "L'Impénétrable Mrs. Clinton."

30. Kevin Merida, "Investigating the President: Some Love Left? Seemingly Unruffled and Focused Hillary Carries On," *Washington Post*, September 21, 1998, 3.

31. Joan Smith, "Thy Name Is Woman," as cited in Heather Nunn, "Violence and the Sacred: The Iron Lady, the Princess and the People's PM," *new formations* 36 (1999): 98–99.

32. Tom Junod, "You'll Never Look at Hillary Clinton the Same Again," *Esquire* (October 1999).

33. Kofman, "The Narcissistic Woman: Freud and Girard," 211.

34. Ibid., 219.

35. Pascal Riché, "Condoleezza Rich, Bush en coeur," *Libération*, January 17, 2005, 39; Daniel Schneidermann, "L'escarpin de Condoleezza Rice," *Libération*, February 11, 2005, 37.

36. Laura Flanders, *Bushwomen: Tales of a Cynical Species* (London: Verso, 2004), 31–35.

37. "Bushwomen" is Laura Flanders's felicitous formulation in her eponymous book. They are "women appointed to the inner circle of the President's cabinet and sub-cabinet." She describes how they "are the extremist administration's female front. Cast in the public mind as maverick or moderate or irrele-

vant or laughable or benign, their well-spun image taps into convenient stereotypes, while the reality remains out of sight" (2). "Theirs is the politics of masquerade" (28).

38. Maureen Dowd, "Why Can't a Woman?," *New York Times,* October 24, 1999, 4:15.

39. Maureen Dowd, "Hot Zombie Love," *New York Times,* June 15, 2003, 4:13.

40. Peggy Noonan, *The Case Against Hillary Clinton* (New York: Regan, 2000).

41. Rose, "Thatcher," 19.

42. Riché, "Condoleezza Rice," *Liberation,* 38–39; Elisabeth Bumiller, "Bush's Tutor and Disciple: Condoleezza Rice," *New York Times,* November 17, 2004, A1.

43. Flanders, *Bushwomen,* 29.

44. Ibid., 30.

45. Dowd "Why Can't a Woman?"

46. Hillary Clinton, *Living History* (New York: Simon and Schuster, 2003). More remains to be done on Kosovo and the feminine, as Kosovo is linked to Albright and was labeled "Madeleine's War" in a *Time* news story (written by Walter Isaacson) with a cover of Secretary of State Albright in a bomber jacket. See Albright's memoir, *Madam Secretary,* 408–428. (The bomber jacket is on 410.)

47. Nunn, "Violence and the Sacred," 97.

48. Gail Sheehy, *Hillary's Choice.*

49. Lucinda Franks, "The Intimate Hillary," *Talk* (September 1999): 248.

50. Nunn, "Violence and the Sacred," 103.

51. Judith Butler, *Gender Trouble* (New York: Routledge, 1999), xiv. References in the text to this edition of *Gender Trouble* will be abbreviated as (*GT*).

52. Joan Copjec, "Sex and the Euthanasia of Reason," in her *Read My Desire: Lacan Against the Historicists* (Cambridge, MA: MIT Press, 1995), 211. This chapter provides a compelling Lacanian critique of Butler's *Gender Trouble.* The full sentence reads as follows: "Sex does not budge, and it is not heterosexist to say so." Copjec continues: "In fact the opposite may be true. For it is by making it conform to the signifier that you oblige sex to conform to social dictates, to take on social content. In the end, Butler, wanting to place the subject on the same level as language, ends up placing her *beneath* it, as its realization. Freedom, 'agency,' is inconceivable within a schema such as this."

53. Butler, *Gender Trouble,* xxiii.

54. Eve Kosofsky Sedgwick, *The Epistemology of the Closet,* cited in Judith Halberstam, "F2M: The Making of Female Masculinity," in Laura Doan, ed., *The Lesbian Postmodern* (New York: Columbia University Press, 1994), 211.

55. Ibid., 212.

56. Ibid., 213.

57. Ibid.

58. Sandy Stone, "The Empire Strikes Back: Post Transsexual Manifesto," in Juha Epstein and Kristina Straub, eds., *Body Guards: The Cultural Politics of Gender Ambiguity* (New York: Routledge, 1991).

59. Halberstam, "F2M," 226.

60. Ibid., 222.

61. Butler, *Gender Trouble*, 33.

62. Copjec, "Sex and the Euthanasia of Reason," 202.

63. Parveen Adams, "Of Female Bondage," in Adams, *The Emptiness of the Image: Psychoanalysis and Sexual Difference* (London: Routledge, 1996), 47.

64. Slavoj Zizek, *The Ticklish Subject: The Absent Centre of Political Ontology* (London: Verso, 1999), 273.

65. Judith Butler, *Undoing Gender* (New York: Routledge, 2004), 223. References to this text will be abbreviated as (*UG*).

66. Tim Dean, *Beyond Sexuality* (Chicago: University of Chicago Press. 2000), 213. Zizek locates an analogous confusion in Butler—a mistaking of the "symbolic void" for a gap in reality, a confusion of the order of things with the order of words. Zizek, *The Ticklish Subject*, 274. See also Copjec, "Sex and the Euthanasia of Reason," 204, on the philosophical error of concluding from "the changing *concepts* of women something about the *being*, the *existence*, of women. We can not argue that sex is incomplete and in flux because the terms of sexual difference are unstable."

67. Jacqueline Rose, *The Haunting of Sylvia Plath* (Cambridge, MA: Harvard University Press, 1991), 237–238.

68. Jean Baudrillard, *Symbolic Exchange and Death* (London: Sage, 1993), 133.

69. Dean, *Beyond Sexuality*, 192. Dean brilliantly states the risk of remaining on the terrain of imaginary relations: "All you get from an imaginary relation is an ego and lots of trouble. By 'trouble' I mean imaginary aggressivity—imaginary . . . in the sense of violent policing of inside/outside borders by which the ego maintains itself."

70. Jaqueline Rose, "Where Does the Misery Come From?" in Rose, *Why War? Psychoanalysis, Politics, and the Return to Melanie Klein* (Oxford: Blackwell, 1993), 106.

71. Dean, *Beyond Sexuality*, 193.

72. Rose, "Where Does the Misery Come From?," 112.

73. In addition to the *Undoing Gender*, I am thinking of Butler's contribution in her *Precarious Life: The Powers of Mourning and Violence* (London: Verso, 2004).

74. Tom Junod, "You'll Never Look at Hillary Clinton the Same Again," *Esquire*, October 1999, 115–116.

75. Harpaz, *The Girls in the Van*, 35.

76. Lucinda Franks, "The Intimate Hillary," *Talk*, September 1999, 173.

77. Christopher Buckley, *No Way to Treat a First Lady* (New York: Random House, 2001), 53.

78. Ibid., 11.

79. Ibid., 15.

80. Ibid.

81. Franks, "The Intimate Hillary," 167–168.

82. Maureen Dowd, "Blonde on Blonde," *New York Times*, August 11, 1999, A23.

83. Harpaz, *The Girls in the Van*, 144–145.

84. Franks, "The Intimate Hillary," 173.

85. Sheehy, *Hillary's Choice*, 172.

86. These references to Wills are found in Sheehy, *Hillary's Choice*.

87. Jaqueline Rose, "The Cult of Celebrity," in Rose, *On Not Being Able to Sleep: Psychoanalysis and the Modern World* (Princeton: Princeton University Press, 2003), 203. Rose makes an interesting suggestion à propos of the Truth and Reconciliation hearings about whether one of the best ways to move ahead in the new millennium is to critically interrogate those things where we feel the most shame (14).

88. Ibid., 4.

89. Ibid., 206.

90. Copjec, "Sex and the Euthanasia of Reason," 198.

91. Junod, "You'll Never Look at Hillary Clinton the Same Again," 119.

92. Ibid., 117.

93. Elizabeth Kohlbert, "The Student," *The New Yorker*, October 13, 2000, 70.

94. Ibid., 65.

95. Junod, "You'll Never Look at Hillary Clinton the Same Again," 118.

96. Elizabeth Kohlbert, "Running on Empathy," *The New Yorker*, February 7, 2000, 42.

97. Junod, "You'll Never Look at Hillary Clinton the Same Again," 118.

98. Anonymous, *Primary Colors: A Novel of Politics* (New York: Random House, 1996), 4.

99. Sheehy, *Hillary's Choice*, 139.

100. Melitta Schmideberg, "Intellectual Inhibition and Eating Disorders," an appendix to Rose, *Why War?*

101. Clinton, *Living History*, 4.

102. Joe Conason, "Hillary—On Her Own," *Talk*, October 2000, 80.

103. Garry Wills, "Lightening Rod," *New York Review of Books*, August 14, 2003, 5.

104. Junod, "You'll Never Look at Hillary Clinton the Same Again," 118.

105. Anne Carson, "The Gender of Sound," in *Glass, Irony and God* (New York: Evergreen, 1992), 120.

106. Ibid., 120–121.

107. Wayne Koestenbaum, *Jackie Under My Skin: The Making of an Icon* (New York: Plume Books, 1996), 72.

108. Carson, "The Gender of Sound," 127.

109. Clifford J. Levy, "When He's Not the Better Half," *New York Times,* August 21, 2005, 4:4.

110. Carson, "The Gender of Sound," 130.

111. Ibid., 129.

112. Clinton, *Living History.*

113. Carson, "The Gender of Sound," 130.

114. Dean, *Beyond Sexuality,* 202; Lacan uses the term "respiratory erotogeneity" in his "The Subversion of the Subject and the Dialectic of Desire," *Ecrits,* trans. Bruce Fink (New York: Norton, 2002), 303.

115. Lacan, "The Subversion of the Subject and the Dialectic of Desire," 303.

116. Dean, *Beyond Sexuality,* 203.

117. Harpaz, *The Girls in the Van,* 75. (On swallowing and so on, see 128–129, 269).

118. Junod, "You'll Never Look at Hillary Clinton the Same Again," 119.

119. Parveen Adams, "The Violence of Paint," in Adams, *The Emptiness of the Image* (London: Routledge, 1996), 114–117.

120. Adams, *The Emptiness of the Image,* 116.

121. Ibid., 89.

122. Joanna Field (pseudonym for Marion Milner), *On Not Being Able to Paint* (Los Angeles: Jeremy P. Tarcher, 1957).

123. It appears the *Commander-in-Chief* has more or less attained its expected popularity. At this post–Golden Globe moment (January 2006), Geena Davis has won a Golden Globe for her portrayal of the president. Her portrayal is not a first, as there have been sci-fi women presidents in space or in a future time. Back on Earth, even a formerly homeless African American woman can become, like Geena Davis, president by default; see Stephen Bury's *Interface* (New York: Bantam, 1994), touted as "A *Manchurian Candidate* for the Computer Age." However, it is still Jack Bauer and 24 that have most captivated the viewing public.

Index

About the Author

Diane Rubenstein is Professor of Government and American Studies at Cornell University and the author of *What's Left? The Ecole Normale Supérieure and the Right.*